Judaism's Encounter *with* Other Cultures

Judaism's Encounter *with* Other Cultures

Rejection or Integration?

Gerald J. Blidstein
David Berger
Shnayer Z. Leiman
Aharon Lichtenstein

edited by
Jacob J. Schacter

JASON ARONSON INC.
Northvale, New Jersey
Jerusalem

This book was set in 10½ pt. Columbus by Alabama Book Composition of Deatsville, Alabama, and printed and bound by Book-mart Press of North Bergen, New Jersey.

10 9 8 7 6 5 4 3 2 1

Library of Congress Cataloging-in-Publication Data

Judaism's Encounter with Other Cultures : rejection or integration? /
edited by Jacob J. Schacter.
p. cm.
Includes bibliographical references and index.
ISBN 0-7657-5957-8 (alk. paper)
1. Judaism and science—History of doctrines. 2. Jews—
Civilization. I. Schacter, Jacob J.
BM538.S3J83 1997
296.3'875—dc20 96-28982

Manufactured in the United States of America. Jason Aronson Inc. offers books and cassettes. For information and catalog write to Jason Aronson Inc., 230 Livingston Street, Northvale, New Jersey 07647.

Contents

INTRODUCTION

Jacob J. Schacter

On February 22, 1934, Rabbi Abraham Isaac Bloch, head of a Jewish educational institution of higher learning in Telshe, Lithuania, wrote a letter in which he presented his opinion about the place of secular studies in Jewish tradition. His opening programmatic statement is significant and serves as an appropriate point of departure for this volume:

> Regarding your request to clarify the ruling concerning the study of "the wisdom of the nations" . . . it is extremely difficult to render a clear precise decision (*ki-halakhah*). For matters like these are based very largely on ideologies and opinions that are associated with the aggadic [or nonlegal] portions [of the Torah]. . . . Even though there are several positive and negative commandments associated with them, it is impossible to establish firm rulings with regard to them as [one can do] in the halakhic portions, that is, to issue a ruling applicable to all. They depend very much upon the temperament of the individual person and upon his unique mode [of life], and also depend upon the conditions of time, place, circumstance, and environment.[1]

Indeed, the attitude of Jews throughout history to Gentile learning and culture is not monolithic and unidimensional and cannot be reduced to any simplistic, facile generalization. On the contrary, it is complex, changing, and nuanced, very much

---

1. Rabbi Bloch's letter was first published by L. Levi, "An Unpublished Responsum on Secular Studies," *Proceedings of the Association of Orthodox Jewish Scientists* 1 (1966): 107–12 and was reprinted by Levi in his "Shetei Teshuvot 'al Limud Ḥokhmot Ḥiẓoniyot," *Ha-Ma'yan* 16:3 (1976): 11–16, and his *Sha'arei Talmud Torah* (Jerusalem, 1981), 296–301. It was most recently reprinted in *Ha-Pardes* 64:8 (May 1990): 9–12.

For a discussion of the context in which this letter was written, see my "Torah u-Madda Revisited: The Editor's Introduction," *The Torah u-Madda Journal* 1 (1989): 1–2, and nn. 1–3.

reflecting "conditions of time, place, circumstance, and environment." Affirmation and acceptance in one part of the world or during a specific century was countered by rejection and denial or simple benign disinterest in other times and places. Often differences existed even within the same cultural milieu and identical chronological time frame. All sorts of factors directly influenced how Jews in any given place or time throughout their history reacted to non-Jewish culture. It is this interesting and fascinating story, with a specific emphasis on those factors which militated in favor of an openness of traditional Judaism to non-Jewish sources, which serves as the focus of this volume.

This issue of Judaism's relationship to non-Jewish *wisdom* (Lamentations Rabbah 2:13) is one of, if not the most basic concern of Jewish intellectual history from antiquity to modern times. Indeed, it is difficult to identify an issue of greater centrality and duration in the history of Jewish thought throughout the ages. It is fundamental to an understanding of the way a minority Jewish culture confronted the majority cultures within which it functioned, struggling to retain its own identity, integrity, and authenticity under the pressure of other and often hostile environments. On occasion, Jews responded positively, even going so far as to appropriate ideas, concepts, and values from the outside and creatively integrate them into its own cultural—and even religious—matrix. There were also many cases of principled objections to such an enterprise, often generating heated controversies that emerged and reemerged throughout the course of Jewish history and did much to define the intellectual and religious profile of Judaism itself.

The authors presented here provide fresh insight into this longstanding discussion and debate. In stimulating and compelling presentations, they discuss both sides of the issue but, particularly, provide a rich sampling of source material and offer an eloquent and convincing case for the perpetuation of Judaism's dialogue and cultural interaction with the world outside of it.

In the first essay, Dr. Gerald Blidstein treats the attitude of the talmudic Sages to the ideas, legal systems, and realia of the gentile culture of their times.[2] After briefly dealing with the slippery question of how influence is to be determined or proven in such cases, Dr. Blidstein engages in a close textual analysis of various rabbinic sources which directly address the issue: the talmudic prohibition against involvement in *Greek wisdom* or *the wisdom of the other nations*, the banning of *the reading of outside books*, and the dictum outlawing a father from teaching his son *higgayon*. Besides precisely defining the meaning of these phrases and the parameters they were meant to encompass,[3] Dr. Blidstein discusses whether they are to be avoided because they are intrinsically worthless, deficient, or dangerous (potentially under-

2. See also Louis H. Feldman, "Torah and Secular Culture: Challenge and Response in the Hellenistic Period," *Tradition* 23:2 (Winter 1988): 26–40.

3. See also Joshua Bloch, "Outside Books," *Mordecai M. Kaplan Jubilee Volume* (New York, 1953), 87–108; Dov Rappel, "Ḥokhmat Yevanit-Retorika," *Meḥkerei Yerushalayim bi-Maḥshevet Yisrael* 2:3 (1983): 317–22.

mining the absolute superiority or centrality of Torah study) or because they are simply superfluous and irrelevant for someone whose religious obligation requires him to study Torah all day long. One thing is clear: In classical rabbinic Judaism there was no higher value than the study of Torah.

But beyond these programmatic statements about gentile culture which are generally negative in tone, Dr. Blidstein notes that the talmudic rabbis did not live in a hermetically sealed world, and they achieved—and sometimes even sought—familiarity with significant elements of Roman and Hellenistic culture. Gentiles were expected to abide by the Seven Noahide Commandments, which share a common morality with the more developed *halakhah*; some identified gentile civil law with the *dinnim* (i.e., "law") of those commandments. Dr. Blidstein also points out how the talmudic sages were aware of various Greek words and terms, even incorporating them into their normative legal framework, and he shows how they were open to and accepting of gentile descriptions of the physical world and its workings, acknowledging an overall "sphere of culture" shared by Jews and gentiles alike. As Dr. Blidstein documents, the rabbis knew and used universal folk motifs and were very much aware of contemporary assumptions regarding medicine, science, astronomy, and physiology.

Dr. Blidstein concludes that the rabbis during the talmudic period were not necessarily hostile to gentile culture, nor were they ignorant of it. It was just that they did not consider it necessary for themselves. The views of their gentile contemporaries were essentially irrelevant to the rabbis who operated within a self-contained Jewish system governed exclusively by the Torah. They saw no need to recommend gentile sources for insights into ritual, ethical behavior, or legal norms. In sum, their attitude was not a negative one; they simply considered gentile culture as peripheral and superfluous.

The issue of Judaism's attitude toward and use of aspects of gentile or secular culture from tenth-century Baghdad through the transition to modernity in the middle of the eighteenth century is treated next by Dr. David Berger. While explicit concern with the legitimacy of Greco-Roman culture remained sporadic and marginal in the vast talmudic corpus, this was not the case at all in medieval times. In fact, in the Middle Ages, this issue moves from the periphery to the center of Jewish concern. In a wide-ranging article, Dr. Berger describes the rich tapestry of Jewish and non-Jewish cultures on three continents. He points out how the medievals, especially in the Islamic orbit, provided a new and crucially significant answer to the ancient quest for justifying involvement in general culture from the perspective of a tradition where Torah study was still considered to be an all-encompassing religious imperative. They developed the notion that extratalmudic disciplines, particularly philosophy, were not only important per se, but were actually an integral part of Torah itself. It is thus wrong, writes Dr. Berger, to speak of secular studies in a general sense since, for a substantial number of medieval thinkers, the study of philosophy in and of itself was elevated to the level of religious obligation. In fact, he shows how the study of philosophy was so highly considered during this period that even those who took the conservative position in the debates over philosophy in the thirteenth and early fourteenth centuries, which he discusses in great detail, were often devotees of that discipline, albeit in a more moderate fashion.

The central figure in this positive attitude toward philosophy was, of course, Maimonides. Already by the thirteenth century, shortly after his death, Maimonides' reputation as a preeminent halakhist and philosopher had reached heroic proportions, and all who succeeded him were forced to reckon with the power and force of his stature and authority. Dr. Berger points out how it was extremely difficult to be opposed to the legitimacy of philosophical inquiry in Judaism when the great, towering, and influential Maimonides clearly considered rational investigation of Judaism to be a crucial religious imperative and an indispensable component of genuine religious experience.

Dr. Berger also contrasts the unusually fruitful and positive cultural symbiosis between Judaism and Islamic civilization with the much more limited and circumscribed contacts between Judaism and Christian culture. While pointing out that a characterization of Ashkenazic Jewry as culturally insular and narrow is a simplistic and misleading oversimplification, Dr. Berger nevertheless charts those factors which accounted for a much more extensive involvement of Jews in Islamic culture. Spanish Jewry, in particular, was "unambiguously hospitable to the pursuit of philosophy, the sciences, and the literary arts." Finally, in the course of his widely focused analysis, Dr. Berger also treats the relationship between Jews and the dominant cultures in which they lived in Southern France (where a massive controversy about the works of Maimonides erupted in the thirteenth century and left its mark on Christian Spain and on all of subsequent Jewish history); in the Ottoman Empire and Poland (where the successors of medieval Sephardim and Ashkenazim struggled toward a new cultural equilibrium); in Renaissance Italy (where a unique Jewish community simultaneously absorbed and resisted a dazzling Christian environment); and in eighteenth-century Europe (where the threat and promise of a new, transformed "modern" culture confronted Judaism with one of the most difficult challenges it ever faced).

At the threshold of modernity, the great battles between the members of the traditional society and those in the forefront of the Jewish Enlightenment were fought over this precise issue. By the nineteenth century, when the movement toward religious Reform and secularization in general was well established, the legitimacy of secular learning became a settled question for large segments of world Jewry. For them the case was closed. For traditionalist groups, however, the issue was not merely alive but it took on an unprecedented force and urgency.

Dr. Shnayer Z. Leiman begins his essay with the formidable figure of the Gaon of Vilna who was seen as a model—justly or otherwise—by all sides in the dispute over secular learning at the end of the eighteenth and beginning of the nineteenth centuries. The bulk of his essay concentrates on several key nineteenth century rabbis—David Friesenhausen, Isaac Bernays, Jacob Ettlinger, Samson Raphael Hirsch, and Azriel Hildesheimer—who combined unimpeachable traditionalist credentials with the pursuit of a sophisticated understanding of modern Western culture.[4] But there was something very significant that distinguished them from their like-minded predecessors in the medieval world. Not only did every one of them affirm the conceptual importance and legitimacy of secular culture, each one, with the exception of Friesenhausen, attended a university, something unheard of in medieval times. And not only did they all personally demonstrate their commitment to secular knowledge, they went further than that. Without exception, each attempted to formalize this integration in the curriculum of an educational institution which they founded. In medieval times, interest in secular culture was essentially a personal and individual enterprise, and the single example of an institution in sixteenth-century Mantua, Italy devoted to Judaism and secular studies[5] is simply the exception that proves the rule. Now, however, with the beginning of the modern period and all the changes in Jewish life it represented, described by Dr. Leiman at the beginning of his essay, the quest became institutionalized. These great scholars clearly did not believe that it was necessary to wait until a person "filled his belly with the meat and wine" of pure Torah learning before turning to secular wisdom. Little children in the youngest grades should already be exposed to it, they felt.[6] This new trend began with the founding of an integrated-curriculum elementary school by Ẓevi Hirsch Koeslin, a Halberstadt merchant, in 1795 and only gained momentum in the nineteenth and twentieth centuries.

The figure which merits the most of Dr. Leiman's attention is Rabbi Samson Raphael Hirsch, the German communal leader and educator who devoted his life to the principle of *Torah 'im derekh ereẓ*, the integration of Torah and aspects of non-Jewish culture. Dr. Leiman goes to great lengths to prove that this notion was not meant by Hirsch as a grudging concession to the unique exigencies and needs of his immediate community, intended solely for mid-nineteenth century Germany, but was a fundamental and irrevocable component of his understanding of Judaism, "intended for all Jewish communities, for all times, and for all places." Dr. Leiman goes out of his way to demonstrate that revisionist efforts, especially in the case of Rabbi Hirsch, to truncate and minimize the breadth of that commitment cannot be squared with the historical record.[7]

---

4. In addition to the sources cited by Leiman, see Mordecai Eliav, "Gishot Shonot le-Torah 'im Derekh Ereẓ," *Sefer Aviad,* ed. Yiẓḥak Raphael (Jerusalem, 1986), 77–84; Mordecai Breuer, "Ḥokhmat Yisrael-Shalosh Gishot Ortodoksiyot," *Sefer Yovel li-Khvod Morenu ha-Gaon Rabi Yosef Dov Halevi Soloveitchik Shlita* (Jerusalem, 1984), 856–65; Julius Carlebach, "The Foundations of German-Jewish Orthodoxy: An Interpretation," *Leo Baeck Institute Year Book* 33 (1988): 78–88.

5. See David Berger, n. 121; Jacob R. Marcus, *The Jew in the Medieval World* (Cincinnati, 1938), 381–88.

6. For the important distinction between a personal interest in secular knowledge and introducing it into an elementary school curriculum, which first took root in the nineteenth century, see R. Simon Schwab, *These and Those* (New York, 1966), 15–16.

7. In addition to the sources cited in Leiman's essay, see also I. Grunfeld, *Three Generations*

The existence of such revisionism brings us to the twentieth century and to the current state of the controversy. Dr. Leiman makes reference in his afterword to several major rabbis who continued the traditions of the chief protagonists of his study. Some of these, such as Rabbi David Ẓevi Hoffmann, were outstanding academic scholars, while others, such as Rabbis Abraham Isaac ha-Kohen Kook and Joseph B. Soloveitchik, were original thinkers of the highest rank. Nonetheless, historical and sociological forces have today created a situation in which most leading talmudists in the contemporary world advocate a curriculum restricted to "Torah only" even as the overwhelming majority of world Jewry has long ago abandoned any inhibitions with respect to their involvement in secular culture.

The final essay in the volume is a general conceptual overview of the place secular studies should have in the religious consciousness and daily schedule of a Jew whose value system is shaped by traditional Jewish texts and teachings.[8]

(London, 1958), 114–19; Zvi E. Kurzweil, "Samson Raphael Hirsch: Educationist and Thinker," *Tradition* 2:2 (Spring 1960): 295; R. Yaakov Yeḥiel Weinberg, "Mishnato shel R. Shimshon Raphael Hirsch," *Talpiyot* 8:1–2 (1961): 189; idem., "Torat ha-Ḥayyim," *Ha-Rav Shimshon Raphael Hirsch: Mishnato ve-Shitato* (Jerusalem, 1962), 190–91; Cyril Domb, "Torah and the Revolutionary Spirit," *Encounter*, ed. H. Chaim Schimmel and Aryeh Carmell (Jerusalem/New York, 1989), 175–76; Immanuel Jakobovits, "Torah im Derekh Eretz Today," *L'Eylah* 20 (Fall 5746): 37–39; idem., "Torah im Derekh Eretz," in *The Jewish Legacy and the German Conscience*, ed. Moses Rischin and Raphael Asher (Berkeley, 1991), 159–66; Noah H. Rosenbloom, "Religious and Secular Co-Equality in S. R. Hirsch's Educational Theory," *Jewish Social Studies* 24:4 (October 1962): 231; Shelomo Danziger, "Rav S. R. Hirsch—His 'Torah im Derekh Erez' Ideology," in *Moreshet Ẓevi: The Living Hirschean Legacy* (New York/Jerusalem, 1988), 93; idem., "Is Torah im Derekh Eretz Relevant in our Time?", *Jewish Action* 49:3 (Summer 5749): 15; Ernst L. Bodenheimer and Nosson Scherman, "Rabbi Joseph Breuer," *The Jewish Observer* 15:6 (May 1981): 6; Moshe Zuriel, "'Al Shitat 'Torah 'im Derekh Ereẓ,'" *Ha-Ma'ayan* 29:1 (1988): 61–63; Joseph Munk, "Samson Raphael Hirsch on Judaism and Secular Culture," *L'Eylah* 28 (Fall 5749): 31; Nachman Bulman, "A Healthy Sun," *The Jewish Observer* 26:1 (February 1993): 24; Shelomoh E. Danziger, "Rediscovering the Hirschian Legacy," *Jewish Action* 56:4 (Summer 5756/1996): 23–24; Judith Bleich, "Rabbi Samson Raphael Hirsch: Ish al Ha'edah," *Jewish Action* 56:4 (Summer 5756/1996): 27–29.

For the opinion that Hirsch's ideology "may have been a *hora'as sha'ah*" [i.e., a temporary act], see Yehuda Levi, "Torah 'im Derekh Ereẓ," *Ha-Ma'ayan* 22:4 (1982): 5; idem., "Torah 'im Derech Eretz: Torah Proper or Hora'as Sha'ah?", *The Jewish Observer* 21:9 (December 1988): 12; idem., "Torah 'im Derekh Ereẓ: Amitah shel Torah o Hora'at Sha'ah?", *Mamlekhet Kohanim ve-Goy Kadosh*, ed. Yehuda Shaviv (Jerusalem, 1989), 98.

8. For previous analyses of the issue, citing a number of relevant sources, see the works by Yehuda (Leo) Levi: *Vistas From Mount Moria* (New York, 1959), 60–98; "Ḥokhmat ha-Torah ve-Sha'ar he-Ḥokhmot," *Yad Re'em* (Jerusalem, 1975), 189–216; "Torah ve-Derekh Ereẓ," *Ha-Ma'ayan* 17:1 (1976): 12–32; "Torah and Secular Studies: The Humanities," *Proceedings of the Association for Orthodox Jewish Scientists* 5 (1979): 153–67; *Sha'arei Talmud Torah* (Jerusalem, 1981 and reprinted several times); *Torah and Science* (Jerusalem/New York, 1983); *Torah and Science: Their Interplay in the World Scheme* (Jerusalem/New York, 1987);

Unconfined to any particular chronological period, Rabbi Aharon Lichtenstein paints a broad picture, ranging widely over a variety of sources from the Bible to the twentieth century, and passionately argues for the legitimacy—nay, even the necessity—of secular studies for the committed Jew.

Rabbi Lichtenstein first seeks to demonstrate the value of secular knowledge as helping a person to fulfill his or her responsibility to the world in which he or she lives, to reach personal self-fulfillment, and to work toward the perfection of a redeemed world. Included in this scheme are not only the sciences but the humanities as well, both important in achieving the highest realms of human and Jewish self-realization. Furthermore, Rabbi Lichtenstein shows how secular knowledge is also indispensable for Jewish religious study, practice, and even spirituality or religious sensibility. Once again, history, the social sciences, and the humanities are all considered to be as central to this effort as are the sciences.

After showing how valuable and important secular knowledge is on a variety of levels, Rabbi Lichtenstein turns to the question of justifying recourse to it in a tradition which considers Torah "the truest and richest of [all] spiritual treasures." If all of knowledge is included within Torah, why seek elsewhere for perfection? In response, Rabbi Lichtenstein points out that, indeed, some areas of human creativity, especially poetry and literature, reached higher degrees of expression outside Jewish tradition. In an early article on this subject written over thirty years ago, he wrote:

> Nor should we be deterred by the illusion that we can find all we need within our own tradition. As Arnold insisted, one must seek "the best that has been thought and said in the world," and if, in many areas, much of that best is of foreign origin, we shall expand our horizons rather than exclude it. "Accept the truth," the Rambam urged, "from whomever states it." Following both the precept and practice of Rabbenu Bachye, he adhered to that course himself; and we would be wise to emulate him. The explicit systematic discussions

---

Yahadut u-Madda (Jerusalem, 1988); "The Torah and Sciences," *Moreshet Ẓevi: The Living Hirschian Legacy*, 125–71; *Torah Study* (Jerusalem/New York, 1990); "Torah 'im Derekh Ereẓ bi-Dorenu," *Ha-Ma'ayan* 31:1 (1991): 1–21.

Additionally useful are: Moshe Munk, "Torah 'im Derekh Ereẓ bi-Yamenu," in *Ha-Rav Shimshon Raphael Hirsch: Mishnato ve-Shitato*, 200–33; David S. Shapiro, "Secular Studies and Judaism," *Tradition* 8:2 (Summer 1966): 15–39; reprinted with some brief changes in idem., *Studies in Jewish Thought* 1 (New York, 1975), 400–424; Moshe Swift, "Sefarim Ḥiẓonim bi-Halakhah," in *Sefer ha-Yovel Tiferet Yisrael* (London, 1967), 205–18; Moshe Arend, "Limud Ḥokhmat ha-Goyim bi-'Enei Ḥakhmei Yisrael," *'Iyyunim bi-Ḥinukh* 28 (1980): 51–62; Yeshayahu Director, *Sefer Likkutei Tal* (New York, 1976); Moshe Weinberger, "On Studying Secular Subjects," *Journal of Halacha and Contemporary Society* 11 (1986): 88–128; Aaron Rakefet-Rothkoff, "Torah Study and Secular Endeavor," *Niv ha-Midrashia* 20–21 (1987–1988): 39–47; and the articles by Dov Rappel, Mordecai Breuer, Eliyahu Zeeni, Hai Mish'an Montefiore and Rabbi Lichtenstein himself in *Mamlekhet Kohanim ve-Goy Kadosh*, pp. 13–85, 136–144.

> of Gentile thinkers often reveal for us the hidden wealth implicit in our own writings. They have, furthermore, their own wisdom, even of a moral and philosophic nature. Who can fail to be inspired by the ethical idealism of Plato, the passionate fervor of Augustine, or the visionary grandeur of Milton? Who can remain unenlightened by the lucidity of Aristotle, the profundity of Shakespeare, or the incisiveness of Newman? There is *chochma bagoyim,* and we ignore it at our loss. Many of the issues which concern us have faced Gentile writers as well. The very problem we are considering has a long Christian history, going back to Tertullian and beyond. To deny that many fields have been better cultivated by non-Jewish rather than Jewish writers, is to be stubbornly—and unnecessarily—chauvinistic. There is nothing in our medieval poetry to rival Dante and nothing in our modern literature to compare with Kant, and we would do well to admit it. We have our own genius, and we have bent it to the noblest of pursuits, the development of Torah. But we cannot be expected to do everything.[9]

But even this does not conclude the discussion. In the last part of his essay, Rabbi Lichtenstein turns his attention to one final crucial question. For even if it can be shown that secular knowledge and culture have a distinct value for the Jewish religious personality, one must still determine if it should be pursued given: (*a*) the limitations of time and resources which perhaps should better be spent on "pure" Torah and (*b*) "the danger that religious commitment may be diluted by exposure to secular culture." After a careful halakhic analysis of the parameters of the *miẓvah* [biblical commandment] of Torah study and the concomitant prohibition against *bittul Torah* [neglecting Torah study], Rabbi Lichtenstein concludes that secular studies very definitely have a significant place in the life of a fully committed Jew. Openness to secular culture is, therefore, not a modern phenomenon reflecting an unjustified concession and even capitulation to the current forces of secularism. It is very much a legitimate part of Jewish tradition from its very beginnings.

What is most striking about Rabbi Lichtenstein's essay is not just the arguments he presents but the sources he adduces in support of his position. Tennyson, Byron, Wordsworth, Whitehead, Arnold, Shaftesbury, Spenser, Newman, Hawthorne, Yeats, Milton, Keats, Sidney, De Quincey, and C. S. Lewis are liberally cited alongside Maimonides, Halevi, R. Moses Isserles, R. Joseph Karo, Nahmanides, R. Asher b. Yeḥiel, R. Menaḥem Meiri, R. Baḥya b. Asher, R. Aharon Halevi, R. David ibn Zimra, R. Ḥayyim of Volozhin, R. Shnayer Zalman of Lyady, R. Isser Zalman Meltzer, and R. Barukh Ber Leibowitz. This, alone, is Rabbi Lichtenstein's strongest argument.

The first three parts of this volume, then, present a comprehensive and authoritative overview of a central theme in the millennial history of Jewish thought; the final part will become an instant primary source in a discussion which continues to

9. A. Lichtenstein, "A Consideration of Synthesis from a Torah Point of View," *Gesher* I (1963): 10–11.

resonate deeply among many committed Jews with all the force and power that it generated in premodern and early modern times.

This volume is being published as part of the Torah u-Madda Project of Yeshiva University. I want to express my thanks to Rabbi Robert Hirt for his involvement in all aspects of the project and to The Bruner Foundation for a significant grant which made this volume possible. I also appreciate the input of Dr. Janet Carter and Dr. Egon Mayer, both formerly of The Bruner Foundation, and that of Dr. David Ruderman. In addition, I gratefully acknowledge the support of the Joseph J. Green Memorial Fund at the Rabbi Isaac Elchanan Theological Seminary, an affiliate of Yeshiva University. Of course, my great gratitude goes to the authors of the essays presented here. They are each recognized authorities in their fields and collectively have made a great contribution to Jewish learning and scholarship. It has been a privilege working with them. I especially want to thank Dr. David Berger for his ongoing personal involvement in all stages of this volume.

1

Rabbinic Judaism and General Culture: Normative Discussion and Attitudes

Gerald J. Blidstein

Contents

Introduction: Setting the Parameters

It is possible to approach the topic of talmudic openness to non-Judaic cultures in two ways. One can focus on *rabbinic consciousness* and examine the Talmud's discussion of whether non-Jewish culture is a legitimate resource for Jewish spirituality and civilization. Obviously, explicit talmudic acknowledgment of borrowing would be relevant to this rubric. "What did the rabbis *say* about . . . ?"is then our proper question. A second approach focuses on *rabbinic absorption* of non-Judaic motifs, values, and patterns; it studies implicit cultural diffusion—not "What did the rabbis *say*?", but rather: "What did the rabbis *do*?" The major task, then, is to survey rabbinic creativity and civilization in terms of its roots, investigating if and how the rabbis whose opinions are cited in talmudic literature (hereinafter: the Sages) learn and borrow from surrounding cultures. The assumption here is that one can learn much more about the interaction of rabbinic and general culture by observing the data of this interaction themselves, rather than by ferreting out the relatively rare explicit utterance. This pragmatic test would seemingly be more significant than the scholastic question of what the rabbis said when they considered the issue.

More significant, and certainly more challenging. Producing a record of what the Sages said is not an especially subtle task; it relies more on legwork than on analysis or judgment. But the modern mentality, especially, assumes that there is much more to a person than what he communicates explicitly, and that the same is likely to be true of a culture as a whole. (Of course, this is not an exclusively modern attitude—*lo ha-midrash 'ikkar ela ha-ma'aseh*—"the main thing is the doing, not the teaching," as the ancient rabbinic sage says. [Avot 1:17]) To study the roots of a culture then, one must dig beneath the surface, and that means exploration of delicate and virtually impalpable connections, reactions, responses, influences, and adaptions. Furthermore, as I have indicated, the explicit statement is sporadic and rare; but we are really concerned with the broad impact of an entire civilization. Material culture aside, the range of the question is staggering: Hellenistic philosophies and religions; law, science, and folklore; literary forms and techniques—as well as substantive literary motifs.

Unfortunately, this quantitative dimension puts the question of whether (and how) the Sages absorbed values, concepts, and patterns of behavior from the surrounding culture beyond the parameters of this essay and, indeed, outside the grasp of this author. But the difficulty is not merely quantitative. For the issue of *influence* has become rather thorny in recent years. It is increasingly clear that the criteria for establishing cultural diffusion must be drawn rigorously and that many erstwhile claims for influence must be reexamined. Rule-of-thumb resemblance is obviously not adequate, nor is *post hoc ergo propter hoc.* Patient research uncovers ever-earlier sources for ostensibly later phenomena; the possibility of parallel development can rarely be ruled out; deeper inquiry reveals significant if delicate differences between phenomena, and so on.

Thus, Elias Bickerman makes these suggestive comments in the Retrospect to his final book:

> We have often contrasted Hebrew and Greek thought . . . but we have rarely pointed to Greek influences. In the first place, Jerusalem was no more unchanging than Athens. Many unexpected traits that appear to be un-Jewish . . . may result from . . . the existence of an unknown force of the first magnitude that disturbs any calculation of influences . . . a common Levantine civilization stubbornly persisted under Macedonian rulers. . . . On the other hand, Greek ideas did percolate down to the Jews in Judea, even to those who lacked the advantages of a Greek education. Although in isolated and fragmentary manner . . . the Jews drew upon new insights, adopting those elements of Greek culture that appeared to them useful or stimulating, and neglecting the rest . . . discoveries of borrowings and influences have only a modest heuristic value unless we can learn why and to what purpose the new motif was woven into the traditional design. . . . As Vico observed more than two centuries ago, people accept only the ideas for which their previous development has prepared their minds, and which, let us add, appear to be useful to them.[1]

And Bernard Jackson concludes his survey of the methodological problems surrounding the investigation of the impact of foreign systems of Jewish law (*halakhah*) with a different, but equally suggestive, metaphor: "The effect of Greece was also that of a catalyst—a fertility drug rather than a parent."[2]

Needless to say, the topic provokes basic debate. Martin Hengel, for example, sees a deeply Hellenized Judaism by Maccabean times.[3] Morton Smith states,

1. E. Bickerman, *The Jews in the Greek Age* (Cambridge, 1988), 298–305.

2. B. Jackson, "Sources and Problems," in his *Essays in Jewish and Comparative Legal History* (Leiden, 1975), 1–24. For a much more extensive and annotated discussion, see Jackson's "On the Problem of Roman Influence on the Halakhah and Normative Self-Definition in Judaism," in E. P. Sanders, et al., eds., *Jewish and Christian Self-Definition* 2 (Philadelphia, 1981), 157–203.

3. M. Hengel, *Judaism and Hellenism*, 2 vols. (London, 1974). For references to critical

"Palestine in the first century was profoundly Hellenized . . . the Hellenization extended even to the basic structure of much rabbinic thought."[4] Henry Fischel puts it pithily (though far from absolutely): "The Pharisees may have been the most Hellenized group in Judea. . . . The strongly Israel-centered and devout makeup of the Pharisees and Tannaim does not preclude Hellenization."[5] Arnaldo Momigliano, on the other hand, provides a different judgment: "By writing in Hebrew and preserving their spiritual independence, men like Kohelet and Ben Sira saved the Jews from the intellectual sterility which characterized Egyptian and Babylonian life under the Hellenistic kings. . . . In terms of political and economic organization the Jews were certainly more Hellenzied after the Maccabean revolution than before it. But each of the leading Jewish sects of Palestine developed a style of life which . . . kept Hellenization on the surface."[6]

But we ought to remember that the meaning of statements often depends on their

---

reviews of this influential book, see D. Schwartz, *Studies in the Jewish Background of Christianity* (Tubingen, 1992), p. 40, n. 31.

4. M. Smith, "Palestinian Judaism in the First Century," in M. Davis, ed., *Israel: Its Role in Civilization* (New York, 1956), 71.

5. H. A. Fischel, "Story and History: Observations on Greco-Roman Rhetoric and Pharisaism," in D. Sinor, ed., *American Oriental Society, Middle West-Branch, Semi-Centennial Volume* (1969), 82. Further on, though (pp. 85–86), Fischel identifies seven modes by which the Sages adapted that which they adopted. Nonetheless, the major thrust of Fischel's work (in this and other essays) is to demonstrate the Hellenistic impact on the literary culture of the Sages.

6. A. Momigliano, *Alien Wisdom: The Limits of Hellenization* (Cambridge, 1975), 95–96, 114. See, as well, Saul Lieberman's introduction to his *Yevannit ve-Yavnut be-Ereẓ Yisra'el* (Jerusalem, 1962), xi–xiii. These comments, as well as Lieberman's "How Much Greek in Jewish Palestine?" (below, n. 82) seem to minimize the extent of Hellenistic influence in comparison with the impression left by his earlier *Greek in Jewish Palestine* (New York, 1992) and *Hellenism in Jewish Palestine* (New York, 1950) (see also nn. 23, 38). For a critique of these seminal works, see G. Alon, *Meḥkarim be-Toledot Yisrael* 2 (Tel Aviv, 1958), 248–77; also published in *Kiryat Sefer* 20 (1943): 76–95.

For reasons that do not concern us here, the overwhelming bulk of research in our topic concerns the impact of Hellenistic culture on Judaism, and my discussion will follow that pattern. The Babylonian Talmud was not created, however, in the Hellenistic orbit, and Ezra returned to the Land of Israel from Babylon and its culture. To further complicate matters, it is thought likely that Hellenism itself incorporated Babylonian elements, that Iranian concepts continued to flow into Greco-Roman culture (even in Qumran?), and that the rabbis of Babylon and the Land of Israel shared many elements of a Near Eastern culture that included Babylonian components (see my n. 105). For some recent writing on the subject, see I. Gafni, *Yehudei Bavel be-Tekufat ha-Talmud* (Jerusalem, 1991), 161–76; J. Neusner, "How Much Iranian in Jewish Babylonia?", in his *Talmudic Judaism in Sassanian Babylonia* (Leiden, 1976), 139–49; S. Shaked, "Hashpa'ot ha-Dat ha-Iranit 'al ha-Yahadut," in H. Tadmor, ed., *Ha-Historiah shel 'Am Yisra'el—Shivat Ẓiyyon* (Jerusalem, 1986), 236–50, 315–17; idem, "Iranian Loanwords in Middle Aramaic," *Encyclopedia Iranica* II (London, 1987), 259–61.

context and their point of departure. The Western historian who minimizes the extent of Hellenization in ancient Judaism does not intend to adopt the traditionalist's view that all Oral Law is from Sinai, with nary an element of alien influence (if that, indeed, is the traditionalist's view). Momigliano's "surface," for example, might be painfully deep for believers—his historical and ideological assumptions unacceptable. Furthermore, to argue for the Semitic as against the Hellenistic roots of rabbinic institutions may not preserve the pristine, noncontaminated image of talmudic culture. The issue is not merely terminological, however, it is a matter of basic method. Contemporary methodologies of historical research rule out statements of faith. But the believer claims, to the contrary, that historical research which has not taken the assertions of faith seriously, has simply ignored relevant facts. The gap may be well-nigh unbridgeable, then. Or should we say, as scholars delight in doing, that the answer lies somewhere between the two poles? Historical method, too, makes its own faith-assertions. And, on the other hand, it is no simple matter to limn the parameters of the Sinaitic Oral tradition (*Torah she-be'al peh*), and even the more systematic of the great medieval thinkers do not provide conclusive definitions. All in all, there is little discussion which takes both poles of the question seriously and attempts to provide an integrated picture.

The question of historical consciousness may also be relevant to our enterprise. If the Sages were not possessed of historical consciousness (whose origins will be assigned either to the Greeks or to nineteenth-century Europeans), then their willingness to accept ideas and patterns of behavior that are Greek at their source becomes less significant. Not, of course, from the historical point of view, which records shifts in cultural preferences over the years, suggests causes, plots patterns. But the Sages' consciousness becomes a crucial category if we view their historical behavior as probative. Unconscious assimilation of cultural patterns is not very instructive from a normative point of view, for it happens unawares and does not reflect those characteristics on which the normative discussion is based. The issue which provides the backdrop for this book rises, after all, in the full light of contemporary consciousness, as we ask what is to be our knowing relationship with non-Jewish cultures. Paradoxically then, the mere existence of cultural diffusion—even of a broad and sweeping kind—may not be terribly significant; the most isolationist may well admit that talmudic authorities or latter rabbis absorbed much from the "outside" yet not feel that his position is compromised.[7]

In raising the issue of rabbinic self-consciousness I do not intend, of course, to prejudge the matter. One ought not to assume out of hand that the Sages did not reflect on the character of their enterprise. Indeed, there are a number of indications

7. See for example, J. D. Bleich, *Contemporary Halakhic Problems* I (New York, 1977), xv: "The foregoing should not in any sense generate the impression that subjective considerations . . . should ever be allowed consciously to influence scholarly opinion." For extensive discussion of the role of nonconscious activity in this area, see Jackson, "Roman Influence."

to the contrary. One example is the famous anecdote which tells of Moses' visit to the academy of R. Akiva, his disappointment when he could not understand the lesson taught, and his relief when he was told that all R. Akiba taught was not less than "a teaching [*hakakhah*] given to Moses at Sinai."[8] The famous Mishnah hovers at the brink of self-consciousness as it ponders the roots of substantive Jewish law: "Release from vows hovers in the air and have naught to support them; the rules about the Sabbath, Festal offerings, and Sacrilege are as mountains hanging by a hair, for Scripture is scanty and the rules many."[9] In a less well-known remark, R. Akiba replies to the charge that his legal ruling effectively eliminates a topic of Torah law (the possibility of *zab*): "You are not responsible for the laws of *zab*," suggesting, almost, that interpretation can declare its independence of the concrete reality intended by the text.[10] Some discussions indicate an awareness of the sophisticated character of other aspects of rabbinic creativity; one thinks of the midrashic explorations of the nature of midrash itself, the different modalities by which Scripture may be understood, and the possible mutuality of *peshat* (literal meaning) and *derash* (nonliteral). Or, to choose another topic, the Talmud's consciousness of rabbinic disagreement in matters of *halakhah* and its implications; the resolution of such problems by the statement that all the contending views are "the words of the living God"[11] or the way that the human majority of Sages overrules the declared opinion of God himself.[12] Yet, it remains the case that very little of this energy is spent on the issue of foreign versus native influences. Even when we detect an awareness of the gap between the pristine meaning of Scripture and the teaching of the talmudic authorities, the rabbis do not—and need not—assume that this gap was opened by the impact of non-Jewish cultures. Rather, it is the nature of rabbinic creativity itself which is explored.

The contemporary historian's question, in any case, is far broader than the earlier simplistic: "Who took from whom?" Increasingly the task is to describe the development of cultures in holistic terms, to look for phenomena that are shared across boundaries, and to see how different peoples are parts of overarching patterns. At the same time, of course, the historian is sensitive to the *different ways* in which different peoples adopt or synthesize a common perspective. Finally, he or she will also cultivate an awareness of how and why groups *reject* the beliefs and mores which may dominate their environment. Now, the historian's agenda may yet be relevant even from a normative point of view. But this would be the case only if we assume that the career of rabbinic creativity is a controlled and disciplined venture, that it possesses either a large rational component or at least projects a pattern (even if of intuitive behavior) that can be imitated, that it can serve as model.

8. *Menaḥot* 29b. Already Rashi, *s.v. nityashvah*, attempts to pull the sting of the aggadah.
9. *M. Ḥagigah* 1:8.
10. *M. Zabim* 2:2.
11. *'Eruvin* 13b.
12. *Baba Meẓia* 59b; *p. Mo'ed Katan* 3:1 (81d).

Clearly these are major issues, and they—along with the guesswork involved in identifying the presence of cultural diffusion, and the scope of the question itself—lead me to focus in this essay on the obiter dicta of the Sages, on their explicit consideration of the relationship of Judaism and Jews to non-Jewish culture.

The Study of Nontoraitic Materials

The Wisdom of the Nations—Banned Study?

Explicit discussion of the legitimacy of knowledge that is not anchored in the Judaic tradition generally takes place in the context of the norm of Torah-study. That is to say, the question will be generally framed as to whether one may study non-Judaic material (or nontoraitic materials); a common phrase relates to the study of "Greek wisdom" as the topic mooted. This, itself, is characteristic of the rabbinic perspective which attaches fundamental significance to study as a primary activity of the Jew, and as the matrix from which flow value and meaning. If one wants to ask whether non-Judaic culture is a legitimate component of a Jew's consciousness, one begins by asking whether it is a legitimate object of study. As we shall see, to be more precise one asks how such knowledge relates to the overarching imperative that Torah be *the* object of study. The possible illegitimacy of non-Judaic knowledge is the flip side, then, of the totalizing legitimacy of Torah. What is derived from a Greek source is ipso facto contaminated; it can certainly not be normative. But the reluctance to banish "Greek wisdom" on its own merits may have other, different, implications.

The most explicit discussion of our topic by the Sages focuses on the legitimacy of studying "Greek wisdom" (*ḥokhmat Yevanit*) or "the wisdom of the nations," alongside or instead of the "wisdom of Israel" (*ḥokhmat Yisrael*). Though no talmudic source indicates what is included in this wisdom, it is likely that literature, rhetoric, and philosophy are what is meant, while language instruction is a matter of further debate.

1. A basic, unambiguous stand on our issue is presented in the Tannaitic midrash to Deuteronomy 6:7 (". . . talk of them when you stay at home and when you are away, when you lie down and when you get up"), a verse traditionally understood as undergirding the imperative of Torah study:

> *And thou shalt talk of them* (6:7): Make them matters of basic importance and not merely incidental by discussing nothing but them, and by not mixing other matters with them, as some one did. You might say, "I have learned the wisdom of Israel, so now I will go and learn the wisdom of the other nations;" hence Scripture says, *To walk therein* (Leviticus 18:4) and not get free of them. Similarly Scripture says, *Let them be only thine own, and not*

strangers with thee (Proverbs 5:17). *When thou walkest, it shall lead thee; when thou liest down, it shall watch over thee; and when thou awakest, it shall talk with thee* (Proverbs 6:22). *When thou walkest, it shall lead thee* in this world; *when thou liest down, it shall watch over thee,* in the hour of death; *and when thou awakest,* in the days of the Messiah, *it shall talk with thee,* in the world-to-come.[13]

The study of Torah is not to be diluted by other sources of knowledge, nor is it to be abandoned for other, non-Jewish materials. Our statement begins ambiguously enough, to be sure. It is unclear, in fact, whether the opening sentence deals with the study of competing cultures or simply with other, secular pursuits. Is "some one" a heresiarch seduced from Torah by Greek wisdom? Indeed, the fear that the study of alien wisdom can turn a man from the path of God ought not to be taken lightly, for the connection of such study and heresy is made throughout the talmudic period.[14] Or is "some one" simply a rabbi who turned professor or even stockbrocker?

Be this as it may, our midrash then proceeds to describe the student who says he "has learned" the wisdom of Israel and is now eager to learn the wisdom of the nations as well. This is immediately seen as, in effect, an attempt to free oneself of Torah. Perhaps we are to understand our student as saying, "I have learned all there is to Torah." Or, more radically, perhaps even the attempt to complement Torah with the study of other materials is, ipso facto, a rejection of Torah, and hence reflects an attempt to liberate oneself from the "wisdom of Israel." Clearly, our passage takes an all-or-nothing position: it is to be *either* the wisdom of Israel *or* the wisdom of the other nations—one cannot have both. For it is the wisdom of Israel which alone accompanies the Jew though life and death, guides him to the Messianic era,

13. *Sifre* Deuteronomy, sec. 34. I have adapted somewhat the translation of R. Hammer, *Sifre* (New Haven, 1989), 64–65. A virtually identical comment is found in the *Sifra* to Leviticus 18:4 (*Sifra Aḥarei* 13:11 [86a–b]). For rabbinic discussion of the materials in this section, see *Enzyklopedia Talmudit* XV, col. 59–64, 68–78.

14. R. David Ẓevi Hoffmann reads "someone" as a reference to R. Eliasha ben Abuyah, the famous renegade from Judaism who was also accused of favoring "Greek books" (see *Midrash Tannai'im,* p. 27); see also Finkelstein's note in his edition of *Sifra,* p. 61, and the comment of R. Hillel to *Sifre.* Others understand the opening of our passage not as referring to competing areas of study at all, but simply to business or social activities; see Rashi, *Yoma* 19b, *s.v. ve-lo;* R. Samson of Sens, as given in S. Lieberman's review of the Finkelstein edition, *Kiryat Sefer* 14 (1937–38): 333; *Korban Aharon* to *Sifra.* The fear that the study of Hellenistic culture will lead the Jew to abandon his people or corrupt his faith is made explicit elsewhere. Finkelstein points to the comment of R. Simeon b. Menasyah (*Sifre,* sec. 48, ed. Finkelstein, p. 110): ". . . drink from your creator's waters (i.e. Torah) and do not drink of muddy waters, lest you be pulled in the direction of *minut* (gnosticism?)," and one may add the more oblique statement in *M. Avot* 1:11. *Sifre* Deuteronomy (sec. 345) also speaks of the scholar (*talmid ḥakham*) "who abandoned the study of Torah and went off to other matters," a phrase describing apostasy, according to M. Ber, who argues that the phenomenon was not all that unusual (*Ẓion* 55:4 [1990]: 410). See also R. Yoḥanan, *p. Peah* 1:1 (15c).

and is present with him in eternal life. There can be nothing else nor need there be. It is possible, of course, to explain our passage, in the light of its opening phrase, as asserting axiological priority; insisting that Torah is the only source of value and allowing the student to devote effort to the wisdom of the nations so long as he recognizes its inferior status. But irrespective of the conceptual or practical feasibility of this approach, it clearly goes beyond the plain meaning of the remainder of our text, which paints a more uncompromising picture.

The terminology used here is itself revealing. Phrases like "wisdom of Israel" and "the wisdom of the other nations" are not commonplaces and also seem to be circuitous ways of referring to Torah and secular knowledge. The significant point is not, I think, the contrast drawn between the origins of one type of wisdom as against the origins of another, as though national loyalty is at issue. We ought to note, rather, that these phrases are part of a quotation; this is how the individual who wishes to study the non-Judaic materials presents his program. (Indeed, such phrases are generally found in this context, as we shall see.) In doing so, he already establishes the verbal—and substantive—equivalence of the two bodies of knowledge. Both are "wisdom"; they merely differ in their points of origin. (Perhaps, even, both points of origin are human, simply representing different cultures.) The medium, then, is virtually the message, and the midrash has no choice but to demur. One wonders whether a different descriptive mode, one which would have posed the query in terms of "God's Torah" and the "wisdom of the other nations" would deserve a different answer. Indeed, when the *baraitha* (rabbinic passage) approvingly describes the school of the Patriarch, where in fact both types of wisdom were taught, it balances "Greek wisdom" with "Torah."[15]

Two other terminological points are in order: first, our midrash does not single out *Greek* wisdom for specific rejection (as do other sources). It is the "wisdom of the *nations*" that is not a proper topic of attention. Secondly, the nations *do* possess a wisdom. True, the phrase may be sarcastic; or it may only reflect the perspective of our ambitious student. But inasmuch as we find the phrase in simple declarative sentences as well,[16] we may fairly take it at face value. Expanding on this last point, it is interesting that our midrash does not condemn the wisdom of the nations per se or declare it evil. Rather than devote attention to non-Jewish culture, the Jew is to devote himself to Torah alone: that is the crux. This objection can itself, of course, be interpreted in different ways. We may say that other studies are *bittul Torah,* time taken away from the rightful pursuit of Torah. Taken more seriously, we may say that the two cultures stand in unalterable opposition, that the imperative that one study Torah consequently implies that one study nothing else, and that Torah is sufficient unto its devotee. Nonetheless, our midrash does not go so far as to attack

15. *Baba Kamma* 83a and parallels.
16. *M. Sotah* 9:14.

non-Jewish culture, or even to offer any evaluative comment—unless the declaration that other cultures are not Torah is enough!

2. Talmudic discussions of the issue are much more varied than our univocal Tannaitic midrash. Here is the classic passage in the Babylonian Talmud:

> GEMARA. It was taught. R. Jose says, Even if the old [shewbread] was taken away in the morning and the new was set down in the evening there is no harm. How then am I to explain the verse, "*Before me continually*" (Exodus 25:30)? [It teaches that] the table should not remain overnight without bread.
>
> R. Ammi said, From these words of R. Jose we learn that even though a man learns but one chapter in the morning and one chapter in the evening he has thereby fulfilled the precept of "*This book of the law shall not depart out of thy mouth*" (Joshua 1:8).
>
> R. Joḥanan said in the name of R. Simeon b. Yoḥai, Even though a man but reads the Shema morning and evening he has thereby fulfilled the precept of "[*This book of the law*] *shall not depart.*" It is forbidden, however, to say this in the presence of an *'am ha-areẓ* [ignoramus]. But Raba said, It is a meritorious act to say it in the presence of *'am ha-areẓ.*
>
> Ben Damah the son of R. Ishma'el's sister once asked R. Ishma'el, May one such as I who has studied the whole of the Torah learn Greek wisdom? He thereupon read to him the following verse, *This book of the law shall not depart out of thy mouth, but thou shalt meditate therein day and night.* Go then and find a time that is neither day or night and learn then Greek wisdom.
>
> This, however, is at variance with the view of R. Samuel b. Naḥmani. For R. Samuel b. Naḥmani said in the name of R. Jonathan, This verse is neither duty nor command but a blessing. For when the Holy One, blessed be He, saw that the words of the Torah were most precious to Joshua, as it is written, "*His minister Joshua, the son of Nun, a young man, departed not out of the tent*" (Exodus 33:11). He said to him, "Joshua, since the words of the Torah are so precious to thee, [I assure thee,] *this book of the law shall not depart out of thy mouth.*"
>
> A Tanna of the School of R. Ishma'el taught: The words of the Torah should not be unto thee as a debt, neither art thou at liberty to desist from it.[17]

The substantive issue is rooted here in the charge of God to Joshua (Joshua 1:8): "This book of the law shall not depart from your mouth, but thou shalt meditate therein day and night," which is pursued on a number of planes.

There is first the assertion of R. Simeon b. Yoḥai that he who reads the Shema

17. *Menaḥot* 99b. My discussion conforms, in large measure, to the analysis advanced by Azariah de Rossi (16th century) in his *Me'or 'Einayim, Imre Binah,* Chap. II (R. Bonfil, ed., *Kitvei 'Azariah min ha-'Adumim* [Jerusalem 1991], 220–21).

morning and evening "fulfills" the charge that he study Torah "day and night." Shema is Torah, and Joshua 1:8 can be understood minimally. Even as minimum, though, it is a normative statement. And, needless to say, one who studies more Torah is all the more virtuous; R. Simeon himself proclaims a much more demanding standard and urges elsewhere that a person spend all his time on the study of Torah.[18] But if R. Simeon taught that Joshua 1:8 articulates a minimum, R. Ishma'el taught that it proclaims a total demand.

The context in which R. Ishma'el—a contemporary of R. Simeon's master, R. Akiba—urged his reading of Joshua 1:8 was, of course, quite different. R. Ishma'el responded to a question put him by his nephew Elazar who, having "studied all the Torah," wished to study "Greek wisdom" as well. We are not surprised to recall, given this provocative question, that Ben Damma was willing to be cured of a snakebite by a Christian charm, only to be prevented—the snakebite proved fatal—by his uncle R. Ishma'el.[19] In our own instance, too, R. Ishma'el sought to curb his nephew's inclinations, proclaiming on the basis of Joshua 1:8 that none of the twenty-four hours sacred to Torah ought to be diverted to Greek wisdom.

A closer reading of our text is revealing. It is clear, for example, that R. Ishma'el does not directly relate to the question of how and when a person fulfills the expectation (obligation?) expressed in Joshua 1:8. Put normatively, R. Ishma'el might be reading the verse as allowing all ordinary activities, but as demanding that any time not so occupied be devoted to study of Torah; consequently, we may not spend any part of the day or night studying "Greek wisdom." Torah is to be a person's exclusive spiritual diet and in this sense Joshua 1:8 does make an intensive demand, which is not satisfied by study morning and evening alone. Put more pointedly, it is "Greek wisdom" which is the target. Perhaps, even, the questioner who claims to have learned "all the Torah" invites a negative reply, for he thus demonstrates how facile his grasp of Torah is, and how little he ought to be encouraged to roam in alien fields.

R. Jonathan is understood by the Talmud to reject the reading of R. Ishma'el—and possibly even that of R. Simeon b. Yoḥai—by urging that Joshua 1:8 not be read in a normative vein at all. There is no command to study Torah day and night, and, the Talmud implies, no consequent ban on the learning of Greek wisdom. Clearly, though, uninterrupted study of Torah *is* a "blessing," and a person who studies Greek wisdom has foregone this blessing. But that remains his prerogative. Perhaps, also, the blessing of Joshua 1:8 is specifically appropriate to Joshua, for

18. As is well known, the positions of R. Simeon b. Yoḥai and R. Ishma'el are reversed on the related problem of Torah study and the pursuit of an occupation; see *Berakhot* 35b, where it is R. Ishma'el who takes a less than literal view of Joshua 1:8. R. Simeon b. Yoḥai's demand in that context that *all* one's time be devoted to Torah study is generally read as directed to the exceptional individual. See *Keren Orah, Menaḥot,* ad loc.; *Neẓiv* to *Sifre,* ad loc. For a recent survey, see M. Ber, "Talmud Torah ve-Derekh Ereẓ," *Bar Ilan* 2 (1964): 134–63.

19. *Tosefta Ḥullin* II, 23; 'Avodah Zarah 16b.

whom the words of Torah were "most precious," and one ought not to generalize beyond that.

Overall, the talmudic discussion does not come down on the side of those who consider the study of "Greek wisdom" a forbidden encroachment on Torah study. On the contrary, Joshua 1:8 is read in this vein by R. Ishma'el alone, and he is sandwiched between two Tannai'im (R. Simeon b. Yoḥai and R. Jonathan) who read the verse less literally or stringently. Needless to say, we do not know how these Tannai'im would have responded to the concrete question put by Ben Damma or even how they approached the issue of "Greek wisdom." But the use to which their statements are put by the Talmud integrates them into a structure which crowds R. Ishma'el into a corner. Indeed, it is inferred from the Mishnah itself (that is, R. Jose) that Joshua 1:8 can be read minimalistically.

Interestingly, the Talmud does not embark on a broad, systematic discussion (either here or anywhere else, to the best of my knowledge) of the dimensions of the imperative to study Torah. Many homiletical or aggadic statements on the topic can be garnered; and the Talmud does discuss, briefly, questions like how (or if) one balances work and study, or the fulfillment of other normative commandments and study.[20] But no talmudic passage integrates the various issues, a task left to subsequent medieval and modern commentaries. Our text, typically, goes no further than the various exegeses of Joshua 1:8 take it.

3. Though the discussion of our topic in Palestinian sources does add some significant considerations to the Babylonian passage, it also parallels it in other particulars. Here is *Midrash Tehillim* to Psalms 1:2 (". . . the teaching of the Lord is his delight, and he studies that teaching day and night"):

> R. Eliezer asked R. Joshua: "Then according to you, in what way can the words *And in His law doth he meditate day and night* be obeyed?" R. Joshua answered: "By reading of the *Shema*, for when a man reads the *Shema* morning and evening, the Holy One, blessed be He, reckons it for him as if he had labored day and night in the study of Torah."
>
> Bar Kappara taught: When a man reads two chapters of Scripture in the morning, and reads two more chapters in the evening, he obeys the words, *And in His law doth he meditate day and night.* R. Ḥiyya bar Abba said that what Bar Kappara taught could apply only to a man who was in the habit of expounding in two chapters. For only when he adds two expositions of the chapters he reads in the morning and two of the chapters read in the evening, is it reckoned as if he had labored day and night in the study of Torah.
>
> R. Berekhaih said: Our forefathers instituted the practice of studying Mishnah at dawn and at dusk.

20. See the sources assembled in E. E. Urbach, *The Sages* I (Jerusalem, 1975), 603–20; M. Ber (n. 18); and S. Safri, "Ḥassidim ve-Anshei Ma'aseh," *Ẓion* 50 (1985): 138–54.

> It was asked of R. Joshua, "May a father teach his son the wisdom of the Greeks?" He answered: "It may be taught at a time which is neither day or night, for it is said *This book of the Law shall not depart out of thy mouth, but thou shalt meditate therein day and night*" (Joshua 1:8).
>
> R. Joshua said: A father should not even take time to teach his son a craft lest he cause his son to neglect the words of Torah, of which it is said *Therefore choose life* (Deuteronomy 30:19).[21]

Here R. Joshua[22] provides a focus for a number of the issues we have seen discussed in the Babylonian passage. To begin with, he allows that the study of Torah "day and night" can be discharged by the reading of Shema morning and evening (though he also allows that God does wish that a man in fact "labor day and night in the study of Torah"). Yet, despite this flexibility, the same R. Joshua reads Joshua 1:8 as forbidding the study of Greek wisdom, for it willy-nilly encroaches on the fullness of time which should be devoted to Torah alone. "Greek wisdom" clearly does not qualify as a surrogate for Torah study; and if it is Torah's rival, Torah ought to be a twenty-four-hour-a-day regimen. Finally, R. Joshua (himself a blacksmith) urged, seemingly, that a father may not even use his son's time to teach him an occupation. This would put our entire discussion on a different footing; the intensive study of Torah, rather than the rejection of "Greek wisdom," would then be at the center of the matter. But it is likely that the text of *Midrash Tehillim* is corrupt at this point, as we shall see. Finally, we note that the issue has become what a father may teach *his son*—not what a person may study himself. Though some have urged that this distinction is crucial, and that Greek wisdom was never ruled out as a topic for one's own study but only as a subject unfit for the young,[23] I am not convinced. The proof-text, as well as the apparent rationale, are simply too broad: Joshua 1:8 is directed at each individual.

---

21. W. Braude, trans., *Midrash Tehillim* I (New Haven, 1959), 23–24. R. Joshua had previously rejected the view of R. Eliezer, according to which one fulfilled Joshua 1:8 by wearing *tefillin,* doubtless because these are to be worn constantly, a reading which also takes certain liberties with that verse. It is likely that R. Joshua's own reading of the verse took account not only of its conclusion but also of its beginning: "This book of the Torah shall not depart from your mouth . . . ," certainly not so as to utter words of Greek wisdom!

22. Note that in *Tosefta 'Avodah Zarah* 1:20 (Zukermandel, p. 461), the opinion that Greek wisdom may be studied only at a time that is neither night nor day is given in the name of R. Joshua, not R. Ishma'el as in the Babylonian Talmud. The query of Ben Damma could have been directed only at R. Ishma'el, as the Babylonian Talmud had it.

23. The matter was so understood by R. Israel of Toledo in the thirteenth century, as is noted by S. Lieberman, who accepts this position (*Hellenism in Jewish Palestine* [New York, 1950], 101–3). This explanation was also adopted by R. Ḥanokh Zundel (d. 1860), in *'Anaf Yosef* to *Ein Ya'akov, Menaḥot* 99b; and by R. David Friedman of Karlin, *'Emek Berakhah* (Jerusalem, 1881), chap. 4. See too the statement of R. Jacob Anatoli cited in B. Z. Dinur, *Yisrael ba-Golah,* 2nd ed. (Jerusalem, 1972), 2, Part 6, p. 72, #26.

4. Though the materials in the Palestinian Talmud are virtually identical with those found in *Midrash Tehillim,* the one significant variation allows us to see how the issue is brought to a head. What is most interesting, though, are the contexts in which the topic is discussed. Here, first, is the talmudic text itself:

> It was asked of R. Joshua: "May a father teach his son Greek?" He answered, "It may be taught at a time which is neither day nor night, for it is said, '. . . *for you shall meditate therein day and night*.'" If so, a man ought to be forbidden to teach his son a trade, since it says '*You shall meditate therein day and night.*" Yet R. Ishma'el has taught "*'And you shall choose life'* (Deuteronomy 30:19), that is a trade?"
>
> R. Ba son of R. Ḥiyya b. Ba in the name of R. Yoḥanan: "[It is forbidden] because of informing."
>
> R. Abbahu [said] in the name of R. Yoḥanan: "A man may teach his daughter Greek, because it is an ornament for her." Simeon b. Ba heard this and said, "Since R. Abbahu wants to teach his daughter Greek, he pins it on R. Yoḥanan." [R. Abbahu answered] "I'll be damned if I didn't hear it from R. Yoḥanan."[24]

We are already familiar with R. Joshua's reading of Joshua 1:8 as a ban on Greek—or any secular—wisdom which competes with Torah. But the Talmud seemingly rejects this approach, citing the imperative that a father teach his son a trade.[25] This may either be a frontal challenge, proving that Joshua 1:8 cannot be taken literally, or it may be a more subtle attack, suggesting that Greek may be taught if it provides an occupation.[26] Be this as it may, the study of Torah is no longer seen as unexceptionally all-consuming and devotion to Torah does not ipso facto rule out the study of Greek.

This does not mean that the Palestinian Talmud concludes that Greek may be taught. Though rejecting the claim that the very primacy of Torah demands a ban, it then cites R. Yoḥanan who argued that the study of Greek led to cooperation with the enemy. In context, R. Yoḥanan's rationale supports the ban, but it must be admitted that it introduces an element of historical relativity, suggesting that it applies to Greek wisdom specifically and at a particular historical juncture, at that. It is no longer a matter of principle, but of prudence; though even the decision as

---

24. *p. Peah* 1:1 (15c); *p. Sotah* 9:16 (24c).

25. *Midrash Tehillim* (above, n. 21) probably ought to be corrected in light of this passage; see Buber's edition of *Midrash Tehillim,* 16, n. 227.

26. This latter explanation is found in the twentieth century responsum of R. Barukh Ber Leibowitz on the topic of secular studies in his *Birkhat Shemuel, Kiddushin,* no. 27; it is also adopted by S. Lieberman, *Hellenism,* 101. (It may also be possible to explain the passage differently: the homily of R. Ishma'el resolves the contradiction between Joshua 1:8 as understood by R. Joshua and the permissibility of teaching an occupation, for the latter is also sanctioned by Scripture.)

to when and where prudence is in order is a subjective one. The continuation also introduces an element of uncertainty (and an interesting peep into rabbinic life): were women less likely to turn informers? Was the ban itself less than absolute? Or, perhaps, did R. Yoḥanan say less than what R. Abbahu reported in his name?

The literary context of this talmudic discussion is also revealing. Actually, we ought to speak of the different contexts in which it appears. We first encounter it in relationship to the *Mishnah Pe'ah* 1:1: "These are things for which no measure is prescribed . . . the study of Torah." If the question of "Greek wisdom" is related to the presumption that Torah is to be studied day and night, its relevance to the mishnaic declaration that Torah has no limit is clear.[27] Our talmudic discussion is also found, appended verbatim to the *Mishnah Sotah* 9:14: "During the war of Quietus[28] they forbade . . . that a man should teach his son Greek."

In this latter context, the talmudic editor has made an interesting use of midrashic exegesis as a base for rabbinic legislation. Furthermore, it is possible that R. Yoḥanan's "It is forbidden because of informing" is actually a rationale for the legislated ban of the Mishnah (with which it is coherent, since the Mishnah dates the ban to the war with Rome) rather than a continuation of the discussion of R. Joshua's principled attempt to curtail the study of "Greek wisdom," a discussion which concludes (as it does in *Midrash Tehillim*) with the counterclaim that Joshua 1:8 allows instruction in a trade and that this is, indeed, required. Indeed, by offering this rationale, R. Yoḥanan may indicate that the ban itself is relative to the historical situation and was not intended for periods and places where informers are not a likely hazard.

5. The Mishnaic tradition that a specific ban that "a man not teach his son Greek" was imposed is, indeed, a provocative piece of information. Actually, such a ban is reported as having been promulgated at a number of historical junctures:

---

27. Another Mishnah teaches: "Search it [the Torah] and search it, for everything is to be found in it (*Avot* 5:25)." This has frequently been taken as opposing the study of non-Jewish texts, which are at best superfluous to the Jew's quest; thus R. Obadiah of Bertinoro refers to the (presumed) ban on Greek wisdom in this context, and perhaps even Maimonides (!) nods in this direction in his *Commentary to the Mishnah*. R. Menahem Me'iri reads this Mishnah in a more limited way, as assuring that Torah literature is fully coherent, perhaps even in the sense posited by M. P. Golding ("Reasoning and the Authoritative Expansion of the Law" in N. Samuelson, ed., *Reason and Revelation as Authority in Judaism* [Philadelphia, n.d.], 69): "The Torah not only is an integrated legal system, but also is complete in the sense that it contains *in potentia* all that is necessary for the further development of the law." This is parallel, he urges (p. 83, n. 28), to the assertion of the Code Napoleon (art. 4) that a "judge who shall refuse to decide a case under pretext that the law is silent . . . or inadequate, may be prosecuted for denial of justice." In these readings, the Torah is not pitted *against* another body of literature.

28. So in Cambridge and Parma mss.; this reading is preferred by many historians. See, for example G. Vermes et al., eds., E. Schurer, *A History of the Jews* (Edinburgh, 1973), 531–34; G. Allon, *Toledot ha-Yehudim be-Ereẓ Yisra'el* I (Tel Aviv, 1958), 255–56.

during the Hasmonean period, in the decade preceding the war against Rome in 68–70, and during the campaigns of Lucius Quietus preceding the Bar-Kokhba revolt.[29] The precise content of the ban is, to be sure, not defined; the Babylonian Talmud asserts that it included Greek "wisdom" but not study of the Greek language.[30] Indeed, R. Judah the Patriarch urged Jews to speak either "good Hebrew" or "good Greek" (*Sotah* 49b). The Patriarchs also maintained schools in which "Greek wisdom" was taught, but the Talmud argues—a testimony to the seriousness of the ban—that these were maintained to train a cadre of Jews capable of contact with the Roman administration.[31]

Now the significance of these traditions lies more in what they imply than in what they say. From a historical point of view, the need to promulgate the ban repeatedly suggests that many Jews did not abide by it.[32] From a normative point of view, the existence of a rabbinic ban (*gezerah*), or in our case a number of such successive bans, strongly implies that the study of secular wisdom is not forbidden by Torah law. Rather, it is a matter of rabbinic legislation, legislation which is clearly tied to historical events and consequently directed against a specific alien culture (the Greek) but not against all such cultures. True, the passage in the Palestinian Talmud does attempt to apply R. Joshua's exegesis of Joshua 1:8 to this issue, thus giving the ban Scriptural authority.[33] Perhaps, though, this very attempt—which apparently failed—is now to be understood as *asmakhta*,[34] hermeneutics which justify, after the event, the establishment of a norm which is admittedly rabbinic and, in this case, relative. Midrashic vehemence may indicate how sensitive our issue was historically, or may testify to an attempt to present the ban as basic. But, ultimately, as the issue unravels in talmudic texts, it does not bestow normative status.

To sum up, then: the midrashic tradition—*Sifre, Sifra, Midrash Tehillim*—is much

---

29. *M. Sotah* 9:14; *p. Shabbat* 1:4 (3c); *Baba Kamma* 82b.

30. *Baba Kamma* 83a. The Palestinian Talmud does not make this distinction, and both it and the *Tosefta* (*Sotah* 15:8; ed. Zuckermandel, p. 322) speak of the teaching of Greek. *Tosefta 'Avodah Zarah* 1:20 speaks of *Sefer Yevanni* (Greek book). R. Yoḥanan's explanation of the ban as directed against informers makes good sense on the assumption that even language instruction (rhetoric?) is included in the ban. See S. Lieberman, *Hellenism*, 101, n. 12, and p. 113.

31. *Baba Kamma* 83a extends the idea already found in *Tosefta Sotah* 15:8; the *Tosefta* speaks of Greek and not Greek wisdom.

32. Interestingly, R. Isaac Herzog, the late Chief Rabbi of the State of Israel, assumed that these decrees (*gezerot*) were never accepted by the community, and, hence, were voided. See I. Herzog, *Pesakim u-Ketavim* 2 (Jerusalem, 1989), 557. On the overall impact of the Greek language on the Jewish community as a whole, see J. N. Sevester, *Do You Know Greek?* (Leiden, 1968).

33. See *Tosafot, Menaḥot* 64b, *s.v. arur.*

34. See *Yefeh Mar'eh* to *p. Pe'ah*, 1:1 (15c).

more surefooted and univalent on the issue of "Greek wisdom" or more broadly (and consistently) "the wisdom of the nations" than is the talmudic tradition. But for the talmudic tradition, the very disapproval of such study is a matter of debate, and its seriousness, a matter of degree.

It is well worth placing the talmudic traditions in some broader perspectives as well. Jonathan Goldstein has pointed out, for example, that the conservative Roman reaction to Greek language and culture was far more persistent, principled, and harsh than the talmudic response which, he notes, is sporadic and largely stimulated by specific events.[35] We have also seen that the Sages are concerned, on the whole, with the degree to which the study of Greek culture might dislodge the centrality of Torah study; they deal with formal instruction in Greek materials. With one exception—the Palestinian report of the "18 decrees" passed shortly before the destruction of the Second Temple—no talmudic source bans the use of the Greek language per se.[36] Jews are not forbidden to speak Greek, nor is its use even discouraged. Even the famous midrash which praises the Israelites for "not changing their language" while in Egypt (and thereby meriting redemption from slavery) is sensitive to the danger that Jews might abandon their own language; it is not directed against use of an additional, second tongue.

But too much ought not to be made of this last point. The proof-texts cited indicate that the model Jew speaks Hebrew, not Greek. More broadly, the basic thrust of this teaching is to encourage Jews to hold firmly to their native national traditions. The significance of this aggadah and its message may be gauged, incidentally, by the fact that it appears in numerous collections. Another indication of the seriousness with which the tradition of Israelite devotion to their national identity in Egypt was taken is the fact that one item, that Jews did not change their names, appears in a number of different versions (as Saul Lieberman has pointed out): that no foreign names were adopted at all, or that only names which sounded similar to the Hebrew original were taken, or that only names which translated the Hebrew original were adopted. Clearly, the adoption (or nonadoption) of non-Jewish names was a delicate issue in talmudic times! The backdrop to all these hortatory midrashim lies in the fact, known well to the Sages, that "the majority of Jews outside the land of Israel have the same names as do non-Jews." Coming back to the question of language per se, let us recall that R. Me'ir promised "the world to come" to any who lived in the Land of Israel, recited the Shema twice daily, and spoke Hebrew.[37] All in all, then, the issue of language may have been more charged than the normative materials, taken narrowly, indicate.

35. J. Goldstein, "Jewish Acceptance and Rejection of Hellenism," in E. Sanders et al., *Jewish and Christian Self-Definition* 2, 64–87. The Roman and Jewish reactions had been contrasted, as well, by M. Hadas, *Hellenistic Culture* (New York, 1959), 45–46.

36. *p. Shabbat* 1:4 (3c), and see *Korban ha-'Edah*, ad loc. and S. Lieberman, *Yerushalmi Kifshuto* (Jerusalem, 1935), 44.

37. *Mekhilta de-Rabbi Ishmael* to Exodus 12:6 (ed. Horowitz-Rabin, p. 14); *Sifre* to

Actually, of course, use of Greek abounds. Saul Lieberman has pointed to Greek proverbs and bon mots found verbatim in the Talmud and midrash; and midrashic exegesis even finds Greek puns in Scripture.[38] Abraham's famous and touching reply to Isaac (in the midrashic reading) that he, Isaac, would serve as the sacrificial lamb, is based on the similarity of *seh* (lamb) to the Greek *su* (you): *ha-seh le-'olah beni* meaning "you will be the sacrifice, my son." And when Rav explains that God gave Cain a dog to accompany him in his wanderings, this is probably a midrashic pun as well; the biblical *ot* (sign) means "letter" in mishnaic Hebrew, and adding the Greek *s* to *Cain* we get (in Greek) *kunos,* or dog.[39] Needless to say, the assumption that languages other than Hebrew can be discovered under the surface of the biblical text is most revealing; hardly a consistent method, it does indicate an openness that should be kept in mind in describing the rabbinic mentality. But the phenomenon is not only aggadic; we recall that R. Akiba connected the meaning of *totafot* in "African" to the shape of the halakhic phylacteries.[40]

Most of this material reflects literary play and borrowing of fixed formulae—not

---

Deuteronomy 32:43 (ed. Finkelstein, p. 383 [R. Me'ir]); this teaching doubtless had a practical thrust and was not concerned with the metaphysical virtues of Hebrew alone. So, too, R. Yose b. Akiba (*Sifre* to Deuteronomy 11:19) declared that a father who did not start teaching his son Torah and speaking to him in Hebrew as soon as he began to talk would cause his death. Is this directed against parents who preferred a Greek education? The many aggadot praising the merits of the Holy Language may also serve as an indication that the Sages were struggling to preserve the primacy of Hebrew; but the popular antagonist may have been Aramaic no less than Greek. Perhaps the strongest version of the motif of Jewish linguistic faithfulness in Egypt tells of a covenant that Jews "would do acts of kindness (*gemillut ḥassadim*) for each other, preserve circumcision . . . , and not abandon the language of the house of Jacob and go learn the language of Egypt, because of idolatry" (*Seder Eliyahu Rabbah* XXII [ed. M. Ish-Shalom, 124–25]). S. Lieberman, "Ḥazzanut Yannai," *Sinai* 4 (1939): 277–28; *Tosefta Gittin* 6:4 (ed. Lieberman, p. 270). For bibliography on Greek names among diaspora Jews, see G. Mussies, in S. Safrai, ed., *The Jewish People in the First Century* II (Philadelphia, 1976), 1063–64. S. Lieberman also notes (*Tosefta ki-fshuta* 8 [New York, 1973], 790, n. 63), that Jews living in the Land of Israel in Amoraic times typically carried two names, one Jewish and the other Roman (in their role as citizens of the empire). The most recent discussion is M. D. Herr, "Hashpa'ot Ḥiẓẓoniyot be-'Olamam Shel ḥakhamim," in Y. Kaplan, ed., *Hitbollelut u-Temi'ah* (Jerusalem 1989), 94–102.

38. S. Lieberman, *Greek in Jewish Palestine* (New York, 1942), 15–67.

39. *Bereshit Rabbah* 56:4 (ed. Theodore-Albek, p. 599; see their commentary, ad loc.); *Bereshit Rabbah* 2:12 (op. cit., p. 219), and *Yefeh To'ar,* ad loc. Naturally, these examples barely scratch the surface.

40. *Sanhedrin* 4b. Textual variants and explanations of this enigmatic comment abound, but these are not our concern here. Another halakhic example is found in the connection seen by the rabbis between the belief that a premature infant born in the seventh month lives while a similar birth in the eighth month is fatal with the Greek term for life which is related to the Greek number seven. See *Bereshit Rabbah* 14:2 (op. cit., p. 127). This comment was made by R. Abbahu, somewhat playfully, to his gentile interlocutors.

free conversation, even as a second language. It seems, then, that the Sages were not dogmatically opposed to the Greek language and even enjoyed a cultured bon mot now and then. But, if the many homiletical statements (*aggadot*) about Hebrew are to be taken probatively, the Sages certainly did not want Jews abandoning Hebrew as a language of internal communication and were possibly not happy with Jews who conversed in Greek. Obviously, this last observation can be further pursued from a methodological point of view in different directions—that of the metaphysical value of language, and that of the sociology of subject peoples.

Outside Books—Secular Works?

Another interesting indicator of the attitude of the Sages to secular knowledge is found in the discussions surrounding the reading of "outside books" [*sefarim ḥiẓoniyim*], that is, books not included in the biblical canon. The term and category derive, of course, from R. Akiva's declaration that among those who "have no share in the world to come" is to be included "one who reads the outside books."[41] This statement is ambiguous on at least two scores: What does *read* mean? And what are "outside books?" As to our first question, halakhists have unanimously understood the word *read* in its broadest sense; that is to say, they have not seen it as referring to the much narrower activity of using the text under discussion for liturgical purposes in the synagogue or for instructional purposes in the school. This interpretation, favored by some modern scholars, has R. Akiva denying Scriptural status to "outside books," but not objecting to their use in general. Yet, even if halakhists do not restrict the meaning of *read* in this way, the term is nonetheless not free of ambiguity—as the talmudic discussions themselves reveal. These discussions center, as we shall see, on our second question: what are the banned "outside books"?

Both Talmuds ask this question. The Palestinian Talmud amplifies R. Akiva's declaration, prohibiting:

> one who reads the "outside books" such as the books of *Ben Sira* and the books of *Ben La'anah*.[42] But he who reads the books of Homer and all other books that were written

41. *M. Sanhedrin* 10:1. For rabbinic discussion, see *Enzyklopedia Talmudit*, 15, col. 61–64. In the following I follow the translations and general interpretation offered in S. Z. Leiman, *The Canonization of Hebrew Scripture* (Hamden, Conn., 1976), 86–92; itself indebted to S. Lieberman, *Hellenism in Jewish Palestine*, 106–11. For a recent discussion (and different suggestions) see J. Faur, "Le-Bi'ur ha-Munaḥ 'Kore be-Iggeret'," *'Alei Sefer* 15 (1988–89): 21–30.

42. *Ben Sira* was written in Jerusalem in pre-Hasmonean times and was known and used by the Sages. See *EJ* 4:550–53, and E. Schurer, op. cit. (n. 28), 3 (Edinburgh, 1986), 190–212; for talmudic use and attitudes, see also M. Z. Segal, *Sefer Ben Sira ha-Shalem*

> "from then on,"[43] is considered like one who is reading a secular document. . . . Hence casual reading of Homer is permissible but intensive study is forbidden.[44]

"Outside books," then, are those that might claim biblical status, especially if written ostensibly in biblical times; and it was such whose reading (whether liturgical or personal) R. Akiva banned, perhaps in opposition to the popular trends in his day. But be this as it may, R. Akiva would clearly allow the reading of Homer—and if Homer, so populated with gods and goddesses, amour and war, is permissible, any secular literature is legitimate reading matter! One restriction does remain true: Homer is to be read, but casually, for entertainment. It is not to be studied. Only Torah is an appropriate object of study, or more substantively: only Torah is the source of norms and values.

The Babylonian Talmud reads:

> R. Akiva adds: one who reads the outside books. . . . A Tanna taught: this means the books of the heretics (*minnim*). R. Joseph said: It is forbidden to read the books of Ben Sira.[45]

Once again, the declaration of R. Akiva does not ban all books other than Torah. For the anonymous Tanna, the banned books are heretical works, likely works of Judaeo-Christians. R. Joseph adds *Ben Sira* to the list, probably because it aspired to—but was denied—Scriptural status.[46] Clearly, purely secular works were not the target of R. Akiva's ban. One may argue, of course, that today's *secular* plays the role of the talmudic *heretical*, and ought to be treated in the same fashion as were books of *minnim*. But this step involves a creative halakhic appropriation of our text, as well as a significant value judgment; and both moves would take us beyond our immediate frame of reference. In any case, Homer should not have been easy to swallow in talmudic times either; nonetheless this model of pagan culture was considered appropriate reading matter by the Sages.

There is, however, one early rabbinic text that may take a more rigorous position on our question. *Midrash Kohelet Rabbah* (to Kohelet 12:12) remarks that "whoever brings into his house more than twenty-four books (of the Bible) introduces confusion into his house, as, e.g., the book of *Ben Sira* and the book of

(Jerusalem, 1959), 36–47, and S. Z. Leiman, *Canonization*, 92–102. *Ben La'anah* (and *Ben Tiglah*) are otherwise unknown Apocryphal works; see *EJ* 4:539.

43. That is, from the cessation of prophecy. See S. Lieberman, *Tosefeth Rishonim* 4 (Jerusalem, 1939), 157, who refers to *Seder 'Olam Rabbah*, chap. 30.

44. *p. Sanhedrin* 10:1 (28a).

45. *Sanhedrin* 100b.

46. The Talmud itself argues for the substantive impropriety of *Ben Sira,* but this argument is compromised, as is well known, by the use and citation of *Ben Sira* by talmudic sages themselves; see S. Z. Leiman, *Canonization*, 92–102.

Ben Taglah."[47] Here the Sages ostensibly say that any book which is not in the biblical canon is not fit to be in a Jewish home, creating a total ban, indeed, on all secular materials. Yet, even this midrash continues and specifies the books of *Ben Sira* and *Ben Taglah*, much as did the talmudic texts with which we are familiar. Saul Lieberman has argued, moreover, that the midrash as we have it is textually corrupt at this point, and concludes that its original intent was to permit the reading of the Homeric epics.[48] This squares perfectly with what we have seen in the Talmud.

Higayyon—The Study of Logic?

Dealing as we are with explicit talmudic rulings on access to secular and even pagan materials, we cannot avoid noting R. Eliezer's warning: "Keep your children away from *higayyon*."[49] The last term is of course crucial—and it is also enigmatic. In medieval and modern Hebrew, *higayyon* is the term for *logic*, and even for philosophical logic. Indeed, R. Eliezer was already read in geonic times as banning the study of philosophy for the young and corruptible at least. Yet, this was hardly the regnant understanding among medieval authorities, as Mordechai Breuer has shown at length.[50] Rashi, for example, took R. Eliezer as opposing undue concentration on biblical study or, alternatively, as warning against allowing children to pratter unduly (when they should be studying); and one can hardly accuse Rashi of having been corrupted by Greek philosophy or of having a bias in that direction. The majority of modern scholars similarly see no connection between our term (as used in talmudic times) and philosophy,[51] though it should be added that Saul Lieberman does allow that "the explanation of *higayyon* as dialectics, sophistry, . . . and even logic is . . . plausible."[52] All in all, then, it would be difficult to generalize a ban

47. See n. 42 above.

48. Cited in n. 41 above.

49. *Berakhot* 28b.

50. M. Breuer, "Min'u Benekhem Min ha-Higayyon," *Sefer Zikkaron ha-Rav David Ochs* (Ramat Gan, 1978), 242–61.

51. To be more precise, the comment of R. Eliezer is not read as a warning against the study of philosophy in general but it is often taken to mean: do not stress the role of logic in the study of Torah itself. This understanding does rely on the classic medieval (though see S. Lieberman, below, n. 52) use of *higayyon*. It also recalls the intellectual profile of R. Eliezer, who gives pride of place to tradition rather than creativity; and it notes his statement in its entirety: "Keep your sons away from *higayyon* and seat them in the laps of rabbinic scholars [*talmidei ḥakhamim*]." See, e.g., H. Graetz, *Geschichte der Juden* (Leipzig, 1908), 393; L. Ginzberg, *An Unknown Jewish Sect* (New York, 1970), 49–51. Others place the term in a social, rather than an academic, context. See G. Alon, "Gaon," *Tarbiẓ* 21 (1950): 107. See now J. Faur, "Le-Bi'ur" (n. 41), 28–30.

52. Lieberman, *Helllenism*, 109, n. 62.

on secular study from R. Eliezer (whose position is, in any case, that of an individual); even if *higayyon* were to mean dialectics, sophistry, or logic, it is likely that these topics were seen as especially subversive (or attractive as areas of study that could compete with Torah) for the young, and for them specifically.

Hebrew Scripture and Greek Text

One text that is frequently cited as an exemplar of rabbinic approval of Greek culture and its integration into Jewish life is the midrash to Genesis 9:27. On the whole, this midrash is less crucial than it is often made out to be; it is typically singular, as a midrash frequently is; and it contains little normative content. Despite all this, our midrash does make a point that is worth noticing and is appropriately discussed at this juncture.

"May God enlarge [*yaft*] Japhet, and let him dwell in the tents of Shem" was commented on and understood in various ways by the Sages. *Enlarge* meant for some that Cyrus, the Persian descendent of Japhet, would build the Second Temple; yet God (*He*, not *he*) would dwell only in the tents of Shem (Israel).[53] But Bar Kappara homilized that it was Japhet himself who would dwell in the tents of Shem, and, by virtue of his language: "Let the words of Torah be uttered in the language of Japhet," that is, in Greek. This, as R. Judan commented, referred to the translation of the Bible into Greek.[54] Bar Kappara himself may even have referred to the use of Greek in the very study of Torah (as "tents" is frequently midrashic code for places of Torah-study; recall Jacob, the "dweller in tents," the student, contrasted with Esau the hunter).[55] This midrash approves, then, of the use of Greek to translate the Bible, but it does not yet explicitly express an attitude towards the non-Judaic language itself, which merely facilitates the communication of Torah to ignorant Jews or curious, impressionable gentiles. (Actually, of course, translation never takes a merely instrumental view of language, and a translator's relationship to the language into which he renders his text is richly creative and even intimate—but our midrash need not take account of all that.)

Talmudic discussion, however, carries us considerably further for it attempts to explain the favored position of Greek, a priority already implied by our midrash.

53. The idea that the Divine Presence (*Shekhinah*) was absent from the Second Temple because it was built by Cyrus is found in *Yoma* 10a (R. Yoḥanan), but it may very well be at the root of this midrash too.

54. *Bereshit Rabbah* 36:7; *p. Megillah* 1:9 (71b). See also Targum Onkelos and ps. Jonathan to Genesis, ad loc.

55. S. Lieberman, *Greek in Jewish Palestine* (n. 38), 15–67, gives many examples of rabbinic use of Greek proverbs, literary expressions, etc., but there is no evidence that Torah was taught in Greek, as our midrash may imply, and as S. Baron, *Social and Religious History of the Jews* 2 (Philadelphia, 1958), 142, asserts.

These discussions take as their point of departure R. Simeon ben Gamliel's insistence that the Torah may be translated—and, apparently, read in the synagogue—only into Greek. R. Yoḥanan cited the midrashic reading of Genesis 9:27 with which we are already familiar, but the Talmud retorted that Scripture ought then to be rendered into the tongues of "Gomer and Magog," also children of Japhet, as well. The discussion concludes, now, that *yaft* derives not from *enlarge*, but from *beauty*, and Genesis 9:27 thus announces that only the most beautiful of Yaphet's languages—Greek—will win a place in the tents of Shem.[56] A similar point is made in the Palestinian Talmud, where Aquilas the translator is praised by his rabbinic mentors in the words of Psalms 45:3: "You are fairer [*yafyafita*] than all men; your speech is endowed with grace; rightly has God given you an eternal blessing." *Yafyafita* is doubtless taken as an echo of Genesis 9:27; the "eternal blessing" lies in the fact that Aquilas rendered Torah into Greek.[57] The basic point which emerges from all this, of course, is that the Sages appreciated the charm and elegance of Greek, perhaps even took particular pleasure in the fact that the Torah would be translated into that language. R. Eliezer and R. Joshua, who praised Aquilas so fulsomely, clearly knew enough Greek to appreciate that the only linguistically *adequate* language into which the Torah could be rendered was Greek, this being the outcome of investigations undertaken by the Sages.[58] Here, then, it is not the beauty of Greek but its precision and suppleness that is the point.

These comments sit uneasily with the various bans on Greek language and culture. None dispute the normative reality of the latter. But we now see that the Sages were open to the beauties of Greek, and that their ambience was not boorish or crude.

Certainly, all these rabbinic statements were made after the fact, that is, centuries after the Greek Septuagint was a fact.[59] Indeed, the Tanna R. Judah said that it became permissible to translate the Torah into Greek simply because it was not

56. *Megillah* 9b. The rabbis acknowledge that the Torah may be read in translation; see *Tosefta Megillah* 3(4):11 (ed. Liberman, p. 356), and S. Lieberman, *Tosefta Kifshuta* 5 (New York, 1962), 1179–80. This is also the plain sense of the *M. Megillah* 1:8 and of talmudic discussions, such as *Megillah* 18a. For further review of opinion and discussion of this matter, see later commentators such as R. Aryeh Leib of Metz, *Turei Even*, and especially R. Naftali Z. Y. Berlin, *Meromei Sadeh*, both to *Megillah* 8b–9b.

57. *p. Megillah,* op. cit. As to the identity of the translator, see S. Lieberman, *Greek,* 18.

58. *p. Megillah,* op. cit. The claim that the Sages "investigated the matter and found that the Torah could be translated adequately only into Greek" is a clear counter to the disapproving statement in *Soferim* 1:7 (ed. M. Higger, 101–2): "for the Torah could not be translated adequately."

59. It has been claimed that disapproval of the Septuagint translation is a later development, related perhaps to its use by the Christian movement. For a recent treatment of the subject, see I. Gruenewald, " Ha-Polemos be-'Inyan Tirgum ha-Torah li-Yevvanit," *Te'udah* 4 (1986): 65–78.

possible to reject Ptolemy's request for such a translation.[60] But this is not the drift of rabbinic discussion as a whole. R. Simeon ben Gamliel, a contemporary of R. Judah and the only other early Sage to offer a rationale for the unique position of Greek, points to its linguistic virtues;[61] and the midrashic play of Yefet meaning beauty/Greek is used widely by the early Sages of the Talmud (*Amoraim*).[62] On the whole, then, the Sages claimed that Greek well deserved its role as vehicle of revelation, with the *amoraim* arguing that even the Bible hinted at the destiny of the language.

It is worth noting that the Sages did not take easily to the idea of translation, or, more precisely, the reading from a translation as a written text in the synagogue in place of the original Hebrew. While the anonymous Mishnah does permit such translation into all languages, the point of R. Simeon ben Gamliel's allowance of Greek is to *disallow* translations into other languages. Similarly, both he and R. Judah use the term *heter* (permit) to describe the rabbinic policy even towards favored Greek—hardly an enthusiastic endorsement; and this doubtless reflects hesitations about the use of translation rather than a negative stance towards Greek. Indeed, the Sages banned the reading of supplementary Aramaic translation (read after the original Hebrew) from a scroll, holding that translation, as Oral Torah, must remain oral; this is apparently the primary meaning of the rule: "Matters [of Torah] that are oral should not be said from a written text."[63] Thus, the use of a written translation as substitute for the Hebrew Torah itself is itself noteworthy. It would seem, then, that a written text that *replaces* the Hebrew original can be perceived as Written Torah, and will have an easier time of it than a translation that accompanies the reading from the original Hebrew![64] Alternatively, these materials may reflect a tradition that did not have the rule banning the reading of "matters that are oral" from a written text or, at least, did not apply that rule to translations.

---

60. *Megillah* 9a; and see *Turei Even* to *Megillah* 8b, *s.v. RSBG.*

61. Do these differing Tannaitic views start from differing attitudes towards Greek culture? It has been argued (despite *Shabbat* 33b) that R. Judah is generally hostile (see I. Ben-Shalom, "Rabi Yehudah bar Ila'i ve-yahasoel Romi," *Ẓion* 49 [1984]: 9–24); R. Simeon ben Gamliel, a scion of the Patriarchal house, is more favorably disposed towards the surrounding culture.

62. See at notes 54, 56, *supra.* Even Bar Kappara's original homily on Genesis 9:27 was applied by R. Judah to the idea of translation, to which it did not necessarily itself refer.

63. *p. Megillah* 4:11 (74d); *Temurah* 14b and *Gittin* 60a; and see Y. N. Epstein, *Mavo le-Nusaḥ ha-Mishnah* (Jerusalem, 1948), 696–97. Thus, Maimonides includes this rule in his Code only in the context of reading a supplementary translation in public (*Hil. Tefillah* 12:11), though he does mention it in other contexts as well (see G. Blidstein, "Maimonides on Oral Law," *Jewish Law Annual* 1 [1978]: 110, n. 5). See also I. Gruenewald, "Ha-Polemos," 71–72.

64. The paradoxes—both practical and conceptual—inherent in this situation are obvious and need not be belabored.

Law of the Gentiles: Continuum or Contrast?

"He issues His commands to Jacob, His statutes and rules to Israel. He did not do so for any other nation; of such rules they know nothing. Hallelujah" (Psalms 147:19–20). This may sound like a rather extreme statement; but let us recall that even though the Bible expects moral behavior of all people (and not only Jews), it nowhere asserts that God revealed His law to any but Jews. The Sages, of course, would have to square these verses in Psalms with the belief in Noahide Law that is commanded to all men.[65] Be this as it may, the assertion of the psalmist certainly summed up Israel's special responsibility and favored position. It would also reflect the assumption that Israel could learn nothing about God's will or the proper way to live from pagans or non-Jews who were never blessed with God's Torah.

This, indeed, is the working assumption of talmudic literature. The Sages, so intent on defining the right thing to do in both ritual and ethics, do not turn to the work of their non-Jewish contemporaries for guidance or even comparison; in fact they seem barely interested in how other systems of thought and life handled similar problems. Indifference is the rule, on the whole, as they go about their business. Yet if the Sages do not expect to learn anything from the gentile legists or religionists, they still acknowledge the existence of gentile law and morality and its relationship to Jewish Torah. This awareness expresses itself in two contrasting—but not necessarily contradictory—patterns. There is a body of teaching which indicates that gentile law and morality form a continuum with that of the Jews; and there is a body of teaching which emphasizes the gap between the two.

We shall first outline the pattern formed by those sources which describe the continuum of Jewish Torah and gentile law; and, to be precise, let me add the proviso that we may really be speaking of *law commanded the gentile,* rather than of *gentile law,* though this latter phenomenon occurs as well. Be this as it may, a fundamental point at which to start is with Noahide Law, that is *sheva mizvot benei Noaḥ* (the seven commandments given Noahides).[66] Despite some initial debate as to the precise identity of the norms included in the list, a consensus was eventually established and the list crystalized: idolatry, blasphemy, eating the flesh of a living creature, robbery, murder, adultery, and incest were banned; and the rule of law (*dinnim*) was to be established. This list parallels in large measure the Ten Commandments (with the exception that the Sabbath and honor of parents, are omitted). It also indicates those three norms which a Jew is expected to honor even at the cost of his life, namely the ban on murder, idolatry, and *'arayyot* (adultery and

65. See below, n. 73.

66. The most recent treatment of this topic is D. Novak, *The Image of the Non-Jew in Judaism* (Toronto, 1983). See also the essays by S. H. Bergman, R. Loewe, and K. Wilhelm, in R. Loewe, ed., *Studies in Rationalism, Judaism and Universalism* (London, 1966).

incest). The absence of any positive religious or moral content is striking and significant. No ritual activity is expected nor, for that matter, any positive acknowledgment of God at all. Similarly, on the social level, the Noahide is not to harm his fellow—but he is not expected to love him. Such, at least, is the message of the Seven Noahide Commands. The prophet Ezekiel, on the other hand (16:49), knew that Sodom was destroyed because its people "had plenty of bread and untroubled tranquility, yet . . . did not support the poor and the needy" suggesting that non-Jews, too, were expected to care for their neighbors.[67] All in all, one has the impression that this Noahide agenda describes a lesser Judaism. Thus, the regimen of the "resident alien" (*ger toshav*), who is seen by some as having started on the path to conversion, is identified by the Sages with the Noahide commandments.[68]

Our topic may be profitably approached from the opposite direction as well. Some talmudic texts may indicate that, in receiving the Torah, the Jews built on and continued their identity as Noahides; they did not start afresh. This is expressed in typically formal language:

> Any normative commandment (*mizvah*) which was given to Noahides and not repeated at Sinai is obligatory upon Israel alone and not upon Noahides. Those commandments, however, which were given to Noahides and repeated at Sinai are intended for both Noahides as well as for Israel.[69]

Had they not been repeated at Sinai, therefore, Noahide commands would have obliged Israel alone, for Israel is the fullest continuation of the Noahide covenant and would also preserve the Noahide identity. This point is made more directly in the midrash: "Ten commands were given to the Children of Israel at Marah: the seven which Noahides had accepted to which were added . . ."[70] The continuum of Noahide law and Jewish *halakhah* is palpable.

Noahide law has sometimes been understood as the talmudic equivalent of

---

67. This is noted in *Sanhedrin* 58b. From the talmudic context it appears that Noahides may well be obliged in certain positive commandments even if these are not found in the list of the Seven Noahide Laws. Thus, R. Aḥai Gaon claimed that Noahides were commanded to "be fruitful and multiply," much as Jews are (*She'iltot* 165). For an explication of the maximalist view of the Noahide Laws, see D. S. Shapiro, *Oraḥim* (Jerusalem, 1977), 55–75.

68. *'Avodah Zarah* 64b.

69. *Sanhedrin* 59a.

70. *Sanhedrin* 56b. See also the description of the "Book of the Covenant" from which Moses read to the people at Sinai and to which they responded, "We shall do and we shall obey" (*Mekhilta* to Exodus 24:7): "He read to them the laws commanded to Adam [*sic*], the commandments given to the Israelites in Egypt and at Marah, and all the other commandments" (trans., J. L. Lauterbach [Philadelphia, 1933] 22, 211); and see note following. See, as well, D. Frimer, "Israel, the Noahide Laws, and Maimonides," *Jewish Law Association Studies* 2 (1986): 89–102.

natural law; to which rejoinder is frequently made that the talmudic appellation is always Noahide *commands* (*miẓvot benei Noah*), thus emphasizing God as the source of these norms. In any case, before embarking on a discussion of the relevance of natural law to talmudic thought, one would have to select the precise variant of natural law at issue and contend with the fact that the Talmud has no handy term for *nature.* None of these considerations are really crucial, but they ought to be kept in mind. Assuming, then, that the term *miẓvot* in our context is deliberate, it is nonetheless unclear whether the Sages predicate an actual historical bestowal of these commands or rather claim that the human person is inherently obliged to these ethical/religious norms by the Creator. (Maimonides, who declared that Noahide obedience must be derived from a belief in Sinaitic revelation—a position derived in part from a single, late midrash—is not necessarily typical on this point.)[71]

A no less significant aspect of this terminology is that the Noahide is obliged in precisely the same way as the Jew is: by God's command.[72] In this sense, it ought to be possible for a Jew to recognize in a gentile's normative behavior (and legal system) a response to the same commands by which he and his society are formed. Indeed, the midrash is forced to back off from the psalmist's expansive claim that God issued his commands to Jacob alone, "not for any other nation; of such rules they know nothing." The nations, we are now told, know the rules but are ignorant of their finer points.[73] This implies, as well, that the nations are expected to adopt much of the Jewish halakhic structure, except for those particulars from which they are

---

71. *Hil. Melakhim* 9:11.

72. An interesting attempt has been made by Saul Berman ("Noahide Laws," in M. Elon, ed., *Principles of Jewish Law* [Jerusalem, 1975], 709) to show that talmudic sources are not of one mind on this point, some indicating that these precepts were *commanded,* and others claiming that they were based on *consent.* But even these latter materials include the noun, *miẓvot* (and generally speaking, *consent* accompanies *command* in rabbinic thought; the two concepts do not clash).

73. "'He spoke his words to Jacob . . .'—But weren't the nations of the world (also) commanded to establish the rule of law [*dinnim*], which is one of the Seven Noahide Commands? . . . Rather, Scripture refers to the finer specifics of the law [*dikdukei ha-din*], such as Ben Zakkai's examination of witnesses regarding the color of date-stems. Furthermore, Noahides are executed on the testimony of a single witness and by the decisions of a single judge . . . while the people of Israel are judged by three judges in civil cases and twenty-three judges in capital cases" (*Tanḥuma,* ed. S. Buber, Deuteronomy 14b). Interestingly, the distinction between Noahides and Israel focuses on what are primarily procedural matters, though these are not in the least trivial. See also *Shemot Rabbah* 30:9: "'He spoke his words to Jacob . . . He did not do so for any other nation, and He did not make his laws known to them,' but He chose Jacob above gentiles, to whom He gave only some of the laws; He gave Adam six commands, added a seventh to Noah, an eighth to Abraham, to Jacob a ninth, but to Israel He gave all." The difference between Israel and the nations is relativised though the midrash emphasizes the gap between the two. All this in the seemingly absolute context of Psalms 147! See too n. 87.

explicitly excluded. This has some bearing on another puzzle: does Noahide Law reflect a rabbinic assumption that the gentile world was in fact committed to the rule of law (as Kadushin and Lieberman, among others, assert)?[74] This would indicate that the gentile systems were a legitimate concretization of the divine command, though differing from the Torah given Israel. Or is it, rather, a list of ideal norms, reflecting the moral/religious definition of a minimal human ethos? The Talmud itself claims that gentile society has rejected the norms of Noahide Law; this is also the import of the well-known midrash that tells how God first offered the Ten Commandments to the nations of the world, who all found its moral and religious demands unacceptable.[75]

There are other indications, too, that the Sages presumed a continuum of human morality. *Mishpatim*, they teach, are those requirements to which gentiles raise no objection, and which, were they not written in the Torah, "It stands to reason [*be-din hayah*] that they should have been written."[76] The issue for us is not the sort of "reason" here assumed, but rather the apparent agreement of Jewish and gentile society that certain norms are required: "theft and incest and idolatry and blasphemy and murder" are outlawed. Perhaps, too, we can view Jewish ethical obligations which the Mishnah grounds "in the interests of peace"[77] in a similar light. These are frequently understood to be a mere expression of self-interest, cynically clothed in noble ethical verbiage. But taking a more generous attitude, we may say that seeing that Jews and gentiles did live together in the cities of Hellenistic Palestine, the Sages found a policy of mutuality and fraternity to be not only sensible but even virtuous. Similarly, a midrash teaches that moral behavior (*derekh ereẓ*) preceded the giving of Torah by twenty-six generations, that is, for the career of humanity from Adam to Sinai.[78] In context, the function of this teaching is to praise the common morality of the unlearned—in this case, a man who never spread malicious gossip and who made peace between the quarrelsome—as taking priority over the attainments of the learned. But it also carries the message that humanity shares a common pre-Sinaitic morality. Indeed, the very phrase *derekh ereẓ* (the way of the land) is an idiomatic reminder of the universality of the human ethos, ranging from morality to propriety and good manners, and even to practical reason. This, of course, is good biblical doctrine; the narratives of Genesis assume that all men and women are responsible to be "God-fearing" and would be called to account (as were Cain, the contemporaries of Noah, Abimelekh, and Pharaoh) for their immoral-

74. M. Kadushin, *Worship and Ethics* (Northwestern U. Press, 1964), 145; S. Lieberman, *Greek in Jewish Palestine* 81.

75. *Baba Kamma* 38a; *Mekhilta* to Exodus 20:2 (op. cit.), 234–36; *'Avodah Zarah* 2b.

76. *Sifra* to Leviticus 18:4 (ed. Weiss, 86a); *Yoma* 67b.

77. *M. Gittin* 5:8; *Tosefta Gittin* 5(3):4–5.

78. *Vayikra Rabbah* 9:6. For an overview of the term and its varied meanings, see M. Kadushin, *Worship and Ethics*, 49–57.

ity.[79] So, when R. Simeon ben Gamliel asserted that society (literally, "the world," *ha-'olam*) survives because of truth, justice (or law) and peace, he may well have meant human society as a whole.[80]

Yet, we must distinguish between the existence of a moral continuum, even the belief in a common human nature, and the willingness or need to create a community of thought or reflection. Even if norms are held in common, the gentile world will rarely be called upon to provide a model for Jewish imitation. Thus, the all-too-famous instance where the Sages point to a gentile—Dama b. Netinah, an Ashkelonite—as an exemplar of filial piety and indeed allow his behavior to create the heroic norm, is the exception, not the rule.[81]

The issue of Jewish openness to gentile models, the willingness of *halakhah* to learn from the non-Jewish world, may also be examined on the verbal, linguistic level. Earlier, we discussed the Sages' attitude to the Greek language per se, suggesting it might be an indicator of their posture vis-à-vis non-Jewish culture as a whole. Here, where we pursue the narrower question of their willingness to learn from gentiles in the halakhic realm, we may profitably survey a more specific linguistic phenomenon, and that is the wide use of Greek and Latin legal terms for the corresponding talmudic institutions. The use of loan-words is selective, as is well known. "Greek philosophic terms are absent from the entire ancient Rabbinic literature"; a fortiori that no Jewish religious idea or practice is described by a Greek term. The situation is different, however, as regards legal terminology. Not only are "rabbinic books full of Greek words," but rabbinic ideas and institutions are denoted by Greek terms.[82] Furthermore, these terms do not merely translate the names of institutions otherwise known to the rabbis themselves by native Hebrew terms; they are sometimes the *only* nomenclature provided for these ideas and practices.

All this suggests the obvious dilemma: Is the institution in question fully native, a part of earlier Jewish rabbinic creativity, yet so consistent with non-Jewish practice that a foreign term—with its attendant attractiveness—is used? Alternatively, does the terminology indicate that the practice is a thoroughgoing import? Certainly, the modern career of Judaism offers examples of both these options, though it is admittedly rare that a foreign term not only serves to translate the Jewish concept but actually to name it. There is, of course, a third possibility, more subtle than the preceding. Foreign terminology *does* indicate the utilization of a foreign concept or practice; but it only provides a device which is coherent with rabbinic thought on the topic. The import may, indeed, provide a solution which rabbinic thought on

79. See M. Greenberg, "Mankind, Israel, and the Nations in the Hebraic Heritage," in J. Nelson, ed., *No Man is Alien* (Leiden, 1971), 15–40.

80. *M. Avot* 1:18.

81. *Kiddushin* 31b; elsewhere, Esau [that is, Rome] is seen as a paragon of filial piety. For other texts and background, see my *Honor Thy Father and Mother* (New York, 1976), 35–36.

82. S. Lieberman, "How Much Greek in Jewish Palestine?" in A. Altman, ed., *Biblical and Other Studies* (Cambridge, Mass., 1963), 332, 334.

its own may not have been able to devise, as we shall later suggest in the case with *prozebol.* Yet it is not, on that score alone, disruptive or illegitimate. Rather, its acceptance reflects the disciplined growth of one culture through the assimilation (and, frequently, adaptation) of appropriate elements of another, remaining faithful to its own overarching and immanent trajectory.

The recent publication of Daniel Sperber's *Dictionary of Greek and Latin Legal Terms in Rabbinic Literature* not only provides an up-to-date lexicographic tool; it also enables a broad survey of the phenomenon under consideration and of its implications. Ranon Katzoff's review essay of Sperber's work devotes itself, in part, to the broader issues raised by the presence of some two hundred legal "loan words" in the rabbinic corpus; his conclusions are a sobering reminder that surface images often deceive. "Only a very few of these two hundred words actually entered the rabbis' legal vocabulary. The vast majority appear in aggadic contexts . . . less than one quarter in halakhic contexts, and of these, only a handful . . . actually became part of the legal vocabulary. *What emerges is a picture of considerable familiarity with foreign laws, but very little acceptance of it.*"[83] Though this conclusion describes our overall perspective as well, it is instructive to examine some topics where foreign institutions most likely impinged on *halakhah,* a process which (as Katzoff points out) was more common before the destruction of the Temple.

A convenient example is found in the familiar *prozebol* of Hillel. *Prozebol* is often cited in discussions of halakhic flexibility and is not infrequently the subject of tendentious debate; but we are concerned with its etymology and origins. The term apparently is Greek, though—significantly—an exact and conclusive parallel to the Jewish institution is still lacking.[84] The *prozebol* was an instrument which allowed the collection of debts after the Sabbatical year, the idea being that the debt in question was now owed the court or was being collected through it. Now, debts presented before a court were collectible after the Sabbatical year as a matter of Mishnaic law; the institution was derived midrashically (from Deuteronomy 15:2–3), as well. For some, then, Hillel's *prozebol* was merely a concretization, broadly disseminated, of this earlier institution which is then a part and parcel of the Oral Law. Rashi, however, understood *prozebol,* a piece of rabbinic legislation, to be at the very root of the other mishnaic regulations, with the midrash in question a mere *asmakhta.* Indeed, this understanding makes the best sense of the talmudic discussion.[85] If, now, the basic practices of presenting debts to the court is of Hellenistic

83. D. Sperber, *A Dictionary of Greek and Latin Legal Terms in Rabbinic Literature* (Ramat-Gan, 1984); R. Katzoff's review essay appeared in the *Journal for the Study of Judaism in the Persian, Hellenistic and Roman Period* 20:2 (Dec. 1989): 195–206, esp. pp. 202–6. The passage cited is on p. 202; the italics are mine.

84. See Sperber, *Dictionary,* 154–56, for discussion and bibliography.

85. Rashi, *Makkot* 3b, *s.v. moser*; Rashi, *Gittin* 36a, *s.v. moserani*; *Tosafot* at both places. See Y. Gilat, "le-Hishtalshelutah Shel Takkanat ha-Pruzbul," *Sefer Barukh Kurzweil* (Jerusalem, 1975), 93–96.

provenance (as the terminology would indicate), then the Sages have appropriated *prozebol* from the surrounding legal culture. At the same time, it is obvious that the foreign practice has been enlisted to serve a purpose which was an organic need of Jewish law itself; and, moreover, that the solution proposed by *prozebol* was coherent with the basic structures of Jewish law. This, of course, is exclusive of the fact that Hillel's *prozebol* apparently adapts the Hellenistic institution, rather than copies it.

Another instance is found in the practice of giving "gifts in contemplation of death" as a way of avoiding the strenuous biblical regulations on the distribution of property to heirs after death. Here the crucial Hellenistic term is *deyathiqi.* But note the careful summation of Reuven Yaron, the major investigator of the topic: "From our discussion of Tannaitic definitions of *deyathiqi* and *mattana* the reader may have gained the impression that the work of the Tannaim, in connection with dispositions in contemplation of death, consisted mainly in the translation of various Greco-Egyptian documents. In reality, however, the Tannaim used the Greco-Egyptian documents merely as raw materials for the building up of legal institutions of their own, which in important aspects were quite different from the original." These sentences introduce a discussion of the structure and specifics of rabbinic law on the topic.[86]

On the whole then, the Sages do not occupy themselves overly much with the nature of the continuum linking Jewish law and teaching and that of the surrounding world. Nor, on the other hand, do they exert themselves too intensely in constantly denying the phenomenon. I am not convinced, for example, that the idea of *Torah she-be'al peh* (Oral Law), which supplements Scripture, was intended to assert the distinctiveness of the totality of Jewish *halakhah,* stressing that, since it is all Sinaitic, it can have nothing in common with non-Jewish systems.[87] However one interprets the nature and scope of Oral Torah, the idea seems more fundamentally a guarantor of the legitimacy, and indeed sanctity, of *halakhah* than of its distinctiveness. Indeed, certain periods of talmudic history betray more concern lest Oral Law become known to gentiles (Christians) than that Oral Law be contaminated by non-Jewish accretions.[88]

There is, actually, little discussion of the substantive drawbacks of gentile law, little disapproval of its standards or procedures. The major point, rather, is that it is alien, that it is not Jewish; and Jews are expected and required to order their lives and society by the Torah and its institutions. An interesting (though not especially

86. R. Yaron, *Gifts in Contemplation of Death* (Oxford, 1960), 46.

87. See B. Jackson, "On the Problem of Roman Influence on the Halakha," in E. P. Sanders, et al., *Jewish and Christian Self-Definition* 2, p. 197. Jackson reads the idea of Noahide Law in similar fashion: "the notion of Noahide Law emphasized that even where there was common moral content, Gentile law lacked the status that attached to superior technical development." Cf. the midrashic materials cited in n. 73 above; these indicate that this very claim is a two-edged sword, as it also points to the commonality of both bodies of law.

88. See, for example, *Tanḥuma, Ki Tissa,* sec. 34.

typical) case in point concerns a claim for damages made before the Exilarch (*resh galuta*), whose decision is rejected by the defendant on the grounds that it is no more than what Persian law would decide ("who needs an exilarch who gives us Persian law?"). R. Naḥman is then approached, and he, in fact, renders a different verdict, one ostensibly in keeping with Jewish law. The talmudic bottom line, however, is that in certain cases, "the law is with the exilarch."[89] It certainly does not help then to identify Jewish law with its Persian counterpart, and the disappointed party can expect popular sympathy when he asks, "Who needs an exilarch who gives us Persian law?" But it is not impossible either for the halakhic decision to dovetail with that of the Persians.

Another instance is given in the Mishnaic debate as to the mode of execution by the sword. The anonymous Tanna described it as decapitation, "as the kingdom [i.e., the Romans] are wont to do." R. Judah replied that this could not be the practice, for the Torah forbids us to "walk in the ways of the gentiles"; to which the answer is given that Jews did not learn decapitation from the Romans but from the Torah.[90] This talmudic passage has given rise to much discussion as to the parameters of prohibited and permitted borrowing, as one might imagine. For our purposes, it is sufficient to point to the suggestive fact that certain practices will be found unacceptable if borrowed from gentiles, but no exception will be taken to them if Judaism arrives at them on its own.

Thus, whatever continuum may exist phenomenologically, the Talmud will not seek out the foreign parallel or attempt to learn from it. And, inasmuch as Jewish society is expected to provide for its own needs, individual Jews are not to accept the solutions of an alien system. This is true not only when these solutions are at odds with the native Jewish position, but even when the Jewish and gentile laws dovetail: Jews are not to turn to the gentile judiciary even if it will render a verdict acceptable in Jewish law.[91] The barrier is institutional, structural, national.

Having come this far, it is impossible to skirt that most concrete instance of the impact of non-Jewish law on the halakhic system: *dina de-malkhuta dina* (the law of the kingdom is law). The Jew is to abide by the laws of the land in which he lives. The scope of the rule is not fully clear even in the relatively few talmudic sources devoted to the topic. It is quite certain that it applies to areas of civil and criminal law, particularly those areas which were of special interest to governments, such as taxation and penalties; but the law of the kingdom is not law if it interferes with the specifically religious obligations of the Jew. The rule is occasionally applied, as well, to matters of procedure in the context of civil law, and it will affect, directly or

89. *Baba Kamma* 58a–59a; see also *Baba Bathra* 173b.

90. *Sanhedrin* 52b.

91. *Mekhilta* to Exodus 21:1 (op. cit., III, 1–2); *Gittin* 88b. See my comments in "Medinat Yisrael ba-Pesikah ha-Hilkhatit," *Diné Yisra'el* 13–14 (1986–88): 34–39.

indirectly, relations between Jews. None of this suggests the *reception* of gentile law by the halakhic system.

The entire *topos* can be seen, of course, as the legal counterpart of diaspora existence, the ineluctable acquiescence to foreign domination. But medieval commentators discussed the legitimacy of *dina de-malkhuta*, and were not satisfied to take it as an expression of the reality of power alone. After all, *dina de-malkhuta* not only impinged on intra-Jewish relationships; it could, according to some, directly order them. Some measure of moral justification is necessary, then, if one Jew is to make demands of another in the name of *dina de-malkhuta* even contrary to Torah law. For some medieval thinkers, royal power purchased obedience through some variation or other of medieval social contract theory. Rashi, though, took an even more principled tack: the normative legitimacy of *dina de-malkhuta* derives in his view precisely from the fact that gentiles, as Noahides, are obliged in *dinnim* (law); it is even possible (though no more than that!) that this fact establishes the Jewish obligation to obey this law.[92] Now, Rashi's doctrine may carry the implication that *dina de-malkhuta* must abide by basic criteria of justice for it to be valid, since *dina* ought to conform to Noahide *din,* itself a command of God. A second implication of this doctrine may be that *dina de-malkhuta* will then form a continuum with Jewish law itself. Nonetheless, one is hard pressed to find explicit acknowledgment of this continuum or, and even more so, discussion of its implications.

Yet, this ought not to be taken to mean that the Sages were unaware of gentile law. In their business dealings with gentiles, Jews obviously had to abide by gentile law and rabbis were no different than other Jews in this regard. When such interaction required halakhic regulation from the Jewish side, gentile law became an intrinsic part of the picture and the Sages took account of it as a given fact. Thus, we find them discussing, in a comparative vein, common situations, assuming at times that the gentile procedure was in fact rooted in Judaic legislation. Similarly, sexual relations of Jews and gentiles (even if forbidden by the law itself) require clarification from the legal perspective of the different systems. Occasionally, the comparative interest seems fueled by the intellectual interest alone. Awareness of the details of gentile law crops up, then, in discussions of modes of conveyance (*kinyan*) and collection of debts; the forms by which marriage is effected and dissolved; standards in the law of torts; and procedures in capital trials. By and large, Jewish law and gentile laws are laconically placed in formal apposition; there is little polemic or evaluation of the different systems.

Thus, the Sages discuss the nature of *kinyan* in gentile law: how do gentiles acquire property? The two alternatives are by payment of money or by physical

---

92. Rashi, *Gittin* 9b *ḥuẓ*. For a survey of views on the legal basis of the principle, see S. Shilo, "Dina DeMalkhuta Dina," in M. Elon, ed., *Principles of Jewish Law*, 711–13. I discuss the historical impact of this principle on Jewish legal behavior in "A Note on the Function of 'The Law of the Kingdom of Law' in the Medieval Jewish Community," *Jewish Journal of Sociology* 15:2 (December, 1973): 213–20.

movement of the object to be acquired (*meshikhah*). Significantly, one basic talmudic discussion assumes that all this lies in the context of Torah law; that is, that the Torah itself teaches how gentiles are to acquire property. Furthermore, gentile conveyance is coordinated, in the discussion, with the Jewish mode: for Abaye, Jews and gentiles acquire by different modes; for Amemar, they acquire in identical fashion.[93] A different discussion assumes that it is actual gentile practice which is the subject, and merely attempts to prove anecdotally what contemporary gentiles consider binding conveyance without any explicit coordination with Jewish practice.[94] Naturally, these two perspectives do not necessarily contradict each other; the Sages may assume that gentile practice in fact reflects biblical legislation, and we shall see other indications of this habit of thought. The motive for these discussions is also noteworthy, as it derives from the need to decide concrete issues faced by Jewish law rather than a theoretical interest in gentile law per se. (In discussion of Noahide law, though, the regulations governing non-Jews are treated as matters of intrinsic interest.) A firstling (*bekhor*) owned by a Jew in partnership with a gentile need not be given to the priest; when, then, is gentile ownership effected? Similarly, the Talmud discusses how gentiles make conveyance of landed property; once again, the concrete issue concerns business deals involving Jews and gentiles.[95] R. Safra uses gentile law as an indicator for Jewish law of usury; "what in their law is actionable and must be paid as interest will be returned to the debtor in our law." All interest is illegal; but if it was paid, it is returned only if payment was a result of a binding prior agreement. Gentile legal behavior is a good test of whether a given commercial arrangement constitutes such binding prior agreement.[96]

Our final instance is perhaps the most well-known of all, at least in its Maimonidean interpretation. The Mishnah rules that if the ox of a Jew gores that of a gentile, no payment is made; but if it is the gentile's ox which gores that of the Jew, then full payment is exacted, whether the damage is caused by a "goring" ox or by an "innocent" one (which usually entails half, rather than full, payment). One of the comments made in explanation of this Mishnah is R. Yoḥanan's brief statement: "as in their laws." Maimonides understood this to mean that gentile law releases the owner of a goring ox from all responsibility, and therefore when a Jew's ox gores a gentile's, one simply turns the tables and imposes their own standards on them. Others explain the passage differently. The important fact, from the perspective of our inquiry, is that the Sages possessed and deployed this additional bit of knowledge of non-Jewish law of torts, using it to explain an otherwise perplexing

93. *Bekhorot* 13a–b. The discussion attributed to Amemar is an extrapolation from his comment in *'Avodah Zarah* 71a.

94. *'Avodah Zarah* 71a (Amemar).

95. *Baba Bathra* 54b–55a.

96. *Baba Meẓia* 62a–b. *Baba Bathra* 173b–174b similarly discusses the different rules governing collection of loans from guarantors in Jewish and gentile practice.

regulation. The Mishnaic rule in this reading was formulated in reaction to the rule operative in gentile law.[97]

Certainly, one should not exaggerate the extent of rabbinic knowledge of gentile law or the rabbis' interest in the topic. On the other hand, the materials just cited represent explicit discussions of gentile law; it is conceivable that much more lies under the surface, as we saw in our consideration of Jewish borrowing from the gentile world. Such rabbinic knowledge explains, perhaps, the assumption of one famous Tannaitic passage that Jewish judges were competent to render decisions based on either Jewish or gentile law![98]

The Sages also treat the gentile law of personal status. It is generally agreed that only the sexual connection itself effects marriage between gentiles; the purely formal *kiddushin* and *nissuin* (components of the Jewish marriage ceremony) are reserved for Jewish society.[99] Once again, gentile law (in this case, Noahide law) is derived from the biblical statement: from Adam on "a man will cleave to his wife," and that, indeed, is how she is taken to wife. Gentile law of divorce is also different from that of Jews, though here the Sages suggest two options: either gentiles have no formal divorce at all, or husbands and wives divorce each other in a perfectly egalitarian way. Here too Scripture—Malachi 2:16—is called into play. These discussions seem to answer to no practical need of Jewish society (they differ in that respect from the matters of civil law raised earlier) and seem to represent a theoretical interest in the moral shape of the non-Jewish world; this despite the fact that, as Boaz Cohen put it, "the rabbis were hardly interested in comparative law."[100] Yet, though these rabbinic positions are anchored in Scripture, we may also ask whether they do not also reflect contemporary social mores. Thus, Cohen

97. *M. Baba Kamma* 4:3, and *Palestinian Talmud*, 4:3(4b); Maimonides, *Hil. Nizkei Mammon* 7:5. For non-Jewish law in the twelfth century as background to the Maimonidean ruling, see B. Jackson, "Maimonides' Definitions of Tam and Mu'ad," *Jewish Law Annual* 1 (1978): 171, n. 13.

98. *Palestinian Talmud*, 4:3 (4b); *Baba Kamma* 113a.

99. This is clearly the position of the Babylonian Talmud; see *Sanhedrin* 57b. I believe it is the position of the Palestininian Talmud as well (*p. Kiddushin* 1:1[58c]), which also seems to allow for cohabitation alone as the form for effecting marriage by gentiles (*contra* B. Cohen, *Jewish and Roman Law* I [New York, 1966], 378). The sense of that passage is, then, that gentiles have no means for constituting marriage. Needless to say, this flies in the face of actual practice (which is doubtless the reason why Cohen reinterprets the passage) and can refer only to the ideal scheme as it is halakhically conceived. *Bereshit Rabbah* 18:5 (ed. Theodore-Albeck, p. 166) supports Cohen with its distinction between *nesu'ot* and *arusot*, but perhaps even in that text *nesu'ot* means: by cohabitation. Be that as it may, the fact that the Talmud then asks whether gentiles do or do not have formal means for divorce must mean that marriage does exist for them, even if only constituted through cohabitation.

100. Cohen, *Jewish and Roman Law*, 378. One wonders whether the specific point of contrast between gentile law and Jewish reality raised by R. Ḥiyya (in *Kiddushin*, op. cit; a gentile couple which divorces, the wife remarries and is divorced, both then convert and

plausibly suggests that R. Yoḥanan's report that gentile wives divorce their husbands by presenting them with a *rifudin* is a reference to the *repudium* of Roman law. Other aspects of this discussion—the fact that infidelity by a betrothed person did not constitute adultery, for example—may also reflect gentile law as practiced in the environment of the Sages.[101] But it is also clear that the attempt to provide a realistic, historical parallel to each rabbinic opinion leads to rather forced interpretations, as when the statement that God has given divorce to Jews but not to gentiles is taken to mean only that divorce is a part of religious law in the Jewish system, while in pagan jurisprudence it is a civil transaction.[102] Clearly, this analysis is an attempt to account for the embarassing reality of divorce in Roman law, a reality supposedly absent according to rabbinic theory (unless one assumes that the Sages found Roman law illegitimate on this point). Be all this as it may, it appears that the Sages did have some interest in gentile law of personal status, both as ideal construct and as it was actually put into practice.[103]

The discussion of legal procedure also evokes an interesting glance at gentile law. The Mishnah rules that when opinions are presented in capital cases, the junior judges speak before their seniors. The question is then argued whether "our law is like their law" in this respect or not. Typically, their law is established by citing Scripture (Genesis 38:24; Esther 1:16) rather than by referring directly to actual practice, thus blurring its meaning; is it what gentiles actually do in reality, or what they should be doing? Nor is the point of the discussion too clear; that is to say, why are the Sages interested here in the congruence (or noncongruence) of Jewish and gentile practice? Rather than assuming rabbinic curiosity on a comparative level, some have integrated this discussion into its talmudic context. If gentiles follow this same procedure, argues *P'nei Moshe,* then it is apparently a matter of reason (*sevarah*), and hence common to Jews and non-Jews alike; consequently, no specifically Jewish source for the procedure need be sought.[104] In this understanding of our passage, gentile practice becomes an indicator of universal reason, and both Jewish and gentile law are presumably derived from that identical source.

---

wish to remarry) was the full stimulus for the question as to gentile divorce. Interestingly, this preconversion activity influences the future status of the couple as Jews.

101. B. Cohen, *Jewish and Roman Law,* 384–85, 378, 337–41.

102. B. Cohen, *Jewish and Roman Law,* 383–84. On the other hand, both the question raised by R. Ḥiyya (n. 100 above) and R. Yoḥanan's reference to *repudium* (n. 101) indicate that the Sages knew full well that in practice non-Jewish law made provision for formal divorce.

103. Needless to say, the rabbis were familiar enough with pagan sexual mores and practices (including those that were legalized) to be critical of their immorality. See S. Baron, *Social and Religious History of the Jews* 2, 223–26, and, at greater length, Y. Cohen, "Demut ha-Nokhri . . . be-Tekufat ha-Tanna'im," *Eshel Be'er Sheva* 2 (1980): 39–63.

104. *p. Sanhedrin* 4:7 (22b). Novak (op. cit., p. 65) states that the talmudic debate is whether Jewish procedure follows non-Jewish law in this instance. This is not explicit in the text; and see *P'nei Moshe* (to whom Novak refers) who offers a different (if somewhat strained) reading.

Of Facts and Values

The Sages doubtless felt that they did not need the gentiles where values or norms were concerned. They probably thought otherwise concerning matters of fact. Here, truth was to be accepted—and, indeed, sought—whatever its source. This distinction between facts and values (wooly as it may be) is perhaps at the heart of the rabbinic assertion that the nations of the world do not possess Torah, but that they do possess wisdom;[105] we recall the normative rabbinic benediction "upon seeing a wise gentile."[106] I do not mean that the Sages claimed that the gentile world was devoid of moral values. Rather, the Jew had divine Torah, and the gentile did not; consequently, the Jew need not learn anything from the gentile in this regard. The situation was different as far as wisdom was concerned: here God did not necessarily bestow any advantage on His people Israel.[107] Such wisdom includes, of course, information about the physical world and its workings. It would also include insight about the human world and its dynamics. Consequently, non-Jewish aphorisms and anecdotes pepper the Talmud and midrash (as Saul Lieberman has shown)[108] and more extensive literary borrowing is also a reasonable assumption. *Aggadot* adopt and adapt common motifs and stories in a process of mutual borrowing and exchange. Needless to say, the line separating facts from values (or normative judgments) may often be unclear. In a famous and influential passage, for example, the Talmud asserts that death is dependent on the observed cessation of breathing.[109] Is this a normative judgment? Or is it a statement of fact which represents the scientific wisdom of the day? Classic halakhic discussion assumes the former.[110]

---

105. *Midrash Eikhah Rabbah*, 2. For the ancients, "wisdom" doubtless included the "science" of astrology, which found adherents among sages in both Babylonia and the Land of Israel, as S. Lieberman, *Greek*, 97–100, points out. See *Berakhot* 64a, *Shabbat* 119a and 156b, *Yevamot* 21b.

106. *Berakhot* 58a. It is also possible that *Birkat ha-Ḥokhmah*, which opens the intermediate blessings of the daily *'Amidah*, refers to universal wisdom as well as to Torah. Note its reference to *enosh* and *adam*, generic terms for man, in its opening phrase. But see Samuel's abbreviated version, *Berakhot* 29a, and especially the expansion of that blessing for Sabbath night. This formula seems to exclude the broader possibilities raised by *Pesaḥim* 104a, for example. For a broader collection of sources, see M. Wienfeld, "Ha-Bakashot Le'Da'at," *Tarbiẓ* 48 (1979), 186–200; "Ikkevot shel Kedushat Yozer," *Tarbiẓ* 45 (1976), 15–26, esp. 19–23.

107. I am too dogmatic. After all, "Ten measures of wisdom were given to the world; the Land of Israel received nine" (*Kiddushin* 49b).

108. *Greek*, 1–67, 144–82; *Hellenism*, 3–19.

109. *Yoma* 85a.

110. See, e.g., J. D. Bleich, *Contemporary Halakhic Problems* I, 372–93.

Literary Borrowing

The observation of human nature finds imaginative literary expression, and rabbinic openness to the literary forms and motifs of the gentile world is probably the equivalent then, of their openness to contemporary science. At the same time, it is clear that any culture assimilates only such materials as are appropriate to its own basic world view. Thus, the Sages hardly borrow much from the erotic romances of the time; indeed, even Josephus exercises restraint on that score. It is reasonable to expect, moreover, that the Sages will adapt or even transform—perhaps automatically and without much conscious thought—such materials as they absorb. Furthermore, it has been suggested that certain of the Sages' literary forms are uniquely structured ("with no parallel in . . . world literature"), due to the existential implications of Judaic theology and anthropology.[111] These cautionary notes aside, though, it appears that the Sages shared in the literary culture of their day, especially in its folkloristic and popular elements.

Midrash and aggadah will frequently cite popular adages and words of worldly wisdom; they are introduced with the standard phrase, "as people say," and there is no reason to assume that such "people" are exclusively Jews. But, it is clearly impossible to treat this topic from the obiter dicta of the Sages alone, despite my general resolve to avoid speculative discussion of *influence* in rabbinic literature. For it is not so much a matter of asserting direct influence, as a recognition that the rabbis are part of a sphere of culture whose materials pass with considerable freedom between all its members.

A good example is the legend that Joseph's body had been placed deep in the Nile River, and that the Exodus could take place only after Moses was finally informed of its whereabouts by the mysterious Seraḥ and had induced it to rise to the surface, fulfilling the pledge to Joseph that his body would be returned for burial in Canaan when his brethren left Egypt. Now, Egyptian lore had told that Typhon had similarly put the dead Serapis in the Nile, from which he had to be liberated. And the Talmud itself identifies the Egyptian Serapis with Joseph. Now, it seems likely that the motif, though borrowed by the Sages from the Egyptian milieu, was used for their own purposes. It may well be the case, as Joseph Heinemann points out, that this bit of "creative historiography" serves the esthetic interest of the Sages by adding suspense to the Exodus narrative, but it is quite difficult to maintain that it can be derived simply from the hermeneutic process of reading the Bible. Rather, the Sages seem to be in contact here with universal folk motifs and, perhaps, with a specific aspect of Egyptian lore.[112] So, too, R. Simeon b. Yoḥai's description of Eve

111. Yonah Frankel, *Darkei ha-Aggadah ve-ha-Midrash* (Massada, 1991), 338. The parables in the Gospels show similar characteristics, but that is because they adhere to the early Jewish pattern (p. 391).

112. *Mekhilta* to Exodus 13:19, *'Avodah Zarah* 43a; Lieberman, *Hellenism,* 136–38.

as a woman who opens the jar which her husband had sealed after warning her not to tamper with it by any means; as Lieberman notes: "this parable was certainly appreciated by the people who were familiar with the Greek Eve–Pandora."[113] Thus, Pandora releases evil upon the world, while Eve (in this tale) is herself stung by the serpent (the jar itself is full of goodies); but the resemblance cannot be accidental, and the pointed difference is probably deliberate.

Nor is rabbinic contact with the surrounding world displayed only in materials that relate to the heroes of the distant past. The cycle of stories describing the encounter of the Tanna R. Joshua with the Elders of Athens bears many resemblances to the ancient *Book of Ahikar,* which has been dated to the seventh century B.C.E. To choose but one detail, both Ahikar and R. Joshua are required to build castles in the air.

> Ahikar orders eagles to be brought to him and ties to them a basket containing masons. He then commands Pharoah's slaves to bring building materials to the masons, so that they can start building . . . they confess that they cannot do this, and so they are defeated. So it is in the talmudic story, with the difference that R. Joshua suspends himself between heaven and earth by pronouncing the Name of God; he then tells the Elders of Athens to supply him with building materials which they cannot do, and they must admit their defeat.[114]

The characteristic difference in detail does not mask the similarity. Sometimes differences are much more pointed, but these too disclose the common universe of discourse. It has been suggested that the Nazarite whose vow was respected by Simeon the Righteous is the mirror image of (and retort to) Narcissus; both are passionately struck by their reflection in a pool of water, but while Narcissus pines away in self-adoration, the Nazarite dedicates his seductive hair to God and saves himself.[115] Needless to say, all this raises most interesting questions concerning the aggadic activity of the Sages, their use of story, and their understanding of the creative process in which they took part. We merely intend here to point to the likely interface between the Sages and the surrounding culture as indicator of their openness to that culture and their use of its resources.[116]

---

113. J. Goldin, trans., *The Fathers According to Rabbi Nathan* (New Haven, 1955), 12 (which translates as *Aboth de-Rabi Nathan,* Version A, Chap. 1, ed. Schechter, p. 6); S. Lieberman, *Hellenism,* 136, n. 86.

114. *Bekhorot* 8b; E. Yassif, "Traces of Folk Traditions of the Second Temple Period in Rabbinic Literature," *Journal of Jewish Studies* 39:2 (1988): 227–29.

115. *Nedarim* 9b and parallels.

116. The work of H. A. Fischel on literary structure and content ought to be noted here as well. See his "Studies in Cynicism and the Ancient Near East," in J. Neusner, ed., *Religions in Antiquity* (Leiden, 1968), 372–411; "Story and History: Observations on Greco-Roman

Physical Facts

The Sages had little difficulty in accepting knowledge of the physical world from gentiles; more broadly, we may say that Jews have no advantage when it comes to matters of fact (whether physical or not). Put theologically, Torah is not the exclusive source for scientific knowledge, though it too can, if understood correctly, reveal worldly wisdom. I hardly intend to define *fact* as over against *value,* but I think it is clear that the Sages felt comfortable with gentile knowledge of the former and drew the line intuitively when grey areas posed difficulties. Despite the general assumption that medieval Jewish philosophy stands at a considerable remove from talmudic culture, it is likely that the great medieval rationalists would also argue that they were students of gentiles only so far as factual knowledge was concerned, though it is clear that the range of the factual had been broadened considerably.[117] Be this as it may, there were certain topics on which the Sages found their gentile contemporaries to be their equal, if not superior.

One such area was medicine and its associated arts. A superficial glance at J. Preuss's classic volume on talmudic medicine reveals hundreds of instances in which rabbinic physiological and anatomic knowledge parallels that of their Hellenistic or Semitic contemporaries; the same is true as regards their pharmaceutical expertise and their skill in the art of healing.[118] Indeed, this is as much as conceded by early medieval authorities (*Geonim*) who argue that talmudic medicine is not normative—indeed, that it is downright dangerous—because it merely reflects the wisdom available historically to the Sages of the Talmud.[119] Certainly, the Talmud is not teeming with instances; indeed, medical information as a whole, while highly valued by the Sages, is not abundant in rabbinic literature. But one instance is most revealing, I think. The Sages, as is well known, disapproved of pagan superstition (*darkei ha-emori*), and treated it as a form of idolatry. Nonetheless, acts that would otherwise have been condemned were acceptable (said R. Yoḥanan) if they served medical purposes; their empirical utility proved them to be not superstition but part

Rhetoric and Pharisaism," in H. Fischel, ed. *Essays in Greco-Roman and Related Talmudic Literature* (New York, 1977), 443–73.

117. R. Baḥya ibn Pequdah and R. Abraham Maimonides are somewhat exceptional in this regard as they acknowledge the spiritual superiority of gentile (Sufi) models. R. Abraham, interestingly, will claim that the Sufi masters have returned to biblical patterns.

118. J. Preuss, *Biblisch-Talmudische Medezin* (Berlin, 1911). Dr. Fred Rosner has published an English translation of this fascinating work.

119. The references have been collected by Reuven Margaliot in his edition of R. Abraham Maimonides, *Milḥamot Hashem* (Jerusalem, n. d.), 84, n. 18. Here is Maimonides on rabbinic knowledge of the physical sciences: "The Sages . . . did not speak about this as transmitters of dicta of the prophets but rather because . . . they had heard these dicta from the men of knowledge who lived in those times" (*Guide* 3:14). See also *Hil. Kiddush ha-Ḥodesh* 17:28.

of the science of the day. Now, since this behavior would (except for that saving grace) have been condemned as pagan superstition, the Sages clearly realized that it entered the Jewish bailiwick from the pagan neighborhood. This characteristic was not, obviously, held against it.[120] Nor should we be surprised, finally, if R. Yoḥanan craftily extracted the medical secrets of a wise gentile woman and announced them to his students.[121]

Certain specific topics were clearly of more interest to the Sages than others, and their investigation was a *desideratum,* though we find varying evaluations of the significance of these inquiries. "Astronomic calculations," which were apparently relevant to calendric regulation, "are aftercourses of wisdom"—but they are not its essence.[122] On the other hand:

> R. Simeon b. Pazzi said in the name of R. Joshua b. Levi on the authority of Bar Kappara: He who knows how to calculate the cycles and planetary courses, but does not, of him Scripture saith, *but they regard not the work of the Lord, neither have they considered the operation of his hands* (Isaiah 5, 12). R. Samuel b. Naḥmani said in R. Joḥanan's name: How do we know that it is one's duty to calculate the cycles and planetary courses? Because it is written, *for this is your wisdom and understanding in the sight of the peoples* (Deuteronomy 4, 6). What wisdom and understanding is in the sight of the peoples? Say, that is the science of cycles and planets.[123]

Here, R. Joshua b. Levi apparently sees intrinsic religious significance in astronomic knowledge, demonstrating, as it does, the coherence and wonder of God's creation. For R. Joḥanan, ironically, the wisdom which the Jew can demonstrate to the gentile is his scientific expertise, or perhaps, the scientific expertise required for the proper application of Jewish *halakhah* (rather than *halakhah* itself, as Deuteronomy 4:6 might indicate).

Considerable knowledge of physiology is indicated in the regulations for deciding whether animals are unfit for consumption as *terefah* (that is, an animal having a fatal disease or condition).[124] We are also informed that the students of R. Ishma'el engaged in the dissection of a human cadaver (the body of a prostitute executed by "the king"). Here, too, the motive seems to have been halakhic rather than medical or intellectual, as they produced the kind of inventory useful for halakhic discus-

120. *p. Shabbat* 6:9 (8c); *Shabbat* 67a and *Ḥullin* 77b. See *Enzyklopedia Talmudit* VII, 709–12.

121. *'Avodah Zarah* 28a.

122. *M. Avot* 3:18, as interpreted by *Tif'eret Yisra'el,* ad. loc., and by S. Lieberman, "How Much Greek?" (above, n. 82), 131–32.

123. *Shabbat* 75a.

124. On a different subject, Rav tells that he spent eighteen months in the company of shepherds, learning how to distinguish a *passing* blemish from a *permanent* one—information necessary in applying the law of firstlings (*Sanhedrin* 5b). For information on matters agricultural garnered from gentiles, see *Shabbat* 85a, and Rashi, loc. cit.

sion.[125] Now, there is no good reason to assume that in cultivating these areas of knowledge, the Sages were totally self-sufficient and did not garner the wisdom and expertise of the surrounding cultures and traditions.

The extent of physiological information possessed by gentiles was surprisingly broad apparently. Here is a discussion between Antoninus[126] and R. Judah the Patriarch as to when the evil urge (*yeẓer ha-ra*) and the soul (*neshamah*) each enter a person:

> Antoninus asked our Rabbi [R. Judah the Patriarch]: When is the evil urge placed in man? As soon he is formed [in embryo], he replied. If so, he objected, he would dig through the womb and emerge; rather is it when he emerges [from the womb]. Rabbi agreed with him, because his view corresponds with that of Scripture, viz., *For the imagination of man's heart is evil from his youth [mine'urav]* (Genesis 8:21). R. Judah said: This is written *mine'arav* [from his awakening], which means, from when he awakes to the world.
>
> He asked him further: When is the soul planted in man? When he leaves his mother's womb, replied he. Leave meat without salt for three days, said he, will it not putrefy? Rather, when his destiny is determined. Our Teacher agreed with him, for Scripture too supports him: *All the while my breath is in me, and the spirit of God is in my nostrils* (Job 27:3), while it is written, *And Thy Providence hath preserved My spirit* (ibid. 10:12); hence, when didst Thou place the soul in me? When Thou didst determine my fate.[127]

The passage itself is far from simple; it also demonstrates the complexities inherent in our topic. *Evil urge* is not exclusively a moral category here; but neither is it exclusively vitalistic. Rather, it is on the border of the spiritual and biological, as the egotistical drive will force the embryo out of the womb before its necessary biological maturation has been completed. Nor is *soul* simply a matter of the vital life force, for it must have been evident to all—even on the basis of biblical narratives!—that the fetus is alive, that it moves in the womb. Thus, the discussion of Antoninus and R. Judah was not about physical science in the narrow sense but dealt with the development of personality and, perhaps, moral traits.[128] Yet, a common language was found. Characteristically, it was not Antoninus's logic that

---

125. *Bekhorot* 45a. The matter is reported by Samuel, himself a physician and astronomer.

126. On Antoninus (who has been identified with a number of Roman emperors), see L. Ginzberg, *JE*, I, 656–57.

127. Genesis *Rabbah* 34:10.

128. The parallel to *Bereshit Rabbah* 34:10 in *Sanhedrin* 91b provides *Bereshit* 4:7 with its explicit mention of *ḥatat* (that is, sin) as prooftext, indicating that physical nature alone is not the topic. See *Mattenot Kehunah* to the midrash, ad loc. For further discussion of this passage, see D. Feldman, *Birth Control in Jewish Law* (New York, 1968), 271–73. Rabbi and Antoninus continue to discuss the fate of the soul and its relationship to the body after death, but here R. Judah is exclusively the teacher, answering Antoninus's questions. See *Mekhilta* to Exodus 15, 1.

convinced the rabbi, but the congruence of his ideas with biblical verses. The irony goes in both directions: the gentile may have hit the truth on the head, but his method is not really authoritative; the Jew will appeal to Scripture, but only to discover that the gentile was there first, in a sense, because of his superior logic. These matters, then, may be understood by a gentile as well as—indeed, in our case, better than—by a Jew, and by no common Jew at that. The dialogues of Antoninus and R. Judah the Prince are usually amicable (as distinguished from other polemical interchanges between rabbis and Romans). In this case, R. Judah is willing to learn from his Roman friend. Interestingly, the story assumes that Romans, too, spoke in terms of *yeẓer ha-ra* and *neshamah*.

The possibility of a discussion between Jewish sages and Roman wise men in which the Romans are judged to be in the right, is, as we might expect, restricted to such "scientific" topics. Here is another discussion, this time one that focuses on astronomic realities; and here R. Judah the Prince is not a participant but rather the referee:

> Our Rabbis taught: The Sages of Israel maintain that the *galgal* [celestial sphere] is stationary [fixed], while the *mazzaloth* [constellations] revolve; while the Sages of the nations of the world maintain that the *galgal* revolves and the *mazzaloth* are stationary. Rabbi observed: This disproves their view [viz.] we never find the Wain in the south or Scorpio in the north. To this R. Aba b. Jacob demurred: Perhaps it is like the pivot of a millstone, or like the door socket?
>
> The Sages of Israel maintain: The sun travels beneath the sky by day and above the sky by night; while the Sages of the nations of the world maintain: It travels beneath the sky by day and below the earth at night. Said Rabbi: And their view is preferable to ours, for the wells are cold by day but warm at night.
>
> It was taught, R. Nathan said: In summer the sun travels in the heights of the heaven, therefore the whole world is hot while the wells [springs] are cold; in winter the sun travels at the lower ends of the sky, therefore the whole world is cold while the wells are hot.[129]

The specifics of this discussion are intimately connected to ancient cosmological assumptions and will not detain us here. Gad Zarfati's summary will suffice: the Jewish sages, he reports, represent Babylonian cosmology which generally governs various talmudic statements on the topic; that of the gentile sages is the geocentric, Ptolemaic view. R. Judah the Prince does not only side with the gentile sages as over against his compatriots then, but also rejects the traditional cosmology in favor of

129. *Pesaḥim* 94b.

the "modern" (for its time, of course) perception.[130] Now, this last topic may even have had some halakhic implication. R. Asher (thirteenth-century, Germany-Spain) claimed that the rule according to which dough for Passover *mazzah* may be kneaded only with water which was drawn from the well the night before kneading (*mayyim she-lanu*), reflects the view of the gentile sages; since the sun travels "under" the earth during the night, it warms the water in the wells, and this might hasten the leavening of the dough and cause it to turn into *hamez* (leavened bread).[131]

But the ability of the Jewish sage to discover scientific fact in Scripture can also demonstrate the superiority of the Sages' insular methods to the empirical science of the day, and frustrate the gentile "philosopher":

> A certain philosopher wished to know after what period of time a serpent bears. When he saw them copulating, he took them and placed them in a barrel and fed them until they bore. When the Sages visited Rome, he asked them how long it takes a serpent to bear. R. Gamaliel turned pale [with shame] and could not answer him. R. Joshua, meeting him and seeing his face wan, asked him, "Why is your face wan?" "I was asked a question," replied he, "and I could not answer it." "And what is it?" "After how long does a serpent bear?" "After seven years," he told him. "How do you know that?" he inquired. "Because the dog, which is a wild beast, bears at fifty days, while it is written, *More cursed art thou than all cattle, and than all beasts of the field* (Genesis 3:14). Hence, just as the cattle are seven times more accursed than the beast, so is the serpent seven times more accursed than the cattle." At eventime he [R. Gamaliel] went and told it to him [the philosopher], who began to beat his head against the wall [in grief], crying out, "All that for which I toiled seven years, this man has come and offered to me on the end of a cane!"

It is not merely R. Joshua's homiletic method which is being celebrated here, or even the richness of Scripture when mined correctly; it is also gentile science, limited by its human parameters, which is lampooned.[132]

Indeed, it is this conversation which is typical of the interchange with gentile wise men which is described in the Talmud. Intrinsically, of course, the very existence of any such discussion is evidence of rabbinic exposure to gentile culture and, ostensibly, of rabbinic eagerness to learn from its proponents. But the actual contents of these conversations as recorded by the Talmud (whether always historically accurate or not) lead to a different conclusion. To begin with, the description of the Sages' interlocutors as "philosophers" is far from definitive. Many of the conversations are, in fact, conducted with Roman officials, sometimes with

---

130. G. B. Zarfati, "Shalosh He'arot 'al Divrei Tanna'im," *Tarbiz* 32 (1963): 140–42; idem, "ha-Kosmographia ha-Talmudit," *Tarbiz* 35 (1966): 137–48.

131. *Pesahim* 42a and R. Asher, ad loc. But note Rashi, *s.v. shelanu*, who cites the *baraitha*, and not the opinion of the gentile sages. My argument in this section is fundamentally Maimonidean; for Maimonides' use of *Pesahim* 94b, see *Guide* II:8.

132. *Bereshit Rabbah* 20:4. Not surprisingly, this midrash was a favorite of R. Yosef Yavez (*Or ha-Hayyim*, chapter III).

Hadrian himself. Occasionally, a single discussion will be found in a number of versions, one identifying the gentile partner as a philosopher, the other identifying him as a Roman emperor; this is true, for example, of the discussion of serpentine reproduction cited earlier.[133] The literary structure of rabbinic sage matched against Roman emperor duplicated, ironically enough, a familiar *topos* of Hellenistic literature, with the rabbi functioning in the role of philosopher!

The ease with which *philosopher* shades into *emperor* dovetails with the basic quality of most of these conversations. Most are polemical, with the gentile (sometimes even a Roman *matrona*) questioning Judaic theology or the veracity of biblical assertions, ranging from the way God created the world (or Eve) to His dealings with the people Israel. Others are frankly folkloristic. But common to almost all is a conclusion in which the Jewish sage successfully counters his antagonist's challenge and roundly demonstrates the superiority of the Jewish tradition.[134] It is possible, of course, that the historical reality was quite different, and that the Sages conversed amiably and profitably with their gentile counterparts. But talmudic and midrashic literature labor to produce an opposite impression.

Yet, let us recall that the talmudic conversations do relate to issues of religious significance, and it is precisely in this area that the tradition must defend itself against paganism; it will certainly not be corrected by gentile arguments. The realm of facts is more open and less threatening, and here a rabbi may well be willing to learn from a gentile philosopher, a R. Judah the Prince preferred the opinion of the gentile sages to that of the rabbis in astronomic questions.[135] The most we can say, then, is that the talmudic literary tradition has little interest in preserving these academic conversations, just as it has little interest in preserving scientific information in general.

Imitation of Material Culture

Openness to or closure before the gentile world also expresses itself in the attitude to material culture: dress, food, artifacts, utensils, art, domicile. Do the Sages require the Jew to reject items that are distinctively Hellenistic or Roman? Needless to say, *halakhah* does sometimes impinge on the shape of physical culture. It has been noted, for example, that stoneware is frequently found in Jewish archaeological remains of

133. See the parallel passage at *Bekhorot* 8b.

134. For a survey of these conversations, see M. D . Herr, "The Historical Significance of the Dialogues Between Jewish Sages and Roman Dignitaries," *Scripta Hierosolymitana* 22 (1971): 123–51. A most significant number of such dialogues are reported of the Tanna R. Joshua b. Ḥananiah; these are presented in Z. Bacher, *Aggadot ha-Tannai'im*, I/i (Berlin, 1922), 121–37. The conversations of R. Akiba and the Roman prefect Tineius Rufus are another case in point.

135. See Lieberman, "How Much Greek?", 131–32.

the period; this reflects the fact that stone (unlike other materials) does not become impure and is, therefore, much more practical for use by *kohanim* (priests) and others who abide by their standard. Halakhic regulations also affect the use of art forms, in certain instances even decorative art. They cause, obviously, differences in diet. None of these restrictions derive, though, from a rejection of gentile patterns of behavior, per se. And, all in all, they had little impact on the *realia* of talmudic civilization. The three volumes of S. Krauss's *Talmudische Archaeologie* amply document the common physical infrastructure of Jewish and gentile culture during talmudic times; the many sporadic references in Lieberman's *Tosefta Ki-Fshutah* produce a similar portrait.[136] Jews and gentiles dressed, to a large degree, in similar fashion, and they lived in similar homes.

A small number of Tannaitic texts do challenge this assumption of indifference, however, and it is to these that we shall now turn. It should be said that these are concerned with what is apparently a narrow aspect of the material culture of the time. Yet, even if understood restrictively, it is no easy matter to specify the parameters within which these norms function; and if understood broadly, they fly in the face of much found elsewhere in talmudic literature. Indeed, some medieval authorities claim that the Talmud itself is not of one mind as regards the norms involved.[137]

Sifre comments on Deuteronomy 12:30, "*Take heed that thou be not ensnared to follow them, and that thou inquire not after their gods, saying: 'How do these nations worship their gods,' even so will I do likewise. Thou shalt not do so to the Lord thy God.*"

> *Take heed (to thyself)*—this indicates a negative commandment—*and that thou inquire not after their gods, saying*—you should not say, "Since they go out clad in a toga, so will I go out clad in a toga; since they go out wearing purple, so will I go out wearing purple; since they go out wearing a *tulas*, so will I go out wearing a *tulas*"—*even so will I do likewise* (12:30).[138]

Sifra comments as follows on Leviticus 18:3–4: *"You shall not copy the practices of the land of Egypt where you dwelt nor of the land of Canaan to which I am taking you nor shall*

136. S. Krauss, *Talmudische Archaeologie*, 3 vols. (Leipzig, 1910). A Hebrew version exists in four volumes: *Kadmoniyyot ha-Talmud* I/i, I/ii (Berlin, 1924); II (Tel Aviv, 1929); II/ii (Tel Aviv, 1945).

137. *Tosafot, 'Avodah Zarah* 11a, *s.v. ve-iy*; and see at n. 147.

138. *Sifre* Deuteronomy, sec. 81; ed. Finkelstein, p. 147; trans. Hammer, p. 135. There is no certain explanation for *tulas*, but most commentators identify it as an item of dress. This passage appears as a comment to the biblical phrase, "Inquire not after their gods," but the practices mentioned have no religious content (attempts to push the passage in that direction do not impress me as successful). Perhaps *elohim* is taken in the secular sense of judges, distinguished individuals, as elsewhere in rabbinic literature? For this topic as a whole, see M. D. Herr, "Hashpa'ot Ḥiẓẓoniyot," (n. 37 above), 88–93.

you follow their laws. My rules alone shall you observe and faithfully follow my laws. I the Lord am your God":

> Perhaps you should not build buildings or plant crops as the gentiles do? Scripture says: "nor follow their laws"—that is, laws that are firmly established (engraved) for them, their parents, and ancestors. What do they do? A man marries a man, and a woman marries a woman. A man marries a woman and her daughter, a woman marries two men.
>
> What has Scripture not yet said? For it has already said: *Let no one be found among you who consigns his son or daughter to the fire, or who is an augur, a soothsayer, a diviner, a sorcerer . . .* (Deuteronomy 18:10–11).[139] What then is the meaning of, *nor shall you follow their laws?* That you not behave according to their practices, things which have become firmly established [engraved] among them, such as theatres, circuses, and arenas.
>
> R. Meir says: this refers to the "Emorite practices" [that is, pagan superstitions, on the whole] listed by the Sages.
>
> R. Judah ben Bathyra says: that you grow no sidelocks or trim the front . . .
>
> Perhaps you will say then, "They have their practices but we have none." So Scripture says, *My rules . . . shall you observe.* But there is still hope for the Evil Urge, which can muse: "their practices are finer than ours." So Scripture says: *Observe them faithfully, for that will be proof of your wisdom and discernment to other peoples* (Deuteronomy 4:6).[140]

Although the Scriptural verses to which *Sifre* relates deal with the cultic temptations posed by the peoples of Canaan and their culture, the midrash assigns part of the verse to matters concerned not with religion but rather with fashion. Jews were not to wear the toga or dress in purple. Were Jews to avoid, then, any item of dress worn by gentiles? It does not seem so. Perhaps, at the time this midrash was formulated, these were in fact the only items of dress which had not already been adopted by Jews. The toga, we may add, was a national dress. Toga and purple, moreover, were the formal habit of the Roman upper class, the administrators and functionaries who came to Palestine. For a Jew who wore a toga did not wear a neutral, serviceable item of clothing; he made a statement about his identity. And,

139. The verses cited follow on Deuteronomy 18:9: "you shall not learn to imitate the abhorrent practices of those nations," and so are legitimately cited in the context of our topic.

140. *Sifra Aḥarei*, Par. 9:9, Perek 13:9, Par. 13:9 (ed. Weiss, 85d–86a). My rendering relies on translations found in the dictionaries of Jastrow and Sperber. Interestingly, the succeeding sections of *Sifra* deal with different aspects of Jewish-gentile relations in the broadest sense, and form a short essay on the topic, as it were. Thus, 13:10—which laws are required by reason and which are unique to revelation; 13:11—wisdom of the gentiles and wisdom of Israel; 13:13—the status of a gentile who studies Torah; 13:14—martyrdom in the face of gentile threats.

in fact, our sources do not know of Jews who wear the toga; the typical Jewish outer garment is the *tallit*, which resembles the Roman *pallium.*[141] *Sifre* does not insist that the Jew dress distinctively, that he be known as such by his clothing. But it does make the point that there will be items of clothing whose symbolic valence puts them out of bounds for a Jew. Here, perhaps, the fact that the clothes in question designated the Romans, who were both pagan and conquerors, may have been crucial.

Sifre does insist, then, that there is a line which cannot be crossed; that, irrespective of the objective, substantive nature of a cultural pattern or item, it also serves as symbolic indicator. Our case is difficult to characterize, as we have seen, so we cannot decide whether *Sifre* simply forbids a Jew to wear what no other Jew of his time wore, thus choosing to mask his Jewish identity; or whether it rejects a specifically Roman style, Romans being what they were for Jews. But there is a line. Perhaps, too, the consciously articulated, "Since they . . . so will I," focused the ire of the Sages. (We recall a similar literary form in their ban on the wisdom of the nations: "You might say, 'I have learned . . . so now I will go and learn.'") For the Jew this reveals his motive—not need or utility, but imitation.

Sifra is much more complex and varied. The opening passages make it clear that the Jew is not expected to behave differently than his gentile neighbor in matters that have no religious or moral significance. He will farm the same way and put up the same buildings, and he may even take his neighbor as a model. But he may not imitate the sexual perversion he saw around him (and these were matters forbidden by the Torah in any case); that is the point of Leviticus 18:3–4, then. As to the second passage, it is unclear whether the different tannaitic authorities are in dispute or each simply adds to the opinion of his fellow; needless to say, the former understanding would imply considerable debate as to the parameters of cultural openness. Be this as it may, it appears that all agree that Scripture here bans activities or patterns of behavior that are not grossly idolatrous and perhaps are not idolatrous at all. Pagan superstitions are banned (R. Meir);[142] so are specifically upper-class Roman haircuts (R. Judah b. Bathyra).[143] Attendance at the theatre, circus, or arena

141. Krauss, *Kadmoniyyot* II/ii, 200–01; Jastrow, *Dictionary*, 537. A midrash does deal with the obligation to attach *ẓiẓit* to the toga, indicating that certain Jews did, in fact, wear it. See *Arukh Completum*, s.v. *tg* (ed. Kohut, 4, p. 19). See also *Sifre* Deuteronomy, Piska 234 (pp. 266–267).

142. Elsewhere, the category invoked by R. Meir, *darkei ha-emori*, also includes the Roman haircut mentioned independently in our midrash by R. Judah. See *Tosefta Shabbat*, chapter 6(7).1 (ed. S. Lieberman, p. 22). For overall discussion of the items found in this rubric, which fill two chapters of *Tosefta Shabbat*, see Lieberman, *Tosefta Kif-shuta*, 3, 79–106. Subsequent halakhic discussion is summarized in *Enẓyklopedia Talmudit* 7, 706–12. The distinction between *superstition* and *religion* is, as usual, difficult to define. All I mean here is that *darkei ha-emori* does not include worship of pagan deities.

143. The specific Roman hairstyle here intended is a matter of discussion. The *kome*, if

is also forbidden; these all could frequently involve participation (passive, at least) in objectionable activities (either idolatrous or immoral); or they may have been banned as centers of Roman frivolity.[144] With the exception of the Roman haircut, then, the examples given in *Sifra* all focus on patterns of behavior which are not only historically associated with gentiles, but are also substantively objectionable.

Our two Tannaitic sources stake out different territory. For *Sifrei*, the activities to be avoided are intrinsically suspect, if not downright bad; the fact that they are gentile habits is largely an accident of birth. For *Sifre*, on the other hand, the gentile connection is at the heart of the matter; the issue is not one of religious or moral impropriety but of national, cultural identity. This overall contrast has far-reaching implications, for it poses the question of whether gentile origins or practice are enough to disqualify patterns of behavior or culture for Jews.

The sparse talmudic discussion devoted to our topic continues, as it were, this ambivalent tradition which unfolds through medieval and modern times. R. Judah, we recall, had rejected decapitation by the sword as a form of halakhic execution ("as the Romans do") because Jews are not to "follow their laws."[145] The Sages replied that since this procedure is already found in the Bible, it does not originate with the Romans and is acceptable for Jews. They also argue that another such phenomenon exists in the practice of funeral *burning* at rites for the kings of Israel;[146] though found among pagans, it also has biblical roots. The basic assumption of both parties to this discussion is that the pagan, or Roman, or gentile provenance of the practice would be enough to place it out of bounds for Jews (were it not for its original and legitimating biblical roots). True, the issue—in the case of decapitation—involves fixing (and borrowing) a legal norm, and this may heighten rabbinic sensitivity. But all in all, it seems that the admittedly gentile origin of the practice, the fact that it is clearly identified as Roman, is the crucial aspect of the problem.

---

identified with the Greek style of that name (see Lieberman, *Tosefta Kif-shuta,* 80–81), was not idolatrous but, as F. W. Nicholson, "Greek and Roman Barbers," *Harvard Studies in Classical Philology* 2 (1891): 51, wrote, "seems . . . to have been affected by the fops of the day." Growing a *belorit,* "on the other hand, may well have been a prelude to idolatrous devotion" (see Lieberman, op. cit.), but may also be an indifferent adoption of the style. It is not found in the *Sifra,* but is given in the list of *Tosefta Shabbat.* See also *Shir ha-Shirim Rabbah* 2:2:2, where the *belorit* is seen as parallel to *kil'ayim,* a clear violation of Torah law.

144. Talmudic materials indict the theatre, etc., on all these grounds. For a summary, see S. Krauss, *Paras ve-Romi ba-Talmudim* (Jerusalem, 1945), 282–85. Maimonides, incidentally, may have understood this source as forbidding construction of such buildings by Jews; see *Hil. 'Avodah Zarah* 11:1.

145. *Sanhedrin* 52b. Alternative ways of understanding R. Judah suggested by other tannaitic materials are not our concern here.

146. *Burning* may refer to the burning of clothing and other items, or to the burning of incense; again, the matter does not concern us here.

A second talmudic discussion points in a different direction, however. It relates to the very same problem noted above, the use of funeral burning at royal rites. The context is a discussion as to whether such practice is idolatrous (when it occurs in non-Jewish instances, of course). Proof is brought that such burning is not idolatrous, for if it were, how could it have been adopted by Jewish kings? "Is it not written, 'you shall not follow their laws?' Hence all agree that 'burning' is not an idolatrous rite but merely a mark of high esteem."[147] The point, for us, is clear: Leviticus 18:3–4 bans only that which has idolatrous origins (even when done innocently by Jews); that which is merely a cultural pattern or social norm, even if associated with gentiles, is unobjectionable.[148]

If only gentile practices that smack of the idolatrous, the superstitious, the indecent, or the immoral are placed out of bounds by the Sages, the message is clear. True, it may not always be easy to define the "immoral," for example, but that problem is faced daily and is not unique to items of gentile origins. But if the Sages also demand that the Jew avoid aspects of material culture that smack of the gentile world, and for that reason alone, we would like to have precise definitions, clear parameters, and firm identifications. These are lacking.

It ought to come as no surprise that the aggadic tradition makes its contribution to our discussion as well. The prime locus, I think, concerns a topic with which we are already familiar—the behavior of the Israelites while in Egypt. Earlier on we saw discussion of Israelite devotion to language and names. Aggadists also related to the question of dress.

So far as I can see, the question does not come up in the Tannaitic or Amoraic collections, where no attention is paid to the question of whether Jews wore Egyptian or native clothing. The idea first appears, apparently, in the medieval *Lekaḥ Tov,* which declares that just as the Jews retained their language and names, so too they did not adopt Egyptian clothing. (The idea reappears in the high medieval commentaries, but it sometimes changes form; Ritba [fourteenth century Spain] writes that the Israelites were recognizable in Egypt because of the *ẓiẓit* they wore—but not because they wore distinctive clothing.)[149] Another instance is presented by Moses' appearance as an "Egyptian" to the daughters of Reuel (Exodus

147. *'Avodah Zarah* 11a.

148. This reading of the sources reflects *Tosafot, 'Avodah Zarah,* ad loc. A different reading is advanced by *Tosafot, Sanhedrin* 52b, *s.v. ela.* These problems—which, as I have suggested, are adumbrated in the earliest tannaitic comments in *Sifre* and *Sifra*—wind down the ages. See the materials collected in *Enzyklopedia Talmudit,* XVII, 305–25. For a more systematic treatment, see H. J. Zimmels, "'Inyan Ḥukkot ha-Goyyim be-Shut," *Sefer Yovel le-Rabbi Ḥanokh Albeck* (Jerusalem, 1963), 402–24.

149. *Midrash Lekaḥ Tov* (compiled by Toviah b. Eliezer, 11th cent.) to Exodus 6:6, Deuteronomy 26:5. For further materials, see M. M. Kasher, *Torah Shelemah* 8 (New York, 1954), 239.

2:19), a fact which is usually held against him—so much so that this alienation becomes an aggadic reason for his not being allowed to enter the Land of Israel. One midrash explains this incident by saying that Moses was dressed as an Egyptian, hence the mistaken identity; and Moses is taken to task for his error. This tradition is a singleton, however. Elsewhere, this detail is not specified, or Moses is criticized for allowing the Midianite maidens to present him to their father as an Egyptian without correcting them; his sin of denial went deeper than his Egyptian costume.[150]

To sum up: occasionally *aggadot* do focus on the question of gentile clothing, but the vast majority of the parallels simply do not consider the point. Clearly it was not an issue for the Sages.

Concluding Comment

I confess that I have not attempted an analytic treatment of the relationship of *Torah* to *madda* [general culture], that is to say, I have not attempted to discuss the relationship of materials which, in native halakhic terms, would be designated *Torah* and those which would lack this designation. Indeed, the first task of such a discussion, to provide guidelines as to how these designations would be made and how such status would be assigned, is no mean assignment. It is likely, moreover, that such guidelines would relate in part to context and could not simply be descriptive alone. Be this as it may, my task has turned out to be more literary than philosophical. What I have done is to consider the express relationship of the Sages and their work to gentile culture. The wisdom of the nations, in its varied forms, has stood in for *madda,* as I have asked: How do the Sages relate to non-Jewish ideas and literary materials? To be more precise: what is their *explicit policy* on this issue? What do they say when they express themselves on the topic, and when they consider the matter from a normative perspective?

In terms of their own work, the Sages neither appeal to the views of their gentile contemporaries (and it might be anachronistic to expect them to do so), nor do they debate them or polemicize against them. This is the major fact. Each page of the Talmud speaks it loud and clear, most certainly when the topics of discussion are halakhic. In this sense, the talmudic consciousness is self-contained. Its major concerns are religious ritual and ethics, both personal and social, and its normative system is worked out without express benefit of non-Jewish wisdom or sources. The discussion focuses, usually, on literary materials, and these are drawn from within the sacred tradition itself (Bible, Mishnah, etc.).

150. *Shemot Rabbah* 39:1. For the dominant tradition, see Kasher, *Torah Shelemah,* 94, nn. 147–148. Both Egyptians and Jews wore *kil'ayim* in Egypt (*Shir ha-Shirim Rabbah* 2:2:2), but there is no accusation that Jews aped Egyptian clothing per se.

This insistence on a specific textual matrix is analogous (and perhaps related) to the general talmudic disinclination to consider topics from the perspective of universal reason alone. Yet, this parallel is not fully borne out. For, read carefully, the Talmud does disclose countless value judgments and reasoned attitudes in and between many a line.[151] This simply means (the views of some traditionalists notwithstanding) that the Jewish Sage considers reason, good judgment, common sense, and perception of moral truths, to be Jewish attributes no less than gentile; they are simply human traits. The Sages do not compromise their Jewish identity when they appeal to these and incorporate them into the talmudic process. But the situation as regards the use of opinions explicitly labelled Greek or Roman, and deriving their reputation from that affiliation, is quite different. These do not have any authoritative weight in a normative discussion, and they do not find their way into the talmudic give-and-take. The process by which norms are established and elaborated simply has no room for contributions that do not originate within the tradition and its bearers; the "rules of recognition" do not include them.

It would be a mistake, though, to equate this disregard with hostility. Nor does it indicate total ignorance, as we have seen indications that the Sages were not unaware of the normative realities (as opposed to the philosophic views) of their gentile neighbors. The Sages were insular in terms of their own work and thought, then, because God had given His Torah to the Jewish people and that was enough. Its study and elaboration could proceed in a fairly self-sustaining fashion, building on both the richness of the tradition itself and the perceived common truths of human reason.

Factual information, as distinct from values or norms, could be appropriated, on the other hand, from any who possessed it, gentile no less than Jew. Science is not Torah. Knowledge of the physical world, psychological, and sociological truths—these are frequently integrated into the normative discussion and are necessary for the concrete application of norms to specific instances. Yet, taken in their own right, they would not qualify for a *birkhat ha-Torah* (the blessing recited over the

---

151. This topic is one of the most discussed in the literature on halakhic theory and literature. All too frequently, I believe, the discussion proceeds from positions developed in the abstract and ignores the testimony (or at least the implications) of the talmudic give-and-take itself, which is often unsuited to dogmatic theorizing. A good reading of some sources can be found in E. Goldman, "Ha-Mussar, ha-Dat, ve-ha-Halakhah," *De'ot* 22 (Winter, 1963): 65–76. For recent presentations of the various arguments, see Volumes 6 (1987) and 7 (1988) of the *Jewish Law Annual*, which was dedicated to "The Philosophy of Jewish Law." Much writing on the topic has crystallized around Aharon Lichtenstein's now-classic paper, "Does Jewish Tradition Recognize an Ethic Independent of Halakha?" in M. Fox, ed., *Modern Jewish Ethics* (Ohio State University Press, 1975), 62–89; for a critique see E. Borowitz, "The Authority of the Ethical Impulse in the Halakha," in N. Samuelson, ed., *Reason and Revelation as Authority in Judaism* (Philadelphia, n.d.), 104–14. See N. Rabinovitch, "Halakha and Other Systems of Ethics," in M. Fox, op. cit., 89–102, as well.

study of Torah), and they need not derive from sacred sources. And if science is not Torah, neither is Torah science; Torah does not claim to present authoritative empirical information, certainly not in the total sense true of its normative claim. Needless to say, the scheme just presented is too neat, too good to be true, somewhat shallow. The Sages explicitly turn to non-Judaic authorities for sources of information only very infrequently; most of the time, their reports as to human nature and social reality are drawn from personal observation and long-accepted consensus. Conversely, norms may well be based from the outset on certain assumptions about how human beings do, in fact, function; in that sense, the tradition may make certain claims as to matters of fact even though these claims rarely, if ever, surface as part of the normative process itself. But, despite all these disclaimers, the Sages do not, in principle, rule out the possibility that their discussion can be enriched by information drawn from the outside world.

As I pointed out earlier, the Sages rarely condemn gentile culture in principled, sweeping terms. There are famous exceptions, to be sure. A good example is R. Isaac Nafḥa's dramatic assertion that Roman Caesaria and Jerusalem can each rise only on the other's ruins, a statement which suggests that Judaism and Hellenistic-Roman culture are totally antithetical. Nonetheless, it is not clear that Caesaria represents non-Judaic culture per se or, as seems more likely, an urban paganism with its attendant immoralities and idolatries, compounded by the political conflicts and historical realities of the time. Caesaria was, after all, the seat of Roman rule over the Land of Israel at the time R. Isaac Nafḥa lived.[152] Generally, in fact, the Sages contend with nations and peoples rather than with ideas and cultures, and while this may amount to the same thing, as peoples are in essence bearers of culture, their comments may primarily reflect political rather than ideological tensions, conflicts, and memories.

Gentile culture will be strongly attacked when it is immoral or idolatrous. It may seem that it is always precisely such for the Sages; but this is not really an accurate impression, as much of our presentation has shown. Literary motifs, we have seen, are frequently assimilated. In any case, non-Jewish culture is not condemned by virtue of its alien origins, as though it were contaminated by simply being non-Sinaitic. Is it unrealistic to expect the Sages to speak in such abstract terms when the more significant categories of idolatry and immorality are available and appropriate? Perhaps, then, I am making a weak sort of argument from silence. Nonetheless, whatever halakhic materials exist reinforce my analysis.

All in all, the Sages devote minimal attention to the question of whether gentile materials are fit for Jewish use; the issue was not terribly pressing and perhaps not terribly significant, either. But whatever little halakhic discussion exists does not

152. *Megillah* 6a. For R. Isaac Nafḥa's (generally hostile) views of the gentile peoples, see Z. Bacher, *Aggadat Amor'ei Ereẓ Yisra'el* (Tel Aviv, 1927), II/1, 204–9. On Roman Caesaria, see L. Levine, *Caesarea Under Roman Rule* (Leiden, 1975).

condemn gentile culture out of hand. A clear distinction is made, for example, between forbidden *sefarim ḥiẓoniyim* and permitted gentile works, including such pagan materials as Homer. The talmudic discussion of the study of Greek wisdom (*ḥokmat Yevanit*) is indecisive; indeed, if a conclusion is necessary, it is probably permissive. The fact that Greek wisdom is not forbidden for all Jews and in all seasons in its own right, as an intrinsic refraction of idolatrous paganism, say, must be appreciated. Similarly, the legislated bans (*gezerot*) on Greek, however understood, reflect specific historical junctures; they are not, by definition, immutable expressions of Torah law. Finally, the fullness of the talmudic testimony indicates that the normative impact of even this negative posture was quite limited. The upshot, then, is that the Sages do not fundamentally restrict the intellectual liberty of the Jew or require him to confine his curiosity, his inquisitiveness, or his search to Torah and its allied materials. This is true despite the fact that, as far as their own work is concerned, the Sages show little interest in matters outside Torah.

To sum up: gentile culture was peripheral to the rabbinic enterprise, at least insofar as the Sages present that enterprise. It was superfluous in terms of their own agenda, either as a resource or as a problem. Yet, by the same token, there is little attempt to distance the Jew from all things gentile. And there is even less attempt to distance him from matters which are intrinsically unobjectionable but are not rooted in the Judaic tradition.[153]

153. A most suggestive paper on our topic is Z. W. Harvey, "Rabbinic Attitudes Towards Philosophy," in H. J. Blumberg, et al., eds., *"Open Thou Mine Eyes. . . .": Essays in Aggadah and Judaica Presented to Rabbi William J. Braude"*, 83–101.

2

Judaism and General Culture in Medieval and Early Modern Times

David Berger

CONTENTS

Prefatory Note

The attempt to provide an analytical overview of Jewish attitudes toward the pursuit of general culture in the millennium from the Geonic Middle East to the eve of the European Jewish Enlightenment is more than a daunting task: it flirts with the sin of hubris. The limitations of both space and the author required a narrowing and sharpening of the focus; consequently, this essay will concentrate on high culture, on disciplines which many medieval and early modern Jews regarded as central to their intellectual profile and which they often saw as crucial or problematic (and sometimes both) for the understanding of Judaism itself. Such disciplines usually included philosophy and the sciences, sometimes extended to poetry, and on at least one occasion embraced history as well. The net remains very widely cast, but it does not take all of culture as its province.

Not only does this approach limit the scope of the pursuits to be examined; it also excludes large segments of the medieval and early modern Jewish populace from consideration. Thus, I have not addressed the difficult and very important question of the cultural profile of women, who very rarely received the education needed for full participation in elite culture, nor have I dealt with the authors of popular literature or the bearers of folk beliefs.

Paradoxically, however, the narrower focus also has the effect of enlarging the scope of the analysis. The issue before us is not merely whether or not a particular individual or community affirmed the value of a broad curriculum. The profounder question is how the pursuit of philosophy and other disciplines affected the understanding of Judaism and its sacred texts. Few questions cut deeper in the intellectual history of medieval and early modern Jewry, and while our central focus must remain the affirmation or rejection of an inclusive cultural agenda, the critical implications of that choice will inevitably permeate every facet of the discussion.

The Dynamics of a Dilemma

The medieval Jewish pursuit of philosophy and the sciences was marked by a creative tension strikingly illustrated in a revealing paradox. The justifications, even the genuine motivations, for this pursuit invoked considerations of piety that lie at the heart of Judaism, and yet Jews engaged in such study only in the presence of the external stimulus of a vibrant non-Jewish culture. Although major sectors of medieval Jewry believed that a divine imperative required the cultivation of learning in the broadest sense, an enterprise shared with humanity at large could not be perceived as quintessentially Jewish. Thus, even Jews profoundly committed to a comprehensive intellectual agenda confronted the unshakable instinct that it was the Torah that constituted Torah, while they simultaneously affirmed their conviction, often confidently, sometimes stridently, occasionally with acknowledged ambivalence, that Jewish learning can be enriched by wider pursuits and that in the final analysis these pursuits are themselves Torah. On the other side of the divide stood those who saw "external wisdom" as a diversion from Torah study at best and a road to heresy at worst, and yet the religious arguments that such wisdom is not at all external often made their mark even among advocates of the insular approach. The dynamic interplay of these forces across a broad spectrum of Jewish communities makes the conflict over the issue of general culture a central and intriguing leitmotif of Jewish history in medieval and early modern times.

The Islamic Middle East and the Geonim

The first cultural centers of the Jewish Middle Ages were those of Middle Eastern Jewry under Islam, and the Islamic experience was crucial in molding the Jewish response to the challenge of philosophical study. In the seventh century, nascent Islam erupted out of the Arabian peninsula into a world of highly developed cultures. Had this been the typical conquest of an advanced society by a relatively backward people, we might have expected the usual result of *victi victoribus leges dederunt*: as in the case of the barbarian conquerors of the Roman Empire or the ninth- and tenth-century invaders of Christian Europe, the vanquished would have ultimately imposed their cultural patterns, in however attenuated a form, upon the victors. The Islamic invasion, however, was fundamentally different. The Muslim armies fought in the name of an idea, and a supine adoption of advanced cultures would have robbed the conquest of its very meaning. At the same time, a blithe disregard of those cultures bordered on the impossible. Consequently, Islam, which was still in an inchoate state in the early stages of its contact with the Persian, Byzantine, and Jewish worlds, and whose founder had already absorbed a variety of influences, embarked upon a creative confrontation that helped to mold its distinctive religious culture.

The legacy of classical antiquity was transmitted to the Muslims by a Christian society that had grappled for centuries with the tensions between the values and doctrines of biblical revelation and those of Greek philosophy and culture. For the Fathers of the Church, there was no avoiding this difficult and stimulating challenge. As intellectuals living in the heart of Greco-Roman civilization, they were by definition immersed in its culture. The very tools with which patristic thinkers approached the understanding of their faith were forged in the crucible of the classical tradition, so that the men who molded and defined the central doctrines of Christianity were driven by that tradition even as they strove to transcend it. This was true even of those Fathers who maintained a theoretical attitude of unrelieved hostility toward the legacy of Athens, and it was surely the case for patristic figures who accepted and sometimes even encouraged the cultivation of philosophy and the literary arts provided that those pursuits knew their place.[1]

As Muslims began to struggle with this cultural challenge, a broad spectrum of opinion developed regarding the desirability of philosophical speculation. To suspicious conservatives, "reason" was a seductress; to traditionalist theologians, she was a dependable handmaiden, loyally demonstrating the validity of the faith; to the more radical philosophers, she was the mistress and queen whose critical scrutiny was the final determinant of all truth and falsehood.[2] Jews in the Islamic world confronted a similar range of choices, but what was perhaps most important

1. Despite—or precisely because of—its excessively enthusiastic description of patristic humanism, the rather old discussion in E. K. Rand, *Founders of the Middle Ages*, 2nd ed. (Cambridge, Mass., 1941), provides the most stimulating reminder of the importance of this issue to the Fathers of the Church.

2. For an account of the Muslim absorption of "the legacy of Greece, Alexandria, and the Orient," which began with the sciences and turned toward philosophy by the third quarter of the eighth century, see Majid Fakhry, *A History of Islamic Philosophy* (New York and London, 1983), 1–36. Note especially p. xix, where Fakhry observes that "the most radical division caused by the introduction of Greek thought was between the progressive element, which sought earnestly to subject the data of revelation to the scrutiny of philosophical thought, and the conservative element, which disassociated itself altogether from philosophy on the ground that it was either impious or suspiciously foreign. This division continued to reappear throughout Islamic history as a kind of geological fault, sundering the whole of Islam."

In describing the manifestations of this rough division in a Jewish context, I have succumbed to the widespread convention of utilizing the admittedly imperfect term *rationalist* to describe one of these groups. As my good friend Professor Mark Steiner has pointed out, philosophers use this term in a far more precise, technical sense in an altogether different context. Intellectual historians, he argues, have not only misappropriated it but often use it in a way that casts implicit aspersions on traditionalists who are presumably resistant to reason. Let me indicate, then, that by rationalist I mean someone who values the philosophical works of non-Jews or of Jews influenced by them, who is relatively open to the prospect of modifying the straightforward understanding (and in rare cases rejecting the authority) of accepted Jewish texts and doctrines in light of such works, and who gravitates toward

was that they faced those choices in partnership with the dominant society. In ancient times, the philosophical culture was part of a pagan world that stood in stark opposition to Jewish beliefs. Under such circumstances, committed Jews faced the alternatives of unqualified rejection of that civilization or a lonely struggle to come to grips with the issues that it raised. Although the philosophical culture of antiquity retained its dangers for medieval Jews under Islam, the culture with which they were in immediate contact confronted the legacy of the past in a fashion that joined Muslims and Jews in a common philosophic quest.

Needless to say, there were fundamental, substantive reasons for addressing these issues, but it is likely that the very commonality of the enterprise served as an additional attraction for Jews. Members of a subjected minority might well have embraced the opportunity to join the dominant society in an intellectual quest that was held in the highest esteem. This consideration operated with respect to many religiously neutral facets of culture from poetry to linguistics to the sciences. It was especially true of philosophy, which succeeded in attaining supreme religious significance while retaining its religious neutrality. Among the multiplicity of arguments that one hears from Jews opposed to philosophical study, the assertion that it involves the imitation of a specifically Muslim practice played no role precisely because the problems addressed were undeniably as central to Judaism as they were to Islam.

The existence of a religiously neutral or semi-neutral cultural sphere is critically important for Jewish participation in the larger culture. The virtual absence of such a sphere in Northern Europe before the high Middle Ages—and to a certain degree even then—ruled out extensive Ashkenazic involvement in the elite culture of Christendom and may well have been the critical factor in charting the divergent courses of Ashkenazim and Sephardim. The issue, of course, is not religious neutrality alone. During the formative period of Middle Eastern and Iberian Jewry, the surrounding civilization was dazzling, vibrant, endlessly stimulating. During the formative years of Ashkenazic Jewry, the Christian society of the North was primitive, culturally unproductive, and stimulated little more than the instinct for self-preservation.[3]

---

naturalistic rather than miraculous explanation. As the remainder of this essay will make abundantly clear, I do not regard this as a rigid, impermeable classification.

3. Historians of the Carolingian Renaissance and other scholars who have rendered the term *Dark Ages* obsolete will no doubt take umbrage at this description, but even on a generous reading of the evidence, cultural activity took place within such narrow circles that I do not think apologies are necessary. For an overview and reassessment of the current status of research on early medieval Europe, see the discussion and extensive bibliography in Richard E. Sullivan, "The Carolingian Age: Reflections on its Place in the History of the Middle Ages," *Speculum* 64 (1989): 267–306.

For some observations on the importance of a neutral cultural sphere under Islam, see Joseph M. Davis, "R. Yom Tov Lipman Heller, Joseph b. Isaac Ha-Levi, and Rationalism in

These central considerations were reinforced by a linguistic factor. In the Muslim orbit, the language of culture and the language of the street were sufficiently similar that access to one provided access to the other. By the end of the first millennium, Arabic had become the language of most Jews living under Islam, and mastery of the alphabet was sufficient to open the doors to an advanced literary culture. In Northern Europe this was not the case. Knowledge of German or even of early French did not provide access to Latin texts, and the study of such texts had to be preceded by a conscious decision to learn a new language.

The Jewish intellectual and mercantile class under Islam did not merely know the rudiments of the language. The letters of Jewish merchants that have survived in the Cairo Genizah are written in a good Arabic style, which must reflect familiarity with some Arabic literature.[4] The stylistic evidence is reinforced by the use of expressions from the Quran and *ḥadith*. In tenth-century Mosul, a group of Jewish merchants convened regularly to study the Bible from a philosophical perspective.[5] This level of knowledge underscores an additional, crucial point about the relationship between the cultural level of a dominant civilization and the degree to which Jews will be integrated into their environment. In a relatively backward society, an outsider can achieve economic success without attaining more than a superficial familiarity with alien modes of thought. In an advanced culture, maintaining ignorance while achieving success requires enormous dedication to both objectives; it may be possible, as some contemporary examples indicate, but it is extraordinarily difficult. The upper echelons of medieval Muslim society valued cultural sophistication, and a Jew who wanted access to the movers and shakers of that society even for purely pragmatic reasons could not allow himself to remain unfamiliar with its language, its literature, and its thought. This is true not only for merchants; communal leaders who wanted to lobby for essential Jewish interests also required a sophisticated command of the surrounding culture, and the phenomenon of the acculturated Jewish courtier, which reached maturity in Spain, was born in this environment.

Familiarity with Arabic language and literature exercised a significant influence on the development of a new phase in the history of Hebrew poetry and prose. Here too the primary locus of this achievement was Muslim Spain, where Hebrew literature attained dazzling heights, but the beginnings were clearly rooted in the Geonic Middle East. Not surprisingly, the most significant figure in this development was R. Saadya Gaon, whose works often follow Arabic models and who

---

Ashkenazic Jewish Culture 1550–1650" (Harvard University dissertation, 1990), 26–27. (Davis's dissertation, which I shall have occasion to cite again in the section on Ashkenazic Jewry, was submitted after this essay was substantially completed.)

4. See S. D. Goitein, *A Mediterranean Society* 2 (Berkeley, 1971), 180–81. This is not to say that every Jewish merchant could read Arabic (cf. p. 179).

5. See Haggai ben Shammai, "Ḥug le-ʿIyyun Pilosofi ba-Miqra be-Mosul ba-Me'ah ha-ʿAsirit," *Peʿamim* 41 (Autumn, 1989): 21–31.

explicitly expressed admiration for the accomplishments of the dominant culture, and there is reason to believe that the Gaon refined and embellished a new literary trend that had already begun in the Jewish communities in Egypt and Israel.[6]

Another pursuit which combined intellectual sophistication, prestige, integration into the larger society, and economic success was medicine. Medical education could be obtained privately and was part of any advanced curriculum, and so no significant impediment limited minority access to the field. Moreover, the service provided by a physician is so crucial that any tendency to discriminate will be brushed aside by the all-powerful will to live; it is no accident that those who wished to discourage the use of Jewish doctors in Christian Europe could do so only by instilling the fear of death by poison. It is consequently perfectly natural that both religious minorities in the Muslim world entered the medical profession to a degree that was entirely disproportionate to their numbers; by the thirteenth century, this phenomenon was sufficiently striking to impel a Muslim visitor to observe that most of the prominent Jews and Christians in Egypt were either government officials or physicians.[7]

The flexible character of the educational system was not confined to medicine. The absence of governmental or communal control as the Islamic world was formulating its approach to the philosophical enterprise meant that no societal decision had to be made about proper curriculum, and diverse approaches could therefore coexist without formalized pressure for homogenization. In twelfth- and thirteenth-century Northern Europe, when medieval Christians first confronted the issue of philosophical study seriously, the situation was quite different. Ecclesiastical control of cathedral schools and the nascent universities created a more homogeneous position, which both legitimated and limited the philosophic quest. Thus, despite the persistence of diversity even in the Christian West, one can speak of a quasi-official, religiously domesticated philosophical approach, while Muslims and Jews faced an array of possibilities in which virtually no option was foreclosed.

It is hardly surprising, then, that the atmosphere of tenth-century Baghdad, which was the intellectual as well as political capital of the newly matured Muslim civilization, resonated with a bewildering variety of fiercely argued philosophical and religious doctrines. Two scholars attempting to convey a sense of the environment in which R. Saadya Gaon worked have reproduced a striking description which is well worth citing once again. A Muslim theologian who visited Baghdad explained why he stopped attending mass meetings for theological debate:

6. See the eloquent remarks of Ezra Fleisher in his "Hirhurim bi-Devar Ofyah shel Shirat Yisrael bi-Sefarad," *Pe'amim* 2 (Summer, 1979): 15–20, and especially in his "Tarbut Yehudei Sefarad ve-Shiratam le-Or Mimẓe'ei ha-Genizah," *Pe'amim* 41 (Autumn, 1989): 5–20.

7. Goitein, *A Mediterranean Society* 2, pp. 242–43, 247–50. See also Goitein's "The Medical Profession in the Light of the Cairo Genizah Documents," *Hebrew Union College Annual* 34 (1963): 177–94.

> At the first meeting there were present not only people of various [Islamic] sects, but also unbelievers, Magians, materialists, atheists, Jews and Christians, in short, unbelievers of all kinds. Each group had its own leader, whose task it was to defend its views, and every time one of the leaders entered the room, his followers rose to their feet and remained standing until he took his seat. In the meanwhile, the hall had become overcrowded with people. One of the unbelievers rose and said to the assembly: we are meeting here for a discussion. Its conditions are known to all. You, Muslims, are not allowed to argue from your books and prophetic traditions since we deny both. Everybody, therefore, has to limit himself to rational arguments. The whole assembly applauded these words. So you can imagine . . . that after these words I decided to withdraw. They proposed to me that I should attend another meeting in a different hall, but I found the same calamity there.[8]

Both the vigor of the intellectual debate and the opposition to its excesses left their mark on contemporary Jewish texts. In R. Saadya's *Book of Beliefs and Opinions,* we find the first major philosopher of the Jewish Middle Ages arguing for the legitimacy of philosophical speculation against explicit criticism of the entire enterprise. Any attempt to assess the size and standing of the various parties to this dispute during the Geonic period faces serious obstacles. Saadya himself cited the argument that philosophical study bore the seeds of heresy and maintained that this position is proffered only by the uneducated.[9] Salo Baron has dismissed Saadya's assertion as "whistling in the dark."[10] Even if the Gaon's assessment does not result from wishful thinking alone, we cannot easily use it to determine the extent and character of the opposition since it may reflect Saadya's conviction that anyone making this argument is uneducated virtually by definition. At the same time, the passage is not historically useless. For all of Saadya's confidence, polemical aggressiveness, and exalted communal standing, I doubt that he could have written this sentence if recent Geonim or highly influential figures in the yeshivot had maintained a vehement, public stand against philosophical study. On the level of public policy in Saadya's Baghdad, philosophical speculation was either encouraged or treated with salutary neglect.

The introduction to *The Book of Beliefs and Opinions* vigorously sets forth some of the basic arguments for this pursuit:

> [The reader] who strives for certainty will gain in certitude, and doubt will be lifted from the doubter, and he that believes by sheer authority will come to believe out of insight and

8. Cited from *Journal Asiatique,* ser. 5, vol. 1 (1853): 93 by M. Ventura, *Rab Saadya Gaon* (Paris, 1934), 63–64, and by Alexander Altmann in *Three Jewish Philosophers* (New York and Philadelphia, 1960), part II, 13–14. At the same time, the authorities did have a sort of inquisitorial mechanism for the enforcement of correct belief.

9. Saadia Gaon, *The Book of Beliefs and Opinions,* translated by Samuel Rosenblatt (New Haven, 1948), Introductory Treatise, 26.

10. *A Social and Religious History of the Jews* 8 (New York, 1958), 69. Baron (pp. 67–68) also cites a ninth-century Muslim who maintained that Jews were uninvolved in scientific pursuits because they considered "philosophical speculation to be unbelief."

understanding. By the same token the gratuitous opponent will come to a halt, and the conceited adversary will feel ashamed.

The conviction that philosophical certainty is attainable and that reasoned faith is superior to faith based on tradition alone underlies this argument and reflects the views of the Muslim *mutakallimun* whose approach Saadya shared. Indeed, he anticipated the assertions of later Jewish thinkers by maintaining that the Bible itself requires such investigation. Isaiah, after all, proclaimed, "Do you not know? Do you not hear? . . . Have you not understood the foundations of the earth?" (40:21). And the Book of Job records the admonition, "Let us know among ourselves what is good" (34:4). Not only does Saadya take the term *know* as a reference to the understanding that results from philosophical speculation; he is so convinced of this that he regards these verses as decisive evidence that the talmudic rabbis could not possibly have intended to ban such speculation when they forbade investigation into "what is above and what is below, what is before and what is behind" (*M. Ḥagigah* 2:1).[11]

Saadya's confidence that reason can yield certainty is strikingly illustrated by his application to philosophy of a talmudic statement whose primary context was clearly that of Jewish law. The Rabbis inform us that legal questions used to be settled through an appeals process leading up to the high court in Jerusalem, but "ever since the number of disciples of Hillel and Shammai increased who did not attend scholars sufficiently, many disagreements have arisen in Israel"(*Tosefta Sanhedrin* 7:1). "This utterance of theirs," says Saadya, speaking of the benefits of philosophical speculation, "indicates to us that when pupils do complete their course of study, no controversy or discord arises among them."[12] It is difficult to argue against the sort of inquiry that is sure to lead to piety and truth.

Nonetheless, not everyone shared Saadya's certainty. The greatest of the Geonim other than Saadya was undoubtedly R. Hai, who flourished in the late tenth and early eleventh centuries. In some respects, his views on these issues paralleled those of Saadya. He permitted Jewish teachers to instruct children in mathematics and the art of writing Arabic, and in the same ruling he agreed to allow non-Jewish children to study in the synagogue (presumably with Jewish students) if there is no way to prevent this without jeopardizing peaceful neighborly relations. As Shlomo Dov Goitein has pointed out, it would appear to follow that considerable time might be devoted to subjects other than Torah.[13] A famous report informs us that R. Hai sent

11. *Beliefs and Opinions*, 9, 27.

12. *Beliefs and Opinions*, 13.

13. Goitein, *A Mediterranean Society* 2, p. 177. At the same time Goitein notes that genizah evidence does not indicate much formal study of arithmetic on the elementary level (pp. 177–78). For the text of R. Hai's responsum, see Simcha Asaf, *Meqorot le-Toledot ha-Ḥinnukh be-Yisra'el* 2 (Tel Aviv, 1930), 4–5.

a student to consult the Christian *catholikos* for assistance in understanding a biblical verse, and while this does not bear directly on the question of general culture, it reflects habits of mind that might well lead to a willingness to explore beyond the boundaries of classical Jewish texts.[14]

At the same time, R. Hai had reservations about the results of philosophical study, and our assessment of his reservations depends to a critical extent on the authenticity of an important letter that he reportedly addressed to R. Samuel ibn Nagrela of Spain. The letter itself has come down to us in several versions. In the central passage that appears in all the sources, R. Hai admonishes R. Samuel to

> know that what improves the body and guides human behavior properly is the pursuit of the Mishnah and Talmud; this is what is good for Israel. . . . Anyone who removes his attention from these works and instead pursues those other studies will totally remove the yoke of Torah from himself. As a consequence of such behavior, a person can so confuse his mind that he will have no compunctions about abandoning Torah and prayer. If you should see that the people who engage in such study tell you that it is a paved highway through which one can attain the knowledge of God, pay no attention to them. Know that they are in fact lying to you, for you will not find fear of sin, humility, purity, and holiness except in those who study Torah, Mishnah, and Talmud.

A longer version of the letter preserved in the thirteenth-century *Sefer Me'irat 'Einayim* of R. Isaac of Acre places the issue in a concrete historical context. R. Hai forbids the study of *higgayon,* which undoubtedly means philosophy in this letter, and urges the constant study of Talmud in accordance with the practice of

> the beloved residents of Qairuwan and the lands of the Maghreb, may they be blessed in the eyes of Heaven. Would that you knew of the confusion, disputes, and undisciplined attitudes that entered the hearts of many people who engaged in those studies in Baghdad in the days of 'Adud al-Dawla [977–983] and of the doubts and disagreements that were generated among them with respect to the foundations of the Torah to the point that they left the boundaries of Judaism.

He goes on to say that "there arose individuals in Baghdad [apparently somewhat later] who would have been better off as Gentiles"; indeed, they went so far that they aroused the anger of non-Jews who were presumably concerned about the spread of philosophical heresy that might contaminate Muslims as well. Because of the damage that this caused, R. Hai intervened to stop these miscreants in particular

---

14. See Joseph ben Judah ibn Aqnin, *Hitgallut ha-Sodot ve-Hofa'at ha-Me'orot: Perush Shir ha-Shirim,* ed. by A. S. Halkin (Jerusalem, 1964), 495.

Whatever the provenance of the poem *Musar Haskel* attributed to R. Hai, it is worth noting the advice to teach one's son a craft and to study "wisdom," mathematics, and medicine. See Asaf, *Meqorot* 2, p. 8.

and Jewish intellectuals in general from engaging in such pursuits. The letter goes on to assert that even the Gaon R. Samuel b. Ḥofni, who had read such material, saw the damage that resulted and refrained from doing so any longer.

Since the days of Graetz, the authenticity of this document has been the subject of scholarly debate. In the most recent discussion, two new, conflicting considerations have been raised. On the one hand, the name of the ruler in Baghdad is reported with a level of accuracy that might not have been available to a late forger; on the other, the section preserved in *Me'irat 'Einayim* often uses the first person singular, while it was the practice of the Geonim, without exception, to write in the first person plural. If this letter in its entirety was written by R. Hai, it provides fascinating information about extreme rationalism among Jews in late tenth-century Baghdad and about a very strong Jewish counterreaction. My own inclination, however, is to treat the document with considerable skepticism. The unique appearance of the first person singular is surely a weighty consideration, and an expert in the history of medieval Islam assures me that 'Adud al-Dawla's name was not so obscure as to be unavailable to a thirteenth-century Iberian forger (not to speak of an earlier one) even in its precise form. The unconditional denunciation in the letter is considerably stronger than what we would expect from R. Hai's other writings: there were a number of other appropriate opportunities in the Gaon's voluminous correspondence for him to have expressed such views, and yet this passage remains unique; the assertion that R. Samuel ben Ḥofni, for whom speculative pursuits were clearly of central importance, would have abandoned them because of this incident is both implausible in the extreme and reminiscent of other rereadings of history of the sort that produced a document attesting to Maimonides' late embrace of kabbalah; and the specific reference to the abandonment of prayer, an issue which is unattested as far as I know in this early period, echoes similar charges in the literature of the Maimonidean controversy.

Whatever the authenticity of the original document, there is an illuminating aspect to the later textual history of this letter. One of the versions contains a brief addition clearly introduced by a reader who wanted to soften the antiphilosophical message of the Gaon. Where R. Hai criticized those who "pursue those other studies," our philosophically oriented copyist wrote "those other studies *alone*," and where R. Hai spoke about the purity and holiness of those who study Mishnah and Talmud, our copyist wrote that these qualities will be found only in those who study "Mishnah, Talmud, *and wisdom together, not wisdom alone*." These revisions, which were introduced by the interpolater into a letter of Naḥmanides that quotes R. Hai, have been embraced to our own day by scholars who welcome an attenuation of the original message. In the event that the letter itself is inauthentic, there is a certain poetic justice in the undermining of its central point by yet another creative artist.[15]

15. R. Hai's letter is most conveniently available in *Oẓar ha-Geonim* to *Ḥagigah*, pp. 65–66. The most recent discussion of the problem of authenticity, which cites earlier

Whatever we make of the highly dubious report that R. Samuel ben Ḥofni stopped perusing philosophical books as a result of a particular incident, his study of such works is clearcut and their influence upon him was profound. He rejected a literal understanding of the raising of Samuel's spirit by the witch of Endor, and according to R. Hai he denied various miracles that the Talmud attributes to the ancient rabbis, arguing that such miracles are associated only with prophets and that the Talmudic reports are not "halakhah." The point here, if I understand the expression correctly, is not that the content of these passages classifies them as aggadic but rather that they are not normative in much the same way that a rejected legal position is not normative. Here, however, normative seems synonymous with "true," and the utilization of this category to reject the truth of a rabbinic narrative is striking, especially in the absence of any apparent effort at allegorization. Indeed, the most recent study of R. Samuel's thought argues that his position denying these talmudic miracles stemmed from a specifically Mu'tazilite position on the relationship between miracles and prophecy.[16]

Although various Geonim were favorably inclined toward the study of philoso-

---

studies, is in Amos Goldreich's disssertation, *Sefer Me'irat 'Einayim le-Rav Yizḥaq de-min Akko* (Jerusalem, 1981; Pirsumei ha-Makhon le-Limmudim Mitqaddemim, 1984), 405–07. Goldreich notes Shraga Abramson's observation about the Geonim and the first person plural, which was made in a different context; see Abramson, *Rav Nissim Gaon* (Jerusalem, 1965), 307. When I raised the issue in a conversation with Prof. Abramson, he confirmed that there are no exceptions to this usage; since R. Hai became Gaon when Samuel ibn Nagrela was a small child, the possibility that the letter was written before the author assumed his position must, of course, be ruled out. (In a personal communication, Menahem Ben Sasson has suggested the possibility that a shift from plural to singular might have taken place in the course of translation from Arabic into Hebrew.) See too Zvi Groner in *'Alei Sefer* 13 (1986): 75, no. 1099. I am grateful to Ulrich Haarmann, my colleague at the Annenberg Research Institute when this essay was written, for his assessment of the degree of familiarity with 'Adud al-Dawla in the thirteenth century.

For an example of the fortunes of the pro-philosophy version of the letter, see the various printings of C. D. Chavel, *Kitvei Rabbenu Mosheh ben Naḥman* (henceforth *Kitvei Ramban*), beginning with Jerusalem, 1963, 1, pp. 349–50. For the initial challenge to the letter's authenticity, see H. Graetz, "Ein pseudoepigraphisches Sendschreiben, angeblich von Hai Gaon an Samuel Nagid," *Monatsschrift für Geschichte und Wissenschaft des Judenthums* 11 (1862): 37–40. There is no concrete basis for Graetz's suspicions that the citation from R. Hai was inserted into Naḥmanides' letter by a later copyist; consequently, if the letter is a forgery, we probably need to assume that it was produced no later than the early months of the controversy of the 1230s and that it already deceived Naḥmanides.

16. See David Sklare, *The Religious and Legal Thought of Samuel ben Ḥofni Gaon: Texts and Studies in Cultural History* (Harvard University dissertation, 1992), 74. Sklare's dissertation, which appeared well after the completion of this study, presents a broad characterization of Jewish high culture in Geonic times from "extreme rationalism" to traditionalism; see chapter four, pp. 145–210. For attitudes toward *aggadah*, see pp. 64–75.

On the witch of Endor, see Radaq's discussion on I Samuel 28:25. For R. Hai's responsum,

phy, it is clear that the curriculum of the advanced yeshivot was devoted to the study of Torah alone. I am unpersuaded by Goitein's suggestion that the reason for this was the feeling that only those whose professional training would expose them to Greek science needed the protection afforded by the proper study of philosophy and theology. The private nature of philosophical instruction in the society at large made it perfectly natural for Jews to follow the same course; more important, the curriculum of these venerable institutions went back to pre-Islamic days, and any effort to introduce a curricular revolution into their hallowed halls would surely have elicited vigorous opposition. In any case, the absence of a philosophical curriculum in the academies has led to the recent suggestion that openness to Arabic culture by the later Geonim resulted precisely from the weakening of the yeshivot which freed someone like R. Samuel ben Ḥofni from the restraints of the traditional framework.[17]

We are even told in an early Geonic responsum that Bible was not taught in the academies. R. Natronai Gaon informs us that because of economic pressures which required students to work, the talmudic directive (*Kiddushin* 30a) that one-third of one's time be devoted to biblical study could no longer be observed, and the students relied upon another talmudic statement (*Sanhedrin* 24a) implying that Bible, Mishnah, and Midrash are all subsumed under Talmud. One wonders whether this was only a result of insufficient time. The all-consuming nature of talmudic study led to a very similar conclusion among Ashkenazic Jews; moreover, the fact that Judaism shared the Bible with Christianity and, to a degree, with Islam may have helped to generate an instinct that this was not a quintessentially Jewish pursuit. Only the Talmud was the special "mystery" of the Jewish people.[18]

The assertion that the Jews of Qairuwan studied Torah exclusively may well reflect their general orientation accurately. At the same time, we have evidence of some broader pursuits. Dunash ben Tamim of tenth-century Qairuwan wrote several

see *Oẓar ha-Geonim* to *Ḥagigah,* p. 15. On R. Hai's own reservations about the authority of *aggadah,* see R. Abraham b. Isaac Av-Beit Din, *Sefer ha-Eshkol,* ed. by A. Auerbach (Halberstadt, 1868), 2, p. 47. There is some confusion about R. Samuel's views on the talking serpent in Genesis and the talking donkey in Numbers; see the discussion in Aaron Greenbaum, *Perush ha-Torah le-Rav Shmuel ben Ḥofni Gaon* (Jerusalem, 1979), 40–41, n. 17. Whatever R. Samuel's position may have been, there were Geonic views that endorsed a nonliteral understanding of these accounts. For the expectation that R. Samuel would facilitate a student's pursuit of the sciences in addition to Mishnah and Talmud, see I. Goldziher, "Mélanges Judéo-Arabes, XXIII," *Revue des Études Juives* 50 (1905): 185, 187.

17. So Sklare, *The Religious and Legal Thought of Samuel ben Ḥofni,* 96–99, 139–40. As Sklare notes, R. Saadya himself was educated "outside the orbit of the Gaonic yeshivot." For Goitein's remark, see *A Mediterranean Society* 2, p. 210.

18. For R. Natronai's observation, see Asaf, *Meqorot* 2, p. 4. Cf. Rabbenu Tam's remark in *Tosafot Qiddushin* 30a, *s.v. la ẓerikha leyomei.* On the oral law as the mystery of Israel, see *Pesiqta Rabbati* 5. On later reservations about biblical study, see below, n. 109.

astronomical works, one of which he composed to honor the local Muslim ruler, as well as a mathematical treatise and a commentary to *The Book of Creation (Sefer Yeẓirah)*. Moreover, the famous question from Qairuwan about the composition of the Talmud that elicited a classic responsum by R. Sherira Gaon may have been inspired as much by an interest in history, which is also attested in other ways, as by Karaite pressures.[19] Needless to say, the sort of interest in history that expresses itself as a question about the Talmud is itself a manifestation of the study of Torah, but the definition of the boundaries between the sacred and the profane is precisely what is at issue in much of the medieval discussion of pursuits that transcend a narrow definition of Torah.

Muslim Spain and Maimonides

The cultural symbiosis between Judaism and Islamic civilization grew to maturity in the Middle East during the time of the Geonim, but its classic expression and most dazzling achievements emerged from Muslim Spain in the tenth, eleventh, and twelfth centuries. We have already seen that linguistic acculturation is a precondition for such a symbiosis, and familiarity with Arabic literature was one of the most important stimuli to the development of a distinctive Jewish literary voice. Moses ibn Ezra's treatise on Jewish poetry contains a striking passage which reveals a frank recognition of this process by medieval Jews themselves:

> When the Arabs conquered the Andalusian peninsula . . . our exiles living in that peninsula learned the various branches of wisdom in the course of time. After toil and effort they learned the Arabic language, became familiar with Arabic books, and plumbed the depths of their contents; thus, the Jews became thoroughly conversant with the branches of their wisdom and enjoyed the sweetness of their poetry. After that, God revealed the secrets of the Hebrew language and its grammar.[20]

The relationship between the study of Hebrew grammar, with all that it implies for the development of biblical exegesis, and the knowledge of a different Semitic language is self-evident. Medieval Jews had always known Hebrew and Aramaic, but the addition of Arabic, with its rich vocabulary and literature, enabled grammarians to understand the meaning of a host of difficult Hebrew words and to uncover the mysteries of the Semitic root. Unlocking the structure of the language

19. See Menahem Ben Sasson, *Ḥevrah ve-Hanhagah bi-Qehillot Yisrael be-Afriqah ha-Ẓefonit bi-mei ha-Beinayim—Qairuwan, 800–1057* (Hebrew University dissertation, 1983), 179, 185–86. R. Sherira's epistle is now available in N. D. Rabinowitch's English translation, *The Iggeres of Rav Sherira Gaon* (Jerusalem, 1988).

20. *Shirat Yisrael*, ed. by B. Z. Halper (Leipzig, 1924), 63, cited in Asaf, *Meqorot* 2, p. 23.

provided a revolutionary tool for the indisputably religious enterprise of understanding the Bible. There can be no more eloquent testimony to the significance of this development than the extensive appeal to grammatical analysis by R. Abraham ibn Ezra, easily the greatest biblical exegete produced by the Jewry of Muslim Spain. It is consequently both remarkable and revealing that the greatest of medieval Jewish grammarians, Jonah ibn Janaḥ, alludes to Talmudists who regard the study of language as "superfluous," "useless," "practically . . . heretical."[21]

The unavoidable connection between grammatical investigations and the study of non-Jewish works may well account for this attitude, which continued in certain circles through the Middle Ages and persists to our own day. It is difficult to think of any other consideration that could account for so extreme an assertion as the imputation of virtual heresy to grammarians. Considering the undeniable value of this pursuit for biblical study, opposition could be expressed only by Jews who attached little importance to the systematic study of the Bible itself and regarded the Talmud as the only proper subject of intense, regular, prolonged scrutiny. The denigration of biblical study, which we have already touched upon and which also persists in the same circles to this day, may well result not only from the fact that the Bible is shared with non-Jews but from the inevitable contact that it fosters with gentile scholarship and culture. A further consideration, which is not directly related to our theme, may have been the concern that biblical study undisciplined by the everpresent restraints of authoritative talmudic commentary could itself lead to heretical conclusions in matters of both theology and law.

Despite this evidence of opposition, the dominant culture of Andalusian Jewry embodied an avid pursuit not only of linguistic sophistication but of literary expression in the fullest sense. Ahad Ha-Am long ago coined the felicitous term *competitive imitation* (*hiqquy shel hitḥarut*) to describe the motivation and character of this culture,[22] and later scholars have elaborated the point with an accumulation of evidence of which Ahad Ha-Am was only dimly aware. In the words of a recent study, "Golden Age Hebrew poetry . . . can be viewed as a literary discourse designed to mediate cultural ambiguity because it signifies both the acculturation to Arabic cultural norms *and* [emphasis in the original] the resistant national consciousness of the Jewish literati who invented it."[23]

Far more than ordinary intellectual competitiveness was at stake here. The beauty of Arabic was a crucial Muslim argument for the superiority of Islam. Since the Quran was the final, perfect revelation, it was also the supreme exemplar of

21. *Sefer ha-Riqmah*, ed. by M. Wilensky (Berlin, 1929), p. v, cited in Asaf, *Meqorot*, 2, pp. 19–20.

22. "Ḥiqquy ve-Hitbolelut," in *'Al Parashat Derakhim*, 2nd ed., 1 (Berlin, 1902), 175.

23. Ross Brann, "Andalusian Hebrew Poetry and the Hebrew Bible: Cultural Nationalism or Cultural Ambiguity?" in *Approaches to Judaism in Medieval Times* 3, ed. by David R. Blumenthal (Atlanta, 1988), 103. See also Brann's book, *The Compunctious Poet: Cultural Ambiguity and Hebrew Poetry in Muslim Spain* (Baltimore, 1991).

aesthetic excellence, and its language must be the most exalted vehicle for the realization of literary perfection. When Jews compared the richness and flexibility of Arabic vocabulary to the poverty of medieval Hebrew, the Muslims' argument for the manifest superiority of their revelation undoubtedly hit home with special force. The quality of Arabic was evident not merely from a mechanical word count or even an analysis of the Quran; it shone from every piece of contemporary poetry and prose.

Consequently, Jews were faced with a dual challenge. First, they had to explain the undeniable deficiencies of the vocabulary of medieval Hebrew. For all its terrible consequences, the exile has its uses, and Andalusian Jews maintained that the untold riches of the Hebrew language had gradually been lost due to the travails of the dispersion. The numerous words that appear only rarely in the Bible and whose meaning we must struggle to decipher are but the tip of the iceberg; they testify to a language far more impressive than the one bequeathed to us by our immediate ancestors.

Moreover, and far more important, Jews were challenged to demonstrate that even the Hebrew at their disposal was at least as beautiful as Arabic and that Hebrew literature could achieve every bit as much as the literature of medieval Muslims. This created a religious motivation to reproduce the full range of genres and subjects in the Arabic literary repertoire, which meant that even the composition of poetry describing parties devoted to wine, women, men, and song could be enveloped by at least the penumbra of sanctity. There can be no question, of course, that even if the genre was born out of apologetic roots, it took on a life of its own, and not every medieval wine song was preceded by a *le-shem yiḥud;* at the same time, every such poem was a conscious expression of Jewish pride, which in the Middle Ages had an indisputably religious coloration. Furthermore, the power and beauty of the religious poetry of the Jews of medieval Spain were surely made possible by the creative encounter with Arabic models. Some of the deepest and most moving expressions of medieval Jewish piety would have been impossible without the inspiration of the secular literature of a competing culture.

Jews could have accomplished their fundamental goal by establishing parity between Hebrew and Arabic, but such an achievement is psychologically insufficient and polemically tenuous. Consequently, we find the glorification of Hebrew over Arabic and the assertion, which we shall find in other contexts as well, that Arabic culture, including music, poetry, and rhetoric, was ultimately derived from the Jews.[24]

24. The footnotes in Brann's article provide a recent bibliography of the substantial work on this theme. See especially A. S. Halkin, "The Medieval Jewish Attitude Toward Hebrew," in *Biblical and Other Studies*, ed. by Alexander Altmann (Cambridge, Mass., 1963), 233–48, and Nehemiah Allony, "Teguvat R. Moshe ibn Ezra la-' 'Arabiyya' be-Sefer ha-Diyyunim ve-ha-Siḥot (Shirat Yisrael)," *Tarbiẓ* 42 (1972/73): 97–113 (particularly the challenge

On a less exalted level, poetry also fulfilled a social function. Businessmen had poems written in their honor which served the pragmatic purpose of useful publicity as well as the psychological purpose of boosting the ego. The ability to write poetry was the mark of an accomplished gentleman, and this too encouraged the cultivation of the genre.[25] As I have already indicated in passing, the existence of the class of Jewish courtiers created a firm social base for a Jewish literary and philosophic culture. Jewish communities in Muslim Spain became dependent upon the representation afforded by courtiers, and that representation was impossible without a command of the surrounding culture. Since courtiers came to expect poetic flattery, their presence and patronage gave the poet both support and standing, although it hardly needs to be said that the relationship between patron and poet is never an unmixed blessing.

Despite all this, disparagement of poetry and opposition to reliance on Arabic models were not unknown among the Jews of Muslim Spain. In some instances, however, even those who criticized what they perceived as an overemphasis on language and rhetoric did not reject the enterprise entirely, and there can be little doubt that the dominant social and intellectual class regarded literary skill as a fundamental component of a proper education. The ideal of *adab,* which roughly means general culture, was embraced by many Jews, and the praises of a great man would point to his mastery of the full range of medieval disciplines.[26]

Samuel ha-Nagid's description of God's kindness to him contains the central elements to be sought in the well rounded Jewish intellectual: "He endowed you [i.e., Samuel] with wisdom of His Scripture and His Law, which are classified first among the sciences. He instructed you in Greek knowledge and enlightened you in Arabic lore."[27] In this passage we find only the most general categories of learning, and the sole hierarchy of values places Torah above other pursuits. When the

---

from the beauty of the Quran on p. 101). Cf. also Norman Roth, "Jewish Reactions to the *'Arabiyya* and the Renaissance of Hebrew in Spain," *Journal of Semitic Studies* 28 (1983): 63–84.

Le-shem yiḥud describes a dedicatory prayer recited by later Jews before fulfilling a religious obligation. Despite the anachronism and the resort to Hebrew, I cannot think of a better way to make the point.

25. See S. D. Goitein, *Jews and Arabs* (New York, 1955), 162.

26. For references and discussion, see Bezalel Safran, "Baḥya ibn Pakuda's Attitude toward the Courtier Class," in *Studies in Medieval Jewish History and Literature* [1], ed. by Isadore Twersky (Cambridge, Mass., 1979), 154–96. For some tentative reservations about the thesis of Safran's article, see Amos Goldreich, "Ha-Meqorot ha-'Arviyyim ha-Efshariyyim shel ha-Havḥanah bein 'Ḥovot ha-Evarim' ve-'Ḥovot ha-Levavot'," in *Meḥqarim be-'Ivrit u-ba-'Aravit: Sefer Zikkaron le-Dov Eron,* ed. by Aharon Dotan (Tel Aviv, 1988), 185, 199, nn. 22, 95.

27. Brann's translation (p. 108) from *Divan Shmuel ha-Nagid,* ed. by Dov Yarden, 1 (Jerusalem, 1966), 58.

general sciences are broken down in greater detail, a more nuanced picture emerges in which philosophy takes pride of place while the remaining disciplines are necessary both for their own sake and for their usefulness in preparing the student for ever higher forms of study. As a result of this concept of "propaedeutic studies," virtually every field can bask in the reflected glory of the queen of the sciences.

"It is certainly necessary," writes Maimonides, "for whoever wishes to achieve human perfection to train himself at first in the art of logic, then in the mathematical sciences according to the proper order, then in the natural sciences, and after that in the divine science."[28] More complete lists include logic, mathematics, astronomy, physics, medicine, music, building, agriculture, and a variety of studies subsumed under metaphysics. So much significance was attributed to the propaedeutic studies that one of the polemicists during the Maimonidean controversy maintained that the only people who became heretics as a result of reading *The Guide of the Perplexed* were those who came to it without the proper preliminaries. This argument led him to a new application of a famous Maimonidean admonition. No one, said Maimonides, should approach the study of philosophy without first filling his stomach with the "bread and meat" of biblical and talmudic law. In our context, says Yosef b. Todros Halevi, that metaphor should be applied not to "the written and oral Torah" but to

> the other sciences like the sciences of measurement and physics and astronomy. These are known as the educational, pedagogic sciences . . . which lead the human intellect to approach the understanding of the divine science with a generous spirit, with passion and with affection, so they they can be compared to this world in its capacity as a gateway to the world to come.[29]

Not all philosophers assigned such weight to these preparatory studies. Thus, Abraham ibn Daud derided excessive preoccupation with medicine, with the "still more worthless. . . . art of grammar and rhetoric," and with "strange, hypothetical" mathematical puzzles, when the only valuable aspect of mathematics is the one that leads to a knowledge of astronomy. Endless concentration on the means would

28. *The Guide of the Perplexed,* translated by Shlomo Pines (Chicago and London, 1963), I:34, p. 75.

29. *Qevuẓat Mikhtavim be-'Inyenei ha-Maḥaloqet 'al Devar Sefer ha-Moreh ve-ha-Madda'*, ed. by S. Z. H. Halberstam (Bamberg, 1875), 10. See *Mishneh Torah, Hil. Yesodei ha-Torah* 4:13. On the propaedeutic studies, see inter alia, Harry A. Wolfson, "The Classification of Sciences in Medieval Jewish Philosophy," *Hebrew Union College Jubilee Volume* (Cincinnati, 1925), 263–315; A. S. Halkin, "Li-Demuto shel R. Yosef ben Yehudah ibn 'Aqnin," in *Sefer ha-Yovel li-khevod Ẓevi Wolfson*, ed. by Saul Lieberman (Jerusalem, 1965), 99–102; Halkin, "Yedaiah Bedershi's Apology," *Jewish Medieval and Renaissance Studies*, ed. by Alexander Altmann (Cambridge, Mass., 1967), 170; Halkin, "Ha-Ḥerem 'al Limmud ha-Pilosophiah," *Peraqim* 1 (1967–68): 41; Baron, *History* 8, p. 143.

steal time better devoted to the end, which clearly remained the study of metaphysics.[30]

By far the most significant challenge to the prevailing ideal of the philosophers came in R. Judah Halevi's revolt against Andalusian Jewish culture, a revolt so far-reaching that it actually serves to underscore the centrality of philosophical inquiry for that culture. Halevi's accomplishments as a poet and abilities as a thinker made him a sterling example of what Jewish *adab* strove to produce; when he revolted against the values of the Jewish elite, he challenged the very underpinnings of his society.[31] This challenge finds expression in his poetry, in his decision to abandon Spain for the land of Israel, and in his antiphilosophical philosophical work, the *Kuzari*.

Halevi substituted a deeply romantic, historically founded, revelation-centered, strikingly ethnocentric faith for the philosophically oriented religion of many of his peers. At the same time, the *Kuzari* operates within the matrix of medieval philosophical conceptions. Halevi could no more rid himself of the active intellect than a contemporary religious critic of evolution could deny the existence of atoms or DNA. More important, the antiphilosophical position of the *Kuzari* is an integral part of Halevi's revulsion at fawning courtiers, at Jewish groveling disguising itself as competitive imitation, at much of what "the exile of Jerusalem that is in Spain" stood for. It is no accident that his famous line denouncing Greek wisdom for producing flowers but no fruit and for affirming the eternity of matter is part of a poem justifying his decision to abandon Spain for the land of Israel. To the degree that Halevi's position developed in stages, there can be little doubt that the radical social critique gave birth to the philosophical revisionism; he clearly did not decide to leave Spain as a consequence of his rethinking of the role of philosophical speculation. If he did, however, the point would be even stronger. Nothing could demonstrate more clearly the degree to which the philosophic quest had become part of the warp and woof of Spanish Jewish civilization.

Halevi's insistence on the radical superiority not only of Judaism but also of the Jewish people has disturbed and perplexed many readers, particularly in light of his assertion that even proselytes can never hope to attain prophecy. His position can probably be understood best if we recognize that the roots of his revolt lay not so much in an intellectual reappraisal as in a visceral disgust with the humiliation and self-degradation that he saw in the Jewish courtier culture. He describes acquaintances who attempted to persuade him to remain in Spain as drunk and unworthy of a response.

30. *Sefer ha-Emunah ha-Ramah* (Frankfurt a. M., 1852), Part 2, Introduction, p. 45.

31. For a powerful depiction of Halevi's revolt, see Gerson D. Cohen's discussion in his edition of Abraham ibn Daud, *Sefer ha-Qabbalah (The Book of Tradition)* (Philadelphia, 1967), 295–300.

> How can they offer him bliss/through the service of kings,/which in his eyes/is like the service of idols?/Is it good that a wholehearted and upright man/should be offered the happiness/of a bird tied up in the hands of youths,/in the service of Philistines,/of Hagarites and Hittites,/as alien gods/seduce his soul/to seek their will/and forsake the will of God,/to betray the Creator/and serve creatures instead?

I have already noted the psychological inadequacy of attempting to demonstrate that Jews are just as good as non-Jews; in such a case, the standard of comparison remains the alien culture which Jews strive to match and imitate. Though Halevi was not the only one to assert that Jewish culture was not merely equal but superior, he appears to have regarded the protestations of others as halfhearted, inadequate, even pathetic. There was certainly nothing in the philosophical enterprise in its standard form that had the potential to demonstrate the superiority of Judaism over Islam. In Christian societies, philosophical arguments offered the opportunity of establishing the implausibility, even the impossibility, of distinctive Christian dogmas; in a society with a dominant religion which Maimonides himself described as impeccably monotheistic, this option was precluded. The only way to overcome the status of "despised people," a characterization which appears in the very title of the *Kuzari,* was to cut the Gordian knot and declare one's emancipation from the usual rules of the philosophical game. Judaism rests on a unique revelation, not a common philosophic consensus; Jews are set apart and above, their status ingrained and unapproachable even through conversion. Only such a position could speak to the psychic impulses that lay at the very roots of Halevi's revolt.[32]

Halevi's assertion that one who accepts Judaism because of faith in the revelation is better than one who tries to approach it through the clever application of reason

32. For the poetic passage quoted, see Hayyim Schirmann, *Ha-Shirah ha-'Ivrit bi-Sefarad u-bi-Provence* 1 (Jerusalem, 1954), 498. For the passage about Greek wisdom, see pp. 493–94.

Several very recent studies have grappled with Halevi's position on the second class status of converts. Daniel J. Lasker's "Proselyte Judaism, Christianity, and Islam in the Thought of Judah Halevi," *Jewish Quarterly Review* 81 (1990): 75–91, addresses the issue without any effort to mitigate the sharpness of Halevi's assertion. Attempts to provide such mitigation appear in Lippman Bodoff, "Was Yehudah Halevi Racist?", *Judaism* 38 (1989): 174–84, and in Steven Schwartzschild, "Proselytism and Ethnicism in R. Yehudah HaLevy," in *Religionsgespräche im Mittelalter,* ed. by Bernard Lewis and Friedrich Niewöhner (Wiesbaden, 1992), 27–41.

There is a talmudic passage which could have served as a source for Halevi's position about the denial of prophecy to proselytes. See *Kiddushin* 71b for the assertion that God rests his presence (*shekhinah*) only on families of unimpeachable Jewish lineage.

did not prevent him from maintaining, along with many other medieval Jews, that much of the wisdom of ancient Greece and Rome was derived from Jewish sources. Since the travails of exile have led to the loss not only of much of the Hebrew language but also of ancient Jewish wisdom, that wisdom has come to be associated with the Greeks and Romans. In the hands of rationalists, this argument served not only as an assertion of Jewish pride but as a legitimation of philosophical study. The wisdom of Solomon had to be redeemed from gentile hands. To a later figure like Naḥmanides, whose attitude toward speculation was complex and ambivalent, the fact that gentiles have been influenced by ancient Jewish learning was unassailable, but the lessons to be drawn were less clear. Since the crucial Jewish wisdom had been preserved within the fold, and the material embedded in the books of the Greeks could be recovered only through explorations fraught with spiritual peril, the decision to embark on such exploration required careful, even agonizing deliberation. Despite this ambivalence, the dominant message of the conviction that philosophy was purloined from the Jews was undoubtedly to establish its Jewish legitimacy and perhaps even its standing as a component of Torah itself.[33]

The position of medieval rationalists concerning the relationship between philosophy and Torah is crucial to our entire discussion, and it explains my scrupulous avoidance of the tempting and common term "secular studies." There was nothing secular about metaphysics, and because of the preparatory character of many other disciplines, they too assumed religious value. We have already seen Saadya's arguments for the existence of a religious obligation to engage in philosophical speculation, and similar arguments recur throughout the Jewish Middle Ages. Abraham, we are told repeatedly, attained his knowledge of God through philosophical proofs. We are commanded to "*know* this day . . . that the Lord is God" (Deut. 4:39). David instructed Solomon, "*Know* the God of your father, and serve him with a whole heart and a willing soul" (I Chron. 28:9). Jeremiah wrote, "Let him that glories glory in this, that he *understands and knows me* . . . , says the Lord" (Jer. 9:23).[34] These proof-texts, of course, were not unassailable, and antirationalists argued that there are superior ways of reaching God. Halevi, for example, cleverly reversed the rationalists' argument that Abraham had attained philosophical knowledge of God. The patriarch had indeed pursued philosophical understanding, but the Rabbis tell us that when God told him to go outdoors (Gen. 15:5), he was really telling him to abandon astrology and listen to the divine

33. *Kuzari* 2:26; 66. Cf., *inter multa alia*, *Guide* 1:71. Many of the relevant references have been summarized in Norman Roth, "The 'Theft of Philosophy' by the Greeks from the Jews," *Classical Folia* 22 (1978): 53–67. For Naḥmanides, see *Kitvei Ramban* 1, p. 339, and see below for his overall stance.

34. On these and other arguments, see Herbert A. Davidson, "The Study of Philosophy as a Religious Obligation," in *Religion in a Religious Age*, ed. by S. D. Goitein (Cambridge, Mass., 1974), 53–68.

promise. In this context, astrology is merely an example of "all forms of syllogistic wisdom," which are to be left behind once direct revelation has been attained.[35]

The argument for speculation, however, was not wholly dependent upon proof-texts. If love of God, clearly a quintessential religious value, was to have any real meaning, it could flow only from a knowledge of the Creator's handiwork, and this required a pursuit of the sciences. Moreover, the knowledge of God that comes from tradition alone is inherently insufficient and is in any event secondary rather than primary knowledge. Only those intellectually unfit for speculation can be excused from this obligation; others who neglect their duty are guilty of what R. Baḥya ibn Paqudah called "laziness and contempt for the word of God and his Law" and will be called to account for their dereliction.[36]

A secondary argument pointed to the desirability, even the obligation, of impressing the gentiles with the wisdom and understanding of the Jewish people (cf. Deut. 4:6; *Shabbat* 75a). Baḥya made this point with exceptional vigor by maintaining that gentile recognition of Jewish wisdom can come only if Jews prove the truth of their faith

> by logical arguments and by reasonable testimony. For God has promised to unveil the minds of the nations of their ignorance and to show His bright light to prove the truth of our religion, as it is said, "And many peoples shall go and say, Come yet and let us go up to the mountain of the Lord, to the House of the God of Jacob, and He will teach us of His ways, and we will walk in His paths. For out of Zion shall go forth the Law, and the word of the Lord from Jerusalem" (Isaiah 2:3). Thus it becomes a certainty to us, through logic, Scripture, and tradition, that we are obligated to speculate upon every matter the truth of which is conceivable to our minds.[37]

This is a remarkable formulation. The object to Baḥya is not merely to cause gentiles to admire Jewish wisdom. Jewish philosophical expertise is the medium of an eschatological missionary endeavor. Non-Jews will accept the truth of Judaism at the end of days not because of a supernatural *deus ex machina* but because of the persuasive powers, aided no doubt by God, of Jewish philosophical arguments. Maimonides' well-known view that gentile recognition of the truth at the end of days will come through gradual preparation mediated by Christianity and Islam rather than through a sudden, miraculous upheaval may well be adumbrated in this strikingly naturalistic position in *The Duties of the Heart*. In any event, Baḥya has assigned philosophy nothing less than a messianic function.

In a famous and controversial extended metaphor, Maimonides graphically illustrated his conviction that philosophy alone affords the highest level of religious

---

35. *Kuzari* 4:17, 27.

36. *The Book of Direction to the Duties of the Heart*, trans. by Menahem Mansour (London, 1973), Introduction, p. 94.

37. *The Duties of the Heart*, ch. 1., p. 115.

insight. Near the end of his *Guide,* he tells us that the varying levels of people's apprehension of God can be classified by analogy with the inhabitants of a city who seek the palace of the king. People who have no doctrinal belief are like individuals who have not entered the city at all. Those who have engaged in speculation but have reached erroneous conclusions can be compared with people within the city who have turned their backs on the palace. Then there are those who seek the palace but never see it: "the multitude of the adherents of the Law, . . . the ignoramuses who observe the commandments." We then come to those who reach the palace but do not enter it: "the jurists who believe true opinions on the basis of traditional authority and study the law concerning the practices of divine service, but do not engage in speculation concerning the fundamental principles of religion." At long last we come to those who have "plunged into speculation." Only one "who has achieved demonstration, to the extent that that is possible, of everything that may be demonstrated . . . has come to be with the ruler in the inner part of the habitation."[38]

The supreme value that Maimonides attributed to philosophical speculation does not in itself demonstrate that he classified it as Torah. Several passages in the first book of his code, however, establish this clearly and reinforce the pride of place that he assigned to such speculation in his hierarchy of values. The first two chapters of the code deal in summary fashion with metaphysical questions which Maimonides then tells us represent what the Rabbis called the "account of the chariot." The next two chapters set forth the essentials of astronomy and physics which, says Maimonides, are "the account of creation." In combination, these chapters constitute what the Talmud calls *pardes,* which is clearly a term for the secrets of the Torah. Later he informs us explicitly that "the subjects called *pardes* are subsumed under the rubric *gemara,*" and in the *Guide* he describes the philosophical discussion of divine attributes, creation, providence, and the nature of prophecy as the mysteries and secrets of the Torah.

This, however, is not the end of it. Alone among medieval Talmudists, Maimonides took literally a rabbinic statement that the talmudic discussions between Abbaye and Rava are considered "a small matter" compared with the account of the chariot, which is "a great matter." Since the account of the chariot means metaphysical speculation, the value judgment expressed here is wholly consistent with the palace metaphor in the *Guide* and, to many medieval observers, no less disturbing.[39]

---

38. *Guide* 3:51, pp. 618–19.

39. See *Hil. Yesodei ha-Torah* 2:11–12; 4:10, 13; *Hil. Talmud Torah* 1:11–12; *Guide* 1:35. Isadore Twersky has devoted a number of important studies to Maimonides' views on these questions. See especially his *Introduction to the Code of Maimondes (Mishneh Torah)* (New Haven, 1980), pp. 356–514, esp. pp. 488–507; "Some Non-Halakhic Aspects of the *Mishneh Torah,*" in *Jewish Medieval and Renaissance Studies,* 95–118; "Religion and Law," in *Religion in a Religious Age,* 69–82. That Baḥya regarded metaphysics as Torah may be reflected in his admonition that one must study metaphysics, but it is forbidden to do so (as

What renders Maimonides' position all the more striking is its potential implications for talmudic study. The introduction to his code contains a famous observation that it will now be possible to study the written Torah, followed by "this [book]," from which the reader will know the oral Torah, so that it will be unnecessary to read any other book in between. The possibility that Maimonides meant to render the Talmud obsolete was raised in his own time, and he vigorously denied any such intention in a letter to R. Pinḥas ha-Dayyan of Alexandria. Nonetheless, the tone of even this letter reveals an attitude not wholly typical of medieval Talmudists, and some of Maimonides' epistles to his student Joseph ben Judah express relatively sharp reservations about extreme preoccupation with details of talmudic discussions at the expense of other pursuits.

In the letter to R. Pinḥas he testifies that he has not taught the *Mishneh Torah* for a year and a half because most of his students wanted to study R. Isaac Alfasi's legally oriented abridgment of the Talmud; as for the two students who wanted to study the Talmud itself, Maimonides taught them the tractates that they requested. Although he goes on to insist that he wrote the code only for people who are incapable of plumbing the depths of the Talmud, this description of his students certainly does not convey single-minded devotion to teaching the talmudic text.

Far more striking are the letters to Joseph ben Judah. In one section of this collection, Maimonides predicts that the time will come when all Israel will study the *Mishneh Torah* alone with the exception of those who are looking for something on which to spend their entire lives even though it achieves no end. Elsewhere he permits Joseph to open a school but urges him to pursue trade and study medicine along with his learning of Torah; moreover, he says,

> Teach only the code of R. Isaac Alfasi and compare it with the Composition [i.e., the *Mishneh Torah*]. If you find a disagreement, know that careful study of the Talmud brought it about, and study the relevant passage. If you fritter away your time with commentaries and explanations of talmudic discussions and those matters from which we have excused people, time will be wasted and useful results will be diminished.

Finally, a slightly later citation quotes Maimonides to the effect that talmudic scholars waste their time on the detailed discussions of the Talmud as if those

---

in the case of Torah itself) for worldly benefit. See Safran, "Baḥya ibn Pakuda's Attitude" (above, n. 26), 160. For a halakhic analysis of Maimonides' position on the status of philosophical inquiry as a technical fulfillment of the commandment to study Torah, see Aharon Kahn, "Li-Qevi'at ha-Ḥefẓa shel Talmud Torah," *Beit Yosef Shaul: Qoveẓ Ḥiddushei Torah* 3 (1989): 373–74, 386–403. In Kahn's view, even Maimonides believed that only philosophical discussions centered on sacred texts qualify for the status of Torah. While Kahn's interesting argument is based on instincts that are (and should be) difficult to overcome, the hard evidence for the conclusion remains rather thin.

discussions were an end in themselves; in fact their only purpose was to make the determinations necessary for proper observance of the commandments.[40]

These passages do not make explicit reference to what it is that one should do with the time saved by the study of the *Mishneh Torah*. It is perfectly clear, however, that Maimonides had in mind more than the study of medicine and the merchant's trade. One of the functions of his great halakhic work was to expand the opportunities for the pursuit of philosophical speculation.

Despite the frequency, clarity, vigor, and certainty with which Maimonides affirmed the supreme value of speculation and its standing at the pinnacle of Torah, the poetry and pathos of a single powerful passage reveal how all this can sometimes be overshadowed by the unshakable instinct of which I spoke at the outset: the instinct that it is the Torah that constitutes Torah. In his correspondence with R. Jonathan ha-Kohen of Lunel, Maimonides addressed various questions about specific rulings in his code. He was clearly moved by the informed reverence toward his magnum opus that he found among the rabbis of Provence and looked back with nostalgia on the years that he devoted to its composition. His formulation is both striking and problematic:

> I, Moses, inform the glorious Rabbi R. Jonathan ha-Kohen and the other scholars reading my work: Before I was formed in the stomach the Torah knew me, and before I came forth from the womb she dedicated me to her study [cf. Jer. 1:5] and appointed me to have her fountains erupt outward. She is my beloved, the wife of my youth, in whose love I have been immersed since early years. Yet many foreign women have become her rivals, Moabites, Ammonites, Edomites, Sidonians, and Hittites. The Lord knows that they were not taken at the outset except to serve her as perfumers and cooks and bakers. Nonetheless, the time allotted to her has now been reduced, for my heart has been divided into many parts through the pursuit of all sorts of wisdom.[41]

There are no doubt ways to mitigate the incongruity of this passage. First, the allusion may well be to ancillary, propaedeutic studies whose status as "handmaidens of theology" was well established; neither metaphysics nor, arguably, even physics are necessarily included. Moreover, just a few lines later the letter concludes, "May the Lord, blessed be He, help us and you study His Torah *and understand His unity* so that we may not stumble, and let the verse be fulfilled in our own time, 'I will put my Torah in their inward parts and write it on their hearts'" (Jer. 31:33). Nonetheless, the passionate wistfulness of Maimonides' tone leaves me resistant to efforts at integrating this outburst of religious nostalgia seamlessly into the web of his thought.[42] One almost suspects that as Maimonides recovered from the surge of

40. *Iggerot le-Rabbenu Moshe ben Maimon*, ed. and trans. by Yosef Kafih (Jerusalem, 1972), 126, 134, 136.

41. *Teshuvot ha-Rambam*, ed. by Jehoshua Blau, 2nd ed., 3 (Jerusalem, 1986), p. 57.

42. See the attempt in Yosef Kafih, "Limmudei 'Ḥol' be-Mishnat ha-Rambam," *Ketavim* 2

emotion that overcame him, he purposely inserted the crucial phrase into his final sentence so that no one should suspect that he had renounced some of his central commitments. We are witness here to a fascinating and revealing glimpse of the capacity of an unphilosophical, almost atavistic love for old-fashioned Torah to overwhelm, if only for a moment, the intellectual convictions of the very paradigm of philosophical rationalism.

Aside from the special case of Halevi, we have little direct evidence of principled opposition to philosophy in Muslim Spain. Some of the polemical remarks in the works of Baḥya, Maimonides, and others reveal the unsurprising information that there existed Talmudists who looked upon the enterprise with a jaundiced eye and resisted efforts to reread rabbinic texts in the light of philosophical doctrines. Nonetheless, there was no concerted opposition whose work has come down to us, and Samuel ibn Nagrela is a striking, early example of a figure of some stature in talmudic studies who represented the full range of *adab.* Moreover, we can probably be confident that the greatest Spanish Talmudist of the twelfth century did not maintain a vigorous antiphilosophical stance. R. Joseph ibn Migash, who taught Maimonides' father, did not, as far as we know, produce any philosophical work. At the same time, given Maimonides' oft-expressed contempt for Talmudists who opposed speculation, the great reverence with which he described his illustrious predecessor would be difficult to understand if ibn Migash was counted among them, and R. Abraham Maimonides listed him among the luminaries who "strengthened the faith that they inherited from their fathers . . . to know with the eye of their intellect and the understanding of their mind" that God cannot be conceived in corporeal terms.[43] As in the case of Saadya's Baghdad, many Spanish Talmudists probably treated philosophy with salutary neglect while others, probably including ibn Migash, looked upon it with some favor even though it was not their particular field of expertise. With few significant exceptions, Spanish Jewry under Islam was unambiguously hospitable to the pursuit of philosophy, the sciences, and the literary arts.

(Jerusalem, 1989), 594, where the author nevertheless expresses doubts about Maimondes' authorship of these remarks. See too Rashba's comment in Abba Mari b. Joseph, *Sefer Minḥat Qenaot* (Pressburg, 1838), 40=*Teshuvot ha-Rashba*, ed. by Haim Z. Dimitrovsky 1 (Jerusalem, 1990), pp. 342–43; Profiat Duran, *Ma'aseh Efod* (Vienna, 1865), 15–16. The immense religious value that Maimonides attached to philosophy as well as his ongoing philosophical scrutiny of Jewish religious texts would render this passage problematic even if we were to accept Kahn's conclusion that philosophical inquiry must be based on Jewish sources in order to qualify as Torah. See above, n. 39.

43. See Abraham Maimonides, *Milḥamot Hashem*, ed. by Reuven Margaliyot (Jerusalem, 1953), 49–50. With respect to direct evidence, however, note Israel Ta-Shema's remark that "we do not have a scintilla of information on his pursuit of philosophy, grammar, or science"; see "Yeẓirato ha-Sifrutit shel Rabbenu Yosef ha-Levi ibn Migash," *Kiryat Sefer* 46 (1971): 137. In light of Abraham Maimonides' statement, this formulation may be a shade too vigorous.

The Great Struggle: Provence and Northern Spain from the Late Twelfth to the Early Fourteenth Century

The great religious value of philosophy was inextricably intertwined with its great religious danger. Since reason and revelation were rooted in the same source, they could not conflict with one another;[44] at the same time, the study of philosophic texts generated a host of problems for traditional conceptions, particularly as Aristotelianism launched its triumphant march across the medieval intellectual landscape. To most believers, God had created the world out of nothing; to Aristotelians, a form of primeval matter had always existed. To the traditional believer, God's knowledge extended to the most minute details affecting the lowest of creatures, and his loving providence was over "all his handiwork" (Psalms 145:9); to the Aristotelian, he did not know particulars at all. To the person of faith, celestial reward awaited each righteous individual as a separate entity; to the Aristotelian philosopher, the soul's survival depended upon intellectual attainments and took a collective rather than an individual form. One is tempted to paraphrase Maimonides' exalted assessment of metaphysics by observing that these are indeed not small matters.

Medieval thinkers had a wide range of options in dealing with such issues. At one end of the spectrum were those who rejected philosophical inquiry on principle. On the other were those who accepted virtually the full corpus of Aristotelian conclusions and maintained that revealed religion, which should not be consulted for the answers to ultimate questions, was intended as a political instrument for ordering the life of the masses. Ranged between these extremes were the large majority of thinkers with greater or lesser inclinations toward the preservation of traditional beliefs. In any given instance, one could argue that the philosophical position was unproven and unpersuasive or that the standard religious conception was not essential or had been misconstrued. The last approach was both controversial and fruitful because it required not only a rethinking of doctrine but a reinterpretation of classic texts. The allegorical understanding of both biblical and talmudic material is consequently an integral and significant part of our story. The attitudes of Jews toward general culture had a profound impact on their conceptions of Judaism itself.

The battle over philosophical study became a major theme in medieval Jewish history as a result of a watershed event: the migration of many Spanish Jews to

44. For a sharp formulation of this point, see Norman Roth, *Maimonides: Essays and Texts, 850th Anniversary* (Madison, 1985), 94. He argues that from the point of view of medieval Jewish and Muslim rationalists there can be no conflict because "what prophetic revelation brings in the way of flashes of light to the masses, the philosopher sees in the full blaze of rational illumination."

Southern France in the wake of the Almohade conquest of the late 1140s. This conquest brought the history of Andalusian Jewry to a tragic end and opened a new chapter in the relationship between Sephardic and Ashkenazic Jews. A number of the exiles moved only as far north as Christian Spain, where some of them translated scientific and philosophical works that helped to transfer the advanced culture of the Muslim world into the ever more curious Christian Europe of the twelfth century. While this dimension of cultural activity did not play a central role within the Jewish community itself, it was a development of major importance in the evolution of European civilization.[45]

From an internal Jewish perspective, the major acts in this drama were to be played out in the south of France.[46] For the first time, substantial numbers of Ashkenazim and Sephardim confronted one another in the same community, and the immigrants resisted any assimilation into the cultural patterns of the native Ashkenazim. On the contrary, one senses a degree of self-confident assertiveness that borders on cultural imperialism. The Provençal Jews needed to defend even their halakhic traditions against a Sephardic effort to impose the rulings of R. Isaac Alfasi, and the Spanish Jews brought with them a feeling of almost contemptuous superiority toward those who were untrained in the broader culture of the Andalusian elite. What made this challenge particularly effective was the inability of the Jews of Provence to point to their own unambiguous superiority in Torah narrowly construed. Although the immigrants themselves could offer no Talmudists to compete with R. Abraham b. David of Posquières or R. Zeraḥiah HaLevi of Lunel, they could point to a substantial cohort of distinguished rabbis produced by their native culture along with its philosophical achievements.

Under such circumstances, the argument that pursuit of philosophy enhanced religion by providing insight into the nature of God was difficult to resist. At the same time, the deviations from traditional religious conceptions that philosophy brought in its wake could not but cause concern in a society that was being exposed

45. See M. Steinschneider's classic *Die Hebraeischen Uebersetzungen des Mittelalters und die Juden als Dolmetscher* (Berlin, 1893). For a readable survey of medieval translations and the Jews, see section II of Charles Singer's "The Jewish Factor in Medieval Thought," in *The Legacy of Israel*, ed. by Edwyn R. Bevan and Charles Singer (Oxford, 1927), 202–45. On earlier contacts between Ashkenazim and Sephardim, see the important reassessment by Avraham Grossman, "Bein Sefarad le-Ẓarfat: ha-Qesharim bein Qehillot Yisra'el she-bi-Sefarad ha-Muslemit u-bein Qehillot Ẓarfat," in *Galut Aḥar Golah: Meḥqarim be-Toledot 'Am Yisrael Muggashim li-Professor Ḥaim Beinart*, ed. by A. Mirsky, A. Grossman, and Y. Kaplan (Jerusalem, 1988), 75–101. See now his *Ḥakhmei Ẓarfat ha-Rishonim* (Jerusalem, 1995), 554–71.

46. For a characterization of Provençal Jewish culture in this period, see Isadore Twersky, "Aspects of the Social and Cultural History of Provençal Jewry," in *Jewish Society through the Ages*, ed. by H. H. Ben Sasson and S. Ettinger (New York, 1971), 185–207.

to such ideas for the first time, and the argument from the dangers of philosophical heresy loomed large. It may well be that this dialectic was responsible for one of the most important developments in the history of Judaism: the rise of mysticism as a highly visible factor in the intellectual constellation of medieval Jewry.

The central component of Jewish mysticism in the Middle Ages was its theosophic doctrine. Without detracting from the significance of ecstatic kabbalah, there can be little doubt that one seeking to understand the attraction of esoteric lore in the initial stages of its popularity must look at its doctrinal rather than its experiential aspects. Such an examination reveals that kabbalah provided the perfect solution, at least to people with a receptive religious personality, to the critical intellectual issue that confronted Jews at precisely the time and place in which mysticism began to spread.

The essential claim made by kabbalists was that God had revealed an esoteric teaching to Moses in addition to the exoteric Torah. This secret lore uncovered the deeper meaning of the Torah, and it also taught initiates the true nature of God and creation; it is here, not in Aristotelian physics and metaphysics, that one must seek the meaning of the accounts of creation and of the chariot. Indeed, a recent study has argued that longstanding mystical doctrines were now at least partially publicized because the bearers of these doctrines could not suffer in silence the Maimonidean-style claim that the rabbis had referred to gentile disciplines as the secrets of the Torah. However that may be, kabbalah offered a revealed key to precisely the knowledge that philosophers sought. By locating that key in an inner Jewish tradition, kabbalists could argue that philosophy with all its dangers was superfluous, and even though Rabbinic tradition had attributed spiritual peril to the study of mystical secrets, one could hardly compare the potential for heresy in the pursuit of revealed truth to the dangers of studying Aristotle. Even without reference to the problem of heresy, kabbalah promised the late twelfth-century Provençal Jew all that philosophy offered and more, since human reason is fallible while the word of God is not. Small wonder that Jewish thinkers began to respond, and mysticism embarked on a path that would lead it toward a pre-eminent position in Jewish piety and religious thought by the sixteenth and seventeenth centuries.[47]

The penetration of Sephardic philosophical culture into Southern France in the late twelfth and early thirteenth centuries produced the first great conflict over

47. I made the essential point in "Miracles and the Natural Order in Naḥmanides," in *Rabbi Moses Naḥmanides (Ramban): Explorations in His Religious and Literary Virtuosity*, ed. by Isadore Twersky (Cambridge, Mass. and London, England, 1983), 111. Cf. the citation from A.S. Halkin in note 17 there. On the suggestion that mystics were responding to the claim that Aristotelian doctrines are the secrets of the Torah, see Moshe Idel, *Kabbalah: New Perspectives* (New Haven and London, 1988), 253, and much more fully in sections I and II of his "Maimonides and Kabbalah," in *Studies in Maimonides*, ed. by Isadore Twersky (Cambridge, Mass. and London, England, 1990), 31–50.

the propriety of rationalistic speculation. The Maimonidean controversy erupted in the early 1230s as a result of the perception by R. Solomon ben Abraham of Montpellier that the study of certain works of Maimonides was leading people into heresy. Though the internal Jewish dynamic that we have been examining could have set these events in motion without any external impetus, there can be little doubt that the atmosphere of early thirteenth-century Christian Languedoc aided and abetted the process. The century had begun with the Albigensian Crusade, and the decade of the Jewish controversy was also witness to the birth of an inquisition aimed at Christian heresies.

R. Solomon sent his distinguished student R. Jonah to bring the writings in question to the attention of his natural allies, the rabbis of Northern France. As a result of this initiative, the rabbis of the North proclaimed a ban against *The Guide of the Perplexed* and the first, quasi-philosophical section of the *Mishneh Torah* ("The Book of Knowledge"). At this point, the defenders of Maimonides in the South proclaimed a ban against R. Solomon and his disciples and sent the biblical commentator R. David Kimḥi (Radak) to their natural allies in what was now Christian Spain to obtain support for the second ban.

Radak discovered to his surprise that a mixed reception awaited him. While some Spanish communities affirmed the ban enthusiastically, the distinguished physician R. Judah Alfakar refused to offer support and instead wrote several sharp letters expressing his reservations about Maimonides' *Guide*. The ambivalence that Radak encountered in Spain speaks volumes for the fact that the direction of influence in the Sephardi–Ashkenazi confrontation of the previous decades was not reflected exclusively in the adoption of a philosophical culture by some Ashkenazim. The Ashkenazi impact on many Sephardim was no less profound. In some cases, this influence came through Southern France; in others, it was direct. Whatever the medium, however, Radak discovered a transformed Spanish Jewry whose attitude toward the culture produced by its own forebears could no longer be predicted with confidence.

This transformation is also evident in a letter by Naḥmanides that we shall have to examine later in which he attempted, with some success, to bring the controversy to a close. In the meantime, events in Montpellier overtook developments in Spain. Zealous anti-Maimonists approached local ecclesiastical authorities with what they presented as heretical Jewish books, and the churchmen obliged by burning the controversial works of Maimonides. Indignant Maimonists complained to lay authorities apparently unhappy with ecclesiastical intervention, and the anti-Maimonist delators were promptly punished by having a part of their tongues cut off. Contemporary Maimonists evinced no dismay at the harshness of the penalty; on the contrary, they regarded it as an appropriate divine retribution for an offense whose seriousness in the medieval Jewish context could hardly be exaggerated. Though the internal Jewish controversy did not end immediately after these events, it began to die down, and the works of Maimonides remained undisturbed for decades to come.[48]

The issues raised in the substantial corpus of letters written during this controversy reveal the concerns, the tactics, and the deeply held convictions of most of the parties to the dispute. Regrettably, we possess only one letter from R. Solomon ben Abraham himself. It is of no small interest that he denies requesting a ban against the *Guide* and "The Book of Knowledge" and that he makes a point of his careful, sympathetic study of Maimonides' code in his yeshivah. What concerned him, he writes, was that some Provençal Jews had affirmed extreme philosophical positions that went so far as the allegorization of the story of Cain and Abel and even of the commandments themselves. R. Meir HaLevi Abulafia, who had questioned Maimonides' view of resurrection three decades earlier, reports that R. Solomon was motivated by a concern about rationalists who "wish to break the yoke of the commandments" by denying that God really cares for ritual observances. All God wants, they maintained, is that people know him philosophically; whether the body is pure or impure, hungry or thirsty, is quite irrelevant. R. Meir's brother Yosef b. Todros speaks of Jews who argued that all the words of the Torah and rabbinic tradition are allegories, who mocked the belief in miracles, and who regarded themselves as exempt from prayer and phylacteries. To what degree these assertions reflect reality is far from clear; what is clear is that the argument that rationalism has in fact produced heresy was one of the most forceful and effective weapons in the arsenal of the opposition.[49]

In addition to specific charges of disbelief and violations of law, rationalists also faced the accusation that they abandon the study of Talmud in favor of philosophical speculation. Thus, Radak found it necessary to testify that he studies Talmud assiduously and observes the commandments meticulously; the only reason that people suspected him, he tells us, is that he had indicated that the detailed exchanges in the Talmud will be rendered obsolete in the Messianic age when everything will become clear. Many Talmudists would surely have disagreed even with the assertion to which Radak admits, and Alfakar's letter to him explicitly speaks of the

48. The clarity of this brief summary obscures the obscurity of the events. For an admirable effort to reconstruct the chronology of the controversy, see A. Schochet, "Berurim be-Parashat ha-Pulmus ha-Rishon 'al Sifrei ha-Rambam," *Ẓion* 36 (1971): 27–60, which takes account of the important sources in Joseph Shatzmiller, "Li-Temunat ha-Maḥaloqet ha-Rishonah 'al Kitvei ha-Rambam," *Ẓion* 34 (1969): 126–44. Cf. the earlier works by Joseph Sarachek, *Faith and Reason: The Conflict over the Rationalism of Maimonides* (Williamsport, Penna., 1935), and Daniel Jeremy Silver, *Maimonidean Criticism and the Maimonidean Controversy, 1180–1240* (Leiden, 1965). The best analysis of significant aspects of the debates is in Bernard Septimus, *Hispano-Jewish Culture in Transition* (Cambridge, Mass. and London, England, 1982), 61–103.

49. See R. Solomon's letter in *Qevuẓat Mikhtavim*, pp. 51–52; R. Meir in *Qoveẓ Teshuvot ha-Rambam* (Leipzig, 1859) 3, 6a; R. Yosef in *Qevuẓat Mikhtavim*, 6, 21.

inclination to abolish the discussions of Abbaye and Rava in order "to ascend in the chariot."[50]

On the most fundamental level, Alfakar, whose letters evince an impressive level of philosophical sophistication, denied the controlling authority of reason. Any compelling demonstration, he wrote, requires investigation of extraordinary intensity because of the possibility of hidden sophistry, and an erroneous premise, no matter how far back in the chain of reasoning, can undermine the validity of the conclusion. Consequently, reliance on reason to reject important religious teachings is inadmissible.

Alfakar's specific examples concentrate on the denial or limitation of miracles. Maimonides, he says, regarded Balaam's talking donkey and similar biblical miracles as prophetic visions despite the Mishnah's inclusion of the donkey's power of speech among the ten things created immediately before the first Sabbath. This Maimonidean tendency is symptomatic of the deeper problem of attempting to synthesize the Torah and Greek wisdom. Radak had explicitly praised Maimonides' unique ability to harmonize "wisdom" and faith. On the contrary, says Alfakar, the attempt was a failure. Maimonides, for example, limited the number of long-lived antediluvians

> because his intention was to leave the ordinary operation of the world intact so that he could establish the Torah and Greek wisdom together, "coupling the tent together so that it may be one" (Exod. 26:11). He imagined that the one could stand with the other "like two young roes that are twins" (Song of Songs 4:5); instead, there was "mourning and lamentation" (Lam. 2:5). "The land was not able to bear them, that they might live together" (Gen. 13:6) as two sisters, "for the Hebrew women are not like the Egyptian women" (Exod. 1:19).

As for lesser figures than Maimonides, they reduce the number of miracles because "their soul does not consider it appropriate to believe what the Creator considered it appropriate to do."[51]

Yosef ben Todros Halevi affirmed the dangers lurking in the *Guide* by arguing that no one in his generation has the capacity to read the work without exposing himself to the danger of heresy. Consequently, he can justify the action of the Northern French rabbis without forfeiting his respect for Maimonides. Both "acted for the sake of heaven, each in his place and time." Moreover, he says, the dangers of speculation have even been recognized by the kings of the Arabs, who forbade "Greek wisdom" and philosophical study. If Yosef is referring to the Almohade rulers, we would have a striking appeal by a Jewish conservative to the judgment of persecutors of his people for the sake of validating or at least lending support to a decision affecting the internal spiritual life of Judaism.[52]

50. *Qovez Teshuvot ha-Rambam* 3, pp. 3a–4a.
51. *Qovez Teshuvot ha-Rambam* 3, pp. 1a–2a, 3a.
52. *Qevuzat Mikhtavim*, 21–22, 13–14. The term *malkhei ha-'erev*, based on I Kings

The Maimonist party responded with a vigorous defense of the value of general culture. Radak succeeded in eliciting a ban against R. Solomon and his students from the Jewish community of Saragossa, the text of which contains instructive arguments for the rationalist position taken from Rabbinic literature.

> It is widely known among our people that our sages instructed and warned us to learn the wisdom concerning the unity of God as well as external forms of wisdom that will enable us to answer heretics and know the matters utilized by disbelievers to destroy our Torah. [They] also [instructed us to study] astrology and the vanities of idol-worship, [which] one cannot learn from the Torah or the Talmud, as well as the measurement of land and knowledge of solstices and calculations, as the learned teacher of wisdom said, "The pathways of the heavens are as clear to me as the pathways of Nehardea," and an understanding of the scope with which they measured at a distance on both land and sea. Moreover, they ruled that no one can be appointed to the Sanhedrin to decide the law unless he knows these disciplines and medicine as well.[53]

A particularly interesting aspect of this text is the distinction between "the wisdom concerning the unity of God" (*ḥokhmat ha-yihud*) and "external forms of wisdom" or "external disciplines" (*ḥokhmot ḥizẓoniyyot*). The former requires no defense on instrumental grounds; it is part of the Torah, and the problem is just that the antirationalists do not recognize this. External wisdom, on the other hand, needs to be justified in other ways. The document provides Rabbinic authority for some of these pursuits, whose purpose is often self-evident, but the only concrete argument set forth is the need to respond to heretics. This need, which was legitimized by a Rabbinic text, was routinely cited in other contexts to defend so religiously dubious an enterprise as the study of the New Testament. Its application to our context is attested not only in the Saragossa ban but in the counterargument of Yosef ben Todros that the rabbis' intention in urging Jews to learn the appropriate response to heretics was manifestly "to reconstruct the ruins of the faith, not to destroy it." Yosef, in other words, regarded the use of this argument as the last refuge of scoundrels, a pro forma justification for a pursuit motivated by entirely different considerations.[54]

If the information of the Saragossa authorities was reliable, the text of their denunciation contributes to our knowledge of the ban issued by the antirationalists.

10:15, appears as *malkhei 'arav* in the parallel verse in II Chronicles (9:14) and was no doubt understood by Joseph as Arab kings despite the ambiguity introduced by the juxtaposition of the two phrases in Jeremiah 25:24.

53. *Qovez Teshuvot ha-Rambam* 3, p. 5b.

54. *Qevuẓat Mikhtavim*, 14. On reading the New Testament to answer a heretic, see my comments and references in *The Jewish-Christian Debate in the High Middle Ages* (Philadelphia, 1979; rep., Northvale, N.J. and London, 1996), 309–10.

The earlier ban, we are told, was directed not only against the *Guide* and "The Book of Knowledge" but against "anyone who studies any of the external disciplines." R. Baḥya ben Moses, the chief signatory of the Saragossa ban, repeats this information in a letter to the Jewish communities of Aragon.[55] On the one hand, we could be dealing with an exaggeration designed to facilitate the eliciting of additional counterbans; on the other, the fact that "external books" are denounced in the Mishnah renders it difficult to reject this report out of hand. However that may be, rationalists were clearly uncomfortable with the talmudic prohibition of "Greek wisdom," and we find efforts at redefinition that limit the meaning of the term to a kind of coded communication that has not survived and that therefore poses no limitation whatever to the philosopher's intellectual agenda. One Maimonist argued that however one understands the term, the prohibition can certainly not result from a concern with heresy since the Rabbis would never have excluded potential diplomats from the ban had the reason for it been that weighty.[56]

Defenses of rationalism and its allied disciplines appealed to other considerations as well. The argument that philosophical sophistication was necessary to impress gentiles was fairly widespread, and it occasionally took an even stronger form: the Jewish loss of Greek wisdom, which was, of course, originally Jewish wisdom, makes Jews an object of ridicule in the eyes of their educated neighbors.[57] During the Maimonidean controversy, a more fundamental argument appears in a novel formulation that may reflect the influence of a major Christian work. In the twelfth century, Peter Abelard wrote his celebrated *Sic et Non,* which challenged opponents of speculation to account for a variety of apparent contradictions in authoritative texts. The "authority" which is the presumed alternative to reason is simply not usable without its supposed rival. One Maimonist letter argues for rationalism by citing contradictions in Rabbinic sources that can be resolved only by the sort of speculation that the antirationalists eschew.[58] Patristic contradictions have become Rabbinic contradictions, but the Abelardian argument remains intact.

We have already seen that the anti-Maimonists' concern that rationalism tends to produce heresy constituted one of their most powerful arguments against philosophical study. A striking feature of the controversy is that the Maimonists argued

55. *Qoveẓ Teshuvot ha-Rambam* 3, 5b, 6a.

56. Samuel Saporta in *Qevuẓat Mikhtavim,* 95. On Greek wisdom, see Saul Lieberman, *Hellenism in Jewish Palestine* (New York, 1962), 100–14, and cf. the references in Davidson, "The Study of Philosophy as a Religious Obligation" (above n. 34), 66–67, n. 44.

57. Samuel ibn Tibbon, *Ma'amar Yiqqavu ha-Mayim* (Pressburg, 1837), 173. On the need to impress gentiles, see Twersky, "Provençal Jewry," 190, 204–05.

58. Joseph Shatzmiller, "Iggarto shel R. Asher be-R. Gershom le-Rabbanei Ẓarfat," in *Meḥqarim be-Toledot 'Am Yisrael ve-Ereẓ Yisrael le-Zekher Ẓevi Avineri* (Haifa, 1970), 129–40. Shatzmiller was struck by the argument but not by the Abelardian parallel, which is, of course, speculative. In a recent lecture, Bernard Septimus has noted that R. Asher may well have been making a sharp allusion to the Tosafists' own use of dialectic.

that precisely the reverse was true: it was antirationalism that had produced a heresy more serious than the worst philosophical heterodoxy, because many naïve believers worshipped a corporeal God. The issue of anthropomorphism is therefore crucial to an understanding not only of the Maimonidean controversy but of the role that philosophy played in defining the parameters of a legitimate Jewish conception of God. There can be no higher stakes than these and no better evidence of the powerful, almost controlling presence of the philosophical enterprise at the very heart of medieval Judaism.

Maimonides listed belief in the incorporeal nature of God as one of his thirteen principles constituting the sine qua non of the faith. As he indicated both in his discussion of this creed and in his code, failure to affirm this belief is rank heresy which excludes one from a portion in the world to come. Maimonides has been assigned a highly sophisticated motivation for taking this position. Survival after death requires a cleaving to God that is possible only through the development of that aspect of the soul which perceives certain abstract truths about the Deity; the belief in an incorporeal God is consequently the minimum requirement for attaining eternal life.[59] While Maimonides may well have endorsed this view, the immediate motivation for perceiving anthropomorphism as heresy was probably simpler and more fundamental: the believer in a corporeal God does not really believe in one God at all.

Maimonides drew the connection between unity and incorporeality forcefully and explicitly:

> There is no profession of unity unless the doctrine of God's corporeality is denied. For a body cannot be one, but is composed of matter and form, which by definition are two; it is also divisible, subject to partition. . . . It is not meet that belief in the corporeality of God . . . should be permitted to establish itself in anyone's mind any more than it is meet that belief should be established in the nonexistence of the deity, in the association of other gods with Him, or in the worship of other than He.[60]

Maimonides' son provided an even sharper formulation. Anthropomorphism, he writes, is an impurity like that

> of idolatry. Idolaters deny God's Torah and worship other gods beside Him, while one who, in his stupidity, allows it to enter his mind that the Creator has a body or an image or a location, which is possible only for a body, does not know Him. One who does not know Him denies Him, and such a person's worship and prayer are not to the Creator of the world. [Anthropomorphists] do not worship the God of heaven and earth but a false

59. See Arthur Hyman's important article, "Maimonides' 'Thirteen Principles'," in *Jewish Medieval and Renaissance Studies*, 141–42.

60. *Guide* 1:35, 81. Hyman is, of course, well aware of this passage but argues that the belief in incorporeality is what gives the very profession of unity its salvific value.

image of Him, just like the worshippers of demons about whom the Rabbis say that they worship [such] an image, for the entity that they have in mind, who is corporeal and has stature or a particular location where he sits on a throne, does not exist at all. It was concerning those fools and their like that the prophet said, "He has shut their eyes, that they cannot see, and their hearts, that they cannot understand."[61]

It is especially noteworthy that Maimonides does not appeal to tradition to validate his declaration that anthropomorphism is heretical. On the contrary, his comments on the motivation for his stand clearly reveal the determinative role of philosophy. He tells us in the *Guide* that if he wished to affirm the eternity of the world, he could provide a figurative interpretation to biblical texts that imply the contrary just as he has interpreted anthropomorphic verses figuratively. One reason for distinguishing the case of anthropomorphism from that of eternal matter is that the latter has not been proven. On the other hand, "that the deity is not a body has been demonstrated; from this it follows necessarily that everything that in its external meaning disagrees with this demonstration must be interpreted figuratively." Alfakar, while wrestling with the same problem, pointed to the fact that the Bible itself contains contradictory verses regarding the corporeality of God and argued that this legitimates figurative interpretation. Though Alfakar and Maimonides also cited Onkelos's alleged avoidance of anthropomorphic expressions as a precedent, and Naḥmanides, Abraham Maimonides, and Samuel Saporta provided a list of antianthropomorphic authorities beginning with the time of the Geonim, there can be little doubt that the driving force in the extirpation of a corporeal conception of God was the philosophic enterprise.[62]

The philosophers, in fact, did their job so well that contemporary Jews find it very difficult to acknowledge the existence of medieval Jewish anthropomorphism despite substantial, credible evidence. By far the best known testimony is the assertion by R. Abraham b. David of Posquières that greater Jews than Maimonides believed in a corporeal God because they were misled by the literal meaning of Rabbinic *aggadot.* Maimonist rhetoric during the controversy is replete with assertions that the anti-Maimonists believe in a corporeal God and are consequently heretics. Some of these attacks may well be exaggerated, but they play too prominent a role in the discussion for them to have been invented out of whole cloth. Abraham Maimonides reports that the prominent anti-Maimonist David ben Saul vigorously denied that he conceived of God in crudely anthropomorphic terms;

61. *Milḥamot Hashem,* 52. For a very strong (perhaps just a bit too strong) assertion of this understanding of Maimonides' motivation (without reference to *Milḥamot Hashem*), see Menachem Kellner, *Dogma in Medieval Jewish Thought From Maimonides to Abravanel* (Oxford, 1986), 41: "Maimonides held that . . . one who conscientiously observes the halakhah while believing in the corporeality of God is, in effect, performing idolatry."

62. See *Guide* 2:25, 328; *Qoveẓ Teshuvot ha-Rambam* 3, p. 1b; *Kitvei Ramban,* 1, pp. 346–47; *Milḥamot Hashem,* 49–50; *Qevuẓat Mikhtavim,* 85–86, 90–91.

at the same time, says Abraham, David affirmed his belief that God sits in heaven, where his primary grandeur is to be found, and that a partition separates the Creator from his creatures. In a particularly sharp attack, Abraham comments that Christian support for the anti-Maimonist cause is hardly surprising since the beliefs of the two groups diverge so little.[63]

Finally, we have the works of two Ashkenazic writers who explicitly express conceptions of God which are corporeal by Maimonidean standards. R. Moses Taku is the better known of these figures, and his *Ketav Tamim* is a polemic specifically directed against the Saadyanic and Maimonidean insistence on an incorporeal God. Taku, who is cited in *Tosafot* and was not an entirely marginal figure, not only affirmed a moderate kind of anthropomorphism but also accused the philosophers of heresy in terms strikingly reminiscent of Abraham Maimonides himself. In his vigorous reversal of the Maimonidean argument, Taku wrote,

> Who knows if the redemption is being delayed because of the fact that they do not know who is performing miracles for them. Moreover, if tragedy strikes, they cry out and are not answered because they direct their cries to something other than the fundamental object of faith; for this new religion and new wisdom recently came upon the scene, and its adherents maintain that what the prophets saw was the form of created beings, while from the day that God spoke to Adam and created the world through His word, we have believed it to be the Creator and not a creature.[64]

In addition to *Ketav Tamim,* we now know of a late thirteenth-century French work which maintains the bizarre belief that the substance of God is to be found in the light above the firmament and in the air. The sun is nothing more than a moving window in the firmament, and what we see when we look at it is therefore the very substance of the deity. It is more than a little disconcerting to find a medieval Hebrew text that routinely refers to "the air, blessed be it [He?] and blessed be its [His?] name," but in this case at least, the author describes himself as the object of persecution, and he was no doubt on the theological margins of Ashkenazic Judaism despite the fact that he may have been the author of a rabbinic responsum. Nonetheless, in the late fourteenth or early fifteenth century, an Ashkenazic rabbi was still asking the basic question about the corporeality of God, and there can be little doubt that Ashkenaz in the high Middle Ages did not enjoy a consensus on this most critical of theological questions.[65] Thus, the presence of anthropomorphic

63. Rabad to *Hil. Teshuvah* 3:7; *Qovez̧ Teshuvot ha-Rambam* 3, p. 3b; the letter of the Rabbis of Lunel and Narbonne in *Z̧ion* 34 (1969): 140–41; *Milḥamot Hashem,* 69, 55. Note especially Schochet's vigorous presentation of the Maimonist polemic against anthropomorphism, *Z̧ion* 36 (1971): 54–60. See also the literature cited in Kellner, *Dogma,* 233, n. 159.

64. *Oz̧ar Neḥmad* 3 (1860): 82–83.

65. See Israel Ta-Shema, "Sefer ha-Maskil: Ḥibbur Yehudi Z̧arfati Bilti-Yadua mi-sof

conceptions among some medieval Jews provided the rationalists with a powerful religious argument for philosophical inquiry and even enabled them to reverse the accusation of heresy. Ironically, as the philosophers won their greatest victory, they destroyed the most effective argument for their importance.

For Taku, the major obstacle to the rejection of anthropomorphism was not only the plain meaning of biblical expressions; he was concerned to at least an equal degree with a multitude of Rabbinic texts which he was unwilling to interpret nonliterally. In this and other contexts, conclusions drawn from philosophy and the sciences forced medieval Jews to confront the question of *aggadah* on a fundamental level, so that these pursuits once again impinged upon the study of Torah even in the narrowest sense. We have already seen that Geonim like R. Samuel b. Ḥofni and R. Hai had legitimated rejection of certain *aggadot,* although R. Hai had insisted on the need to make the most strenuous efforts to validate all Rabbinic statements, particularly if they are incorporated in the Babylonian Talmud. The need to reinterpret rather than reject outright was especially acute with respect to an issue like anthropomorphism, where the error was too profound to allow it to stand even as a minority view among the Rabbis. Consequently, by the time of Maimonides and the Maimonidean controversy, substantial precedent existed for a variety of approaches to aggadic texts.[66]

The issue of *aggadah* had already been raised by opponents of Maimonides in the debate over resurrection just after the turn of the thirteenth century, and the Northern French rabbis in the 1230s once again expressed concern. They believed that Maimonides had undermined the traditional understanding of reward after death and specifically criticized his rejection of a literal feast of Leviathan as described in Rabbinic *aggadot.* It is of no small interest that while one defense of Maimonides argued that he had not in fact denied that this banquet would take place, Abraham Maimonides sardonically observed that the Rabbis had proffered this promise so that naïve believers like R. Solomon of Montpellier would have something to look forward to. On a more significant level, Maimonides' assertion that the biblical punishment of *cutting off* (*karet*) signifies the destruction of the soul was attacked as a contradiction of the talmudic perception that it refers to premature

---

ha-Me'ah ha-Yod-Gimel," *Meḥqerei Yerushalayim be-Maḥashevet Yisrael* 2:3 (1982–83): 416–38; Ephraim Kupfer, "Li-Demutah ha-Tarbutit shel Yahadut Ashkenaz va-Ḥakhamehah ba-Me'ot ha-Yod-Dalet-ha-Tet-Vav," *Tarbiẓ* 42 (1972/73): 114.

66. On Taku, see his *Ketav Tamim: Ketav Yad Paris H711,* with an introduction by Joseph Dan (Jerusalem, 1984), Introduction, 24. On the Geonim, see above, n. 16. For a survey of attitudes toward *aggadah,* see Marc Saperstein, *Decoding the Rabbis* (Cambridge, Mass., and London, England, 1980), 1–20, and cf. I. Twersky, "R. Yedaʿyah ha-Penini u-Perusho la-Aggadah," in *Studies in Jewish Religious and Intellectual History Presented to Alexander Altmann,* ed. by S. Stein and R. Loewe (University, Alabama, 1979), Heb. sec., pp. 63–82. See also Lester A. Segal, *Historical Consciousness and Religious Tradition in Azariah de' Rossi's Meor ʿEinayim* (Philadelphia, 1989), 89–114.

death. Maimonides' critics proceeded to denounce those who abandon "*halakhot* and *aggadot*, which are the source of life, to pursue Greek wisdom, which the sages forbade." The point here is not merely the choice of one pursuit over another, but the manner in which the study of the one distorts the understanding of the other. According to a Maimonist report, some of the Ashkenazim went so far as to propose that Rashi's interpretation of *aggadot* be made dogmatically binding.[67]

The centrality of this issue is illustrated not only by the citations of various midrashic passages in the heat of the controversy but by Abraham Maimonides' special treatise on the *aggadot*, which undoubtedly emerged from these debates. This treatise not only proposes reinterpretation but recognizes the occasional need for outright rejection as well. "We are not obligated . . . to argue on behalf of the Rabbis and uphold the views expressed in all their medical, scientific, and astronomical statements, [and to believe] them the way we believe them with respect to the interpretation of the Torah, whose consummate wisdom was in their hands."[68] The essence of this position had already been expressed in the *Guide* itself. Although Maimonides had argued that respect for the wisdom of the Sages requires us to strive to understand even their scientific assertions as consonant with the truth, he nonetheless laid down the following principle:

> Do not ask of me to show that everything they have said concerning astronomical matters conforms to the way things really are. For at that time mathematics were imperfect. They did not speak about this as transmitters of dicta of the prophets, but rather because in those times they were men of knowledge in these fields or because they had heard these dicta from the men of knowledge who lived in those times.[69]

Despite the apparent effort to impose Rashi's presumably literal understanding of *aggadot*, even Ashkenazic Jews were not wholly inflexible on this issue. Moses Taku himself indicated that his teachers had distinguished between Rabbinic statements that appear in the Talmud and those that do not. "If a person sees a strange remark in external [Rabbinic] books, he should not be concerned about it since it does not appear in the *aggadot* in our Talmud upon which we rely." Several disagreements with the Rabbis appear in the admittedly atypical *Sefer ha-Maskil*, and under the pressure of polemics with an apostate attacking the Talmud, R. Yeḥiel of Paris

67. See Saporta, *Qevuẓat Mikhtavim*, 94; *Milḥamot Hashem*, 60–61; Joseph Shatzmiller, "Li-Temunat . . . ," *Zion* 34 (1969): 139; idem, "Iggarto . . . ," in *Meḥqarim . . . Avineri*, 139. Note too Charles Touati's remarks in, "Les Deux Conflits autour de Maimonide et des Études Philosophiques," in *Juifs et Judaisme de Languedoc*, ed. by M. H. Vicaire and B. Blumenkranz (Toulouse, 1977), 177.

68. *Ma'amar 'al Odot Derashot Ḥazal*, in *Milḥamot Hashem*, 84.

69. *Guide* 3:14.

observed, if only for the sake of argument, that the *aggadah* does not have the same binding force as talmudic law.[70]

The most famous medieval assertion that aggadic statements are not binding also emerged out of the crucible of the Jewish-Christian debate, this time from a figure who played a crucial role in the Maimonidean controversy of the 1230s. In 1263, Naḥmanides faced a different apostate who attempted to utilize talmudic evidence for the purpose of demonstrating the truth of Christianity; in their disputation, Naḥmanides argued that midrashic statements should be treated as sermons which command respect but not unqualified assent. The sincerity of that argument has been the subject of controversy to our own day, but an analysis of Naḥmanides' commentary to the Torah leaves little doubt that he meant what he said.[71] Many medieval Jews wished to preserve considerable latitude in dealing with *aggadah,* and although a variety of motives were at work, philosophical considerations took pride of place.

Naḥmanides' role in the controversy and his stand regarding philosophical speculation are especially important both because his efforts appear to have effectively ended the Northern French intervention and because he represents a crucial transitional type in the evolution of medieval Jewish attitudes toward general culture. On the one hand, he was hardly typical of the Andalusian-style Jewish philosopher. He expressed considerable hostility toward "the accursed Greek" Aristotle, described himself as a disciple of the Northern French Tosafists, and fully embraced the "hidden wisdom" of the kabbalah. On the other hand, he mastered the corpus of Jewish philosophical and scientific literature, practiced medicine, and pursued a sort of golden mean during the Maimonidean controversy. His extraordinary commentary on the Pentateuch, which mobilized the full range of his diverse interests, defies neat classification into any prior category of Jewish exegesis or thought.

---

70. *Ketav Tamim,* Paris ms., 7b; *Oẓar Neḥmad* 3, 63; Ta-Shema, "Sefer ha-Maskil," 429; *Vikkuaḥ R. Yeḥiel mi-Paris,* ed. by S. Gruenbaum (Thorn, 1873), 2. See also the citation in Avraham Grossman, *Ḥakhmei Ashkenaz ha-Rishonim* (Jerusalem, 1981), 96, for Rabbenu Gershom's opposition to a deviation from a rabbinic interpretation on a nonlegal matter in a liturgical poem by a distinguished colleague. This may be at least a faint indication that some Jews in early Ashkenaz considered such deviations legitimate. It is, of course, a commonplace that twelfth-century Northern French exegetes proposed interpretations that deviated from those of the rabbis even on matters of law.

71. See *Kitvei Ramban* 1, p. 308, and Bernard Septimus's excellent, though preliminary discussion in "'Open Rebuke and Concealed Love': Naḥmanides and the Andalusian Tradition," in *Rabbi Moses Naḥmanides,* 20–22. Marvin Fox, "Naḥmanides on the Status of Aggadot: Perspectives on the Disputation at Barcelona, 1263," *Journal of Jewish Studies* 40 (1989): 95–109, reaches a conclusion with which I am in fundamental agreement, although I cannot endorse several of his arguments. On one occasion (101), he perpetuates a blurring of the distinction between rejection of *aggadah* and its allegorization; see my remarks in "Maccoby's *Judaism on Trial,*" *Jewish Quarterly Review* 76 (1986): 255, n. 2.

In an oft-quoted passage from his *Sha'ar ha-Gemul*, a work that addresses the problem of theodicy, he denounces people who oppose any inquiry into the nature of divine justice as "fools who despise wisdom. For we shall benefit ourselves in the above-mentioned study by becoming wise men who know God in the manner in which He acts and in His deeds; furthermore, we shall become believers endowed with a stronger faith in Him than others." Despite the vigor of this formulation and its similarity to arguments for philosophical study in general, it is important to recognize that in Naḥmanides' case it is narrowly focused. Speculation about theodicy differs from investigation into the existence or unity of God in a way that illuminates Naḥmanides' fundamental approach to philosophical pursuits. A good philosopher speculates on the basis of empirical data. But the revelation of the Torah is an empirical datum par excellence; consequently, there is no more point in constructing proofs for doctrines explicitly taught in the revelation than for the proposition that the sun rises in the morning. At the same time, philosophical reasoning for the purpose of clarifying those doctrines is not only sensible but critically important. Although Naḥmanides never formulated this position explicitly, I think that it emerges from the pattern of his work and the issues that he addressed. It surely helps to explain why he wrote his magnum opus as a commentary to the revelation and why he was attracted to kabbalah, which provided, as we have seen, revealed information about key philosophical questions.

This nuanced approach placed Naḥmanides in a difficult position during the controversy of the 1230s. He opposed both untrammeled speculation and "fools who despise wisdom"; he admired both Maimonides and the rabbis of Northern France; he felt unreserved enthusiasm for "The Book of Knowledge" and mixed emotions about the *Guide*. His own sophisticated synthesis of speculation and revelation, even in its exoteric form, could not be mechanically prescribed to the masses or, for that matter, to ordinary intellectuals. Consequently, the proposal that he made is a combination of tactful diplomacy and an effort to implement the values that he considered particularly important under the trying circumstances of the dispute.

His most important letter was directed to the rabbis of Northern France. It expresses great admiration for the addressees, defends Maimonides' orthodoxy with respect to key theological issues, explains the purpose of the *Guide*, whose intended audience needs to be appreciated by the Ashkenazim, and launches into a vigorous, even impassioned encomium to "The Book of Knowledge." At this point, Naḥmanides was prepared to offer a concrete proposal: The ban against "The Book of Knowledge" should be annulled, and the ban against the *Guide* should be reformulated to include public study only, which Maimonides himself had disapproved. In the spirit of R. Hai Gaon's letter, the pursuit of philosophy should be discouraged entirely, but since such a level of piety cannot be enforced for all of Israel, no broader ban is advisable.

The distinction between "The Book of Knowledge" and the *Guide* accords well with Naḥmanides' fundamental outlook because the former operates within the context of the revelation while the latter raises questions that approach the tradition from the outside. The difference, then, is as much one of structure as of content. The discouragement of any philosophical study even for the elite goes beyond Naḥmanides' position as it appears in his other writings, and it is likely that he adopted it because of the needs of the moment. Nonetheless, this proposal too reflects a genuine uneasiness with speculation and hostility toward the dominant form of Aristotelianism. Naḥmanides, who sought not so much a religious philosophy as a philosophical religion, embodies an approach that is reflected to a greater or lesser degree in figures like R. Meir Abulafia and R. Judah Alfakar and in some of his great successors among the Talmudists of Christian Spain.[72]

The waning of this phase of the controversy used to be attributed primarily to nearly universal revulsion at the burning of Maimonides' works. We now have reason to believe that Naḥmanides' letter played a major role by persuading the Northern French rabbis to withdraw from the fray.[73] In any event, despite an eruption in the 1280s involving a relatively minor anti-Maimonist agitator, the dispute about philosophical study did not regain its status as a cause célèbre until the first decade of the fourteenth century, when the issue was joined again. In many ways, the debate was unchanged, but in some respects it had been transformed in significant and revealing fashion.

The controversy began when R. Abba Mari of Lunel initiated a correspondence with R. Solomon ibn Adret (Rashba) to complain about the inroads made by extreme rationalism in Provence, especially in the person of Levi b. Abraham of

---

72. For a full exposition of my perception of Naḥmanides' position, see my master's essay, *Naḥmanides' Attitude Toward Secular Learning and Its Bearing Upon his Stance in the Maimonidean Controversy* (Columbia University, 1965). See also my "Miracles and the Natural Order in Naḥmanides" (above, n. 47), 110–11, and Septimus, "'Open Rebuke and Concealed Love'" (above, n. 71). For brief characterizations of Naḥmanides, see my articles in *The Encyclopedia of Religion* 10 (New York, 1987), 295–97, and in *Great Figures in Jewish History* (in Russian [translated by the editorial staff], ed. by Joseph Dan and Judy Baumel [Tel Aviv, 1991], 77–84). On Abulafia, see Septimus, *Hispano-Jewish Culture in Transition*, which also contains an insightful typology of approaches to philosophical study in this period. See also his "Piety and Power in Thirteenth-Century Catalonia," *Studies in Jewish History and Literature* [1], 197–230, for an effort to reconstruct a struggle between rationalists and Talmudists of Naḥmanides' type for political control of a Jewish community.

The interpretation of Naḥmanides' proposal is dependent on the resolution of textual problems in the letter. This is not the place for a detailed discussion. Suffice it to say that the emendation of *teḥazzequ* to *lo teḥazzequ* (*Kitvei Ramban* 1, p. 349), which eliminates the ban entirely, is, in my view, insupportable. For details, see chapter 5 of my master's essay and my forthcoming article, "What did Naḥmanides Propose to Resolve the Maimonidean Controversy?"

73. See the letter of the Maimonists in Lunel and Narbonne, *Ẓion* 34 (1969): 142, and the discussion by Schochet, *Ẓion* 36 (1971): 44.

Villefranche, who advocated an allegorical understanding of some biblical narratives. The first thing that strikes the reader of Abba Mari's work is the impact of philosophy in general and Maimonides in particular on this "antirationalist." Science and metaphysics should be studied only by one

> who has filled his stomach with bread and meat, as we have learned from the Rabbi, the teacher of righteousness, from whose mouth we live through his true statements . . . built upon the foundation of the Torah in "The Book of Knowledge" and *Guide of the Perplexed,* which illuminate the path of those who have been in darkness and cannot adequately be evaluated by the greatest of assessors.[74]

It is true that even in the 1230s, many antirationalists treated Maimonides himself with considerable respect. We have already noted R. Solomon b. Abraham's reference to the study of the *Mishneh Torah* in his yeshivah, and Judah Alfakar had distinguished rather sharply between the author of the *Guide* and those who had made it into a new Torah. At the same time, Alfakar had written that he wished that the *Guide* had never seen the light of day, and Abba Mari's encomium to precisely the two works that were at issue in the earlier controversy is striking testimony to the status that Maimonides himself had attained among all parties to the new dispute.[75]

Not only did Abba Mari express unqualified admiration for Maimonides; he even defended no less a rationalist than Aristotle himself. In a passage about the importance of the belief in creation out of nothing, where Abba Mari was clearly echoing an argument of Naḥmanides, he defended his predecessor's "accursed Greek" by noting that in the absence of the information provided by revelation, a gentile in antiquity could not have been expected to achieve an adequate level of understanding with respect to this issue. On the contrary, Aristotle deserves great credit for disseminating an accurate conception of the one God to a world rife with paganism. Moreover, Abba Mari's endorsement of Maimonides' assertion that creation from nothing cannot be proved philosophically served him as an explanation for the use of the term *ḥoq* as a designation of the law of the Sabbath. The term is usually used for regulations whose reasons are unfathomable; in this case, the purpose of the law, which is to remind us of creation *ex nihilo,* is clear, but the belief

74. *Minḥat Qenaot,* Preface, p. 4 (unpaginated)=Dimitrovsky, 1, p. 228. For a summary of the events and arguments of the early fourteenth-century controversy, see Joseph Sarachek, *Faith and Reason* (Williamsport, Pennsylvania, 1935), pp. 167–264. Despite a variety of subsequent studies that will be noted later, Sarachek's work can still serve as a useful orientation to the dispute.

75. For Alfakar, see *Qoveẓ Teshuvot ha-Rambam* 3, pp. 2b–3a. On respect for Maimonides during the controversy of the early fourteenth century, see the remarks by Charles Touati, "La Controverse de 1303–1306 autour des études philosophiques et scientifiques," *Revue des Études Juives* 127 (1968) : 23–24.

itself cannot be demonstrated by human reason. Maimonidean philosophy has been integrated by a Provençal conservative into the warp and woof of his study of Torah.[76]

Abba Mari provoked sharp disagreement from Rashba when he asserted that gentile philosophical works are not harmful since everyone recognizes their provenance. Since the legitimacy of Maimonides' treatises was surely not at issue, Abba Mari's ire was narrowly focused on what he perceived as the heretical teachings of the Jewish hyperrationalists. As he reports the situation, people like Levi b. Abraham understood Abraham and Sarah as matter and form, the twelve tribes as the twelve constellations, the alliances of four and five kings in Genesis 14 as the four elements and the five senses, and Amalek as the evil inclination.[77]

Such accusations about rationalist allegorization appear in various works during the thirteenth and fourteenth centuries. Even more seriously, we find the assertion that certain rationalists regarded verbal prayer as superfluous and did not observe various commandments either because they allegorized them or thought that they could fulfill their underlying purpose in a different manner. Thus, R. Jacob b. Sheshet maintained that contemporary heretics, in a fashion strikingly reminiscent of Christian polemic against Judaism, argued, "What is the purpose of this particular commandment? Reason cannot abide it. It must have been nothing but an allegory." Elsewhere, Jacob is quoted to the effect that in addition to heresies regarding primeval matter, divine providence, and reward and punishment, these rationalists assert that the purification of one's thoughts is a more than adequate substitute for prayer. Moses de Leon alleged that the adherents of "the books of the Greeks" do not observe the commandment of taking the four species on the festival of *Sukkot*

76. *Minḥat Qenaot*, Introduction, ch. 13–14, pp. 14–15=Dimitrovsky, pp. 255–58. On Abba Mari's philosophical orientation, see A. S. Halkin, "Yedaiah Bedershi's Apology," in *Jewish Medieval and Renaissance Studies*, ed. by Altmann, 178; "Ha-Ḥerem 'al Limmud ha-Pilosofiah," *Peraqim* 1 (1967–8): 48–49.

The intriguing transformation of Naḥmanides' argument into a defense of Aristotle deserves brief elaboration. The original point was that miracles demonstrate creation *ex nihilo* because God would not have limitless control over matter as primeval as He. Since miracles are an empirical datum that became well known throughout the world, the affirmation of the eternity of matter by "the accursed Greek" is a denial of his own vaunted empiricism. Abba Mari accepts the argument with one small correction: miracles are attested in a revelation granted to the Jewish people that was not in fact widely known in Aristotle's world. Hence, although Naḥmanides is correct that creation *ex nihilo* can be proven, the demonstration depends on the knowledge of miracles, which is, or at least was, specifically Jewish knowledge; Maimonides is correct that the doctrine cannot be proven in a philosophical system uninformed by revelation. From this perspective, Naḥmanides' position is not an indictment of Aristotle but an exculpation. For a similar view of Aristotle by a somewhat earlier figure, see Septimus's citation of Judah ibn Matka's *Midrash Ḥokmah*, in *Hispano-Jewish Culture in Transition*, p. 97.

77. *Minḥat Qenaot*, letter 7, pp. 40–41=Dimitrovsky, ch. 25, pp. 343–44, and elsewhere.

because, they say, the reason the Torah provides is that this will enhance the joy of the holiday; well, they are happier with their gold, silver, and clothing than they could possibly be with the four species.[78]

During the controversy, we hear occasional references to a refusal to wear *tefillin* because of a philosophically motivated rejection of the commandment's literal meaning and even to wholesale allegorization of biblical law. In these extreme cases, however, the indictments appear to reflect the behavior of isolated individuals or even what the critic perceived as the logical consequence or underlying intention of the philosophical position. One allegation about *tefillin* refers to a single person, and Rashba is clearly describing a teaching that was not made explicit when he observes that "it is evident that their true intention is that the commandments are not to be taken literally, for why should God care about the difference between torn and properly slaughtered meat? Rather, all is allegory and parable." Although such claims are not entirely unfounded, the statement that the villains in this indictment "have regarded the Torah and its commandments as false, and everything has become permitted to them" was clearly a deduction. Indeed, Rashba explicitly asserts that the hyperrationalists maintain that everything in the Torah is allegory from Genesis until—but not beyond—the revelation at Sinai; nonetheless, he says, it is evident that they really have no faith in the plain meaning of the commandments either.[79]

As a result of these concerns, Rashba issued a ban which itself reflects the changes in this issue since the 1230s. Unlike Naḥmanides, Rashba was sufficiently

78. For Jacob b. Sheshet, see his *Meshiv Devarim Nekhohim*, ed. by Georges Vajda (Jerusalem, 1968), 145, and the citation in Isaac of Acre, *Sefer Me'irat 'Einayim*, ed. by Goldreich, 58–61. For de Leon, see his *Book of the Pomegranate*, ed. by Elliot Wolfson (Atlanta, 1988), 391.

79. On *tefillin*, see *Minḥat Qenaot*, letter 79, p. 152=Dimitrovsky, ch. 88, 721, which bans anyone who understands the commandments in a purely spiritual sense, and cf. letter 81, p. 153=Dimitrovsky, ch. 101, p. 735, where it is fairly clear that the concern was based on a specific statement made by a particular rationalist. Cf. also letter 7, p. 41; Dimitrovsky, ch. 25, p. 344. The passage in *The Book of the Pomegranate* cited in the previous note continues with the allegation that these reprobates also fail to wear *tefillin* because they understand the commandment in a spiritual sense. For the more general assertions, see *Minḥat Qenaot*, letter 20, p. 60=Dimitrovsky, ch. 38, pp. 411–12, and letter 10, p. 45; Dimitrovsky, ch. 28, p. 360. The last assertion is in a text that was distributed in connection with the ban; see Dimitrovsky, ch. 100, p. 727. On neglect of *tefillin*, see the references in Isadore Twersky, *Rabad of Posquières* (Cambridge, Mass., 1962), 24, n. 20. See also Ephraim Kanarfogel, "Rabbinic Attitudes toward Nonobservance in the Medieval Period," in *Jewish Tradition and the Nontraditional Jew*, ed. by Jacob J. Schacter (Northvale, New Jersey and London, 1992), 3–35, esp. pp. 7–12; the issues there, however, are not philosophical. At the eleventh World Congress of Jewish Studies in 1993, Aviezer Ravitsky described a hitherto unknown commentary on the *Guide* by a Samuel of Carcassonne, who indicated quite clearly that the philosopher need not observe commandments whose purpose he regards as no longer relevant.

concerned by the spread of rationalist extremism that he was prepared to go beyond the very narrow ban advocated by his predecessor and to forbid the study of philosophy and some sciences by anyone who had not reached the age of twenty-five. On the other hand, the works of Maimonides were entirely exempted from the prohibition during subsequent discussions clarifying its scope; the only reason this remains in some sense a "Maimonidean controversy" is that the targets of the ban made what Rashba and Abba Mari considered blatantly illegitimate use of Maimonides' works to justify their heresies. Though the distinction between Maimonides and his followers had been made earlier, it is now far sharper and more fundamental. Thus, when modern scholars who see Maimonides as a philosophical radical tell us that the people attacked by Abba Mari were no more dangerous than Maimonides himself, they impose a reading of the Maimonidean corpus which the proponents of the ban did not share.[80]

The validity of the conservatives' perception of Maimonides is, of course, only one side of the coin; the other is the validity of their perceptions of the Maimonists. We have already seen that even the evidence of the antirationalist pronouncements suggests that assertions of wholesale rejection of the commandments by more than a handful of rationalists may be exaggerated. The vigorous response to the ban provides us with a substantial set of arguments for the religious orthodoxy of the philosophers and for the value of the maligned philosophical enterprise. The most extensive of these polemics that remains extant is the apology for philosophy addressed to Rashba himself by R. Yedaiah Bedershi.[81]

Though the work is written in a tone of extreme reverence for the addressee, it concedes virtually nothing to the allegations leveled in the ban. A handful of Provençal Jews may deserve censure for publicizing philosophical teachings best left to the elite, but the content of these teachings is untainted by heresy. The reports of allegorization of biblical narratives and commandments are wholly false; at most, one philosopher is known to have argued that the correspondence between the number of tribes and the number of constellations demonstrates that the Jewish people is bound by the stars, but even this deplorable position takes the reality of the twelve tribes for granted.

Moreover, says Yedaiah, the study of philosophy has overwhelming religious value. It provides proof of the existence and unity of God; demonstrates the falsehood of determinism, magic, and metempsychosis; establishes the truth of prophecy and the spiritual character of the immortal soul; and distinguishes between impossibilities that can be rendered possible through miracles and those which even divine omnipotence itself cannot overturn. First and foremost, philosophy has

80. Touati, "La Controverse," 23–24; A. S. Halkin, "Why Was Levi ben Ḥayyim Hounded?," *Proceedings of the American Academy for Jewish Research* 24 (1966) : pp. 65–77.

81. See Halkin's articles cited in n. 76. The text appears as *Ketav Hitnaẓẓelut, She'elot u-Teshuvot ha-Rashba* (Bnei Braq, 1958), 1: 418, pp. 154–74, and was separately edited by S. Bloch (Lvov, 1809).

extirpated what was once the epidemic of anthropomorphism. Here Yedaiah's formulation is extraordinarily strong:

> In the early generations, the corporeal conception of God spread through virtually the entire Jewish exile . . . ; however, in all the generations there arose *Geonim* and wise men in Spain, Babylonia, and the cities of Andalusia, who, because of their expertise in the Arabic language, encountered the great preparatory knowledge that comes with smelling the scent of the various forms of wisdom, whether to a greater or lesser degree, which have been translated into that language. Consequently, they began to clarify many opinions in their study of Torah, especially with respect to the unity of God and the rejection of corporeality, with particular use of philosophical proofs taken from the speculative literature.[82]

The issue of tradition versus philosophical innovation emerges in even bolder relief than it did in Maimonides' discussion of anthropomorphism. Although Yedaiah explicitly denies that the ancient Rabbis were anthropomorphists, he sees the attaining of a purified conception of God in the Middle Ages as an achievement of a philosophical enterprise unaided by tradition but crucially dependent upon familiarity with Arabic texts. The very essence of the Torah, largely lost through the travails of exile, was restored through the discipline which the antirationalists would now undermine.

Once again we find the advocates of philosophy referring to non-Jews in an effort to legitimate speculation. Jacob ben Makhir pointed to

> the most civilized nations who translate learned works from other languages into their own . . . and who revere learning. . . . Has any nation changed its religion because of this? . . . How much less likely is that to happen to us, who possess a rational Torah.[83]

Jacob's reference to the rationality of Judaism carries significance that goes beyond the specific point in this text. The fact that these discussions now take place in a Christian rather than a Muslim context means that the conviction that Judaism is more rational than its rival can be mobilized to enhance the importance of philosophical study by pointing to its value as a polemical tool. When a Jew justified speculation on the grounds of its usefulness in replying to heretics, the reference was not necessarily to Christians; nonetheless, when Bedershi tells us that one advantage of setting criteria for the possibility of miracles is that it enables us to rule out God's ability to make Himself corporeal, the implications for anti-Christian polemic are self-evident. R. Israel b. Joseph, a fourteenth-century Spanish rabbi who studied

82. *She'elot u-Teshuvot ha-Rashba* 1, p. 166.

83. Cited in Yitzhak Baer, *A History of the Jews in Christian Spain* 1 (Philadelphia, 1961), 296.

with R. Asher ben Yeḥiel, vigorously supported the study of "external disciplines" solely on the basis of their value in supplying "answers to those who err" and providing the ability "to defeat them in their arguments." Here too, while those who err no doubt included philosophical heretics, it is hard to imagine that R. Israel was not also thinking of the utility of philosophy for vanquishing the arguments of Christian missionaries. Ḥasdai Crescas' *Bittul 'Iqqarei ha-Noẓerim* constitutes eloquent testimony to the importance of philosophical sophistication for the late medieval Jewish polemicist in Spain, and it can be asserted with full confidence that no Jewish reader of that work could have come away from it with the slightest doubt that at least some Jews ought to study philosophy.[84]

In light of the usefulness of philosophy for anti-Christian polemic, it is ironic and intriguing that the desire to convert Jews impelled the governor of Montpellier to take the side of the rationalists at the height of the controversy. The advocates of philosophy had issued a counterban against anyone who would refuse to teach the banned disciplines to people under the age of twenty-five in obedience to the antirationalists' proclamation, and they sought legal backing from the civil authorities. Abba Mari informs us that although the governor did not grant all their requests, he lent some support because he was convinced that if Jews were to prohibit anything but talmudic study for a substantial period of a person's life, this would create a situation in which no Jew would ever convert to Christianity.[85]

84. For R. Israel b. Joseph ha-Yisre'eli's remarks, see his commentary to *Avot* 2:14, cited in Israel Ta-Shema, "Shiqqulim Pilosofiyyim be-Hakhra'at ha-Halakhah bi-Sefarad," *Sefunot* 18 (1985) : 105. R. Israel noted that these external disciplines cannot be approached safely before the reader has become a mature talmudic scholar; hence, the rabbis forbade one to teach *higgayon* or Greek wisdom to one's son. The thrust of his observation, however, is permissive: It is prohibited for the father to teach his son, but it is permissible for the father to study on his own. See Saul Lieberman, *Hellenism in Jewish Palestine* (New York, 1962), 102–04. On Crescas, see *Bittul Iqqarei ha-Nozerim*, ed. by Daniel J. Lasker (Ramat Gan, 1990), or Lasker's *Jewish Philosophical Polemics Against Christianity in the Middle Ages* (New York, 1977). On the use of more rigorous philosophical arguments for polemical purposes, see also Shalom Rosenberg, *Logiqah ve-Apologetiqah ba-Philosophiah ha-Yehudit ba-Me'ah ha-Yod-Dalet* (Hebrew University dissertation, 1974), 44. On answering heretics, see also n. 54 above.

85. The phrase that I have translated "talmudic study" literally means "the discipline (*ḥokhmah*) that you call Gamaliel" (*Minḥat Qenaot*, letter 73, p. 142=Dimitrovsky, ch. 92, p. 701). For the identification of "Gamaliel" with Talmud, see Heinrich Graetz, *Geschichte der Juden* (Leipzig, 1863), 7, p. 276; Ch. Merchavia, *Ha-Talmud bi-Re'i ha-Naẓrut* (Jerusalem, 1970), 211, and Dimitrovsky, ad loc. ("apparently this refers to the Talmud"). For the view that "Gamaliel" means medicine, see David Kaufmann, *Die Sinne* (Budapest, 1884), 7, n. 12; D. Margalit, "'Al Galenus ve-Gilgulo ha-'Ivri Gamliel," *Sinai* 33 (1953) : 75–77; Judah Rosenthal's review of Merchavia, *Kiryat Sefer* 47 (1972): 29; Joseph Shatzmiller, "Bein Abba Mari la-Rashba: ha-Massa ve-ha-Mattan sheqadam la-Ḥerem be-Barcelona," *Meḥqarim be-Toledot 'Am Yisrael ve-Ereẓ Yisrael* 3 (Haifa, 1974), 127. I cannot see why a Christian would find it necessary to describe medicine by its presumed Jewish name, especially since the ban

There is strong reason to believe that a majority of the Jews in Montpellier sided with the rationalists.[86] The philosophical culture of Provençal Jewry was so pervasive that rationalist sermons were delivered in synagogues and even at weddings. Opposition to the ban came from the distinguished Perpignan Talmudist R. Menaḥem ha-Meiri, who argued that spiritual damage to a handful of people cannot be allowed to undermine entire fields of study, that even the books of the Greeks have great religious value, that Jews cannot allow gentiles to mock them for their intellectual backwardness, and that Provence can boast a variety of figures who have distinguished themselves in both talmudic and philosophical learning. Here again the antirationalist party demonstrated how much the atmosphere had changed since the 1230s: The reply to ha-Meiri by a disciple of Abba Mari fully conceded the great value of philosophy and pointed out that the ban was directed only at the young.[87]

Ha-Meiri himself was a paradigm of the ideal toward which moderate rationalists strove and to which even extreme rationalists paid lip service: a Talmudist of standing who valued philosophy and the sciences and devoted himself to their study. Ha-Meiri's openness to general culture combined with his well-known

---

does not call it Gamaliel, or even why the exclusion of medicine would need to be mentioned at all in this context. The fact that this would constitute the only attested use of Gamaliel in so broad a sense also militates against the identification. It is true that Talmud was not normally called a *ḥokhmah*, but in the context of this ban, I can easily see a Christian using the equivalent term, presumably *scientia*. Moreover, the Christian argument that the study of rabbinic literature is an impediment to conversion is attested as far back as Justinian's Novella 146 and was reiterated in the 1240s by Odo of Chateauroux. For Justinian, see the text and translation in Amnon Linder, *The Jews in Roman Imperial Legislation* (Jerusalem, 1987), 405–10; for Odo, see the text in Merchavia, 450 (". . . hanc esse causam precipuam que iudeos in sua perfidia retinet obstinatos"). Because the motive assigned by Abba Mari is so congenial to his own position in the controversy, we must read it with some skepticism; note Kaufmann's remark (loc. cit.) that the antirationalist Yosef Yavetz would have given a great deal to have known this quotation. In light of Odo's assertion, however, the report is entirely plausible.

Note too Kaufmann's argument that philosophical allegory may have been influenced by Christian allegory and that this connection led to the hope for conversion through philosophical study; see his "Simeon b. Josefs Sendschreiben an Menachem b. Salomo," in *Jubelschrift zum Neunzigsten Geburtstag des Dr. L. Zunz* (Berlin, 1884), German section, p. 147. I doubt that Christian influence on rationalist allegorization was decisive, and the main point appears to have been that talmudic study retards conversion.

On the counterban and the governor, see the references in Marc Saperstein, "The Conflict over the Rashba's Herem on Philosophical Study: A Political Perspective," *Jewish History* 1:2 (1986) : 37, n. 19.

86. Shatzmiller has argued this point persuasively in "Bein Abba Mari la-Rashba," 128–30.

87. See "Ḥoshen Mishpat," *Jubelschrift . . . Zunz*, Hebrew section, pp. 142–74. For the last point, see especially pp. 162–64.

attitude of toleration toward Christianity suggests an additional dimension of the issue that we have been addressing. Intellectual involvement with the dominant society often goes hand in hand with social involvement of a relatively benign sort. By this time, Christian intellectuals had attained an impressive level of philosophical sophistication to the point where ha-Meiri could express concern about their contempt for ignorant Jews; consequently, familiarity began to breed respect. In ha-Meiri's case, this respect led to the formulation of a wholly novel halakhic category which roughly means civilized people, a category which helped to exempt Christians from a series of discriminatory talmudic statements. While this is not a case of incorporating an external value or doctrine into Rabbinic law—the Christendom that ha-Meiri knew had hardly developed a theory of religious toleration—it probably is an instance of reexamining *halakhah* and Jewish values in light of habits of mind developed by exposure to a culture shared with the gentile environment. Once again, the core of the Torah was touched—or its deeper meaning revealed—through insights inspired by involvement in general culture.[88]

The Sephardim of the Late Middle Ages

The affirmation of the value of philosophy even by the conservatives in this dispute reflects a critically important characteristic of late medieval Jewish culture in Provence and in Spain. Virtually without exception, rabbinic figures of the first rank, whose pursuit of talmudic study was their central preoccupation, either devoted some time to the study of "wisdom" or expressed no opposition to its cultivation.[89]

Rashba himself was not uninfluenced by philosophical ideas. This would be evident even from Bedershi's apology, which clearly assumed that its recipient was receptive to the major thrust of the argument, but it is also explicit in Rashba's own writings. In one elaborate responsum, for example, he analyzed the parameters within which philosophical arguments can be brought to bear on the reinterpreta-

88. On ha-Meiri and Christianity, see Yaakov Blidstein, "Yaḥaso shel R. Menaḥem ha-Meiri la-Nokhri—Bein Apologetiqah le-Hafnamah," *Ẓion* 51 (1986) : 153–66, and the earlier studies cited there. See now the important analysis by Moshe Halbertal, "R. Menaḥem ha-Meiri: Bein Torah le-Ḥokhmah," *Tarbiẓ* 63 (1994) : 63–118, which points to a specific philosophical context for ha-Meiri's position.

89. See Israel Ta-Shema's "Rabbi Yona Gerondi: Spiritualism and Leadership," presented at the Jewish Theological Seminary's 1989 conference on "Jewish Mystical Leadership, 1200–1270," esp. p. 11. A bound volume of typescripts of the proceedings is available in the Mendel Gottesman Library, Yeshiva University. See also Ta-Shema's "Halakhah, Kabbalah u-Pilosophiah bi-Sefarad ha-Noẓerit—le-Biqqoret Sefer 'Toledot ha-Yehudim bi-Sefarad ha-Noẓerit'," *Shenaton ha-Mishpat ha-'Ivri* 18–19 (1992–94): 479–95. For a balanced, moderate defense of a broad curriculum in fourteenth-century Spain, see Profiat Duran's introduction to *Ma'aseh Efod,* 1–25.

tion of sacred texts, and he staked out a position that we would expect from a disciple of Naḥmanides: there is a legitimate place for such arguments as long as the critical demands of tradition are accorded unchallenged supremacy.[90] R. Yom Tov Ishbili (Ritba), perhaps the greatest rabbinic figure in the generation following Rashba, wrote a work exemplifying the same general posture. He defended Maimonides against the strictures in Naḥmanides' commentary to the Pentateuch while at the same time affirming that in the final analysis Naḥmanides is usually correct.[91]

The endorsement of at least a moderate level of rationalism no doubt resulted from the importance of philosophy in traditional Spanish Jewish culture, but we should not underestimate the impact of the heroic image of Maimonides. Just as Naḥmanides' embrace of kabbalah made it very difficult to reject mysticism as a heresy, Maimonides' devotion to philosophy rendered its thorough delegitimation by Sephardic Jews almost impossible. Even some kabbalists attempted to synthesize their discipline with a reinterpreted Maimonidean corpus, though others went so far as to assert that the author of the *Guide* had seen the error of his ways once the secrets of the hidden wisdom were revealed to him. This last example is a rare case of the exception that really proves the rule, because it demonstrates that Maimonides' position stood as such a hallmark of legitimacy that some Jews could comfortably maintain a contrary position only by forcibly redefining the Maimonidean stance.[92]

Moderate rationalism was, of course, not the only approach endorsed by Provençal

90. *She'elot u-Teshuvot ha-Rashba* (1958) 1:9, also edited by L. A. Feldman, *Shnaton Bar-Ilan* 7–8 (1970): 153–61. For a thorough analysis of Rashba's stance, see the unpublished master's thesis by David Horwitz, *The Role of Philosophy and Kabbalah in the Works of Rashba* (Bernard Revel Graduate School, Yeshiva University, 1986). See also Carmi Horowitz, "'Al Perush ha-Aggadot shel ha-Rashba—Bein Qabbalah le-Pilosophiah," *Da'at* 18 (1987) : 15–25, and Lawrence Kaplan, "Rabbi Solomon ibn Adret," *Yavneh Review* 6 (1967) : 27–40. (I should probably not press the argument from Bedershi's perception too hard since *Ktav Hitnaẓẓelut* takes for granted the questionable proposition that Rashba would recognize the value of philosophy because of its ability to refute the belief in metempsychosis, a kabbalistic doctrine that Rashba probably endorsed.)

91. See his *Sefer ha-Zikkaron*, ed. by Kalman Kahana (Jerusalem, 1956), 33–34.

92. For Abraham Abulafia's effort to create a Maimonidean kabbalah, see sections IV–VI of Moshe Idel's "Maimonides and Kabbalah," in Twersky, *Studies in Maimonides*, 54–78. On Maimonides as a kabbalist, see Gershom Scholem, "Me-Ḥoqer li-Mequbbal: Aggadot ha-Mequbbalim 'al ha-Rambam," *Tarbiẓ* 6 (1935): 90–98, and Michael A. Shmidman, "On Maimonides' 'Conversion' to Kabbalah," in *Studies in Medieval Jewish History and Literature*, ed. Twersky, 2, pp. 375–86. For a discussion of this and similar legends in the broader context of folk conceptions about Maimonides, see the study by my father *z"l*, Isaiah Berger, "Ha-Rambam be-Aggadat ha- 'Am," in *Massad: Me'assef le-Divrei Sifrut* 2, ed. by Hillel Bavli (Tel Aviv, 1936), pp. 216–38; and compare his eloquent observations on the contrast between the folk images of Maimonides and Rashi in his "Rashi be-Aggadat ha- 'Am," in *Rashi: Torato ve-Ishiyyuto*, ed. by Simon Federbush (New York, 1958), 147–49.

and Spanish Jews in the later Middle Ages. Despite the exaggerated nature of the conservative manifestoes issued during the controversy, some late medieval thinkers really did espouse radical positions with respect to many philosophical and exegetical issues. When Jacob b. Sheshet denounced rationalists who "assert that the world is primeval . . . , that divine providence does not extend below the sphere of the moon . . . , that there is no reward for the righteous or punishment for the wicked . . . and that there is no need to pray but only to purify one's thoughts,"[93] he was engaging in hyperbole but not in fantasy. The rationalist propensity toward allegorization undoubtedly went beyond anything that rabbis like Rashba would countenance, and we should not allow the Maimonist arguments of Bedershi and his colleagues to blind us to this reality. The works of Samuel ibn Tibbon, Moses Narboni, Joseph ibn Kaspi, Gersonides, and Isaac Albalag constitute but part of a corpus of literature attesting to a flourishing tradition of vigorous rationalism that severely tested the prevailing boundaries of religious orthodoxy.

Philosophers of this stripe were often prepared to make an explicit case against excessive concentration on talmudic study. The most famous example of this attitude is the story ibn Kaspi tells in his will about the problem that arose during a party in his home when "the accursed maid" placed a dairy spoon in a pot of meat. Poor ibn Kaspi had to go to the local rabbi, who kept him waiting for hours in a state of near starvation before apprising him of the *halakhah*. Nonetheless, he tells us, he was not embarrassed by his ignorance, since his philosophical sophistication compensated for the shortcomings in his halakhic expertise. "Why," he asks, "should a ruling or directive regarding the great existence or unity of God be inferior to a small dairy spoon?"[94]

Other expressions of this approach are less amusing but no less striking. Some Jews demonstrated the obscurantism of those who devote their lives to talmudic study by pointing to the Talmud's own assertion that the phrase "He has set me in dark places like the dead of old" (Lamentations 3:6) refers to the Talmud of Babylon. R. Judah ibn Abbas maintained that people who study Talmud constantly "neglect the proper service and knowledge of God" and described talmudic novellae and *Tosafot* as a waste of valuable time. It is a matter of no small interest that Ḥasdai Crescas wrote his philosophical refutation of Christianity in Aragonese or Catalan so that Jews could have ready access to his arguments; there was thus a substantial, sophisticated Jewish audience in late medieval Spain who could follow a difficult vernacular text but not a difficult Hebrew one.

---

93. Cited in *Me'irat 'Einayim*, ed. Goldreich, p. 58.

94. Israel Abrahams, *Hebrew Ethical Wills* 1 (Philadelphia, 1926), 151–52. The somewhat awkward use of the term "great," which technically modifies *unity* in the original, is clearly intended to evoke Maimonides' straightforward understanding of the talmudic contrast between great and small matters. See above, n. 39. On Ibn Kaspi's intellectual stance, see Isadore Twersky, "Joseph ibn Kaspi: Portrait of a Medieval Jewish Intellectual," in *Studies in Medieval Jewish History and Literature* [1], pp. 231–57.

Ibn Kaspi himself, in a work marked by the arresting assertion that Job's suffering was a just consequence of his failure to pursue a philosophical understanding of his faith, utilized the traditionalists' affirmation of the importance of talmudic study to support the indispensability of philosophy. After all, he argued, there exist both physical commandments and commandments of the heart or intellect. Everyone agrees that with respect to the former, an understanding of the intellectual underpinning is eminently desirable. "Why else should we toil to study the Talmud? We might just as well be satisfied with the rulings of Maimonides and R. Isaac Alfasi." Now there is surely no basis for distinguishing the latter commandments from the former with respect to this principle, and books of physics and metaphysics stand in the same relationship to the commandments of the heart as the Talmud does to the physical commandments. Originally, such philosophical works were written by Jewish sages like Solomon, but "we were exiled because of our sins, and those matters have now come to be attributed to the Greeks" except for scattered references in the Talmud. In other words, one cannot affirm the critical importance of talmudic study without being logically compelled to grant at least equal value to the pursuit of philosophy and the sciences.[95]

On the other side of the ledger, R. Asher b. Yeḥiel, who was born and trained in Germany, brought with him a pejorative attitude toward the value of general culture. In responding to the suggestion that no one without expertise in Arabic should render a legal decision, he maintained that his reasoning powers in Torah were in no way inferior to those of Spanish Rabbis, "even though I do not know your external wisdom. Thank the merciful God who saved me from it." The pursuit of such wisdom, he said, leads people away from the fear of God and encourages the vain attempt to integrate alien pursuits with Torah. Still, even R. Asher describes philosophers as very wise men, and an assessment of Spanish Jewish attitudes would

95. On the "dark places" and the Talmud, see *Me'irat 'Einayim*, 62; Isadore Twersky, "Religion and Law," in *Religion in a Religious Age*, 77, and Twersky, "R. Yeda'yah ha-Penini," Altmann Festschrift, p. 71. The talmudic passage is in *Sanhedrin* 24a. For Ibn Abbas, see Goldreich's quotations from the manuscript of *Ya'ir Nativ* (Oxford 1280, p. 50a) in *Me'irat 'Einayim*, pp. 412–13. The oft-quoted curriculum in ibn Abbas's work, which culminates with the study of metaphysics, was published by Asaf, *Meqorot* 2, pp. 29–33. On the vernacular original of *Bittul 'Iqqarei ha-Noẓerim*, see Lasker's edition, pp. 13, 33. Note too the Castilian *Proverbos Morales* by the fourteenth-century R. Shem Tov ibn Ardutiel, *The Moral Proverbs of Santob de Carrion: Jewish Wisdom in Christian Spain*, ed. by T. A. Perry (Princeton, 1988).

If we contemplate for a moment the magnitude of Job's suffering, we can begin to appreciate the importance attached to the philosophic quest by a man willing to propose ibn Kaspi's explanation for such torment. This explanation appears along with the very clever argument linking talmudic and philosophical study in *Shulḥan Kesef: Be'ur 'al Iyyov*, in *'Asarah Kelei Kesef*, ed. by J. Last (Pressburg, 1903), 170–72.

have to assign greater weight to the remarkable suggestion that he rejected than to the negative reaction that he expressed.[96]

That suggestion reflects a real and significant phenomenon: the halakhic decision-making and talmudic study of Provençal and Spanish rabbis were sometimes affected by philosophical considerations. To begin with the most famous example in Maimonides himself, the omission in the *Mishneh Torah* of talmudic laws based on the intervention of the creatures that the rabbis called *shedim* was almost certainly the result of philosophically motivated skepticism. R. Zeraḥiah Halevi cited technical logical terminology and philosophical references in a halakhic discussion. Conceptions of providence were brought to bear on decisions regarding the remarriage of a woman whose first two husbands had died. A more general illustration of the pervasiveness of the philosophical atmosphere emerges from the first sentence of R. Yeruḥam b. Meshullam's introduction to a work of talmudic scholarship, where he informs us how "the scholars of [philosophical] research" have classified the considerations leading to the pursuit of wisdom.[97]

Most strikingly, it now appears that an innovative methodology of talmudic study which conquered Spain in the fifteenth century and dominated the approach of Sephardic communities for two hundred years was rooted in philosophical logic. R. Isaac Kanpanton produced guidelines which required the student to investigate the correspondence between the language and meaning of a talmudic text with exquisite care and to determine the full range of possible interpretations so that the exegetical choices of the major commentators would become clear. In setting forth this form of investigation, or *'iyyun*, Kanpanton made explicit reference to logical terminology, and Daniel Boyarin has recently made a compelling argument that the system as a whole and all its major components originated in the medieval philosophical milieu. He maintains that

96. See *She'elot u-Teshuvot ha-Rosh* (Venice, 1603), 55:9. Cf. Israel Ta-Shema, "Shiqqulim Pilosofiyyim," *Sefunot* 18 (1985): 100–08.

97. On the impact of Maimonides' attitude toward "popular religion" on the *Mishneh Torah*, see Twersky, *Introduction to the Code of Maimonides*, pp. 479–84; see especially Marc B. Shapiro's forthcoming essay in *Maimonidean Studies*. I am unpersuaded by Jose Faur's effort in his generally perceptive *'Iyyunim be-Mishneh Torah le-ha-Rambam: Sefer ha-Madda* (Jerusalem, 1978), 1–2, n. 1, to minimize the philosophical motivation for the omission of *shedim*. For some observations on the impact of Maimonides' scientific posture on his halakhic approach, see Isadore Twersky, "Aspects of Maimonidean Epistemology: Halakhah and Science," in *From Ancient Israel to Modern Judaism: Intellect in Quest of Understanding. Essays in Honor of Marvin Fox*, ed. by Jacob Neusner, Ernest S. Frerichs, and Nachum M. Sarna (Atlanta, Georgia, 1989) 3, pp. 3–23. For R. Zeraḥiah Halevi, see I. Ta-Shema, "Sifrei ha-Rivot bein ha-Ravad le-bein Rabbi Zeraḥiah Halevi (ha-Razah) mi-Lunel," *Qiryat Sefer* 52 (1977) : 570–76. On the problem of remarriage, see Ta-Shema, *Sefunot* 18, p. 110, and Y. Buxbaum, "Teshuvot Ḥakhmei Sefarad be-Din Qatlanit," *Moriah* 7 [78/79] (1977): 6–7. R. Yeruham's comments are in *Sefer Mesharim* (Venice, 1553; rep., Jerusalem, 1975), 2a.

> Jewish scholars in the final days of the Spanish Jewish community saw logic as the road to attaining truth in all sciences, including that of the Torah. Any argument which did not qualify under the canons of logical order was faulty in their eyes. Logical works and principles served as the foundation for scientific and philosophical investigation, and they pointed the way toward valid proof and the avoidance of error in these fields. Since the science of the Talmud differed in its language and its problems from the other sciences—mainly because it is essentially exegetical—the need was felt for general works specific to this field which would direct investigation there.[98]

These were indeed the final days of Spanish Jewry, and the connection between philosophical pursuits and the behavior of the community in extremis has exercised analysts both medieval and modern. Conservatives like R. Isaac Arama renewed the attack against allegorists by asking why they need the Torah at all. When it corresponds to philosophical truths, they accept it literally, and when it does not, they explain it figuratively; in either case, the knowledge they had before the revelation is coterminous with what they know after it. R. Yosef Yavetz attributed the relatively large number of conversions around the time of the expulsion to the corrupting influence of philosophical relativism, a judgment endorsed in the twentieth century by Yitzhak Baer. R. Abraham Bibago, on the other hand, writing in the middle of the fifteenth century, denied that philosophically oriented Jews were any less steadfast than pure Talmudists; spiritual weakness is not dependent upon intellectual orientation. More generally, Bibago's attack against extreme rationalists and especially against opponents of philosophy tends to demonstrate that both groups were active in late medieval Spain. Bibago himself was a relatively moderate rationalist who fits well into the category of Spanish Jews like R. Isaac Abravanel who studied philosophy but attempted to counter rationalist extremism through a conservative interpretation of Maimonides and his legacy. When such a person denounces fools who call "people of intellect and reason" heretics, his remarks deserve special notice; apparently, Spain too was not without thoroughgoing critics of the philosophical enterprise for whom even the rationalism of Bibago was an impermissible deviation from pristine Judaism.[99]

98. Daniel Boyarin, *Ha-'Iyyun ha-Sefaradi* (Jerusalem, 1989), 48–49. The main documentation of Boyarin's general thesis is on pp. 47–68. For a similar development in the field of biblical exegesis, see Shimon Shalem, "Ha-Metodah ha-Parshanit shel Yosef Taitaẓak ve-Ḥugo," *Sefunot* 11 (1971–77): 115–34.

99. See Yavetz's *Sefer Or ha-Ḥayyim* (Lemberg, 1874), ch. 2, and the references in Baer, *A History of the Jews in Christian Spain* 2, 509, n. 12, and in Isaac E. Barzilay, *Between Reason and Faith: Anti-Rationalism in Italian Jewish Thought, 1250–1650* (The Hague, 1967), 148. For Baer's citation of Arama and indictment of Jewish Averroism, see his *History* 2, pp. 253–59. Baer's position was rejected by Haim Hillel Ben Sasson, "Dor Golei Sefarad 'al 'Aẓmo," *Ẓion* 26 (1961): 44–52, 59–64. On Bibago, see Joseph Hacker, "Meqomo shel R. Avraham Bibag ba-Maḥaloqet 'al Limmud ha-Pilosophiah u-Ma'amadah bi-Sefarad ba-Me'ah ha-Tet-Vav," *Proceedings of the Fifth World Congress of Jewish Studies* 3 (Jerusalem, 1972), Heb. sec.,

There is little evidence for the outright Averroist-style skepticism that Yitzhak Baer blames for the apostasy of beleaguered Iberian Jews. Nevertheless, it seems fair to say that an acculturated community is a less likely candidate for martyrdom than an insular one. Imagine two people with equal faith in the truth of Judaism confronting the executioner's sword. The first is an admiring participant in the culture he is being told to embrace, however much he rejects its religion; the second responds to that environment with visceral revulsion. While there are no easy formulas for determining the willingness to be martyred, the second type, who represents the Ashkenazic Jew of the first crusade, is surely more likely to choose death. On this level, the Jews of Spain paid a spiritual price for integration into the cultural milieu of their potential persecutors.

As we have seen in various contexts, the pursuit of the natural sciences went hand in hand with philosophical study, and their status as a mere handmaiden of metaphysics did not prevent them from being investigated with intensity and sophistication. Jewish physicians remained prominent throughout the Middle Ages, and Maimonides' medical treatises contain insights of lasting value. Gersonides made impressive contributions to astronomy, including the preparation of astronomical tables at the request of influential Christians, and fourteenth-century Provençal Jews continued to translate numerous scientific texts. Ibn Kaspi took pleasure in the unvarnished meaning of a talmudic text which asserted that gentile scholars had defeated the sages of Israel in a debate about astronomy; this, he said, demonstrates that non-Jews have something to teach us and that their works should not be ignored.[100]

The relationship between astronomy and astrology raised scientific and theological questions which confound the usually predictable boundaries between

---

pp. 151–58. Cf. also the oft-quoted antiphilosophical responsum by R. Isaac ben Sheshet, *She'elot u-Teshuvot Bar Sheshet* (Vilna, 1878), no. 45.

100. For a succinct summary of Maimonides' contributions to medieval medicine, see S. Muntner, "Gedulato ve-Ḥiddushav shel ha-Rambam bi-Refuah," in *Ha-Ram Bamza"l [sic]: Qovez̧ Torani-Madda'i,* ed. by Y. L. Maimon (Jerusalem, 1955), 264–66. On Jewish physicians in general, see inter alia, I. Munz, *Die Jüdische Ärzte im Mittelalter* (Frankfurt am Main, 1922), and D. Margalit, *Ḥakhmei Yisrael ke-Rofe'im* (Jerusalem, 1962). On science in general and astronomy in particular, see Bernard R. Goldstein, "The Role of Science in the Jewish Community in Fourteenth-Century France," *Annals of the New York Academy of Sciences* 314 (1978): 39–49; reprinted in his *Theory and Observation in Ancient and Medieval Astronomy* (London, 1985); L. V. Berman, "Greek into Hebrew: Samuel b. Judah of Marseilles, Fourteenth-Century Philosopher and Translator," in *Jewish Medieval and Renaissance Studies,* 289–320; Twersky, "Joseph ibn Kaspi" (above n. 94), 256, n. 52, where he cites a variety of references to divergent Jewish interpretations of the passage in *Pesaḥim* 94b concerning the victory of the gentile astronomers. On continuing astronomical study by sixteenth- and seventeenth-century Jews in the Eastern Mediterranean, see Goldstein, "The Hebrew Astronomical Tradition: New Sources," *Isis* 72 (1981): 237–51, also reprinted in *Theory and Observation.*

rationalists and their opponents. From a modern perspective, Maimonides' vigorous opposition to astrology seems precisely what we ought to expect from a person of his intellectual bent. To many medievals, however, astrology was not only validated by Rabbinic texts; it was a science like all others. Gersonides, for example, argued that the discipline was often empirically validated, and it was taken for granted that miracles must overcome not only the regularities of physics but the astrological order as well. At the same time, nonrationalist religious considerations could produce opposition to astrology, so that on this issue the Maimonidean legacy found itself in the unaccustomed company of R. Moses Taku. In the case of Gersonides, astronomy and astrology were kept rigorously separated, so that the affirmation of astrological truths had no adverse affect on his important astronomical studies.[101]

Although Spain and Provence were the major centers of philosophical and scientific pursuits among the Jews of the high and late Middle Ages, they did not enjoy a monopoly. Byzantine Jewry lived in a culture which preserved much of the Greek legacy of antiquity, and its intellectual profile has been described as "catholic in outlook and integrated with its environment. Secular studies were pursued as much as traditional religious studies."[102] Israel Ta-Shema, who has read substantial portions of the massive, unpublished works of Byzantine Jews available in the Institute of Microfilmed Hebrew Manuscripts in Jerusalem, has spoken to me with wonderment of the immense size and scope of the encyclopedic compositions produced by that Jewry, although he is less impressed by their depth or creativity.

---

101. For Maimonides' position, see his letter in Alexander Marx, "The Correspondence between the Rabbis of Southern France and Maimonides about Astrology," *Hebrew Union College Annual* 3 (1926): 311–58. (This letter [p. 351] also contains Maimonides' well-known remark that he had read a multitude of Arabic works on idolatry, an observation which has been regarded as problematic in light of *Hil. 'Avodah Zarah* 2:2. For a discussion of the passage in *Hil. 'Avodah Zarah*, see Lawrence Kaplan and David Berger, "On Freedom of Inquiry in the Rambam—and Today," *The Torah U-Madda Journal* 2 [1990]: 37–50.) For Naḥmanides' arguments from talmudic texts, see his responsum in *Kitvei Ramban* 1, 378–81; see also his *Commentary to Job, Kitvei Ramban* 1, 19, for the assumption that overturning someone's astrological fate requires miraculous divine intervention. Gersonides presented his argument as dreams, divination, prophecy, and astrology in *Milḥamot Hashem* 2:1–3 (Leipzig, 1866), 92–101; Levi ben Gershon (Gersonides), *The Wars of the Lord,* trans. by Seymour Feldman, 2 (Philadelphia, 1987), pp. 27–41. On the frequent but imperfect success of astrologers, see p. 95; Feldman, p. 33. For his separation of astronomy and astrology, see Goldstein, "The Role of Science," 45. On Moses Taku, see *Ketav Tamim, Oẓar Neḥmad* 3, pp. 82–83. (I do not mean to imply that Taku's position, which is reflected in a fleeting remark, was fully identical with that of Maimonides.)

102. Steven B. Bowman, *The Jews of Byzantium: 1204–1453* (University, Alabama, 1985), 168. Bowman goes on to suggest that this integration into Byzantine culture may have served to undermine the cultural independence of the established Jewish community in the face of the Ottoman conquest and Sephardi immigration.

Yemenite Jews, in part because of the influence of the Muslim environment and in large measure because of the inspiration provided by Maimonides, produced works reflecting familiarity with the full range of the medieval sciences. In an exceptionally strong formulation, R. Peraḥiah b. Meshullam wrote that "without the sciences of the intelligibles there would be no Torah," and Ḥoter b. Shlomoh reiterated the standard justification of scientific study as a preparation for metaphysical speculation.[103]

Similarly, the successor culture of medieval Spain was largely true to its heritage. The relative decline and stagnation of Muslim culture in the late Middle Ages had taken its toll on the intellectual creativity of Eastern Jewry, but under the stimulus of the Spanish immigration, the Jews of the Ottoman Empire displayed a renewal of cultural ferment. While this activity was mainly exegetical and homiletical, it included the study and translation of philosophical works. A recently published text provides a striking glimpse into a cast of mind which takes all learning as its province. A young scholar felt insulted when his town was denigrated as climatically unfit for the production of intellectuals. In an indignant response, he challenged the critic to do battle:

> Come out to the field and let us compete in our knowledge of the Bible, the Mishnah, and the Talmud, *Sifra* and *Sifre* and all of Rabbinic literature; in the external sciences—the practical and theoretical fields of science, the science of nature, and of the Divine; in logic . . . , geometry, astronomy, and law; in the natural sciences—the longer commentary and the shorter commentary, *Generatio et Corruptio*, *De Anima* and *Meteora*, *De Animalia* and *Ethics*. . . . Try me, for you have opened your mouth and belittled my dwelling-place, and you shall see that we know whatever can be known in the proper manner.[104]

---

103. The first major scientific work by a Yemenite Jew was Netanel al-Fayyumi's *Bustan al-'Uqul*, and interest in these disciplines persisted into the seventeenth century. See, inter alia, Y. Tzvi Langermann, *Ha-Madda'im ha-Meduyyaqim be-Qerev Yehudei Teiman* (Jerusalem, 1987); Yosef Kafih, "Arba'im She'elot be-Pilosophiah le-Rav Peraḥiah be-R. Meshullam," *Sefunot* 18 (1985): 111–92; David R. Blumenthal, *The Commentary of R. Ḥoter ben Shelomo to the Thirteen Principles of Maimonides* (Leiden, 1974); Meir Havazelet, "'Al ha-Parshanut ha-Allegorit-ha-Pilosofit be-Midrash ha-Ḥefeẓ le-Rabbi Zekharyah ha-Rofe," *Teima* 3 (1993): 45–56; and the references in Amos Goldreich, "Mi-Mishnat Ḥug ha-'Iyyun: 'Od 'al ha-Meqorot ha-Efshariyyim shel 'ha-Aḥdut ha-Shavah'," *Meḥqerei Yerushalayim be-Maḥashevet Yisrael* 6 (3–4) (1987): 150, n. 35.

104. Joseph Hacker, "The Intellectual Activity of the Jews of the Ottoman Empire during the Sixteenth and Seventeenth Centuries," in *Jewish Thought in the Seventeenth Century*, ed. by Isadore Twersky and Bernard Septimus (Cambridge, Mass., and London, England, 1987), 120. (Hacker's translation was printed in a somewhat garbled form, and so I have modified it slightly on the basis of the Hebrew version of his article, "Ha-Pe'ilut ha-Intelleqtualit be-qerev Yehudei ha-Imperiah ha-'Ottomanit ba-Me'ot ha-Shesh-'Esreh ve-ha-Sheva'-'Esreh,"

The polemical vigor and unmitigated pride in such remarks reflect a mentality that does not harbor the slightest twinge of doubt about the legitimacy and significance of all these pursuits.

At the same time, we have interesting evidence of opposition to philosophical study in this community. R. Menaḥem de Lonzano published an attack against philosophy which pointed to serious religious errors that it had inspired even in great figures of the past including Maimonides, R. Joseph Albo, and, strikingly, R. Baḥya ibn Pakuda. We have already seen that Baḥya decidedly belonged among the strongest advocates of speculation, but the piety that suffuses the bulk of his ethical work served to mute his rationalistic message and insulate him from serious attack by most antirationalists. De Lonzano was sensitive to this message and complained that Baḥya, like Maimonides, placed metaphysics at the pinnacle of human endeavor despite the implications for the status of straightforward study of the Torah; indeed, the broadside cites a nameless rabbinic contemporary in Istanbul who wondered why the *Guide* had been burned while *The Duties of the Heart* had remained untouched. On the one hand, it is clear that de Lonzano's attack reflected the view of an influential circle of Talmudists. It is equally clear, however, that he was deeply concerned about the likelihood that he would be subjected to scathing criticism for his position, and he describes contemporaries who advocated the study of halakhic codes rather than the Talmud so that they could devote their time to other disciplines. While we cannot know with any certainty why this critique of philosophy was omitted from the second, early seventeenth-century version of de Lonzano's book, the opposition that it no doubt engendered is as likely an explanation as any.[105] Ottoman Jewry, though on the verge of cultural decline and by no means univocal in its attitude to general culture, remained generally loyal to the legacy of medieval Sephardic thought.

Ashkenaz

The Northern European heartland of medieval Ashkenazic Jewry had a complex relationship with the dominant Christian civilization that defies the often simplistic characterizations describing the Ashkenazim as insular and narrow. There is no question that Northern French and German Jews, unlike their Sephardi counterparts, were deeply resistant to philosophical inquiry, largely because of the absence

Tarbiẓ 53 [1984]: 591.) Note also Hacker's citations from Solomon le-Beit ha-Levi and Abraham ibn Migash on pp. 123–26.

105. See Joseph Hacker, "Pulmus ke-neged ha-Pilosophiah be-Istanbul ba-Me'ah ha-Shesh-'Esreh," *Meḥqarim be-Qabbalah be-Pilosophiah Yehudit u-be-Sifrut ha-Musar ve-he-Hagut Muggashim li-Yesha'yah Tishbi bi-Melot lo Shiv'im ve-Ḥamesh Shanim* (Jerusalem, 1986), 507–36.

of a surrounding philosophical culture during their formative period; a Jewish civilization which reached maturity unaccustomed to speculation will be particularly sensitive to its alien dangers. Certainly the image of the Ashkenazim among Spanish and Provençal advocates of philosophy was that of benighted obscurantists. Radak wrote to Alfakar, "You and other wise men engage in the pursuit of wisdom and do not follow the words of the Ashkenazim, who have banned anyone who does so." R. Isaac of Acre, who became an advocate of such inquiry late in his life, reacted with disdain to those who refuse to examine

> a rational argument or to accept it. Rather, they call one to whom God has given the ability to understand rational principles . . . a heretic and non-believer, and his books they call external books, because they do not have the spirit needed to understand a rational principle. This is the nature of the rabbis of France and Germany and those who are like them.

During the controversy of the 1230s, Maimonists in Narbonne sent a letter to Spain with a particularly vitriolic denunciation of the French rabbis as fools and lunatics with clogged minds, who are devoted to superstitious nonsense and immersed in the fetid waters of unilluminated caves.[106]

Even in the context of philosophical speculation narrowly defined, the situation was not quite so simple. A paraphrase of Saadya's *Beliefs and Opinions* that made its way to early medieval Ashkenaz had a profound effect on the theology of significant segments of that Jewry. Unusual works like *Ketav Tamim* and *Sefer ha-Maskil* demonstrate familiarity with some speculative literature, and the author of the latter treatise was conversant with a variety of up-to-date scientific theories and experiments. In general, technological advances, experimental results, and observations of nature raised no serious religious problems, and there was no intrinsic reason for people unaffected by a theory of propaedeutic studies to connect them to philosophy. We should not be surprised, therefore, that Ashkenazic literature, probably even more than that of the Sephardim, reflects the keen interest and penetrating eye of Jews evincing intense curiosity about the natural and mechanical phenomena that surrounded them.[107] Moreover, the moment we broaden the question to include the

---

106. For Radak, see *Qovez̩ Teshuvot ha-Rambam*, 3b. For Isaac of Acre, see Goldreich's quotation from Oxford ms. 1911 in *Me'irat 'Einayim*, 412. The letter from Narbonne was published by Shatzmiller in *Z̩ion* 34 (1969): 143–44.

107. On the paraphrase of Saadya and its influence, see Ronald C. Kiener, "The Hebrew Paraphrase of Saadiah Gaon's *Kitab al-Amanat Wa'l-I'tiqadat*," *AJS Review* 11 (1986): 1–25, and Yosef Dan, *Torat ha-Sod shel Ḥasidut Ashkenaz* (Jerusalem, 1986), especially pp. 22–24. On science and philosophy in *Sefer ha-Maskil*, see Ta-Shema, "Sefer ha-Maskil," 435, 437–38.

Though the observation about propaedeutic studies is mine, I owe the vigorous formulation about the Ashkenazim's keen interest in the world around them to a conversation with

Jewish response to the surrounding culture in general, we discover the possibility of creative interaction that may have transformed important aspects of Ashkenazic piety and thought.

First of all, the religious confrontation with the Christian world impelled some Jews to study Latin as a polemical tool. More important, the ruthless pursuit of straightforward interpretation, or *peshat,* by twelfth-century Jewish commentators in France can plausibly be seen as a Jewish reaction to nonliteral Christian exegesis. A Jewish polemicist insisting upon *peshat* in a debate with a Christian could not easily return home and read the Bible in a way that violated the very principles of contextual, grammatical interpretation that he had just been passionately defending. Even explanations that are not labeled as anti-Christian can be motivated by the desire to avoid Christological assertions. There is, moreover, substantial evidence of scholarly interchange of a cordial, nonpolemical sort among Jews and Christians attempting to uncover the sense of the biblical text, and the Jewish approach had a considerable impact on the churchmen of St. Victor and other Christian commentators. Finally, the fact that the explosion of Jewish learning and literary activity took place in twelfth-century France may well be related to the concomitant "renaissance of the twelfth century" in the larger society.[108]

Ta-Shema; cf. Noah Shapira, "ʿAl ha-Yedaʿ ha-Tekhni ve-ha-Tekhnologi shel Rashi," *Korot* 3 (1963): 145–61, where Rashi's extensive technological information is treated, probably wrongly, as exceptional. See now the brief but very important note by Y. Tzvi Langermann, "Ḥibbur Ashkenazi Bilti Nodaʿ be-Maddaʿei ha-Tevaʿ," *Kiryat Sefer* 62 (1988–89): 448–49, where he describes a scientific treatise by a fourteenth-century French Jew who was particularly interested in practical science, including various instruments, and who reported that he had written a different work demonstrating how scientific knowledge sheds new light on the understanding of Torah. See also n. 131 below.

The warm, respectful welcome extended to R. Abraham ibn Ezra by prominent Tosafists certainly does not bespeak instinctive hostility to bearers of a broader cultural orientation. For Ta-Shema's more problematic assertion that Ashkenaz boasted full-fledged rationalist allegorizers, see his "Sefer ha-Maskil," 421; if such an approach had really attained an appreciable level of visibility in Northern Europe, it is hard to imagine that we would not find more substantial criticisms of it in the extant literature. Finally, it is worth noting an oral observation by Haym Soloveitchik that the major rabbinic luminaries of Northern France are not among the signatories of the ban against the *Guide* and *Sefer ha-Madda.*

108. See Aryeh Grabois, "The *Hebraica Veritas* and Jewish-Christian Intellectual Relations in the Twelfth Century," *Speculum* 50 (1975): 613–34; David Berger, "Mission to the Jews and Jewish-Christian Contacts in the Polemical Literature of the High Middle Ages," *The American Historical Review* 91 (1986): 576–91; Berger, "Gilbert Crispin, Alan of Lille, and Jacob ben Reuben: A Study in the Transmission of Medieval Polemic," *Speculum* 49 (1974): 34–47 (on the use of Latin texts by a Jewish polemicist); Avraham Grossman, "Ha-Pulmus ha-Yehudi-ha-Noẓri ve-ha-Parshanut ha-Yehudit la-Miqra be-Ẓarfat ba-Me'ah ha-Yod-Bet (le-Parashat Ziqqato shel Ri Qara el ha-Pulmus)," *Ẓion* 51 (1986): 29–60 (for persuasive examples of unlabeled anti-Christian commentaries); Grossman, *Ḥakhmei Ẓarfat ha-Rishonim,*

The stereotype of the narrow Ashkenazi sometimes included the assertion that even biblical study was ignored, and there is a degree of validity in this image, particularly in the later Middle Ages.[109] Nonetheless, the innovative biblical exegesis in twelfth-century France demonstrates that this perception is selective and skewed. Not only did Ashkenazic Jews study Bible; biblical exegesis served as both a battleground and a bridge where Jews and Christians came into frequent, creative contact as enemies and as partners.

In the field of biblical study, interaction is firmly established; what requires elucidation is the extent and nature of its effects. We face a more fundamental problem with respect to the most intriguing question of all: Did the revolutionary use of dialectic in the talmudic methodology of the Northern French Tosafists owe anything to the intellectual upheaval in the larger society? There is hardly any evidence of Jewish familiarity in Ashkenaz with the study of canon law and philosophy, which were the two major areas in which the search for contradictions or inconsistencies and their subsequent resolution began to play a central role. It is

---

473–504; Beryl Smalley, *The Study of the Bible in the Middle Ages* (Notre Dame, 1964); Elazar Touitou, "Shitato ha-Parshanit shel ha-Rashbam 'al Reqa'ha-Meẓiut ha-Historit shel Zemanno," in Y. D. Gilat et al., ed., *'Iyyunim be-Sifrut Ḥazal ba-Miqra u-be-Toledot Yisrael: Muqdash li-Prof. Ezra Zion Melamed* (Ramat Gan, 1982), pp. 48–74 (on the impact of the twelfth-century Renaissance).

For the possible influence of Christian art on Ashkenazic Jews, see Joseph Gutmann's presentation and my response in J. Gutmann, et al., *What Can Jewish History Learn From Jewish Art?* (New York, 1989), 1–18, 29–38. Gabriele L. Strauch's *Dukus Horant: Wanderer Zwischen Zwei Welten* (Amsterdam and Atlanta, 1990) analyzes a fairly typical medieval German romance written or copied by a fourteenth century German Jew in Yiddish (or at least in Hebrew characters with some specifically Jewish terminology). Note also Dan, *Torat ha-Sod*, 37–39, for some general observations on the impact of folk beliefs about magic, astrology, and the like on Ashkenazic Jewry. Finally, Ivan G. Marcus has now presented an analysis of an Ashkenazic ritual for the purpose of illuminating the manner in which responses to Christian society can make their way into the religious life of both scholars and the laity; see his *Rituals of Childhood: Jewish Acculturation in Medieval Europe* (New Haven and London, 1996).

109. See Profiat Duran's introduction to *Ma'aseh Efod*, 41, and the discussion in Isadore Twersky, "Religion and Law," in *Religion in a Religious Age*, ed. by Goitein, pp. 74–77. See also Mordechai Breuer, "Min'u Beneikhem min ha-Higgayon," in *Mikhtam le-David: Sefer Zikhron ha-Rav David Ochs*, ed. by Yitzhak Gilat and Eliezer Stern (Ramat Gan, 1978), pp. 242–64, and Frank Talmage, "Keep Your Sons From Scripture: The Bible in Medieval Jewish Scholarship and Spirituality," in *Understanding Scripture: Explorations of Jewish and Christian Traditions of Interpretation*, ed. by Clemens Thoma and Michael Wyschogrod (New York, 1987), 81–101. On evidence for Ashkenazic biblical study in the precrusade period, see Avraham Grossman, *Ḥakhmei Ashkenaz ha-Rishonim*, 240, 288–89, 323 (inter alia), and cf. my review, "Ḥeqer Rabbanut Ashkenaz ha-Qedumah," *Tarbiẓ* 53 (1984): 484, n. 7. For an overall analysis of the evidence, see Ephraim Kanarfogel, *Jewish Education and Society in the High Middle Ages* (Detroit, 1992), 79–85.

even more difficult to imagine that Christians, whose familiarity with the Talmud was virtually nil, could have been much influenced by Tosafists. At the same time, the very individuals who pursued the new methodologies in fields unknown by the members of the other faith met on the terrain of biblical studies. Rashbam, who was a Tosafist as well as a *peshat*-oriented biblical exegete, is a good Jewish example. In light of these well-documented contacts, it surely cannot be ruled out—indeed, it seems overwhelmingly likely—that some taste of the exciting new approaches was transmitted. When the German pietists wanted to criticize the Tosafist approach, they denounced the utilization of "Gentile dialectic" (*dial tiqa* [*dialeqtiqah*] *shel goyim*); though we are under no obligation to endorse the historical judgment of the pietists, the criticism establishes at least a threshold level of familiarity with the term and its application.[110]

The relationship of these pietists to the surrounding culture is itself highly suggestive. The system of penances that they introduced into the process of repentance is no longer regarded as a defining characteristic of their movement; nonetheless, that system remains a major development in the history of Jewish piety, and despite a smattering of antecedents in rabbinic literature, it is overwhelmingly likely that the influence of the Christian environment was decisive.[111] With respect to quintessentially religious behavior, the inhibition against following Christian models should have been overwhelming, and I think that the psychological factor that overcame it was analogous to the competitive imitation that we have already seen in Muslim Spain. It was critically important for the Jewish self-image that Jews not be inferior to the host society. In Spain, the competition was cultural and intellectual; in Ashkenaz, given the different complexion of both majority and minority culture, it was a competition in religious devotion. I have suggested elsewhere that this consideration may account in part for the assertions by Jewish polemicists that the chastity of monks and nuns is more apparent than real. Celibacy was an area in which Jewish law did not allow competition, and so the problem was resolved by the not entirely unfounded allegation that the religious self-sacrifice of

110. See Kanarfogel, *Jewish Education*, 70–73. The pietists' denunciation of dialectic is in *Sefer Ḥasidim*, ed. by J. Wistinetsky, 2nd ed. (Frankfurt am Main, 1924), par. 752, p. 191. Note too the citation of some parallel methods in *Tosafot* and Christian works in Jose Faur, "The Legal Thinking of Tosafot: An Historical Approach," *Diné Israel* 6 (1975): xliii–lxxii. For intimate familiarity with Christian works in the writings of the probably atypical R. Elḥanan b. Yaqar of London, see G. Vajda, "De quelques infiltrations chrétiennes dans l'oeuvre d'un auteur anglo-juif du XIIIe siècle," *Archives d'Histoire Doctrinale et Littéraire du Moyen Age* 28 (1961): 15–34.

111. On the Christian analogues to the penances of Ḥasidei Ashkenaz, see Yitzhak Baer, "Ha-Megammah ha-Datit ve-ha-Ḥevratit shel Sefer Ḥasidim," *Ẓion* 3 (1938): 18–20. For the new evaluation of the movement's center of gravity, see Haym Soloveitchik, "Three Themes in the Sefer Ḥasidim," *AJS Review* 1 (1976): 311–57. See also Ivan Marcus, *Piety and Society: The Jewish Pietists of Medieval Germany* (Leiden, 1981).

Christians was illusory. With respect to self-mortification for sin, Jewish law was not quite so clear, and Ashkenazi pietists set out to demonstrate that they would not be put to shame by Christian zeal in the service of God.[112]

In the late Middle Ages, Northern European Jewry was subjected to expulsions, persecutions, and dislocations which disrupted its cultural life and moved its center of gravity eastward. By the late fourteenth and early fifteenth centuries, a figure like R. Yom Tov Lipmann Mühlhausen of Prague demonstrates that some Jewish intellectuals had achieved familiarity with philosophy and general culture. In 1973, Ephraim Kupfer published a seminal article which attempted to establish the substantial presence of rationalism in Ashkenaz during this period. There can be no question that much of the evidence that he adduced is significant and stimulating. We can hardly fail to be intrigued, for example, by an argument in an Ashkenazic text that ancient shifts in the *halakhah* of levirate marriage resulted from a rejection of metempsychosis by increasingly sophisticated rabbis. At the same time, it is far from clear that this material reflects the views and interests of substantial segments of Ashkenazic society, and it is very likely that one of the important figures in the article came to Europe from Israel bearing texts and ideas that stem from the Jewish communities of the Muslim East. Both the dissemination and the rootedness of philosophical study in fourteenth- and fifteenth-century Ashkenaz remain an open question, and I am inclined to think that it stood considerably closer to the periphery than to the center.[113]

---

112. On celibacy, see my observations in *The Jewish-Christian Debate in the High Middle Ages*, 27. I have elaborated somewhat in a forthcoming essay, "Hebbetim 'al Tadmitam ve-Goralam shel ha-Goyim be-Sifrut ha-Pulmus ha-Ashkenazit," in Yom Tov Assis, et al., ed., *Qehillot Shum bi-Gezerot Tatnu* (title tentative).

113. See Kupfer, "Li-Demutah," *Tarbiẓ* 42 (1973): 113–47. It is noteworthy that one of the texts cited by Kupfer (p. 129) takes it for granted that the ancient rabbis learned proper methods of demonstration from the works of Aristotle, a position which reverses the standard medieval Jewish assertion about the source of Greek philosophy. See also Kupfer's brief supplementary notes in his "Hassagot min Ḥakham Eḥad 'al Divrei he-Ḥakham ha-Rav R. Yosef b. ha-Qadosh R. Yosef ha-Lo'azi she-Katav ve-Qara be-Qol Gadol neged ha-Rambam," *Qoveẓ 'al Yad* n.s. 11 [21] (1985): 215–16, nn. 2, 4. For some evidence of interest in philosophy outside the "Mühlhausen circle," particularly in *Sefer Hadrat Qodesh* written in Germany shortly before the middle of the fourteenth century, see Davis, *R. Yom Tov Lipman Heller*, 88–103, and see now his "Philosophy, Dogma, and Exegesis in Medieval Ashkenazic Judaism: The Evidence of *Sefer Hadrat Qodesh*," *AJS Review* 18 (1993): 195–222. For an early, brief expression of reservations about Kupfer's thesis, see Joseph Dan, "Ḥibbur Yiḥud Ashkenazi min ha-Me'ah ha-Yod-Dalet," *Tarbiẓ* 44 (1975): 203–06. For a more detailed critique, see Israel Jacob Yuval, *Ḥakhamim be-Doram* (Jerusalem, 1988), 286–311. In an oral communication, Moshe Idel has noted several considerations pointing to the likelihood that Menaḥem Shalem came from Israel: His non-Ashkenazic name usually refers to a Jerusalemite; he makes reference to Emmaus, which he identifies as Latrun; he had a text by Abraham Abulafia and a translation of an Arabic text by Abraham Maimonides. If

The question of the standing of philosophy among fifteenth-century Ashkenazim has a significant bearing on the proper evaluation of major trends and figures in the intellectual life of the burgeoning new center in sixteenth-century Poland. R. Moses Isserles and R. Mordecai Jaffe are the two most prominent examples of distinguished Talmudists who maintained a position of moderate rationalism in which a conservative understanding of Maimonides and a philosophical interpretation of kabbalah served to unite diverse strands of Jewish piety and theology in a manner that removed any threat to traditional religious affirmations.[114] If Kupfer is correct, then this position can be seen as a natural continuation of intellectual trends in late medieval Ashkenaz, and the approach of Isserles and Jaffe would fit well into their generally conservative posture. If he is not, then we must seek other sources for the penetration of philosophical ideas into Polish Jewish thought.

The first of these is the Northern European Renaissance, which affected both Poland and Bohemia and can consequently help to account not only for the elements of rationalism in the works of Polish rabbis but for the significant scientific and philosophical activity among the Jews of late sixteenth and early seventeenth-century Prague. In the case of David Gans of Prague, the relationship with Christian society is crystal-clear: Gans was the first influential Jew to confront Copernicanism, and he did so as a personal associate of Tycho Brahe and Johann Kepler. Gans's illustrious contemporary, R. Judah Loew (Maharal), produced an impressive theological corpus which made extensive, though cautious use of the Jewish philosophical tradition, and described astronomy as "a ladder to ascend to the wisdom of the Torah," while his student R. Yom Tov Lipman Heller, best known for his standard commentary to the Mishnah, displayed considerable interest in the pursuit of mathematics and astronomy. The period from 1560 to 1620 saw a significant increase in works of a philosophical and scientific nature throughout the Ashkenazic orbit, and the contacts between the Jewish communities of Prague and Poland no doubt contributed to the spread of these pursuits. A second significant source of cultural stimulation for Polish Jewry may well have been Renaissance Italy. Polish Jews were in continual contact with Italy in a multitude of contexts; numerous Padua-trained physicians came to Poland, and a constant stream of literary material crossed the border.[115]

Idel is correct, and if Kupfer's suggestion that the two Menaḥems in his study are really one and the same is also correct, then the dominant personality in the article was not an Ashkenazic Jew.

114. See Lawrence Kaplan, "Rabbi Mordekhai Jaffe and the Evolution of Jewish Culture in Poland in the Sixteenth Century," in *Jewish Thought in the Sixteenth Century*, ed. by Bernard D. Cooperman (Cambridge, Mass., and London, England, 1983), 266–82. On Isserles' thought, see Yonah Ben Sasson, *Mishnato ha-'Iyyunit shel ha-Rama* (Jerusalem, 1984).

115. On Gans in particular and Prague in general, see Mordecai Breuer, "Qavvim li-Demuto shel R. David Gans Ba'al *Ẓemaḥ David*," *Bar Ilan* 11 (1973): 97–103, and his edition of *Sefer Ẓemaḥ David le-Rabbi David Gans* (Jerusalem, 1983), esp. pp. 1–9. On Heller,

The use of this material would have been legitimated in the eyes of some conservatives by the heroic image of Maimonides, whose orthodoxy was now beyond reproach. Once again, we find an exception which genuinely proves this rule. In midsixteenth-century Posen, the extreme and eccentric antirationalist R. Joseph Ashkenazi persuaded his father-in-law R. Aaron to deliver an uncompromising attack against the study of philosophy. Ashkenazi, as we know from a later work of his, attacked Maimonides with startling vitriol as an outright heretic who deserves no defense and who is largely responsible for popularizing the allegorization of the Bible and of *aggadah* that has undermined authentic Judaism. Nevertheless, he himself cited with disgust the unanimity of the admiring chorus of Maimonides' supporters, and R. Avraham Horowitz's attack on Ashkenazi demonstrates further the passionate reaction inspired by unrestrained criticism of the author of the *Guide*. Horowitz's work, which contains a vigorous defense of philosophical study, also reflects the presence in sixteenth-century Poland of unabashed exponents of speculation, although the author's partial revision of his rationalist views years later points to the countervailing forces that may well have been dominant even at that time, as they surely were by the dawn of the Jewish enlightenment.[116]

---

see Davis, *R. Yom Tov Lipman Heller*, 339–517; for documentation on the upsurge in Ashkenazic works of a philosophical and scientific nature, see Davis, 121–29. On the contacts between Ashkenaz and Italy, see Jacob Elbaum, "Qishrei Tarbut bein Yehudei Polin ve-Ashkenaz le-bein Yehudei Italia ba-Me'ah Ha-Tet-Zayin," *Gal'ed* 7–8 (1985): 11–40, and, more briefly, his *Petiḥut Ve-Histaggerut* (Jerusalem, 1990), 33–54. On Jews in the medical school at Padua, see Daniel Carpi, "Yehudim Ba'alei Toar Doctor li-Refuah mi-Ta'am Universitat Padua ba-Me'ah ha-Tet-Zayin u-be-Reshit ha-Me'ah ha-Yod-Zayin," in *Sefer Zikkaron le-Natan Cassutto (Scritti in Memoria di Nathan Cassuto)*, ed. by Daniel Carpi, Augusto Segre, and Renzo Toaff (Jerusalem, 1986), 62–91.

116. Lawrence Kaplan has pointed out that despite the impression given by some earlier scholarship, Horowitz's revision does not represent a radical rejection of his earlier views; see "Rabbi Mordekhai Jaffe," 281, n. 8. Horowitz's attack was published and discussed by Ph. Bloch, "Der Streit um den Moreh des Maimonides in der Gemeinde Posen um die Mitte des 16 Jahrh.," *Monatsschrift für Geschichte und Wissenschaft des Judenthums* 47 (1903): 153–69, 263–79, 346–56. For an analysis of Joseph Ashkenazi and selections from his work, see Gershom Scholem, "Yedi'ot Ḥadashot 'al R. Yosef Ashkenazi, ha-'Tanna' mi-Ẓefat," *Tarbiẓ* 28 (1959): pp. 59–89, 201–35. A detailed response to Ashkenazi by a contemporary Italian Jew was published by Kupfer, "Hassagot min Ḥakham Eḥad," *Qoveẓ al Yad* n.s. 11 [21] (1985): pp. 213–88. On Ashkenazi's denunciation even of Maimondes' code, see I. Twersky, "R. Yosef Ashkenazi ve-Sefer Mishneh Torah la-Rambam," *Sefer ha-Yovel li-Khevod Shalom Baron*, ed. by Saul Lieberman (Jerusalem, 1975), 183–94. The moderate rationalism of R. Eliezer Ashkenazi of Posen also deserves mention, although the fact that he spent many years in the East mitigates his significance for a characterization of Polish Jewry; see the analysis of Ashkenazi's exegetical independence in Haim Hillel Ben Sasson, *Hagut ve-Hanhagah* (Jerusalem, 1959), 34–38.

Isserles' conservative philosophical treatise contained considerable scientific discussion as well, and he also wrote a separate astronomical work in the form of a commentary to the standard textbook in that field, Georg Peurbach's *Theoricae Novae Planetarum*. R. Solomon Luria, in an oft-quoted exchange with Isserles, denounced him for citing scientific information derived from gentile sources in a halakhic decision about the *kashrut* of a particular animal and for reading philosophical works at all, and he blames such attitudes for the bizarre and otherwise unattested phenomenon of young Polish Jews who recite an Aristotelian prayer in the synagogue. Isserles' response is revealing. He justified his actions, but made it clear that he gained his scientific knowledge only from Jewish books and that he pursued these studies only at times when most people are out taking walks on Sabbaths and holidays.

Recent research has tended to portray a greater openness to rationalism and science than we had been accustomed to ascribe to this Jewry. Nevertheless, it remains difficult to take the pulse of sixteenth-century Polish Jewish intellectuals with respect to our question: probably a small group of full-fledged rationalists, a substantial number of conservative advocates of a tamed philosophy, and a significant group of rabbis who either shied away from speculation or actively opposed it.[117]

Italian Symbiosis

With respect to Poland and the Ottoman Empire, we could legitimately speak of successor cultures to Ashkenaz and Spain respectively, despite the fact that Middle Eastern Jewry had its own intellectual tradition before the Iberian immigration. Italy is a more complex and more interesting story. Despite their Christian environment, the Jews of medieval Italy appear to have maintained a greater degree of openness to the surrounding culture than did Ashkenazic Jewry. Shabbetai Donnolo is a

117. On Isserles' astronomical treatise, see Y. Tzvi Langermann, "The Astronomy of Rabbi Moses Isserles," in *Physics, Cosmology, and Astronomy, 1300–1700: Tension and Accommodation*, ed. by S. Unguru (Dordrecht and Boston, 1991), 83–98. For the exchange between Isserles and R. Solomon Luria, see *She'elot u-Teshuvot ha-Rama*, ed. by Asher Siev (Jerusalem, 1971), nos. 5–7, pp. 18–38, and cf. the summary in Ben Zion Katz, *Rabbanut, Ḥasidut, Haskalah* 1 (Tel Aviv, 1956), 32–33. It is worth noting that even Luria maintains that he is as familiar with the disputed literature as Isserles (Siev, p. 26). On Poland specifically and sixteenth-century Ashkenazic Jewry in general, see Jacob Elbaum, *Zeramim u-Megammot be-Sifrut ha-Maḥashavah ve-ha-Musar be-Ashkenaz u-be-Polin ba-Me'ah ha-Tet-Zayin* (Hebrew University dissertation, 1977), 120–35; Elbaum, *Petiḥut ve-Histaggerut*, esp. chapter 5; Davis, *R. Yom Tov Lipman Heller*; and the still useful survey by Lawrence H. Davis, "The Great Debate: Secular Studies and the Jews in Sixteenth Century Poland," *Yavneh Review* 3 (1963): 42–58.

well-known, early example of the sort of learned physician and scientist that we usually associate with Jews in the Muslim orbit. To some degree, this phenomenon may have resulted from the significant Muslim impact on Southern Italy, but I am inclined to attribute even greater importance to the fact that pre–twelfth-century Southern Europe maintained a greater continuity with the classical past than did the Christian communities of the North. A case in point is the familiarity of the anonymous tenth-century Italian Jew who wrote *Josippon* with earlier Latin works. By the thirteenth century, Italian Jews displayed a level of sophistication in philosophical and literary pursuits that owed something to contacts with Iberia but at least as much to a receptivity to the cultural developments in their immediate environment. Thus, easily the most philosophically sophisticated anti-Christian polemicist of the thirteenth century was Moses ben Solomon of Salerno, and the often secular, sometimes ribald poetry of Immanuel of Rome could not have been composed in any other Jewry in the medieval Christian world.[118]

Toward the end of the Middle Ages, both Sephardi and Ashkenazi immigrants introduced a mixture of new influences. Elijah del Medigo's late fifteenth-century *Beḥinat ha-Dat* is a clear-cut example of the impact of rationalism, but the fate of Aristotelian philosophy among the Jews of Renaissance Italy is bound up with central questions about their cultural posture. Lists of books in Italian Jewish libraries in the fifteenth and early sixteenth centuries appear to reflect a decline of interest in philosophy from the beginning to the end of that period, with the important and unsurprising exception of Maimonides' *Guide* and some of its commentators. This impression is reinforced by a complaint leveled by R. Isaac Abravanel in Venice as early as the late fifteenth century about the unavailability of Averroes' *Epistle on the Conjunction* and Moses of Narboni's commentary on it. If the requisite work were "*tosafot* or codes, I would borrow it from one of the natives, but in philosophy this is impossible." The declining philosophical content of Jewish sermons in the first half of the sixteenth century provides further evidence of the same significant development.[119]

118. On Donnolo, see the discussion and references in A. Sharf, *The Universe of Shabbetai Donnolo* (New York, 1976). For the greater cultural continuity in Southern Europe, see R. W. Southern's observations in *The Making of the Middle Ages* (New Haven and London, 1953), 20–25. On *Josippon*, see *Sefer Yosifon*, ed. by David Flusser, 2 vols. (Jerusalem, 1978, 1980); in particular, note Flusser's well-documented observation that the author knew Latin works better than rabbinic literature. Moses of Salerno's philosophical polemic was published by Stanislaus Simon, *Mose ben Salomo von Salerno und seine philosophischen Auseinandersetzung mit den Lehren des Christentums* (Breslau, 1931). For Immanuel, see *Maḥberot Immanuel*, ed. by A. M. Haberman (Tel Aviv, 1946).

119. For del Medigo, see his *Sefer Beḥinat ha-Dat*, ed. by Jacob Ross (Tel Aviv, 1984), and D. Geffen, "Insights into the Life and Thought of Elijah del Medigo Based on his Published and Unpublished Works," *Proceedings of the American Academy for Jewish Research* 41–42 (1973–74): 69–86. On libraries, sermons, and the overall phenomenon, see Reuven

The diminution of interest in metaphysics does not bespeak the end of Italian Jewish acculturation. First of all, the continuing use of the scholastic philosophical approach by no less a figure than R. Ovadiah Seforno demonstrates the persistent vitality of that tradition within important rabbinic circles. More important, Renaissance Christians were themselves engaged in disputes about the value of philosophy and tended to emphasize the scientific, ethical, and political dimensions of the Aristotelian corpus rather than its metaphysical component; in a sense, then, the very de-emphasis of the philosophical tradition can be seen not as a turning inward but as a reflection of a larger cultural trend. There is no denying that the gradual displacement of Aristotelianism by kabbalah in the minds of many Italian Jews reflected a desire to emphasize the uniqueness of the Jewish people and its culture in a manner reminiscent of Halevi, whose *Kuzari* underwent something of a popular revival; nonetheless, even R. Yeḥiel Nissim of Pisa, who produced the most impressive reasoned argument for this displacement, recognized the value of philosophical investigations, not to speak of scientific inquiry, provided that they were not assigned primacy in a rivalry with the Torah.[120]

Once we step outside the four ells of Aristotelian metaphysics, the evidence for Renaissance Jewry's immersion in the surrounding culture becomes overwhelming. Indeed, to an observer coming to the subject from the study of another Jewish community, including that of Iberia, the lively and genuinely significant historians' debate over the inner or outer directedness of fifteenth- and sixteenth-century Italian Jews takes on a surreal quality. This is a community with intellectuals entranced by the rhetorical works of Cicero and Quintilian and with preachers who lace their sermons with references to classical authors while insisting that the Bible cannot be properly understood without a literary sensitivity nurtured by careful study of gentile as well as Jewish literature. It is a community with thinkers who set up the Renaissance ideal of homo universalis or *ḥakham kolel* as a paradigm of intellectual perfection attained by King Solomon and sought by anyone with healthy educational priorities. It is a community that produced a plan, at least on paper, of setting up what one observer has described as a Yeshiva University, where the primary emphasis would be on the study of "the written and oral Torah, laws, *tosafot*, and decisors," but instruction would also be provided in the works of Jewish philosophers, Hebrew grammar, rhetoric, Latin, Italian, logic, medicine, non-Jewish philosophical works, mathematics, cosmography, and astrology. It is a community with vigorous, ongoing exchanges with the contemporary Christian elite. Not only did Elias Levita teach Hebrew to Christian scholars; not only did kabbalah itself, which was sometimes taught by Jews, inspire the speculative creativity of Christian

Bonfil, *Ha-Rabbanut be-Italia bi-Tequfat ha-Renaissance* (Jerusalem, 1979), 173–206; *Rabbis and Jewish Communities in Renaissance Italy* (Oxford and New York, 1990), 270–323. For the citation from Abravanel, see Hacker, "The Intellectual Activity of the Jews of the Ottoman Empire" (above, n. 104), n. 47 (pp. 117–18).

120. See Bonfil, *Ha-Rabbanut*, 179–90; *Rabbis*, 280–98.

thinkers; it now appears likely that Pico della Mirandola's version of the quintessentially Renaissance definition of man as a median creature with the power to fashion himself in freedom owes much to a medieval Muslim formulation mediated by Pico's Jewish associate Yoḥanan Alemanno.[121]

At the same time, vigorous opposition to philosophy and the humanist agenda produced a continuing debate. The fact that Joseph Ashkenazi wrote his vitriolic attack against Maimonides while in Italy is no doubt fortuitous, but it made enough of an impact there to have elicited an elaborate refutation. Yosef Yavetz's *Or ha-Ḥayyim* is the work of a Spanish exile in Naples who rejected philosophical pursuits as damaging to faith and did battle with the hallowed rationalist understanding of the biblical admonition to "know" God as a philosophical imperative; a pious individual needs to be rescued from "the ambush of human reason, which lurks in wait . . . at all times." R. David Proventzalo advised the young David Messer Leon to follow the ways of distant Talmudists rather than the philosophical agenda of local rabbis, who appear to assign no value to the Torah and Talmud. R. Ovadiah of Bertinoro denounced the study of Aristotle in particular and philosophy

121. On rhetoric, see *The Book of the Honeycomb's Flow. Sefer Nofeth Suphim by Judah Messer Leon.* A Critical Edition and Translation by Isaac Rabinowitz (Ithaca and London, 1983). See also R. Bonfil's introduction to the facsimile edition of *Nofet Ẓufim* (Jerusalem, 1981). Like del Medigo, Messer Leon was interested in philosophy as well. On homo universalis and King Solomon, see Arthur M. Lesley, *The Song of Solomon's Ascents* (University of California at Berkeley dissertation, 1976), and the citation from David Messer Leon's *Shevaḥ Nashim* in Hava Tirosh-Rothschild, "In Defense of Jewish Humanism," *Jewish History* 3 (1988): 54 (n. 55); note also her remarks on p. 33.

On the proposal in 1564 to set up an academy for Torah and general studies in Mantua, see the text in Asaf, *Meqorot* 2, pp. 116–20; Asaf noted (p. 115) that only an Italian Jew could have thought of such a project. The apt analogy to Yeshiva University was made by Yeḥezkel Cohen, "Ha-Yaḥas le-Limmudei Ḥol me-Ḥazal ve-'ad Yameinu—Seqirah Historit-Sifrutit," in *Yaḥas ha-Yahadut le-Limmudei Ḥol* (Israel, 1983), p. 20. Although this would not have been a degree granting institution, the plan envisioned a preparatory program that would enable the student to enroll subsequently in a formal *studio* and receive a secular degree (*semikhah*!) in a very short time. On Elias Levita and the teaching of Hebrew and kabbalah to Christians, see the discussion in Yitzhak Penkower, "'Iyyun Meḥuddash be-Sefer Massoret ha-Massoret le-Eliyyahu Baḥur: Iḥur ha-Niqqud u-Biqqoret Sefer ha-Zohar," *Italia* 8 (1989): 36–50, and the references in n. 93 (pp. 37–38).

For Alemanno's likely influence on Pico's crucial conception of man, see Moshe Idel, "The Anthropology of Yohanan Alemanno: Sources and Influences," *Topoi* 7 (1988): pp. 201–10. David Ruderman has recently argued that Pico's replacement of a narrow vision of Christian culture with one that was more broadly human created a new challenge and a new opportunity for Renaissance Jews confronting their intellectual environment; see his very useful summary article, "The Italian Renaissance and Jewish Thought," in *Renaissance Humanism: Foundations, Forms, and Legacy, Volume I: Humanism in Italy*, ed. by Albert Rabil Jr. (Philadelphia, 1988), 382–433.

in general in both his commentary to the Mishnah and his correspondence, writing approvingly of the untainted piety that he found in the land of Israel in contrast to the deplorable situation in Italy. In the introduction to his halakhic work *Giddulei Terumah,* R. Azariah Figo lamented his youthful pursuit of general culture in the late sixteenth century and described his decision to "expel this maidservant" and return to the Talmud, although it is noteworthy that he berated himself only for reversing the proper order of priorities, not for pursuing a forbidden path.[122]

Despite the advice that he received, David Messer Leon ultimately opted for humanist pursuits to the point of arguing that the Talmudist who is also a *ḥakham kolel* is more deserving of rabbinic ordination than an ordinary Talmudist. When he left Italy for Constantinople, he found himself under attack for his frequent citation of classical literature in his sermons; in response, he produced a passionate defense of the humanist enterprise, arguing for the value of classical poetry and rhetoric in achieving human perfection, which is bound up with the quest for religious perfection. Two Jewish biographies, one of King Solomon, the other of Isaac Abravanel, written in Italy between the late fifteenth and mid-sixteenth centuries, clearly reflect Renaissance literary trends and further illustrate Jewish involvement in humanistic study and creativity. The seventeenth-century autobiography of Leone da Modena, which can be seen as an extension of this genre, is but one of many indications not only of its author's extraordinary range of interests but of the continuing, even growing Jewish familiarity with the broader culture well into the Baroque period. The glorification of Hebrew reached its peak at the height of the Renaissance, while in the post-Renaissance period even Jewish authors with an excellent command of Hebrew were ever more likely to write in the vernacular.[123]

122. On the response to Ashkenazi, see Kupfer, "Hassagot min Ḥakham Eḥad" (above, n. 113). For the translation from Yavetz's *Or ha-Ḥayyim* (Lublin, 1910), 74–76, see Arthur M. Lesley, "The Place of the *Dialoghi d'amore* in Contemporaneous Jewish Thought," in *Ficino and Renaissance Neoplatonism*, ed. by K. Eisenbichler and O.Z. Pugliese (University of Toronto Italian Studies I, Ottawa, 1986), 75, and cf. Barzilay's discussion, *Between Reason and Faith*, 133–49. For R. Ovadiah of Bertinoro, see his commentary to *Sanhedrin* 10:1 and the letter published in A. Kahana, *Sifrut ha-Historiah ha-Yisre'elit* 2 (Warsaw, 1923), 47, and cf. the commentary to *Avot* 5:22. Cf. also Immanuel Benevento's kabbalistically motivated hostility to philosophy; see the references in Segal, *Historical Consciousness and Religious Tradition*, pp. 61–62 (n. 20). On Proventzalo's advice, see Bonfil, *Ha-Rabbanut*, 173–74; *Rabbis*, p. 270. For Figo, see *Sefer Giddulei Terumah* (Venice, 1643), and Barzilay, pp. 192–209. A similar statement of regret at excessive attention to works of general culture appears in the early seventeenth-century *Shiltei ha-Gibborim* of Abraham Portaleone, but the book itself, despite its presumed character as an act of penitence for these intellectual indiscretions, is replete with references to the classics; see Segal, 52, and the references in n. 23. In a personal communication, David Ruderman has underscored his view of Portaleone and Figo as anti-Aristotelians who nevertheless maintained a positive attitude toward empirical science.

123. Messer Leon's observation on the qualifications for ordination is reminiscent of the

In her study of David Messer Leon's work, Havah Tirosh-Rothschild observes that

> by the end of the fifteenth century, Jewish rationalist tradition had so absorbed Greek philosophy that it had become far less subversive and was even palatable. By David ben Judah's day, however, no such absorption had yet occurred of the poetry, oratory, geography, history and letters of classical antiquity—all introduced to Jews through Renaissance humanism. These subjects, if not philosophy, still seemed to threaten Jewish traditional values, at least in Constantinople if not in Italy.[124]

The point is an important one; nevertheless, most of these pursuits did not have the potential to challenge Judaism in the manner of Aristotelian philosophy. The one which did was history, and the Italian Jew who utilized the discipline dangerously generated a brief but revealing cause célèbre.

In its most common mode, history was a humanistic endeavor no more dangerous than poetry or rhetoric, and some sixteenth- and seventeenth-century Jews in Italy and elsewhere utilized it to provide religious consolation, to place the Jewish

---

assertion that angered R. Asher b. Yeḥiel about the connection between knowledge of Arabic and the right to render a decision in Jewish law. The apologia for humanism is in Messer Leon's unpublished *Shevaḥ Nashim;* for a summary and analysis, see Tirosh-Rothschild, "In Defense of Jewish Humanism." On the biographies, see Arthur M. Lesley, "Hebrew Humanism in Italy: The Case of Biography," *Prooftexts* 2 (1982): 163–77. Da Modena was a multifaceted figure who continues to fascinate. See *The Autobiography of a Seventeenth-Century Venetian Rabbi: Leon Modena's The Life of Judah*, trans. and ed. by Mark R. Cohen (Princeton, 1988), and cf. Cohen's "Leone da Modena's *Riti*: A Seventeenth-Century Plea for Social Toleration of Jews," *Jewish Social Studies* 34 (1972): 287–321. On the persistence and growth of certain forms of acculturation, including use of the vernacular, in the Baroque period, see Robert Bonfil, "Change in the Cultural Patterns of a Jewish Society in Crisis: Italian Jewry at the Close of the Sixteenth Century," *Jewish History* 3 (1988): 11–30. For some observations on Italian Jewish familiarity with Christian philosophy and, more generally, on the relatively painless absorption by this Jewry of a multitude of diverse disciplines and approaches, see Yosef Sermoneta's review of Barzilay's *Between Reason and Faith* in *Kiryat Sefer* 45 (1970): 539–46.

Despite changes in orientation and advances in methodology, the material accumulated in Cecil Roth, *The Jews in the Renaissance* (Philadelphia, 1959), and Moses Shulvass, *The Jews in the Life of the Renaissance* (Leiden, 1973), retains its value and documents Jewish activity in fields like art, drama, music and printing, which I have been unable to treat in this survey. The most vigorous and influential argument for a new perspective is Bonfil's "The Historian's Perception of the Jews in the Italian Renaissance. Towards a Reappraisal," *Revue des Études Juives* 143 (1984): 59–82, which sees Italian Jewish acculturation as part of a competitive struggle affirming Jewish identity in the face of pressure rather than a reflection of an idyllic cultural symbiosis. See now Bonfil's synthetic treatment, *Jewish Life in Renaissance Italy* (Berkeley, Los Angeles, and London, 1994).

124. "In Defense of Jewish Humanism," 39.

experience in a broader context, to validate the tradition, to set the stage for the end of days, to ponder the causes of the Jewish condition, or simply to entertain. Some of these purposes had been pursued even in the Middle Ages by the few Jews who had engaged in the enterprise of setting down events that had, after all, already taken place and whose utility was consequently viewed with considerable skepticism. R. Sherira's epistle took the form of a standard responsum; *Josippon* provided a basic historical survey as well as implicit advice about appropriate Jewish behavior in the face of superior force; R. Abraham ibn Daud's *Book of Tradition* validated the tradition, defended the glories of Andalusian Jewry, and may have pointed esoterically to the date of the redemption; the crusade chronicles provided emotional release and religious inspiration in the wake of unspeakable tragedy.[125]

Whether or not the historical writings of sixteenth- and seventeenth-century Jews reflect a significant historiographical movement has recently become a disputed question. On the one hand, Jewish authors produced ten books of a roughly historical character in the course of about a century, a number that exceeds the entire output of the Middle Ages, and some of these are clearly indebted to the historiographic corpus that emerged in Renaissance society. On the other hand, a rigorous definition of *history* would exclude many, perhaps most, of these works, and even if they are all counted, they do not approach the number that one might reasonably expect in light of the proportion of Christian Renaissance works devoted to historiography.[126] In any event, despite the great interest of several of these books and despite their frequent debt to Christian models, they do not challenge Jewish tradition.

Except one. Azariah de' Rossi's *Me'or 'Einayim*, which is not a narrative history but a series of historical studies, utilized non-Jewish sources to test the validity of historical assertions in Rabbinic texts to the point of rejecting the accepted chronology of the Second Temple and modifying the Jewish calendar's assumptions about the date of creation. The author was clearly sensitive to the prospect of

125. See *Sefer Yosifon*, ed. by Flusser; ibn Daud's *Sefer Ha-Qabbalah*, ed. by Cohen; Shlomo Eidelberg, *The Jews and the Crusaders* (Madison, Wisconsin, 1977), and Robert Chazan, *European Jewry and the First Crusade* (Berkeley and Los Angeles, 1987), 223–97. On R. Sherira, see above, n. 19. For an example of medieval Jewish denigration of the value of history, see Maimonides' *Commentary to the Mishnah, Sanhedrin* 10:1 (almost immediately before the list of the thirteen principles of faith).

126. See Yosef Hayim Yerushalmi's *Zakhor: Jewish History and Jewish Memory* (Seattle and London, 1982), 55–75, and his "Clio and the Jews: Reflections on Jewish Historiography in the Sixteenth Century," *American Academy for Jewish Research Jubilee Volume* (*PAAJR* 46–47 [1979–80]): 607–38; Robert Bonfil, "How Golden Was the Age of the Renaissance in Jewish Historiography?" *History and Theory* 27 (1988): 78–102. Bonfil accounts for what he regards as the relative paucity of Jewish historical works on the grounds that diaspora Jews did not have the sort of political and military history that lent itself to the narrative style most characteristic of Renaissance historiography.

opposition, and he defended the study of history on the grounds of religious utility and the intrinsic value of the search for truth. There is, however, considerable irony in his argument for rejecting historical statements of the Rabbis in favor of gentile authorities. The Sages, he writes, were concerned with important matters; with respect to trivial concerns like history, we should expect to find a greater degree of reliability in the works of gentiles, who after all specialize in trivialities.[127] The difficulty of distinguishing the strands of sincerity and disingenuousness in this assertion speaks volumes for the problematic nature of de' Rossi's undertaking. He can justify his methodology only by minimizing the significance of his discipline.

Contemporary historians differ about the novelty of de' Rossi's challenge. Since the reinterpretation and even rejection of *aggadah* had respectable medieval precedent, Salo Baron and Robert Bonfil have argued that Azariah did little more than broaden the grounds for such a step to embrace historical as well as philosophical or kabbalistic considerations. Yosef Yerushalmi, on the other hand, sees a more radical and significant innovation in *Me'or 'Einayim*; philosophy and kabbalah, he argues, had long been regarded as sources of truth, while Azariah was willing to utilize "profane history . . . drawn from Greek, Roman and Christian writers" to judge the validity of rabbinic statements.[128] The distinction is important and the formulation can, I think, be sharpened. Philosophical truth was not based on the authority of Aristotle; it rested on arguments that Aristotle may have formulated but were now available to any thinker in an unmediated fashion. It was reason, not Aristotle, that required the reinterpretation of whatever Rabbinic text was at issue. History is different. Although reason is very much involved and the decision to follow a gentile account instead of a rabbinic one does not result from a simple preference for Tacitus over Rabbi Yosi, the fact remains that on some level one is accepting the testimony of gentiles rather than that of the Talmudic sages. This may be a legitimate extension of the medieval precedent, but it is hardly a straightforward one.

This point tells us something significant about Italian Jewry and not merely about de' Rossi. Bonfil has demonstrated convincingly that the Italian attack on *Meor 'Einayim* was much more limited in both its ideological scope and its degree of support than historians used to think. Since Bonfil himself does not see the work as radically innovative, he regards the relatively mild opposition as roughly the sort of reaction that we might have expected. Yerushalmi, writing before Bonfil's study, made the cautious observation that "it is perhaps a token of the flexibility of Italian Jewry that the ban upon the book, [which] only required that special permission be

127. *Sefer Me'or 'Einayim*, ed. by David Cassel (Vilna, 1866), 216.

128. See Baron, *History and Jewish Historians* (Philadelphia, 1964), 167–239, 405–42; Bonfil, "Some Reflections on the Place of Azariah de' Rossi's *Me'or 'Einayim* in the Cultural Milieu of Italian Renaissance Jewry," in *Jewish Thought in the Sixteenth Century*, 23–48, esp. pp. 23–25; Yerushalmi, "Clio and the Jews," 634–35, and *Zakhor*, 72.

obtained by those who wanted to read it, was not always enforced stringently." If we accept, as I think we should, both Yerushalmi's perception of the book and Bonfil's findings about the ban, the implications for Italian Jewry become more striking. A substantial majority of the rabbinic leadership accepted with equanimity a work which treated the historical statements of the ancient Sages with startling freedom. The contrast with the intense opposition to *Me'or 'Einayim* from R. Joseph Caro in Safed and R. Judah Loew (Maharal) in Prague highlights the openness of sixteenth-century Italian Jews to non-Jewish sources and the willingness to utilize them even in the most sensitive of contexts.[129]

The Scientific Revolution and the Transition to Modern Times

Apart from the humanistic pursuits that characterized the Renaissance, early modern Europe also witnessed an increasing interest in the natural world. Though the most significant manifestation of this interest was the Copernican revolution and its aftermath, scientifically oriented Jews in the sixteenth, seventeenth, and early eighteenth centuries evinced greater interest in new approaches to chemistry, medicine, zoology, botany, mineralogy, and geography. Hundreds of Jews graduated from the medical school in Padua. Various Jewish works demonstrate familiarity with Paracelsian chemical medicine and Cartesian mechanics, and they display an insatiable curiosity about wondrous beasts and other natural marvels widely reported in an age of exploration. We find a revival and elaboration of the medieval arguments for the Jewish origin of the sciences and their religious utility along with a recognition that the ancient philosophers had attained important religious truths unaided by Jewish instruction.[130]

129. See Yerushalmi, "Clio," 635; *Zakhor*, 72–73. On R. Joseph Karo, see the references in Segal, *Historical Consciousness*, 68, n. 51; on the Maharal, see Segal, 133–61. Another, perhaps fairer way to make the point would be to say that Italian Jewry agreed with Bonfil while the Maharal and R. Joseph Caro agreed with Yerushalmi, but this alone would fail to convey the significance of the Italian position. For a nuanced discussion of major features of de' Rossi's work, see now Bonfil's elaborate introduction to his anthology, *Kitvei 'Azariah min ha-Adummim: Mivḥar Peraqim mi-tokh Sefer Me'or 'Einayim ve-Sefer Maẓref la-Kesef* (Jerusalem, 1991).

130. See David B. Ruderman, *Science, Medicine, and Jewish Culture in Early Modern Europe. Spiegel Lectures in European Jewish History* 7 (Tel Aviv, 1987), and his overlapping article, "The Impact of Science on Jewish Culture and Society in Venice," in *Gli Ebrei e Venezia* (Milan, 1987), 417–48. See also his *Kabbalah, Magic, and Science: The Cultural Universe of a Sixteenth-Century Jewish Physician* (Cambridge, Mass., and London, 1988). In light of Abba Mari of Lunel's salute to Aristotle for achieving genuine monotheism in the absence of

Jewish enthusiasm for these new scientific pursuits was greatly facilitated by a critically important conceptual change. In the Middle Ages, the natural sciences were part of a larger tapestry whose dominant element was metaphysics. During the Renaissance and beyond, philosophy and certain kinds of science grew apart, and the scientific domain itself came to be divided between empiricist and rationalist-mathematical spheres. In this environment, certain scientific fields were uncontaminated by the philosophical baggage associated in some Jewish minds with Aristotelianism, and a Jew could remain a staunch opponent of rationalism in its medieval mode while retaining an intense interest in the new science.[131]

The Jewish absorption of the monumental revolution in astronomy was far more problematic. David Gans of late sixteenth-century Prague, though best known for his historical work *Ẓemaḥ David,* was the first influential Jew to confront Copernicanism, and his attitude to the new astronomy is characteristic of what was probably the dominant reaction by knowledgeable Jews through the early eighteenth century: interested awareness but ultimate rejection.[132] Although Yosef Shlomo Delmedigo, who studied with Galileo and ended his days in Prague, spoke very highly of Copernicus, two major compendia at the very end of our period still reject the heliocentric theory in sharp terms. Toviah Katz described Copernicus's position with some care and even presented a series of Copernican arguments; at the same time, he called him "the firstborn of Satan" and described the adherents of his view as heretics.[133] Similarly, David Nieto dismissed the Copernican conception as an

---

revelation, Ruderman's description of Abraham Yagel's "remarkable" assertion that pagan philosophers "discovered their faith independently of Jewish revelation" (p. 146) needs to be toned down a bit; see above, n. 76. For Jews at the medical school in Padua, see above, n. 115.

On the Jewish origins of the sciences, see, in addition to the references in n. 37 of Ruderman's lecture, the introduction to David Kaufmann's *Die Sinne,* and D. Margalit, "'Al Galenus ve-Gilgulo ha-'Ivri Gamliel," *Sinai* 33 (1953): 75–77. On geography, see L. Zunz, "Essay on the Geographical Literature of the Jews from the Remotest Times to the Year 1840," in *The Itinerary of R. Benjamin of Tudela,* trans. by A. Asher, 2 (London, 1841), 230–317; Ruderman, *The World of a Renaissance Jew: The Life and Thought of Abraham ben Mordecai Farissol* (Cincinnati, 1981), 131–43; André Neher, *Jewish Thought and the Scientific Revolution of the Sixteenth Century: David Gans (1541–1613) and His Times* (Oxford and New York, 1986), 95–165.

For a major synthesis and analysis of the entire subject, see now Ruderman's *Jewish Thought and Scientific Discovery in Early Modern Europe* (New Haven, 1995).

131. David Ruderman is largely responsible for sharpening my awareness of this point. On the division within the sciences, see Thomas S. Kuhn, "Mathematical vs. Experimental Traditions in the Development of Physical Science," *Journal of Interdisciplinary History* 7 (1976): 1–31. As I indicated above, it is important to note that for medieval Ashkenazic Jews, the link between empirical science and rationalist philosophy had never been made, and so their interest in the physical world was never encumbered by this complication.

132. See Neher, *Jewish Thought and the Scientific Revolution.*

133. *Ma'aseh Toviah* (Krakau, 1908), 43b–44b ("'Olam ha-Galgalim," ch. 4).

abomination.[134] By this time, the scientific defense of the Ptolemaic system had become very difficult, but Copernicus had still not carried the day among all intellectuals, let alone among the masses. Since most seventeenth- and early eighteenth-century European Jews, especially outside Italy, were relatively isolated from the burgeoning scientific community, and since they had rabbinic as well as biblical texts to inhibit their receptivity to the new astronomy, it is not surprising that they generally cast their lot with the rear guard action aimed against the Copernican revolution.

During the centuries in which modern Europe was being formed, the major Jewish cultural centers turned inward despite the growing Jewish involvement in national and international commerce. In a recent revisionist work, Jonathan Israel has argued that the period from 1550 to 1713, and particularly from 1650 to 1713, saw "the most profound and pervasive impact on the west which [the Jews] were ever to exert while retaining a large measure of social and cultural cohesion." To the extent that he applies this observation to economics and politics, including the ascendancy of Court Jews in Central Europe and elsewhere and the rough synchronism of Ashkenazi and Sephardi influence on finance and trade, he provides an important new perspective on early modern Jewry. On the other hand, he underestimates and misconceives much of medieval Jewish culture and considerably overrates the achievements of early modern Jews when he writes that "the radical transformation of Jewish culture which occurred during the middle decades of the sixteenth century was, assuredly, one of the most fundamental and remarkable

---

Ruderman (*Science, Medicine, and Jewish Culture*, 21) notes correctly that the chapter ends "limply," without any refutation of the Copernican arguments noted. Nonetheless, the conclusion is slightly more forceful than he indicates. Toviah does not assert that the unspecified counterarguments "are easily confusing [even] to one who understands them"; he says that their validity is easily evident to such a person (*benaqel nekhoḥot*, not *nevukhot*). Moreover, the previous chapter sets forth six standard arguments against the Copernican theory.

On Delmedigo, see Isaac Barzilay, *Yosef Shlomo Delmedigo, Yashar of Candia: His Life, Works, and Times* (Leiden, 1974), and Yosef Levi, "Aqademiah Yehudit le-Madda'im be-Reshit ha-Me'ah ha-Sheva-'Esreh: Nisyono shel Yosef Shlomoh Delmedigo," *Proceedings of the Eleventh World Congress of Jewish Studies*, Division B, vol. 1, Hebrew section, 169–76.

134. This translation may be a trifle too strong for *piggul*, but Neher's effort to soften Nieto's anti-Copernicanism by taking "piggul hu lo yeraẓeh" in the narrow legalistic sense determined by the phrase's biblical context ("a sacrifice which would not be acceptable in the Temple") is an apologetic distortion of a very strong expression; see *Jewish Thought and the Scientific Revolution*, 256. On Delmedigo, Katz, Nieto, and others, see Hillel Levine, "Paradise Not Surrendered: Jewish Reactions to Copernicus and the Growth of Modern Science," in *Epistemology, Methodology, and the Social Sciences*, ed. by Robert S. Cohen and Mark W. Wartofsky (Dordrecht, Boston, and London, 1983), 203–25.

phenomena distinguishing post-Temple Jewish history" and then extends his enthusiastic evaluation into the following century as well.[135]

As we have seen, Italian Jewish culture was indeed marked by an impressive synthesis of Jewish pride and openness to the surrounding culture. In the new Jewish community of seventeenth-century Holland, Sephardic Jews, including some with a Marrano past that made them fully conversant with Christian civilization, contributed philosophical, polemical, and scientific works that utilized wide learning and, when written or available in the vernacular, sometimes influenced European intellectuals. It was not only in Italy that Christian Hebraists held discussions with Jews about scholarly and religious issues. Court Jews were necessarily conversant with the surrounding culture while remaining, at least in many cases, loyal members of the Jewish community.[136]

At the same time, the major seventeenth-century Jewish centers outside Italy were either in a state of cultural decline or evinced relatively little concern with intellectual trends in the surrounding society. Jewry under Islam confronted a Muslim world that was itself culturally stagnant and consequently failed to provide the stimulus that Jewish thinkers needed for creative engagement with disciplines outside of Torah. Theoretically, this Jewry continued to value the sort of intellectual described in an early seventeenth-century chronicle from Fez as

> a complete scholar thoroughly familiar with all the sciences: the science of speculation (*'iyyun*) to an infinite degree, the science of grammar, the science of philosophy, the science of metrical poetry. There was no one like him among all the scholars of Israel. . . . If anyone had an uncertainty regarding a passage in *Tosafot* or the work of R. Elijah Mizraḥi or the Talmud, he would come to this scholar and would not leave until those uncertainties would be fully resolved.[137]

Nevertheless, such scholarship, at least with respect to philosophy, meant mastery of an existing corpus rather than the production of original, creative work.

Ashkenazic Jewry had always felt more of an adversarial relationship with the surrounding society, and even the examples of cultural interaction that we examined

135. Jonathan I. Israel, *European Jewry in the Age of Mercantilism, 1550–1750*, 2nd ed. (Oxford, 1989). The quotations are from pp. 1 and 70.

136. Israel, *European Jewry*, 70–86, 142–44, 216–31. On the former Marranos, see Yosef Kaplan, "The Portuguese Community of Amsterdam in the Seventeenth Century between Tradition and Change," in *Society and Community*, ed. by Abraham Hain (Jerusalem, 1991), 141–71, and Kaplan, "Die Potugiesischen Juden und die Modernisierung: zur Veränderung jüdischen Lebens vor der Emanzipation," in *Jüdische Lebenswelten: Essays*, ed. by Andreas Nachama, et al. (Frankfurt a.M., 1991), 303–17.

137. *Divrei ha-Yamim*, in *Fez va-Ḥakhameha*, ed. by David Ovadia, 1 (Jerusalem, 1979), 47–48. Cf. Elazar Touitou, *Rabbi Ḥayyim Ibn 'Attar u-Perusho Or ha-Ḥayyim 'al ha-Torah* (Jerusalem, 1981), 28.

earlier were often characterized by an element of reserve or competition. With the removal of the Ashkenazic center to the alien environment of Poland, the sense of existential separateness was reinforced, and Jacob Katz has noted that even the martyrdoms in seventeenth-century Poland differ from those of the Crusades as defiant confrontation gave way to a sense of isolation from a hostile environment.[138] Although sixteenth-century Poland was not unaffected by the intellectual currents inspired by humanism and the Reformation, the rationalism that found lukewarm expression in R. Moses Isserles and some of his contemporaries essentially came from a culture outside the immediate environment. As Poland became a cultural backwater in seventeenth- and eighteenth-century Europe, this mild philosophical interest found no reinforcement either in the surrounding society or the indigenous Ashkenazic tradition, and without such reinforcement it largely faded away.

Even in seventeenth-century Germany, which was closer to the center of European creativity, there was insufficient impetus for Ashkenazic Jews to overcome the cultural legacy of their formative period without substantial struggle and considerable delay. In many cases, the communities were being reconstituted in the wake of expulsions and persecutions. The gradual opening of Christian society to some Jews began to undermine the observance of Jewish individuals rather than inspire an intellectual transformation and Renaissance.

Profound differences separated the medieval Iberian experience of a culturally stimulating environment from the situation of early modern Ashkenazim. First, the Jews of Northern Europe came to modernity with a deeply entrenched, fully formed approach that was highly suspicious of external wisdom. Second, the challenges of modern science and philosophical skepticism could not be faced in the kind of partnership with the dominant society that medieval Jews had enjoyed. It is true that Christianity had to face these challenges quite as much as Judaism, but the challenges emanated from Christian society itself, not from a philosophy inherited from classical antiquity. Thus, the search for intellectual allies was severely complicated. Traditional Christians were for the most part heirs to a fully developed, millennial legacy of contempt for Judaism; seventeenth-century skeptics and eighteenth-century *philosophes* regarded Judaism with at least as much disdain as they felt for Christianity and were in any event the authors of the very challenge that had to be faced. When medieval philosophers were called heretics, they usually denied the charge; the moderns often embraced it, indeed, shouted it from the rooftops. The pursuit of speculative thought became associated with irreligion to a far more profound and extensive degree than it had in the Middle Ages.

Moreover, the nature of modern philosophy was so different from that of the medieval past that the religious attractiveness of the discipline was severely under-

138. Katz, *Exclusiveness and Tolerance* (Oxford, 1961), 131–55, and "Bein Tatnu LeTaḥ-Tat," *Sefer Yovel le-Yitzhak Baer*, ed. by S. Ettinger, et al. (Jerusalem, 1961), 318–37.

mined. To the medievals, if philosophy posed serious challenges to religious faith, it also provided indispensable insights into the nature of God. Modern philosophy seemed to supply little more than the problems. At best, religious philosophers could refute attacks against the faith, but they would probably not emerge with new insights about the issues that they were accustomed to regard as the classic subject matter of philosophy. They would find little but heresy on divine providence, hardly anything on attributes or incorporeality, and nothing at all about the recently deceased active intellect and celestial spheres. If all philosophy could achieve was the neutralizing of its own evil influence, then ignoring the enterprise could achieve the same result at a great saving of time and effort, not to speak of averting danger to one's faith. The imperative of answering the heretic was rarely sufficient in itself to inspire philosophical study. In addition to these critical considerations, the religious value of philosophical inquiry was radically diminished by the conviction of many traditional Jews at the dawn of the Enlightenment that the crucial information about God was available through kabbalah.

For the sake of sharpening the analysis, I have intentionally formulated these points with one-dimensional vigor. If modern philosophy did not provide solutions to medieval questions about God and creation, it might nevertheless suggest new areas of fruitful inquiry. The medieval argument that studying the world inspires love of God seemed all the more persuasive to believers beholding the mathematically elegant universe of the new science. We cannot, however, expect the rabbinic leadership of Ashkenazic Jewry to have known the evolving new approaches well enough to have formulated an innovative positive response; indeed, in the early stages they did not know them well enough even to have fully appreciated the new dangers.

Thus, when we do find an interest in philosophical inquiry among the rabbis of early modern Ashkenaz, it tends to take a very traditional form. R. Yair Ḥayyim Bacharach, for example, laid great emphasis on the practical primacy of talmudic study and the theoretical primacy of kabbalah, while demonstrating considerable familiarity with Jewish philosophical literature. In a study of Bacharach, Isadore Twersky observes that "philosophic literature was studied for religious reasons, as part of a spiritual quest, totally separate from external contacts and influences." R. Jacob Emden reports in his autobiography that his father Ḥakham Ẓevi Ashkenazi read secular works "in his spare time" and studied "other knowledge" with the scholars who attended the *klaus* that he headed in late seventeenth-century Hamburg "until they achieved perfection in Torah and wisdom"; here too we are undoubtedly dealing with something other than a fresh and creative confrontation with the world of modern wisdom.[139]

139. On Bacharach, see I. Twersky, "Law and Spirituality in the Seventeenth Century: A Case Study in R. Yair Ḥayyim Bacharach," in *Jewish Thought in the Seventeenth Century*, 447–67 (quotation from p. 455). On Ḥakham Ẓevi, see Emden's *Megillat Sefer*, ed. by D.

By the mid-eighteenth century, Emden's own ambivalent attitude to the study of the "external" disciplines reflects the growing impact of the European opening to the Jews. His essential position is quite negative; at the same time, he speaks of a yearning for the sciences which he fulfilled in part by reading Hebrew books in fields like history and geography and in part by studying the works of non-Jews in the bathroom. His familiarity with the New Testament is striking, and it comes together with a relatively favorable attitude to Jesus and even to Paul. What is most interesting is a recurring justification for secular study that does not appear in premodern times. Jews, says Emden, must achieve some familiarity with gentile language and culture for the sake of mingling comfortably with people. This is a striking reflection of a changed social atmosphere with far-reaching importance for the integration of Jews into European society.[140]

Outside of rabbinic circles, incipient social integration in a world of growing religious skepticism gradually eroded the loyalties of some Ashkenazic Jews. Beginning around the end of the seventeenth century, substantial numbers of Jews began to drift away from accepted religious norms and a smaller number may even have rejected traditional beliefs under the influence of Enlightenment thought. The official community, however, did not begin to change until the second half of the eighteenth century, when leaders of the Jewish Enlightenment began to demand curricular reform and social accommodation.[141]

Despite the fact that these demands were often made in the name of the well-attested rationalist tradition that we have examined throughout this study, the timing, the context, and the orientation of the new movement made it a threat to the established order both politically and religiously. European Jewry, like European Christendom, faced a world in which religion itself could no longer be taken for granted. In the new, largely secular order that established itself in the eighteenth century and continues to our own day, the legitimacy of general culture remained an issue only for the traditionalist segment of the Jewish people, and the terms of the debate were narrowed and transformed. For some, the overwhelming new dangers

---

Kahana (Warsaw, 1897), 11, 16–17, cited in Jacob J. Schacter, *Rabbi Jacob Emden: Life and Major Works* (Harvard University dissertation, 1988), 587–88.

140. See chapter 6 of Schacter's dissertation for a discussion of Emden's general stance, and see especially p. 505, where he notes the novelty of the argument from social interaction.

141. On the timing and extent of these transformations, see the debate between Azriel Schochet, *'Im Ḥillufei Tequfot* (Jerusalem, 1960), and Jacob Katz, *Out of the Ghetto* (Cambridge, 1973). Cf. Schochet's "Reshit ha-Haskalah ba-Yahadut be-Germania," *Molad* 23 (1965): 328–34. See also Israel, who argues very strongly that there was widespread abandonment of tradition, including outright conversion (*European Jewry*, 254–56). On apostasy in the wake of Sabbatianism, see Elisheva Carlebach, "Sabbatianism and the Jewish-Christian Polemic," *Proceedings of the Tenth World Congress of Jewish Studies*, Division C, 2 (1990): 6–7. For a relevant analysis that focuses primarily on a later period, see David Sorkin, *The Transformation of German Jewry, 1780–1840* (New York, 1987).

required an ever more stringent isolation from the evils of modernity. For others, these dangers could be tamed by selective admission of the religiously neutral elements of the new society and culture. For a few, the Torah itself required a heroic confrontation with modernity in all its fullness, a confrontation that would enrich both Judaism and the world.

Acknowledgments

This essay was written when I was a fellow at the Annenberg Research Institute during the academic year 1989–1990. It is a pleasure to thank the staff of the institute and of its library for their courtesy and professionalism. It is a particular pleasure to thank Professor Daniel J. Lasker, who occupied the office next to mine and served as an unfailing source of sound advice and refreshing good humor. I no doubt invaded the offices of two additional fellows of the institute far too frequently, but Professors Anita Shapira and William C. Jordan provided such intellectual stimulation that any expression of regret that I might offer for those interruptions would be insincere. Please forgive me, but I confess that I would do it again.

Outside the institute, Professors Menahem Ben Sasson and David Ruderman read the entire manuscript and provided illuminating, significant suggestions, many of which I had the good sense to incorporate. I am very grateful to Dr. Jacob J. Schacter for his meticulous editorial supervision, which was often substantive as well as technical. After my return from Annenberg, I benefited from the welcoming atmosphere, extraordinary resources, and knowledgeable staff at the Mendel Gottesman Library of Yeshiva University in preparing the final version of the study. While I have added references to more recent scholarship and included many observations reflecting subsequent research, the 1990 text remains at the core of this work.

Finally, my wife Pearl as well as Miriam, Elie, Yitzhak, and Gedalyah not only endured my weekly absences during preparations for the marriage which brought Elie into the family, but, together with Ditza and Miriam, who have joined us more recently, provided love, encouragement, and the inspiration that comes from their own embodiment of Torah and the best of general culture.

3

Rabbinic Openness to General Culture in the Early Modern Period in Western and Central Europe

Shnayer Z. Leiman

Contents

INTRODUCTION

In a very profound sense, the debate between *Torah only* and *Torah and derekh ereẓ* enthusiasts is a misplaced one.[1] The extreme positions are imaginary constructs that no serious Torah scholar embraces. That is, no serious Torah scholar would deny the value of *derekh ereẓ,* whether defined minimally as "gainful employment," or maximally so as to include in its purview secular wisdom and all aspects of general culture that enhance one's understanding and appreciation of God's creation: *the earth in its fullness, the world and its inhabitants* (Psalms 24:1).[2] He could do so only at the risk of undermining Torah itself. On the other hand, no serious Torah scholar who embraced *Torah and derekh ereẓ* ever denied the centrality of Torah, or imagined that *Torah* and *derekh ereẓ* were axiologically separate but equal realms.

Certainly, in the last three hundred years, the preeminent exemplar of *Torah only* was the Gaon of Vilna (d. 1797). The Gaon did not merely refuse to earn a living; he refused to be gainfully employed either as a rabbi or rosh yeshiva. Instead, he devoted a lifetime to the diligent study of Torah for some twenty hours per day. Regarding his daily regimen, his sons reported as follows:

---

1. The binary terminology used here was introduced by R. Shimon Schwab, *These and Those* (New York, 1967), 7.

2. *Derekh Ereẓ* in rabbinic parlance bears a variety of meanings, but never "secular study" or "general culture." See, e.g., the entry *derekh ereẓ* in *Enẓyklopedyah Talmudit* (Jerusalem, 1956), VII, 672–706. The plain sense of the term at its *locus classicus,* M. Avot 2:2: *"yafeh talmud torah 'im derekh ereẓ"* appears to be "worldly occupation" or "gainful employment." See, for example, R. David Ẓ. Hoffmann's German translation of, and commentary to, M. Avot 2:2 in *Mischnaiot*[2] (Berlin, 1924), 332. The broadening of the term *derekh ereẓ* in that context to include secular study, and even more broadly to include general culture, while rooted in medieval commentary, is a modern phenomenon. For the medieval roots, see R. David b. Abraham Maimuni, *Midrash David,* commentary to M. Avot 2:2 (Jerusalem, 1991), 26. For pre-Hirschian broadening of the term in the modern period, see R. Yishmael ha-Kohen (d. 1811), *She'elot u-Teshuvot Zera' Emet* (Livorno, 1796), II, 119a, §107. Cf. the usage by R. Samuel Landau (d. 1834) in a passage from 1816, see n. 40.

Throughout his lifetime, he never slept more than two hours in any twenty-four hour period. He never slept for more than a half-hour at a time, and during that half-hour his lips recited *halakhot* and *aggadot* in a whisper. When the half-hour elapsed, he gathered strength like a lion, ritually cleansed his hands, and began learning in a loud voice, after which he went back to sleep for a half-hour. It was his practice to sleep three half-hours in the evening and one half-hour during the day.[3]

His singular devotion to Torah knew no bounds. Again, the testimony of his sons—who sometimes received the short end of his singlemindedness—is impeccable.

He never inquired of his sons and daughters regarding their occupation or economic well-being. He never sent them a letter inquiring about their well-being. When any of his children came to visit him, even though he rejoiced greatly, for often they had not seen him for a year or two, he never inquired about the well-being of their family or regarding their occupation. After allowing his son to rest for an hour, he would urge him to return immediately to his studies, saying: "You must make amends in my house for the study time forfeited during your journey here."[4]

It is difficult to imagine what else one could do in order to surpass the Gaon as a *Torah only* enthusiast. Nevertheless, the Gaon's attitude toward secular wisdom was hardly rejectionist, as evidenced by the following passages:

R. Barukh Schick of Shklov (d. 1808):

When I visited Vilna in Tevet 5538 [1778] . . . I heard from the holy lips of the Gaon of Vilna that to the extent one is deficient in secular wisdom he will be deficient a hundredfold in Torah study, for Torah and wisdom are bound up together. He compared a person lacking in secular wisdom to a man suffering from constipation; his disposition is affected to the point that he refuses all food. . . . He urged me to translate into Hebrew as much secular wisdom as possible, so as to cause the nations to disgorge what they have swallowed, making it available to all, thereby increasing knowledge among the Jews. Thus, the nations will no longer be able to lord it over us—and bring about the profaning of God's name—with their taunt: "Where is your wisdom?"[5]

3. Introduction to *Be'ur ha-Gra, Shulḥan 'Arukh, Oraḥ Ḥayyim.*
4. Introduction to *Be'ur ha-Gra.*
5. *Sefer Uklidos* (The Hague, 1780), introduction. It is unclear whether the justification given at the end of the passage cited here is to be ascribed to the Gaon of Vilna or to Schick. See David E. Fishman, "A Polish Rabbi Meets the Berlin Haskalah: The Case of R. Barukh Schick," *AJS Review* 12 (1987): 95–121, especially pp. 115–19, who argues persuasively that it is to be ascribed to Schick.

R. Abraham Simḥah of Amtchislav (d. 1864):

I heard from my uncle R. Ḥayyim of Volozhin that the Gaon of Vilna told his son R. Abraham that he craved for translations of secular wisdom into Hebrew, including a translation of the Greek or Latin Josephus,[6] through which he could fathom the plain sense of various rabbinic passages in the Talmud and Midrash.[7]

The Gaon of Vilna's sons:

By the time the Gaon of Vilna was twelve years old, he mastered the seven branches of secular wisdom. . . . [8] First he turned to mathematics . . . then astronomy.[9]

R. Israel of Shklov (d. 1839):

I cannot refrain from repeating a true and astonishing story that I heard from the Gaon's disciple R. Menaḥem Mendel. . . . [10] It took place when the Gaon of Vilna celebrated the completion of his commentary on Song of Songs. . . . He raised his eyes toward

6. Josephus was known to medieval Jewry via a garbled Hebrew version, which was thought to be the original Hebrew version addressed to the Jews, called *Yosippon.* Modern scholarship has established that this Hebrew version originated in the tenth century; see, e.g., David L. Flusser, ed., *Sefer Yosippon* (Jerusalem, 1980), II, 3–252. This was distinguished by the Gaon and others from the original Greek text of Josephus (first published edition: Basel, 1544), and its many Latin translations (first published edition: Augsburg, 1470), addressed to the Romans, which were referred to as *Yosippon la-Romiyyim.* Obviously, the Gaon would have preferred a Hebrew rendering of the original Greek, but one suspects that this call for a translation was addressed to eighteenth century Jews adept in Latin.

7. Letter dated 1862 appended to Kalman Schulman's translation of Josephus' *The Jewish War, Milḥamot ha-Yehudim 'im ha-Roma'im* (Warsaw, 1862), II, v–vi.

8. The term *seven branches of wisdom* (Hebrew *sheva ha-ḥokhmot*) was unknown to classical Jewish literature prior to the medieval period, when it was often read into Proverbs 9:1. The concept, which seems to have originated with Varro (ca. 116–27 B.C.E.), culminated with the seven branches of learning of medieval scholasticism: the trivium of grammar, logic, and rhetoric, and the quadrivium of arithmetic, geometry, astronomy, and music. For two interesting "Jewish" versions of the seven branches of wisdom, see R. Baḥya b. Asher (end of thirteenth century), commentary on M. Avot 3:18, in R. Charles Chavel, ed., *Kitvei Rabbenu Baḥya* (Jerusalem, 1970), 591; and R. Jonathan Eibeschuetz, *Ya'arot Devash*, ed. Makhon Yerushalayim (Jerusalem, 1984), II, 122–23. In general, see Dov Rappel, *Sheva ha-Ḥokhmot: ha-Vikuaḥ 'al Limmudei Ḥol be-Yahadut* (Jerusalem, 1990), 12–66.

9. Introduction to the Gaon of Vilna's commentary on the Torah, *Adderet Eliyahu,* ed. M. Shulsinger (New York, 1950), 6.

10. R. Menaḥem Mendel of Shklov (d. 1827) was instrumental in the renewal of the Ashkenazic community of Jerusalem during the first quarter of the nineteenth century.

> heaven and with great devotion began blessing and thanking God for endowing him with the ability to comprehend the light of the entire Torah. This included its inner and outer manifestations. He explained: All secular wisdom is essential for our holy Torah and is included in it. He indicated that he had mastered all the branches of secular wisdom, including algebra, trigonometry, geometry, and music. He especially praised music, explaining that most of the Torah accents, the secrets of the Levitical songs, and the secrets of the *Tikkunei Zohar* could not be comprehended without mastering it. . . . He explained the significance of the various secular disciplines, and noted that he had mastered them all. Regarding the discipline of medicine, he stated that he had mastered anatomy, but not pharmacology. Indeed, he had wanted to study pharmacology with practicing physicians, but his father prevented him from undertaking its study, fearing that upon mastering it he would be forced to curtail his Torah study whenever it would become necessary for him to save a life. . . . He also stated that he had mastered all of philosophy, but that he had derived only two matters of significance from his study of it. . . . The rest of it, he said, should be discarded.[11]

Even if one allows for a measure of exaggeration in these reports, in fact they were published by contemporaries of the Gaon (with the exception of the second report which, however, is reported in the name of a contemporary of the Gaon) who knew him personally. Moreover, the tradents themselves were men of integrity whose scholarly credentials were impeccable.[12] These, then, should hardly be treated as

11. *Pe'at ha-Shulḥan*, ed. Abraham M. Luncz (Jerusalem, 1911), 5a.

12. R. Bezalel Landau, *Ha-Gaon he-Ḥasid mi-Vilna*, third edition (Jerusalem, 1978), 217 and 225–26, n. 16, questions the authenticity of Schick's report, suggesting that Schick's Haskalah leanings led him either to invent the report in its entirety or, at the very least, to misconstrue whatever it was the Gaon had said. While it is certainly true that some Haskalah enthusiasts recreated the Gaon in their own image—see, e.g., E. Etkes, "The Gaon of Vilna and the Haskalah: Image and Reality," (Hebrew) in *Perakim be-Toledot ha-Ḥevrah ha-Yehudit bi-Yemei ha-Beynayyim u-ve-'Et ha-Ḥadashah* (Jersualem, 1980), 192–217—there is no evidence whatever that Schick engaged in such activity. For the extent of his Haskalah leanings—if they can be called such—see Fishman's study (cited above, n. 5). His integrity, to the best of my knowledge, has never been called into question. The fact remains that Schick, a Polish talmudist who served as *dayyan* in Minsk, published his report during the lifetime of the Gaon. Its content complements and is in harmony with all else that is known about the Gaon's attitude toward *ḥokhmah*. R. Abraham Simḥah of Amtchislav (see above, n. 7), a nephew and disciple of R. Ḥayyim of Volozhin, the Gaon's disciple, refers to Schick's report approvingly; so too the editors of the classic biography of the Gaon, *'Aliyot Eliyahu*, ed. Lewin-Epstein (Jerusalem, 1970), 45, n. 25. Landau's suspicion, at least in this case, appears to be unwarranted. The Gaon's positive attitude toward *ḥokhmah* was sufficiently well known during his lifetime, and immediately afterwards, that many in Eastern Europe assumed he was the author of an anonymous desk encyclopedia of general science and Jewish thought that appeared in Hebrew in Bruenn, 1797. The true author, R. Pinḥas Eliyahu Hurwitz, was forced to reveal his name in the second edition (Zolkiev, 1807) in order to set the matter straight. See R. Pinḥas E. Hurwitz, *Sefer ha-Berit* (New York, 1977), second introduction, 7b.

imaginary tales that were reduced to writing for the first time many generations after the events they purportedly describe. Clearly, the Gaon viewed secular wisdom positively and instrumentally, i.e., its value depended upon the light it could shed on Torah.

In recent years, the Gaon's positive view of secular wisdom appears to have received unexpected support from the publication of R. Hillel of Shklov's *ha-Tor.* R. Hillel (d. 1838) was a disciple of the Gaon who settled in Jerusalem in 1809. His *Kol ha-Tor,* an eschatological work based on the Gaon's teaching, remained in manuscript form until 1946, when several fascicles of the original appeared in print. Fuller versions were published between 1969 and 1994 in Bnei Brak and Jerusalem. R. Hillel cites, in the name of the Gaon of Vilna, an elaborate eschatology in which the spread of secular wisdom among Jews at the end of time plays a decisive role in bringing about the ultimate redemption of mankind.[13]

Conversely, R. Samson Raphael Hirsch (d. 1888) and R. Azriel Hildesheimer (d. 1899), the modern architects of *Torah and derekh ereẓ,* lived, breathed and taught the centrality of Torah. They repeatedly underscored their conviction that *derekh ereẓ* was subservient to Torah (more about which see below, *passim*). The issue, then, is not whether secular wisdom may (or even: ought to) be pursued, but rather: which secular disciplines, under what circumstances, and by whom. The Gaon of Vilna, for example, was not prepared to interrupt his daily regimen in order to master Greek or Latin and read Josephus in the original. But he felt quite comfortable in encouraging other Jews, whose obligation to study Torah—at least in theory—was no different than the Gaon's to translate Josephus into Hebrew.

The extreme positions aside, a spacious middle ground remains, embracing a broad spectrum of opinion—ranging from those who tolerated general culture only under the most circumscribed of conditions, to those who, for example, embraced secular study enthusiastically, and even incorporated it in the yeshiva curriculum.

There can be no question that the dominant position of East European *gedolei yisrael* in recent memory has been the open rejection of general culture. This, despite—and sometimes due to —the advent of modernity and the opportunities and benefits it has provided for the Jewish community at large. The Ḥatam Sofer, R. Yosef Baer Soloveitchik (author of *Bet ha-Levi*), the Ḥafeẓ Ḥayyim, R. Elḥanan Wasserman, the Ḥazon Ish, R. Aharon Kotler—and virtually every Ḥasidic Rebbe of note—are among the many Torah giants who shared this view.

Orthodox teaching, however, has never been in the habit of speaking in only one voice. Diverse figures such as Rabbis Samson Raphael Hirsch, Ẓadok ha-Kohen of

---

13. See *Kol ha-Tor* (Bnei Brak 1969); R. Menaḥem M. Kasher, *Ha-Tekufah ha-Gedolah* (Jerusalem, 1972), 409–575; and the recent, fuller, annotated version of *Kol ha-Tor* (Jerusalem, 1994), esp. pp. 115–126. Much mystery, however, surrounds the publication of *Kol ha-Tor.* The original manuscript has not been made available to the public. Thus, it is unknown how much of the original manuscript was published; how much of it was actually written by R. Hillel of Shklov; and whether or not the quotes in the name of the Gaon of Vilna were actually said by him.

Lublin, Israel Salanter, Abraham Isaac ha-Kohen Kook, and Joseph B. Soloveitchik reflect the incredible richness, depth, and latitude of Orthodox thought in the modern period. Alongside the dominant position of rejection of general culture, there were other *gedolei yisrael*—some sat on the *mo'ezet gedolei ha-Torah* of Agudat Yisrael, others would occasionally join together on broadsides with members of the rabbinic court of the *'edah ha-ḥaredit*—who embraced general culture. Some did so enthusiastically; others reluctantly. Some were natives of Central and Western Europe; others of Eastern Europe. Some thought it esential that the yeshiva curriculum address and incorporate aspects of general culture; others thought it proper for certain individuals to embrace general culture, but not institutions (i.e., yeshivot).

The aim of this essay is to present, if only in outline form, a representative account of *gedolei yisrael* in the early modern period (i.e., the nineteenth century) who sought to relate Torah teaching to general culture. Our focus will be primarily, if not exclusively, on their differing viewpoints vis-à-vis general culture, on the institutions they engendered, and on their impact on the Jewish community at large. This essay does not purport to be an exercise in either history or biography; nor does it make any claim toward comprehensiveness. Rather, it is an attempt to engage in intellectual prosopography, i.e., to present a portrait of one aspect—albeit a crucial one—of the attitudes of a select group of *gedolei yisrael* who confronted modernity with an openness to general culture. Any attempt to portray all *gedolei yisrael* in the modern period who, in one form or another, reacted positively to general culture would have resulted in a lengthy monograph, at the very least. Such a volume would surely have tested the patience of most readers, and—in any event—would have moved well beyond my ability.

No hidden agenda need be sought in the presentation. It is intended to be largely descriptive and, hopefully, accurate. Wherever possible, the positions of the *gedolei yisrael* will be presented in their own words.

One final word. Feelings run high about some of these figures and their respective positions on Torah and general culture. In the heat of argument, their positions have often been misconstrued and misrepresented. It will be no small accomplishment if their views are set out dispassionately and accurately. To the extent that there is an agenda in this presentation, it is a transparent one: to demonstrate that the positions described in this essay are real, not imaginary. They are legitimate alternatives within Orthodoxy, to be accepted, rejected, but not ignored by those genuinely committed to traditional Jewish teaching.

Setting

Rabbinic responses to general culture do not occur in a vacuum. Since our focus is on the modern period, it is essential that we develop a sense of what distinguishes the modern from the premodern periods.[14] After a survey of some of the more important distinctions, we will turn our attention to an historical episode (involving R. David Friesenhausen) that vividly illustrates the tensions that pervaded Orthodoxy during its transition from the premodern to the modern periods. Finally, a brief account of the state of Torah education in Western and Central Europe at the start of the nineteenth century will enable us to view in proper perspective the contributions of the *gedolei yisrael* who followed.

From Premodernity to Modernity

Writing in the seventeenth century, R. Nathan Hanover presented the following idealized portrait of Torah study in Poland:

> Matters that are well known need no proof, for throughout the dispersions of Israel there was nowhere so much learning as in the land of Poland. Each community maintained yeshivot, and the head of each yeshiva was given an ample salary so that he could maintain his school without worry, and that the study of the Torah might be his sole occupation. The head of the yeshiva did not leave his house the whole year except to go from the house of study to the synagogue. Thus he was engaged in the study of the Torah day and night. Each community maintained young men and provided for them a weekly allowance of money that they might study with the head of the yeshiva. And for each young man they also maintained two boys to study under his guidance, so that he would orally discuss the Gemara, the commentaries of Rashi, and the Tosafot, which he had learned, and thus he would gain experience in the subtlety of talmudic argumentation. The boys were provided with food from the community benevolent fund or from the public kitchen. If the community consisted of fifty householders it supported not less than thirty young men and boys. One young man and two boys would be assigned to one householder. And the young man ate at his table as one of his sons. Although the young

14. In preparing this discussion of the setting of the Jewish transition from the premodern to the modern periods, I have learned much from: Robert Chazan and Marc L. Raphael, eds., *Modern Jewish History: A Source Reader* (New York, 1969); Michael A. Meyer, *The Origin of the Modern Jew* (Detroit, 1967); Jacob Katz, *Out of the Ghetto* (New York, 1978); idem, ed., *Toward Modernity: The European Jewish Model* (New Brunswick, 1987); and Paul R. Mendes-Flohr and Jehuda Reinharz, eds., *The Jew in the Modern World: A Documentary History* (New York, 1980). See also Jehuda Reinharz and Walter Schatzberg, eds., *The Jewish Response to German Culture* (Hanover, 1985); David Sorkin, *The Transformation of German Jewry, 1780–1840* (New York, 1987); Frances Malino and David Sorkin, *From East and West: Jews in a Changing Europe, 1750–1870* (Oxford, 1991); and Steven Lowenstein, *The Berlin Jewish Community: Enlightenment, Family, and Crisis, 1770–1830* (New York, 1994). Important studies of the state of Jewish society just prior to the onset of modernity include: Azriel Shochet, *'Im Ḥillufei Tekufot* (Jerusalem, 1960); and Jacob Katz, *Tradition and Crisis; Jewish Society at the End of the Middle Ages* (New York, 1961).

man received a stipend from the community, the householder provided him with all the food and drink that he needed. Some of the more charitable householders also allowed the boys to eat at their table, thus three persons would be provided with food and drink by one householder the entire year.

There was scarcely a house in all of Poland where its members did not occupy themselves with the study of the Torah. Either the head of the family was himself a scholar, or else his son or his son-in-law studied, or one of the young men eating at his table. At times, all of these were to be found in one house. Thus they realized all the three things which Raba said:[15] "He who loves the rabbis will have sons who are rabbis; he who honors the rabbis will have rabbis for sons-in-law; he who stands in awe of the rabbis will himself be a rabbinic scholar." Thus there were many scholars in every community. A community of fifty householders had twenty scholars who achieved the title *morenu* or *ḥaver*. The head of the yeshiva was above all these, and the scholars were submissive to him and they would go to his yeshiva to attend his discourses.

The program of study in the land of Poland was as follows: The term of study consisted of the period which required the young men and the boys to study with the head of the yeshiva. In the summer it extended from the first day of the month of Iyar until the fifteenth day of the month of Ab, and, in the winter, from the first day of the month of Ḥeshvan until the fifteenth day of the month of Shevat. After the fifteenth of Shevat or the fifteenth of Ab, the young men and the boys were free to study wherever they preferred. From the first day of Iyar until the Feast of Weeks, and in the winter from the first day of Ḥeshvan until Ḥanukkah, all the students of the yeshiva studied Gemara, the commentaries of Rashi and Tosafot with great diligence. Each day they studied a *halakhah*—one page of Gemara with the commentaries of Rashi and Tosafot is called a *halakhah*.

All the scholars and the young students of the community as well as all those who showed inclination to study the Torah assembled in the yeshiva. The head of the yeshiva alone occupied a chair and the scholars and the other students stood about him. Before the head of the yeshiva appeared they would engage in a discussion of the *halakhah*, and when he arrived each one would ask him that which he found difficult in the *halakhah* and he would offer his explanation to each of them.

They were all silent, as the head of the yeshiva delivered his lecture and presented the new results of his study. After discussing his new interpretations the head of the yeshiva would discuss a *ḥilluk* (a distinction that explains away an apparent contradiction), which proceeded in the following manner: He would cite a contradiction that emerged from the Gemara, Rashi or Tosafot; he would question deletions or superfluous words and pose contradictory statements and provide solutions which would also prove perplexing; and then he would propose solutions until the *halakhah* was completely clarified.

In the summer they would not leave the yeshiva before noon. From the Feast of Weeks until the New Year, and from Ḥanukkah until Passover, the head of the yeshiva would not engage in so many discussions. He would study with the scholars the Codes such as the *Arba'ah Turim* (the Four Rows) and their commentaries. With young men he would study Rav Alfas and other works. In any case, they also studied Gemara, Rashi, and Tosafot, until the first day of Ab or the fifteenth day of Shevat. From then on until Passover or the New Year they studied the Codes and similar works only. Some weeks prior to the

15. *Shabbat* 23b.

fifteenth day of Ab or the fifteenth day of Shevat, the head of the yeshiva would honor each student to lead in the discussions in his stead. The honor was given both to the scholars and the students. They would present the discussion, and the head of the yeshiva would listen and then join in the disputation. This was done to exercise their intellect. The same tractate was studied throughout the land of Poland in the proper sequence of the Six Orders.

Each head of a yeshiva had a truant officer who daily went from primary school to primary school to look after the boys, both rich and poor, that they should study. He would warn them every day of the week that they should study and not loiter in the streets. On Thursdays all the boys had to be examined by the principal of the primary schools on what they had learned during the week, and he who knew nothing of what he had studied or erred in one thing was flogged by the truant officer at the command of the principal and was otherwise also chastised before the boys so that he should remember to study more diligently the following week. Likewise on Sabbath Eve all the boys went in a group to the head of the yeshiva to be questioned on what they had learned during the week, as in the aforementioned procedure. In this manner there was fear upon the boys and they studied with regularity. Also during the *sheloshet yemei hagbalah* (the three days preceding the Feast of Weeks) and during Ḥanukkah, the young men and the boys were obliged to review what they had studied during that term, and for this the community leaders gave specified gifts of money. Such was the practice until the fifteenth of Ab or the fifteenth of Shevat. After that the head of the yeshiva, together with all his students, the young men and the boys, journeyed to the fair. In the summer they travelled to the fair of Zaslaw and to the fair of Jaroslaw, in the winter to the fairs of Lwow and Lublin. There the young men and boys were free to study in any yeshiva they preferred. Thus at each of the fairs hundreds of yeshiva heads, thousands of young men, and tens of thousands of boys, and Jewish merchants, and Gentiles like the sand on the shore of the sea, would gather. For people would come to the fair from one end of the world to the other. Whoever had a son or daughter of marriageable age went to the fair and there arranged a match. For there was ample opportunity for everyone to find his like and his mate. Thus hundreds and sometimes thousands of such matches would be arranged at each fair. And Jews, both men and women, walked about the fair, dressed in royal garments. For they were held in esteem in the eyes of the rulers and in the eyes of the Gentiles, and the children of Israel were many like the sand of the sea, but now because of our sins, they have become few. May the Lord have mercy upon them.

In each community great honor was accorded to the head of the yeshiva. His words were heard by rich and poor alike. None questioned his authority. Without him no one raised his hand or foot, and as he commanded so it came to be. In his hand he carried a stick, and a lash, to smite and to flog, to punish and to chastise transgressors, to institute ordinances, to establish safeguards, and to declare the forbidden. Nevertheless everyone loved the head of the yeshiva, and he that had a good portion such as fatted fowl, or capons or good fish, would honor the head of the yeshiva with half or all, and with other gifts of silver and gold without measure. In the synagogue, too, most of those who brought honors would accord them to the head of the yeshiva. It was obligatory to call him to the Torah reading third, on the Sabbath and the first days of the Festivals. And if the head of the yeshiva happened to be a Kohen or a Levite, he would be given preference despite the fact that there may have been others entitled to the honor of Kohen or Levi, or the concluding portion. No one left the synagogue on the Sabbath or the Festival until the head of the yeshiva walked out first and his pupils after him, and then the whole congregation accompanied him to his home. On the Festivals the entire congregation followed him to his house to greet him. For this reason all the scholars were envious and studied with diligence, so that they too, might advance to this state, and become the head of a yeshiva in some community, and out of doing good with an ulterior motive, there comes the doing good for its own sake, and the land was filled with knowledge.[16]

We included this riveting, if prolix, passage in its entirety, not only because of its intrinsic merit, but also—and primarily—because it serves as a convenient foil against which one can measure the devastating effects of modernity on the traditional Jewish setting. Hanover's account correctly presupposes that rabbinic authority reigned supreme and went largely unchallenged; that governmental agencies made no attempt to regulate Jewish educational institutions or to impose a minimum set of educational requirements on all citizens of the realm; that religious values dictated priorities in the Jewish community; and that a unified sense of purpose pervaded a more or less uniform and closed social and religious community. With the advent of modernity, all these presuppositions would evaporate into thin air.

In the premodern Jewish world of Nathan Hanover, Jews were neither Lithuanians nor Poles, neither Frenchmen nor Germans. Rabbis moved freely from Lithuania to Germany (e.g., R. Ezekiel Katzenellenbogen [d. 1749] of Brest-Litovsk served as rabbi of the triple community of Altona, Hamburg, and Wandsbeck in Denmark and Germany), from Holland to the Western Ukraine (e.g., R. Ẓevi Ashkenazi [d. 1718], who left Amsterdam to assume a post in Lemberg), and vice versa, thus reflecting the social cohesiveness of the Jewish communities in premodern Europe. By the middle of the nineteenth century—largely due to cultural spheres of influence—it would have been inconceivable for, say, R. Samson Raphael Hirsch (d. 1888) to have served as rabbi of Brest-Litovsk, or for R. Moshe Yehoshua Leib Diskin of Brest-Litovsk (d. 1898) to have served as rabbi of Frankfurt. Indeed, by the end of the nineteenth century, many lay Jews would openly characterize themselves as Frenchmen, Germans, and Englishmen "of the Mosaic persuasion." In short, whereas Jews had once been first and foremost Jews, they now developed multiple identities and loyalties.

In the premodern world, Jews lived in a Christian and alien society. Often, Jews were considered physically revolting, morally depraved, and religiously condemned. This led to a series of political, social, and economic restrictions that kept the Jews a people apart. For example, Jews were not permitted to settle wherever they pleased. The Pale of Settlement in Czarist Russia was a modern vestige of this essentially medieval practice. It took another form in Bohemia and Moravia where, for example, the *Familiantengesetz* of 1726 decreed that only the eldest son in a

16. *Yeven Meẓulah* (Venice, 1653; reissued: Jerusalem, 1965), 42–3. The translation, with minor modification, is taken from Abraham J. Mesch, trans., Nathan Hanover, *Abyss of Despair* (New York, 1950), 110–16.

Jewish household had the right to marry and settle in the locality where his family resided.[17] Jews often had to pay special taxes for the privilege of residing in a particular locality. They also had to pay a special tax, the *Leibzoll* (body tax), when travelling from one country to another. Severe restrictions were placed on the occupations in which Jews were permitted to engage. Jews were often expelled from particular localities as the whim of those in power. Thus, as late as 1744, the entire Jewish community was expelled from Prague, despite the fact that Jews had resided there for centuries.

In general, the Jewish communities were religiously autonomous. Rabbis and rabbinical courts were empowered by the state to adjudicate internal disputes that affected the Jewish community alone. Often, Jewish communal officials were responsible for collecting from all members of the Jewish community the taxes solicited by the governmental authorities. They also maintained internal discipline by means of the authority vested in them by the *kehillah* structure, in accordance with its rules and regulations. In effect, the Jewish and Christian communities were mutually exclusive, with no easy access from the one to the other. A Jew could opt out of the Jewish community almost exclusively by an act of apostasy.

The Age of Enlightenment, the French Revolution, and their aftermath would bring an end to the premodern world, as they ushered in modernity. For the Jews, modernity would be a long process, beginning in the Napoleonic lands, taking root in Germany, and ultimately spreading eastward. Some Jewish communities would first confront modernity in the twentieth century. Key turning points in the history of modernity were the promulgation of the Edict of Tolerance by Emperor Joseph II of Austria in 1781–82, and the granting of citizenship to Jews in France by the National Assembly in 1790–91. These would lead to the granting of citizenship and civil rights to Jews in almost every modern European state by the end of the nineteenth century. The upshot of these political gains was the undoing of all that defined the state of Jewry in the premodern period. Legally, at least, Jews were no longer living in an alien society; in theory, they enjoyed the same rights and privileges as Christians. Unrestricted residency would bring the ghetto walls crumbling down. Taxes that discriminated against the Jews were abolished. Restrictions against specific occupations were rescinded. The Jews entered into European society with a vengeance.

No less significant was the change in attitude toward Jews that accompanied these political reforms, at least initially. Erasmus, Grotius, Pufendorf, and Locke preached toleration, humanism, and the brotherhood of mankind. With Locke, reason became the arbiter of all truth. These teachings laid the foundation for the Enlightenment, which dominated eighteenth-century thought. Under the subsequent influence of Diderot, Voltaire, Rousseau, Hume, Lessing, Herder, and Kant,

17. See, e.g., Hillel J. Kieval, "Caution's Progress: The Modernization of Jewish Life in Prague, 1780–1830," in J. Katz, ed., *Toward Modernity*, 76.

religion was approached rationally. Ultimate faith was placed in rational man, and universal principles that governed nature and society were sought. In intellectual circles, deism displaced traditional Christian teaching and masonic lodges were established to help disseminate the new thinking. The idea of the secular state, and of the separation of church and state, came into being. All this led to a rethinking of the place of the Jew in general society. To the extent that a Jew was rational, and committed to the principles that bind all of mankind together, he could not really be denied his rightful place in society. With the Enlightenment, a new middle ground emerged where Jew and Christian could meet without having to pay the price of apostasy.

While all this was taking place, rabbinic authority was engaged in an act of self-destruction. In 1666, Sabbatai Ẓevi, a Jewish mystic who had been proclaimed the true Messiah, converted to Islam. Despite his conversion and subsequent death (in 1676), the movement he initiated continued throughout much of the eighteenth century. During his lifetime, he enjoyed the enthusiastic support of many prominent rabbinic authorities. After his conversion and death, rabbinic support for the Sabbatian movement waned, but did not disappear entirely. In the eighteenth century, rabbinic opposition would ultimately drive Sabbatianism underground—but not without considerable internecine strife among the rabbis themselves. In 1751, a distinguished rabbinic scholar, R. Jacob Emden (d. 1776), accused one of the leading rabbinic authorities of his generation, R. Jonathan Eibeschuetz (d. 1764), of being a secret believer in Sabbatai Ẓevi. The controversy that ensued—the Emden-Eibeschuetz controversy—would pit rabbi against rabbi in Jewish communities throughout Europe. During the first half of the eighteenth century, R. Israel Baal Shem Tov (d. 1760) would lay the foundations for a new populist Jewish mystical movement, Ḥasidism. Not surprisingly, it met with stiff opposition from the rabbinic establishment. The Sabbatian debacle, the Emden-Eibeschuetz controversy, and the struggle against incipient Ḥasidism left rabbinic authority largely in disarray. Thus, for example, the ultimate symbol, if not expression, of rabbinic power was the ban. During the Emden-Eibeschuetz controversy, Emden and his supporters placed all rabbinic supporters of Eibeschuetz under the ban. Eibeschuetz and his supporters placed all rabbinic supporters of Emden under the ban. Since virtually every major rabbinic figure alive at the time took sides in the controversy, everyone was under the ban, which, of course, rendered the ban meaningless. Ultimately, the ban fell into desuetude. In some places it was legislated out of existence by governmental authority; in others, it was simply no longer circumspect to invoke the ban, and it was allowed to die a natural death. Rabbinic authority would never again regain the stature it held in the premodern period. In the modern period, such rabbinic authority could no longer be imposed; its power would be wielded only among those who voluntarily consented to abide by it, or in the few instances where it continued to derive its authority from the secular state.

Concomitant with these developments, and others that perhaps more properly belong to the twentieth century (such as: advanced technology, secularism, rampant materialism, ethical relativism, and the like, all of which have either contributed to, or are manifestations of, man's alienation from God), the most distinctive feature of modernity vis-à-vis the premodern period has been the precipitous decline in spirituality, or if one prefers, in traditional religion. Whereas for Nathan Hanover religion was the central force of Jewish life—and one suspects that he took for granted that it had always been so in the past and would continue to be so in the future—for the modern Jew, as for modern man, religion is, at best, on the periphery of his consciousness. Religion can become meaningful and fulfilling only with the greatest of effort, always against the grain, in a never ending struggle where absolutely nothing can be taken for granted.

The radical transformation that Jews have witnessed and experienced in the last two hundred and fifty years is perhaps best brought home when one considers the simple fact that Reform Judaism, Conservative Judaism, secular Jews, the academic study of Judaism, the emergence of the American Jewish community as the largest—and one of the most powerful—in the world, political Zionism, and the State of Israel neither existed, nor could have been reasonably predicted, two hundred and fifty years ago.

R. David Friesenhausen: Precursor of *Torah and Derekh Ereẓ*

Doubtless, his colleagues in Berlin called him "Wrong Way" Friesenhausen. During the second half of the eighteenth century, Berlin had become the mecca of enlightened Jewry. Under the aegis of Moses Mendelssohn, leader of and spokesman for the burgeoning Haskalah movement, Berlin became the center of attraction for Jewish intellectuals the world over. Marcus Herz, David Friedlander, Isaac Satanov, Solomon Dubno, Hartwig Wessely, Mendel Lefin, and Solomon Maimon were among the many who made the trek to Berlin, in some instances from as far East as Podolia.[18] Friesenhausen, an intellectual no less talented than many of Mendelssohn's colleagues mentioned above, would, after a residency of close to ten years, leave Berlin for Hunsdorf [Hunfalu], a Hungarian village hidden in the deep backwater of the Carpathian Mountains. That he sought employment and a wife, and eventually found both in Hunsdorf, is clear. But why Hunsdorf? Short of a chance archival discovery, historians will never know the answer to this question. But one suggestive solution has been proffered by Meir Gilon, a modern historian, and after a brief account of Friesenhausen's life, we will present it for the reader's consideration.[19]

Born in the Franconia region of Germany in 1756, Friesenhausen spent the first

18. In general, see Alexander Altmann, *Moses Mendelssohn: A Biographical Study* (London, 1973), 346–420.

19. Meir Gilon, "R. David Friesenhausen: Between the Poles of Haskalah and Ḥasidut,"

thirty years of his life as a Torah Only enthusiast. He studied at the yeshiva in Fuerth, devoting his time entirely to the Talmud and the Codes. Apparently, the effects of the Enlightenment eventually permeated the walls of the yeshiva at Fuerth, and Friesenhausen became an avid reader of treatises on science, mathematics, and even philosophy. He left Fuerth for Berlin in order to pursue his new interests. During his stay in Berlin (1786–1796), he continued to study Torah intensively, allocating no more than two hours per day to secular study. In 1796, his last year in Berlin, he published the first of two books he would publish in his lifetime, *Kelil Ḥeshbon.* A treatise on algebra and geometry written in lucid, almost elegant Hebrew, its unabashed purpose was to make the results of these secular disciplines available to those who could not read modern languages. A letter of approbation from R. Ẓevi Hirsch Levin (d. 1800), Chief Rabbi of Berlin, was appended to the work. In it, R. Ẓevi Hirsch attests that during Friesenhausen's entire stay in Berlin "his Torah study was primary and habitual, whereas his secular study was secondary and sporadic." Shortly after the publication of *Kelil Ḥeshbon,* Friesenhausen left for Hunsdorf, where he was appointed *dayyan* and served with distinction on its rabbinic court until he moved to Ujhely in 1808. There, he served eight years on the rabbinic court of R. Moses Teitelbaum (d. 1841), author of *She'elot u-Teshuvot Heshiv Moshe,* and founder of the first Ḥasidic dynasty in Hungary.[20] Friesenhausen left Ujhely in order to arrange for the publication of his magnum opus, *Mosedot Tevel,* a treatise on astronomy that advocated the acceptance by Jews of the Copernican theory. Indeed, Friesenhausen was among the first Jews to look kindly on Copernicus and his theory.[21] Published in Vienna in 1820, it also included a new proof for Euclid's eleventh axiom, as well as Friesenhausen's autobiographical last will and testament. With the publication of *Mosedot Tevel,* Friesenhausen retired from public activity, spending his last years in the home of his son in Karlsburg in southern Transylvania, where he died in 1828.[22]

Despite his advocacy of *ḥokhmah,* Friesenhausen stressed the centrality of Talmud study throughout his writings. Although *ḥokhmah* clearly had its place in the curriculum, Friesenhausen never got his priorities confused. Indeed, he repeatedly

---

(Hebrew), in Moshe Carmilly-Weinberger, ed., *The Rabbinical Seminary of Budapest* (New York, 1986), Hebrew section, 19–54.

20. R. Yosef M. Sofer, *Ha-Gaon ha-Kadosh Ba'al Yismaḥ Moshe* (New York, 1984).

21. In general, see Andre Neher, "Copernicus in the Hebraic Literature From the Sixteenth to the Eighteenth Century," *Journal of the History of Ideas* 38 (1977): 211–26; Hillel Levine, "Paradise Not Surrendered: Jewish Reactions to Copernicus and the Growth of Modern Science," in R. S. Cohen and M. W. Wartofsky, eds., *Epistemology, Methodology and the Social Sciences* (Boston, 1983), 203–25; and Michael Panitz, "'New Heavens and a New Earth': Seventeenth to Nineteenth Century Jewish Responses to the New Astronomy," *Conservative Judaism* 40:2 (1987–1988): 28–42.

22. R. Yekutiel Y. Greenwald, *Korot ha-Torah ve-ha-Emunah be-Hungariyah* (Budapest, 1921), 40–41 and notes.

criticized those on the (religious) left whose primary energy was expended on *ḥokhmah* at the expense of Torah. A careful reading of his descriptions of those on the left leaves no doubt that he had in mind the radical Haskalah, as it developed in the post-Mendelssohnian era. Friesenhausen, of course, witnessed that development first hand, and could speak about it with authority. With this in mind, Meir Gilon has suggested that Friesenhausen deliberately left Berlin for Hunsdorf as a protest against this new radical Haskalah, and in search of pristine territory where he could realize his educational goals free of its corrupting influences.[23]

Friesenhausen's critique, however, was hardly confined to the left; he also had to contend with the right:

> I appeal especially to all those who fear God and tremble at His word, that they not heed the false claims of those who plot against secular wisdom . . . , unaware that those who make such claims testify against themselves, saying: "We are devoid of Torah, we have chosen folly as our guide." For had the light of Torah ever shone upon them, they would have known the teaching of R. Samuel bar Naḥmeni at Shabbat 75a and the anecdotes about Rabban Gamaliel and R. Joshua at Horayot 10a. Also, they would have been aware of the many talmudic discussions that can be understood only with the aid of secular wisdom. Should you, however, meet a master of the Talmud who insists on denigrating secular wisdom, know full well that he has never understood those talmudic passages whose comprehension is dependent upon knowledge of secular wisdom. . . . He is also unaware that he denigrates the great Jewish sages of the past and their wisdom, as well. Worst of all are those guilty of duplicity. They speak arrogantly in public, either to appease the fools and gain honor in their eyes, or out of envy of the truly wise, disparaging those who appreciate secular wisdom, yet in their hearts they believe otherwise.[24]

Friesenhausen was neither a founder of Reform Judaism, as some have suggested, nor a Maskil.[25] He was a precursor of the *Torah and derekh ereẓ* movement. He was, perhaps, the first traditional Jew in modern times to address the curricular repercussions of *Torah and derekh ereẓ* which, as we shall see, became the hallmark of the various educational institutions—ranging from the Jewish day school to the Jewish university—that combine Torah and secular study under one banner. This occurred when Friesenhausen proposed that a rabbinical seminary be established in Hungary for the training of rabbis and teachers.[26] Friesenhausen was motivated largely by a desire to rescue Jewish youth from the snare of the "smooth talkers, armed with secular knowledge garnered from the handbooks, who ingratiated themselves to the wealthy, and who hold talmudic scholars in disdain," i.e., the Berlin Haskalah

23. Gilon, "R. David Friesenhausen," 26.
24. *Kelil Ḥeshbon* (Berlin, 1796), 8b.
25. See Sandor Buechler, "A zsidó reform úttöröl Magyarországon," *Magyar Zsidó Szemle* 17 (1900): 107–19.
26. *Mosedot Tevel*, 89a–93a.

of the 1790s.[27] His frustration over the failure of his publication to make *ḥokhmah* palatable to the traditional community also encouraged him to seek an alternate, more direct route, in order to advance his cause. Friesenhausen prepared an elaborate curriculum in German and submitted it in 1806 to the Hungarian government for approval. After much procrastination, it was officially rejected by the government in 1813 on the following grounds:

1. There were no Jewish funds available to finance the proposed institution, nor was it feasible to levy new taxes among Jews for this purpose;
2. The government's educational goal was to assimilate the Jew into general society by destroying Jewish insularity. Friesenhausen's proposal would perpetuate and solidify Jewish insularity; and
3. Jewish schools were no longer necessary, as Jews could now study in Christian schools.[28]

While those were the official reasons, it is likely that Jewish influence wielded behind the scenes contributed significantly to the rejection of Friesenhausen's proposal—and perhaps for good reason.[29] In any event, the second reason listed above may well have been the best compliment Friesenhausen ever received in his life. If the Hungarian governmental authorities really believed what they said, then they apparently understood better than most that *Torah and derekh ereẓ* would save, rather than destroy, Judaism in the modern period.

Friesenhausen's mostly utopian proposal called for the establishment of three regional rabbinical seminaries, one each in Hungary, Galicia, and Bohemia-Moravia. In each region, a careful selection process would yield twenty students, aged nine to eighteen, who would make up the entering class. A two-tiered system would be instituted at the seminary: a lower level for ten students aged nine to thirteen, and an upper level for ten students aged fourteen to eighteen. Aside from being knowledgeable in Torah and personally observant, members of the faculty would have to be adept in secular study. The upper level teacher would have to be expert in Talmud; the lower level teacher would have to possess pedagogical talent. Appropriate stipends would be allocated to students in order to provide for all their needs. At age eighteen, a special fund would be established for the student so that he could study undisturbed for a period of ten years. When he married (at age eighteen or later), the funds would be transferred to him. During this ten year period, he would study Torah and *ḥokhmah*, after which he would be qualified to serve as a

27. *Mosedot Tevel*, 89a.

28. Buechler, "A zsidó reform," 118; Gilon, "R. David Friesenhausen," 31.

29. See below, (p. 162) regarding the likely response of the Jewish right and left to Friesenhausen's proposal. Doubtless, some of Friesenhausen's rabbinic colleagues were alarmed by the possibility that it would lead to governmental control of all Jewish institutions of higher learning in the Hungarian empire.

rabbi or teacher in the community. Fifteen years after the founding of the seminary and by government fiat, only graduates of the seminary would be allowed to officiate as rabbis and teachers.

Friesenhausen envisioned the following curriculum: At the lower level: students would arise early and study Bible and Hebrew grammar for one-and-a-half hours prior to prayers and breakfast. After breakfast, they would study Talmud until noon. At noon, they would devote an hour to physical education, followed by lunch and a rest period. The remainder of the afternoon (2:00–8:00 P.M.) would be devoted primarily to Talmud study. From two to three hours of the late afternoon would be set aside for secular study, which over a period of years would include: writing, arithmetic, language of the country of residence, German, and Latin. At the upper level, more intensive study of Talmud would be combined with the study of the Codes. Secular study would now include: geometry, astronomy, physics, biology, history, and speech.[30]

Neither the right nor the left would have supported Friesenhausen's claim at exclusivity, which in effect would have rendered all Torah Only institutions obsolete, and would have forced all rabbis in the Hungarian empire to have been graduates of one of the three government approved rabbinical seminaries.

In his last will and testament, Friesenhausen elaborated on the ideal curriculum he wished his descendants to pursue. He wrote:

> From age thirteen to age seventeen or eighteen, let them focus primarily on those tractates and talmudic discussions relating to *Shulḥan 'Arukh Yoreh De'ah*. From then on, they should study in depth the talmudic tractates from the orders of *Nezikin* and *Nashim*. They should also study the four divisions of the *Shulḥan 'Arukh* in proper sequence, including all the decisions from the earliest times to the present. Among contemporary authorities, none sharpens the mind better than R. Jonathan Eibeschuetz [d. 1764], especially in his *Urim ve-Tumim*, a particularly profound work. *Ẓiyyun le-Nefesh Ḥayyah* by R. Ezekiel Landau [d. 1793], and *Pnei Yehoshua* by R. Jacob Joshua Falk [d. 1756] are well worth studying, especially when examining a *sugya* in depth."[31]

For those of his descendants not able or inclined to pursue a rigorous program of Talmud study, Friesenhausen prepared a no less pious alternate curriculum which, after the age of thirteen, focused on vocational training. In setting out the arguments in favor of learning a trade, Friesenhausen wrote:

> In this age, when we have neither field nor vineyard to cultivate, even talmudists would do well to learn a trade. Unless, of course, their love of Torah leads them to make Torah their occupation, at which point God, in His merciful manner, will arrange for others to do their work for them. . . . Know that any land whose inhabitants are not expert in the

30. *Mosedot Tevel*, 89a–90a.
31. *Mosedot Tevel*, 76a.

various occupations will not succeed. For how can a land thrive without experts in the various occupations? Whatever occupations they are lacking in create lacunae that are not filled. Indeed, when God will gather in the exiles of Israel, we will need experts in the various occupations. If we continue as we are today, how will the Jewish state be able to conduct its affairs? Will God open windows in heaven and lower down experts in the various occupations? Will we import them from the nations surrounding us? This is a sad state of affairs. I too have suffered in my old age because I did not learn a trade in my youth.[32]

Despite his commitment to *ḥokhmah*, Friesenhausen was on cordial terms with the leading *gedolei yisrael* of his time. During his peregrinations, he met and "discussed Torah" with R. Nathan Adler (d. 1800) and R. Pinḥas Horowitz (d. 1805) of Frankfurt, R. David Sinzheim (d. 1812) of Strasbourg, R. Mordecai Benet (d. 1829) of Nikolsburg, and R. Moses Sofer (d. 1839) of Pressburg. One of the more interesting of these discussions is worth repeating here. Friesenhausen, a confirmed Copernican, was troubled by the fact that several kabbalistic works contained astronomical drawings that were clearly Ptolemaic in character. He was assured by the two outstanding kabbalists in Frankfurt—Rabbis Adler and Horowitz—that the Ptolemaic drawings were borrowed from medieval astronomical treaties and inserted into the kabbalistic works; they were not part and parcel of kabbalistic teaching.[33]

In 1819, Friesenhausen met with the Ḥatam Sofer in Pressburg. The latter wrote a letter of recommendation on Friesenhausen's behalf. It reads in part:

> My colleague, the revered Rabbi David ha-Kohen of Fuerth, presently *dayyan* of Ujhely in Hungary, was known to me even when he was a youngster. He was among the most distinguished students in the yeshiva of Fuerth, renowned even then for the soundness and depth of his mind. By now he has added much Torah, for he has spent many years studying Torah, and has served as a decisor of Jewish law in many communities and lands. I have discussed Torah with him, orally and in writing. I have found him to be filled with the word of God, i.e., Torah. He is certainly worthy of appointment as rabbi in a large community and of establishing a yeshiva for older and younger students. Therefore, I take this opportunity to inform all members of the Jewish community about his credentials, so that all will honor him and his Torah, and so that a community seeking a rabbi will know to appoint him to the post.[34]

Friesenhausen's life foreshadows much that would occur in the nineteenth and twentieth centuries. Rabbis Jacob Ettlinger, Samson Raphael Hirsch, and Azriel

---

32. *Mosedot Tevel,* 76b. For similar arguments regarding the necessity for Jews to engage in the various occupations when settled in the land of Israel, see R. Mose Sofer, *Ḥatam Sofer: Sukkah* (Jerusalem, 1974), 92 (*ad Sukkah* 36a); cf. his *Ḥatam Sofer 'al ha-Torah* (New York, 1977), 36a (*parashat Shofetim*).

33. *Mosedot Tevel,* 23a–b.

34. *Mosedot Tevel,* 13a.

Hildesheimer, for example, all attempted to establish rabbinical seminaries whose curricula incorporated secular study and bore a remarkable resemblance to that of Friesenhausen. Only Hildesheimer would succeed in doing so. Essentially, three broad categories of Jewish responses to modernity were possible: assimilation, isolation, and confrontation. Friesenhausen ruled out assimilation and isolation, opting for confrontation as the only viable Jewish response. It was a daring stance, especially then, and a lonely one. He won no friends, influenced few people, and spent a lifetime as a wandering Jew who was almost denied his rightful place—at the very least—as a footnote in Jewish history.

Torah Education in Western and Central Europe at the Start of the Nineteenth Century

One manifestation of the devastating impact of the Enlightenment on West European Jewry was the utter collapse of the traditional yeshivot almost overnight. The famous yeshivot of Metz, Frankfurt, Mannheim, Fuerth, Karlsruhe, Altona-Hamburg, Halberstadt, and Prague were still flourishing in the middle to the late eighteenth century. By the beginning of the nineteenth century all were in a precipitous state of decline. Students were no longer attracted to the yeshivot; traditional *ḥadarim*, which had once served as feeder schools for the yeshivot, were disappearing. The social mobility that was made possible by modernity led students to seek other more "progressive" forms of education, Jewish and secular.[35] Wealthy Jews, now under the influence of a new set of values, withdrew their support of the yeshivot.[36] Another manifestation of the devastating impact of the Enlightenment—certainly from an Orthodox perspective—was the founding and growth of the Reform movement, which introduced denominationalism into what had been a traditional and united Jewish community. The nineteenth century would be marked by internal Jewish polemic, and all the major players, whether Abraham Geiger, Zechariah Frankel, or Samson Raphael Hirsch, would be involved.[37]

A distinguished German Talmudist, R. Mendel Kargau (1772–1842), was a

35. Typical of the new schools that combined secular education with "progressive" religious education, was the Philanthropin in Frankfurt. Founded in 1804, it would mold several generations of Reform Jewish leaders. See Herman Baerwald and Salo Adler, eds., *Geschichte der Realschule der israelitischen Gemeinde (Philanthropin) zu Frankfurt am Main 1804–1904* (Frankfurt, 1904); cf. Mordecai Eliav, *Ha-Ḥinukh ha-Yehudi be-Germanyah bi-Yemei ha-Haskalah ve-ha-Emanzipazyah* (Jerusalem, 1960), 71–141.

36. Eliav, *Ha-Ḥinukh*, 142–55.

37. See Michael A. Meyer, *Response to Modernity: A History of the Reform Movement in Judaism* (Oxford, 1988).

transitional figure who witnessed the rapid changes that were overtaking Orthodoxy. In one of his responsa, he wrote:

> The rabbis who preceded me were exceedingly great in Torah. Nonetheless, had they devoted themselves to even a smattering of secular study—instead of wasting precious time trying to explain away curious midrashic passages by a sophistry consisting of joining together unrelated passages—we would not be inundated now with the destructive forces that are tearing down traditional Judaism.[38]

Despite these ominous developments, there were occasional rays of light. In 1795, the first Orthodox Jewish day school, that is, an elementary school combining Jewish and secular study whose express purpose was the perpetuation of traditional Judaism, was founded by Ẓevi Hirsch Koeslin, a merchant in Halberstadt. Originally a freeschool for the poor, *Hash'arat Ẓevi* (the school was named after its founder and benefactor) eventually became a community school, introduced separate classes for girls in 1827, added a high school in 1866, and continued to thrive until the Nazi period. R. Azriel Hildesheimer was among the many graduates of *Hash'arat Ẓevi*; no better justification for the school's existence is needed. A similar school was founded by R. Samson Raphael Hirsch's grandfather, R. Mendel Frankfurter (d. 1823)—he served as *rosh bet din* of Altona—in Hamburg in 1805.[39] In a sermon delivered in 1816, R. Samuel Landau (d. 1834), son of R. Ezekiel Landau and *rosh av bet din* of Prague, would announce:

> When a child is six or seven years old he should be taught the Torah in Hebrew, together with its translation into German, as it appears in the Hebrew Bibles printed in Berlin, Vienna, and Prague. He should master German and related subjects of importance. Anyone lacking the ability to read and write German cannot succeed in today's world. He will not gain entry to, nor become expert in, any profession. It is obligatory upon every father to teach his son the language and the laws of the state in which he lives. Moreover, parents shall see to it that their children grow in *Torah and derekh ereẓ*. The children shall pursue both, moving from level to level until they are ten to twelve years of age, each according to his ability. When he is twelve years old, a judgment shall be made concerning his ability and character. If it is appropriate that he continue his studies, a determination will be made whether he should pursue secular study or Talmud with Rashi and Tosafot, leading to the rabbinate. If study is not for him, he should be taught a vocation or business skills, each according to his inclination.[40]

Orthodoxy's confrontation with modernity had begun. It is against this backdrop that the two architects of Orthodoxy in the modern period. R. Isaac Bernays and R. Jacob Ettlinger, appear on the horizon of Jewish history.

---

38. *She'elot u-Teshuvot Giddulei Taharah, §7,* printed in Abraham Sofer, *He'arot ve-He'arot'al Shtayim u-Sheloshim mi-Masekhtot ha-Shas* (Jerusalem, 1976), 24.

39. See Eliav, *Ha-Ḥinukh*, 155–61.

40. R. Samuel Landau's sermon is included in R. Ezekiel Landau, *Ahavat Ẓion* (Jerusalem, 1966), 37, sermon 12.

R. Isaac Bernays

On the surface, at least, Rabbi Isaac Bernays' (1792–1849) biography appears to parallel that of his younger contemporary, R. Jacob Ettlinger.[41] Like Ettlinger,

41. Unfortunately, Bernays left almost no writings, or so it would seem, making it extremely difficult to reconstruct his views on almost any topic. The more useful studies are: Leon Horowitz, "A History of Rabbi Isaac Bernays," *Kneset Yisrael* 1 (1886–1887), columns 845–54; Eduard Duckesz, "Zur Biographie des Chacham Bernays," *Jahrbuch der Juedisch-Literarischen Gesellschaft* 5 (1907): 297–322; Hans I. Bach, "Isaac Bernays," *MGWJ* 83 (1939): 533-47; Isaac Heinemann, "The Relationship between S. R. Hirsch and his teacher Isaac Bernays," (Hebrew) *Ẓion* 16 (1951): 44-90; Hans I. Bach, *Jacob Bernays* (Tübingen, 1974); Friedrich Schütz, "Skizzen zur Geschichte der jüdischen Gemeinde Weisenau bei Mainz: mit einer besonderen Würdigung der Familie Bernays," *Mainzer Zeitschrift* 82 (1987): 151–79; Rivka Horwitz, "On Kabbala and Myth in 19th Century Germany: Isaac Bernays," *PAAJR* 59 (1993): 137–83 (cf. the shorter version in Eveline Goodman-Thau, Gerd Mattenklott, and Cristoph Schulte, eds., *Kabbala und Romantik* [Tübingen, 1994], 217–47); and Werner J. Cahnman, "Friedrich Wilhelm Schelling and the New Thinking of Judaism," in Eveline Goodman-Thau et al., eds., *Kabbala und Romantik* (Tübingen, 1994), 167–205. The fullest bibliographical study is Willy Aron, "Hakham Isaac Bernays," *Jewish Forum* 32 (May, 1949), 102–104, 108; (July, 1949), 133.

No discussion of Bernays would be complete without reference to an anonymous two-volume work entitled *Der Bibel'sche Orient* (Munich, 1820–1821), which was an immediate sensation upon publication. The volumes were, in effect, a programmatic essay addressed primarily to enlightened Germans (i.e., Christians)—and only secondarily to Jews—calling for a reassessment of their understanding of the Old Testament and the history of Jewish thought. The author nowhere identifies himself as a Jew; quite the contrary, he tries to create the impression that this was a book by a European intellectual intended for his colleagues. A profound work, it draws on classical Greek and Latin sources such as the Homeric epics and Virgil, Talmud and Midrash, Philo and Josephus, Masoretic studies, medieval Hebrew grammarians, medieval and modern Jewish philosophers—including Spinoza and Mendelssohn, and Lurianic Kabbalah. The book is suffused with the teachings of Bernays, even though his name is nowhere mentioned in it. According to most accounts, Bernays neither admitted nor denied his authorship of the work; though Graetz reports, second hand, that Bernays denied that he was the author. If Bernays wrote *Der Bibel'sche Orient*, it of course becomes the single most important source for Bernays' thought. His authorship would also underscore a radical change in the Orthodox rabbinate as it confronted modernity: here was an Orthodox rabbi, writing in the vernacular and addressing (primarily, at least) Christian intellectuals on philosophical and theological issues of concern to them. If Bernays did not author *Der Bibel'sche Orient*, it of course is not relevant for an intellectual portrait of Bernays. Or, at best, it could be used only with great caution. The most extensive study of the issue is Hans Bach, "*Der Bibel'sche Orient* und sein Verfasser," *Zeitschrift fuer die Geschichte der Juden in Deutchland* 7 (1937): 14–45, who concluded that Bernays authored this work. In recent years, Gershom Scholem ("Ein verschollener juedischer Mystiker der Aufklaerungszeit: E. J. Hirschfeld," *Leo Baeck Institute Yearbook* 7 [1962]: 249) and Arnaldo Momigliano ("Jacob

Bernays studied under R. Abraham Bing (d. 1841)[42] at Wuerzburg, found his vocation in the rabbinate, delivered his sermons in polished German, spent a lifetime in the battle against Reform, and left an indelible imprint on Rabbis Samson Raphael Hirsch and Azriel Hildesheimer. It is reported that Bernays and Ettlinger studied together in their yeshiva days at Wuerzburg; Bernays guided Ettlinger in the study of Maimonides' *Guide for the Perplexed*, whereas Ettinger guided Bernays in the study of *Shulḥan 'Arukh Yoreh De'ah*.[43] Their friendship ended only with Bernays' death in 1849. The graveside eulogy, and later a memorial address at the Great Synagogue in Hamburg, were delivered by Ettlinger.[44] Despite these many parallels and their close relationship, they were very different men; no one ever confused the one for the other.

Bernays was a child prodigy. At age seven, he was awarded the title *ḥaver* by R. Noaḥ Ḥayyim Ẓevi Berlin, then Chief Rabbi of Mainz. This would set the tone for a lifetime of "firsts," almost always accomplished at a youthful age that virtually defies belief. While in his early 20s, he was appointed to the *bet din* of R. Abraham Bing in Wuerzburg.[45] Bernays' interests, however, were not confined to Talmud and rabbinic literature. In 1817, while serving on the *bet din* of Wuerzburg, he published his first scholarly essay. It was a critical review in German of a scholarly book by a Protestant Bible scholar—Gesenius' *Lexicon of the Old Testament* (German edition)—and the review was published in a Protestant journal of theology![46] Clearly, Bernays was standing at the threshold of a new order of Orthodox rabbi.

Bernays," *Mededeligen Der Koninklijke Nederlandse Akademie Van Wetenschappen, Afd. Letterkunde*, 32:5 [1969]: 7), citing Bach, concurred with his conclusion. Neither Scholem nor Momigliano provided any new evidence; and in a personal conversation with Momigliano in London shortly after he published the essay listed above, he admitted to me that he was entirely uncertain about who really authored *Der Bibel'sche Orient!* Bach's study, unfortunately, is methodologically flawed; it proves only that whoever wrote *Der Bibel'sche Orient* was profoundly influenced by Bernays—a fact well-known long before Bach. The book could have been written by any colleague or teacher of Bernays, Jew or non-Jew, who had easy access to Bernays' teaching—and joined Bernays' views to his own. See esp. the study by Rivka Horwitz listed above. The entire issue is hardly resolved and merits careful investigation. Until then, methodological grounds preclude citation from *Der Bibel'sche Orient* for purposes of this essay. Instead, our portrait of Bernays will be drawn almost exclusively from contemporary documents and from citations by eyewitnesses who attended Bernays' sermons and lectures.

42. He also studied under Rabbis Isaac Metz and Herẓ Scheuer at Mainz; see E Duckesz, "Lur Biographie," 297–98.

43. E Duckesz, "Zur Biographie," 298.

44. See Judith Bleich, *Jacob Ettlinger, His Life and Works: The Emergence of Modern Orthodoxy in Germany* (unpublished doctoral dissertation, New York University, 1974), 18. But cf. Moses M. Haarbleicher, *Zwei Epochen aus der Geschichte der Deutsch-Israelitischen Gemeinde in Hamburg* (Hamburg, 1866), 399.

45. See Horowitz, "Toledot Rabbi Yiẓḥak Bernays," column 847.

46. See I. Bernays, "Kritik des kleinen hebraeischen Handwoerterbuchs von Gesenius,"

At the University of Wuerzburg, he studied under Johann Jakob Wagner, a disciple of the German philosophers Hegel, Fichte, and Schelling. In 1819, Bernays spent an entire semester at the University of Munich, where he came under the influence of J. A. von Kalb, a German philosopher and theologian. Bernays learned much from his teachers—and taught them much as well. Both Wagner and Kalb refer to Bernays in their published works. Kalb, who testified that he spent four to five hours daily in discussion with Bernays throughout the semester they shared in Munich, wrote:

> His mastery of Jewish scholarship is bound up with a profound understanding of world history and politics. His proficiency in the latter was to a degree that I have rarely seen among Christian scholars, and have never seen among Jews.[47]

In 1821, at age twenty-nine, Bernays was appointed Chief Rabbi of the free city of Hamburg which at the time, with over 6,000 Jews, was the largest Jewish community in Germany.[48] It was his first and only appointment as a rabbi.[49] Early in 1821, a member of the Hamburg Jewish community solicited a confidential assessment of Bernays—who was residing in Mainz at the time—from Wolf Heidenheim, a noted Jewish scholar and publisher. He wrote:

> My friend, what you ask is difficult indeed. In order to properly assess Bernays one must be Bernays. My limited judgment and meager knowledge do not suffice to measure his

---

in *Neue Theologische Annalen (Jahrbuecher der Theologie und theologischen Nachrichten)* (Frankfurt, 1817), I, 180–95.

47. See Duckesz, "Zur Biographie," 298–301.

48. See Stephen M. Poppel, "The Politics of Religious Leadership: The Rabbinate in Nineteenth-Century Hamburg," *Leo Baeck Institute Yearbook 28* (1983): 439–70.

Interestingly, one of the candidates on the short list who lost out to Bernays was R. Asher Wallerstein (1754–1837) of Karlsruhe, a son of R. Aryeh Leib b. Asher (d. 1785), author of *Sha'agat Aryeh,* and a teacher of R. Jacob Ettlinger.

49. The Board of Directors of the Hamburg Jewish community insisted that the new rabbi be hired under the title *moreh ẓedek,* as distinct from *rav av bet din* or *dayyan.* This was one of many stipulations by means of which the board intended to constrict the powers of the new rabbi and keep him subordinated to lay authority. In his negotiations with the board prior to his acceptance of the post, Bernays rejected the title *moreh ẓedek* and chose instead the title *ḥakham,* hence Ḥakham Bernays. This was a clever move on Bernays' part: it signalled to the board that the new rabbi was hardly docile. Moreover, the choice of *ḥakham* reflected Bernays' perception that the title *Rabbi* by 1821 had depreciated to a point where it was bereft of dignity. Furthermore, in Hamburg, where the Portuguese Jewish community was equivalent to upper class society, the Sephardic title *ḥakham* provided Bernays with instant stature. In German documents, he always used the title *Geistlicher Beamte* (spiritual servant or cleric); it is unclear whether this was his choice, or the suggestion of the board that appointed him. One suspects that the board viewed Bernays as the servant of the community, whereas Bernays perceived of himself as the servant of the Lord.

> stature. He stands above and beyond our rabbis, masters of the Written and Oral Torah; above and beyond our philosophers, and historians of antiquity. It is said appropriately concerning him: "*A wise charmer* (Isaiah 3:3). The moment he begins to discourse on Torah or wisdom all become charmed and silent."[50] Hearing him discuss Hebrew language and biblical exegesis, one believes he is listening to Ibn Ezra himself. If the discussion is about Mishnah, Talmud, Sifra, and Sifre, it is as if he has become Maimonides incarnate. In general knowledge, he is Plato incarnate. Regarding his character, he is pious, noble, and modest. . . . Any community, large or small, that will have the good fortune to come under Bernays' leadership, will not long remain isolated. It will become an *'ir ve-'em be-yisrael* "and all the nations shall flow to it (Isaiah 2:2)."[51]

With such letters of recommendation—and there were more—[52]it is no wonder that Bernays got the job. Nor was it an accident that the offer was made and accepted in 1821. With the turn from the eighteenth into the nineteenth century, Hamburg's Jewish community began to move rapidly from the premodern into the modern period. In 1799, R. Raphael ha-Kohen—an inveterate foe of modernity who had banned the use of Mendelssohn's *Be'ur*—resigned as rabbi of the triple community of Altona, Hamburg, and Wandsbeck, in part because the governmental authorities had withdrawn his unilateral right to place under the ban those Jews who violated ceremonial law.[53] By 1811, the triple community was dissolved, each appointing its own rabbi. From 1807 on, Hamburg had no Chief Rabbi; Rabbis Eleazar Lasi and Barukh Oser officiated as its interim rabbis and as heads of its rabbinic court. During this interregnum, a significant segment of Hamburg Jewry had become acculturated to a point of no return to traditional Judaism. In 1817, a "New

50. *Ḥagigah* 14a.

51. Louis Lewin, "Zum hundersten Todestage Wolf Heidenheims," *MGWJ* 76 (1932): 11–12.

52. See, e.g., R. Abraham Bing's glowing remarks, as reported in Duckesz, "Zur Biographie," 298–99, n. 1.

In Hirschian circles, a tradition was preserved that Bernays was a Talmudist of the same rank as R. Jonathan Eibeschuetz (a distinguished predecessor of his in the Hamburg rabbinate)! See Raphael Breuer, *Unter seinem Banner* (Frankfurt, 1908), 215–16. The tradition is cited in the name of contemporaries of Bernays who were in a position to render such a judgment. Perhaps the tradition originated with Hirsch's grandfather, R. Mendel Frankfurter, one of the few people who attended the lectures and sermons of both Eibeschuetz and Bernays.

53. See E. Duckesz, *Ivah le-Moshav* (Cracow, 1903), German section, xxv–xxvi, for this and other probable causes that led to R. Raphael ha-Kohen's resignation. Jacob Katz has shown that governmental interference with regard to R. Raphael ha-Kohen's use of the ban in Altona and Hamburg dates back at least to 1782. See his "Rabbi Raphael Kohen: Mendelssohn's Opponent" (Hebrew), *Tarbiẓ 56* (1987): 243–64; cf. his "The Changing Position and Outlook of Halakhists in Early Modernity" in Leo Landman, ed., *Scholars and Scholarship: The Interaction Between Judaism and Other Cultures* (New York, 1990), 93–106. Add to the references cited by Katz: Haarbleicher, *Zwei Epochen*, 29–30.

Israelite Temple Association in Hamburg" was established; in 1818, the association dedicated its new Reform temple with organ and choir. The organist, of course, was Christian; the choir consisted of Jewish school boys. In 1819, the Hamburg temple published the first comprehensive Reform prayerbook, and by 1820, membership grew to over 100 families.[54] These developments did not go unnoticed, and the ensuing controversy would involve the leading halakhic authorities of the time, e.g., R. Akiva Eger, Mordechai Benet, and R. Moses Sofer. The unanimous verdict of the traditional rabbinic authorities was unequivocal: The use of the Reform prayerbook was banned; and it was prohibited for any Jew to set foot in the temple.[55] Since the Hamburg Jewish community—like all Jewish communities in Germany at the time—was structured as a single, unified *kehillah* it became obvious that the best way to contain the spread of Reform, and to maintain at least a semblance of communal unity, was to seek a Chief Rabbi, at once traditional and modern, who could address the needs of the entire community. Bernays, who had turned down numerous appointments to rabbinic posts prior to the call to Hamburg, must have realized that destiny was calling. This was the challenge and opportunity for which he had been preparing all his life, and for which he was uniquely qualified. It would be Bernays' task to initiate the Orthodox response to modernity.

If Mendelssohn was the first modern Jew, Bernays was the first modern Orthodox rabbi. This manifested itself not only in the outward concessions he made to modernity, e.g., he wore canonicals,[56] delivered a sermon every Sabbath

---

54. See Meyer, *Response to Modernity*, 53–61.

55. See *Elleh Divrei ha-Berit* (Altona, 1819; reissued by Gregg International Publishers, Farnsborough, 1969).

56. Specifically, Bernays donned a clerical robe (*Ornate*) and collar bands, the attire regularly worn by Christian clerics. (From Horowitz, "A History," column 850, it would appear that Bernays did not wear canonicals at the start of his rabbinic career in Hamburg.) See the various portraits of Bernays, especially the one reproduced in William Aron, *Jews of Hamburg* (New York, 1967), Hebrew section, between pp. 86–97, which hung in the study of Sigmund Freud (who was married to Bernays' granddaughter). Such canonicals were regularly worn by Reform preachers in the early nineteenth century. For a striking portrait of Bernays' Reform counterpart in Hamburg—in full clerical dress—see Alfred Rubens, *A History of Jewish Costume* (New York, 1973), 178; to the naked eye, at least, the Reform rabbi's attire does not differ substantively from that of Bernays. See also Michael A. Meyer, "Christian influence on Early German Reform Judaism," in Charles Berlin, ed., *Studies in Jewish Bibliography, History, and Literature in Honor of I. Edward Kiev* (New York, 1971), 301–2, n. 9, who notes that the use of clerical robes and collar bands by Jewish clergy is already attested in the seventeenth century.

Aside from Bernays, Rabbis Seligmann Baer Bamberger of Wuerzburg and Samson Raphel Hirsch of Frankfurt were perhaps the most prominent Orthodox rabbis who regularly wore canonicals. In the case of Bamberger, he did so with the approval of R. Abraham Bing, Bernays' teacher. Regarding Bamberger, see Naphtali Carlebach, *Joseph Carlebach and His Generation* (New York, 1959), 225–30; cf. Benjamin S. Hamburger; *Nesi ha-Leviyyim* (Bnei

in German,[57] and conducted services in a decorous and aesthetically pleasing manner, but also and more importantly by Bernays' intellectual commitment to modern culture and contemporary scholarship. No less than Mendelssohn, Bernays had mastered contemporary German philosophy and theology. But unlike Mendelssohn, who was not a talmudic scholar of note,[58] Bernays brought to bear his vast rabbinic erudition on modern German thought.[59] The teachings of Schelling, Fichte, Herder, and others were viewed through the prism of classical Jewish literature—and vice versa.

In particular, Bernays came under the influence of early nineteenth century romanticism. As applied to Jewish teaching by Bernays, this resulted in a more critical and less favorable approach to Maimonidean teaching. Bernays viewed R. Judah ha-Levi, Naḥmanides, and the Kabbalah as reflecting more authentically the unadulterated teachings of Scripture and the talmudic rabbis. Indeed, Bernays' most famous public lectures were an extended series of adult education lectures on

---

Brak, 1992), 534–37 (in an anthology of books edited by Ẓevi Bamberger, *Kitvei Rabbenu Yiẓḥak Dov ha-Levi mi-Wuerzburg* [Long Beach, 1992]). See also R. Joseph Carlebach, "Würzburg and Jerusalem: A Conversation between Rabbi Seligmann Baer Bamberger and Rabbi Shmuel Salant," *Tradition* 28:2 (1994): 58–63. Regarding Hirsch, see Jacob Rosenheim, *Samson Raphael Hirsch's Cultural Ideal and Our Times* (London, 1951), 59–62. For a portrait of R. Jacob Ettlinger of Altona in canonicals, see Ulrich Bauche, et al., eds., *Vierhundert Jahre Juden in Hamburg* (Hamburg, 1991), 309. For halakhic discussion of the propriety of canonicals, see R. Marcus Horovitz, *She'elot u-Teshuvot Maṭṭeh Levi* (Jerusalem, 1979), part 2, *Oraḥ Ḥayyim*, §6; cf. R. Ḥayyim 'Ozer Grodzenski, "On Canonicals" (Hebrew), in R. Shlomo Yosef Zevin, ed., *Shiloh* (Jerusalem-Antwerp, 1983), 167–68.

57. Bernays introduced into the Orthodox synagogue in Germany three major innovations regarding the sermon. Whereas Orthodox rabbis ordinarily preached several times a year, Bernays preached every Sabbath. Whereas Orthodox sermons had always been in Yiddish, Bernays preached in German. Whereas Orthodox sermons were grounded in talmudic and midrashic passages and tended to be pilpulistic, Bernays' sermons were lectures on the Bible, Talmud, and Jewish thought, based on philological and historical analysis, never pilpulistic. Thus, Bernays' sermons were unlike those of his predecessors, even as they were unlike the "edifying" sermons of his contemporaries, i.e., the Reform preachers of Hamburg, Frankfurt, Berlin, Vienna, and the like. See, in general: Adolf Kober, "Jewish Preaching and Preachers," *Historia Judaica* 7 (1945): 103–34; and Alexander Altmann, "The New Style of Preaching in the Nineteenth-Century Germany," in A. Altmann, ed., *Studies in Nineteenth-Century Jewish Intellectual History* (Cambridge, 1964), 65–116. Regarding Bernays' sermons in particular, see Moses Mendelson, *Penei Tevel* (Amsterdam, 1872), 50–54.

58. Mendelssohn regularly attended lectures in Talmud (see Mendelson, *Penei Tevel*, 229, 234), but devoted little scholarly attention to Talmud. One of his few talmudic insights, recorded for posterity, appears in R. Levi of Kaidany, *'Ateret Rosh* (Amsterdam, 1766), I, 59b.

59. Indeed, Heinrich Graetz would write: "Bernays was the first to understand—in a far more profound manner than Mendelssohn—the significance of Judaism for world history; moreover, he had a deep understanding of the entire range of Jewish literature." See his *Geschichte der Juden*, ed. M. Brann, second edition (Leipzig, 1900), XI, 388.

the *Kuzari.* Based upon the romantics, Bernays developed an elaborate system of "speculative" etymologies which he applied to Hebrew, and an even more elaborate system of symbolic interpretations which he applied to the biblical narrative and to the commandments. Essentially, he taught, Judaism must be understood from within and against its historical backdrop. He railed against viewing the Bible and Talmud through Greek or Arabic lenses. And while the Jews were a people apart, they also had a mission, namely to spread monotheistic teaching among the pagans. Since Christianity was suffused with pagan elements, the Jewish mission was as relevant in the modern period as it had been in antiquity. Jews, however, could properly undertake their mission only if they remained faithful to classical Jewish teaching (hence Bernays' rejection of the radical Haskalah and Reform Judaism) while engaging humanity at large—the ultimate arena of Jewish activity. For Bernays this meant, in part, that Jews had to participate in general culture, learn from it, and contribute to it.

These lofty teachings of a gifted intellectual and imaginative dreamer fell mostly on deaf ears. One venue for Bernays' teaching was his synagogue. Although his rabbinic contract did not require that he speak more than once a month, he in fact spoke—much to the chagrin of his lay audience—every Sabbath.[60] He was the first Orthodox rabbi to speak regularly in the vernacular (tickets were sold at sixty marks for the privilege of hearing the first German sermon by the "Rabbi and Gaon" Bernays at Hamburg)[61]; and vivid eyewitness accounts of his preaching have been preserved. Heinrich Heine, after hearing Bernays speak, wrote: "He is an ingenious man and has more spirit within him than Dr. Kley, Salomon, Auerbach I and II," but added in the same breath, "None of the Jews understands him."[62] Similar assessments by admirers of Bernays make it clear that he regularly spoke over the heads of his audience.[63] The situation is perhaps best captured in the following anecdote. In a sermon, Bernays mentioned in passing the Roman god Jupiter. After the sermon, a congregant was overheard asking his neighbor: "Who is Jupiter?" The neighbor responded: "I haven't the slightest idea, but if the rabbi mentioned him in a sermon he certainly must have been a famous Jew."[64] Apparently, only the intellectuals—among them Hirsch and Hildesheimer—appreciated Bernays' genius.

Another venue for Bernays' teaching was the day school founded in Hamburg

60. See Poppel, "The Politics of Religious Leadership," 451; cf. Mendelson, *Penei Tevel,* 53 and Haarbleicher, *Zwei Epochen,* 180.

61. See Horowitz, "A History," column 850.

62. See Altmann, "The New Style of Preaching," 78. Eduard Kley (d. 1867), Gotthold Salomon (d. 1862), Issac Levin Auerbach (d. 1853), and Jacob Auerbach (d. 1887) were distinguished preachers at the Reform temples in Berlin, Frankfurt, and Hamburg.

63. See Mendelson, *Penei Tevel,* 53.

64. See Heinemann, "The Relationship," 49.

by R. Mendel Frankfurter in 1805.[65] Despite Frankfurter's efforts, it had reverted back to a traditional *ḥeder* by the time Bernays arrived in 1821. Bernays applied himself with gusto to the day school and revitalized it by revamping the curriculum, expanding its hours, and hiring a new and competent faculty. His early plans called for the establishment of a teacher's seminary as a natural adjunct to the day school, but this would never materialize.[66] Bernays regularly taught the highest Talmud class at the day school—it rarely consisted of more than a handful of students aged fourteen and fifteen—until his death. One of the few documents by Bernays that has been preserved contains the ideal curriculum he drew up for implementation at the day school. Aside from German, history, geography, mathematics, and science, he called for instruction in the history of religions "for religion properly understood is on par with any other science regarding the significance of its content and its antiquity." More importantly, he required of his Jewish faculty that they take into account in their teaching "the religions and beliefs of all other peoples, a comparative study of the languages of antiquity, a profound understanding of Scripture, and extensive study of Midrash."[67]

The day school, much improved, grew modestly under Bernays' aegis to some two hundred students. Deeply concerned about the welfare of his students, he carefully monitored their progress. The full impact of his influence, however, was confined to the few students who chose to study Talmud with him. The vast majority of students left the school at age thirteen or shortly thereafter, to venture into apprenticeships or family businesses. Bernays was particularly proud of the day school and its graduates; he considered it his greatest achievement. After his death, the elementary school would add a high school, and the enlarged school would eventually number over six hundred students and continue to thrive—as shaped by Bernays and others—until the Nazi period.[68]

Clearly, Bernays did not find intellectual fulfillment in the modern rabbinate. When there was talk about the possible appointment of a Jewish talmudist or theologian to a university post, Bernays repeatedly stated that, if invited, he would consider it his duty as a Jew to resign his post as rabbi of Hamburg and to accept the academic appointment instead.[69] Such an attitude presupposes an openness to general culture that was inconceivable among Orthodox rabbis in Germany prior to Bernays, even as it reflects, I suspect, Bernays' less than enthusiastic regard for the

65. See Eliav, *Ḥa-Ḥinukh*, 159–61, and 232–34.

66. See Joseph Goldschmidt, *Geschichte der Talmud Tora Realschule in Hamburg* (Hamburg, 1905), 51–52.

67. See Haarbleicher, *Zwei Epochen*, 248–51.

68. See Goldschmidt, *Geschichte;* cf. Aron, *Jews of Hamburg*, passim; and the references cited below, n. 70 and 74.

69. See Marcus Brann, *Geschichte des Juedisch-Theologischen Seminars in Breslau* (Breslau, 1904), 54, n. 1. The text speaks of an appointment to a "Jewish University"; the exact circumstances regarding this proposed institution appear to be unknown.

Hamburg rabbinate. Despite his frustrations as a rabbi, Bernays was held in esteem by virtually the entire Jewish community of Hamburg,[70] and left an indelible imprint on a small coterie of students who would become leaders of the Jewish community. These included Solomon Frensdorff, principal of the Jewish Teacher's Seminary in Hanover and a Masoretic scholar of note;[71] several *dayyanim* and Jewish educators who would succeed Bernays at Hamburg;[72] and above all, Rabbis Samson

70. In 1846, the Hamburg Jewish community celebrated Bernays' twenty-fifth anniversary as Chief Rabbi. Participants included members of the Hamburg Senate, members of the Jewish Board of Directors, the head of the Portuguese Jewish community in Hamburg, R. Jacob Ettlinger of Altona, and faculty, students, and graduates of the day school. A procession through the streets of Hamburg, musical interludes, and the striking of gold, silver, and bronze issues of a medallion in honor of Bernays—no other rabbi of Hamburg was accorded this honor—were some of the highlights of the celebration. For fuller detail, see Duckesz, "Zur Biographie," 314–19. For the medallion, see Max Grunwald, *Hamburgs deutsche Juden* (Hamburg, 1904), 134–36.

71. See Gerard E. Weil's prolegomenon to Solomon Frensdorff, *Massorah Magna* (New York, 1968), xxv–xxxii, and especially, n. 68. Frensdorff dedicated his first book, an edition of R. Moshe ha-Nakdan's *Darkei ha-Nikkud ve-ha-Neginot*, to his revered teacher Bernays.

72. For example, R. Leib Adler, a noted Jewish educator (see E. Duckesz, *Ḥakhmei AHW* [Hamburg, 1908], 149–50; R. Samson Nathan, Jewish educator and *dayyan* of Hamburg (see Duckesz, op. cit., 152–54); and R. Gottlieb Moses, *dayyan* of Hamburg (see Duckesz, op. cit., 130).

W. Aron, "Hakham Isaac Bernays," *Jewish Forum* 32 (March, 1949): 41, claimed that Nathan Marcus Adler (1803–1890), Chief Rabbi of the British Empire; Solomon Ludwig Steinheim (1789–1866), celebrated physician and philosopher; and Aaron Marcus (1843–1916), publicist for Ḥasidism in Western Europe, were "pupils" of Bernays. These claims appear to have no basis in fact. Nathan Marcus Adler was a student of R. Abraham Bing. The biographies of Adler available to me make no mention of his having studied under Bernays. If he was a student of Bernays, it could only have been prior to 1821, either in Mainz or Wuerzburg. Steinheim—who was three years older than Bernays—was an acquaintance of Bernays, not his student. Aaron Marcus was six years old when Bernays died! And in any event, as indicated above, Bernays taught only the highest classes in the Hamburg day school.

We note in passing that it is often claimed that Nathan Marcus Adler was the first German—and Orthodox—rabbi in the modern period to have earned the Ph.D. degree. See, e.g., Leo Trepp, *Die Oldenburger Judenschaft* (Oldenburg, 1973), 88, and Ismar Schorsch, "Emancipation and the Crisis of Religious Authority: The Emergence of the Modern Rabbinate," in W. E. Mosse, A. Paucker, and R. Ruerup, eds., *Revolution and Evolution: 1848 in German-Jewish History* (Tuebingen, 1981), 208. It would appear, however, that this honor more properly belongs to another rabbi. A likely candidate is Abraham Alexander Wolff (1801–1891), a student of R. Abraham Bing who served with distinction for some sixty years as Chief Rabbi of Denmark. Wolff earned his doctorate at the University of Giessen in 1821 and was appointed *Landesrabbiner* of the province of Oberhessen in 1826. Adler earned his doctorate at the University of Erlangen in 1828 and was appointed Chief Rabbi

Raphael Hirsch[73] and Azriel Hildesheimer,[74] who were able to transform aspects of Bernays' intellectual teaching into a more practical form of Judaism, one that would revive Orthodoxy in Germany and ultimately impact on Orthodoxy the world over.

R. Jacob Ettlinger

Rabbi Jacob Ettlinger[75] (1798–1871) studied under R. Asher Wallerstein (d. 1837)—a son of R. Aryeh Leib b. Asher (d. 1785), the *Sha'agat Aryeh*—at Karlsruhe, and under R. Abraham Bing at Wuerzburg, receiving his rabbinic ordination from the latter. While at the yeshiva in Wuerzburg, Ettlinger attended the university there. During his third year of study at the university, anti-Semitic riots broke out in Wuerzburg and Ettlinger was forced to flee, never completing his program of study. But the mere fact that a *gadol be-yisrael*—later to achieve great renown as the author of *'Arukh la-Ner*, a celebrated commentary on several tractates of the Talmud, and *She'elot u-Teshuvot Binyan Ẓiyyon*, a classic compendium of responsa—pursued a formal program of study at a secular university, and in fact excelled in his secular studies, reflected a change of prodigious proportions for traditional Judaism. Ettlinger, after all, did not pursue secular study because he sought a medical or any other professional degree. For Ettlinger, secular study was deemed significant, perhaps even necessary, for a rabbi who wished to function in

---

of Oldenburg in the same year. Aside from the sources listed above, see the entries on Wolff and Adler in the various Jewish encyclopedias.

73. Hirsch refers to Bernays as his "unforgettable teacher." See, e.g., Hirsch's commentary to Genesis 4:26; cf. his commentary to Numbers 20:8 and to Psalms 16:1. Hirsch's reference to the "one star that guided me somewhat in the beginning" (*Nineteen Letters*, letter 19) is almost certainly to Bernays.

74. See, e.g., Hildesheimer's moving eulogy over Bernays in A. Hildesheimer, *She'elot u-Teshuvot Rabbi 'Azriel* (Jerusalem, 1976), II, 437–40, where Hildesheimer records several exegetical gems he heard from Bernays, and opines—in all seriousness—that Bernays' sermons were divinely inspired. Cf. Hildesheimer's introduction to R. Zalman Bonhard's *Minḥah Tehorah* (Pressburg, 1858), 9, n. 3.

For other eulogies over Bernays, see M. S. Kruegar, *Zekher Ẓaddik: Rede zur Gedaechtniss Feier des sel. Chacham Isaac Bernays* (Hamburg, 1849); and R. Jacob Ettlinger, "Trauerrede," *Der Treue Zions-Waechter* 5 (1849): 161–68.

75. The definitive biography of Ettlinger is by Judith Bleich, *Jacob Ettlinger, His Life and Works: The Emergence of Modern Orthodoxy in Germany* (see n. 44); we have relied heavily on her research for the account presented here. Important materials relating to Ettlinger are gathered together in R. Yehudah A. Horovitz, ed., *She'elot u-Teshuvot he-Arukh la-Ner* (Jerusalem, 1989), 2 vols. See also Yonah Immanuel, "Chapters in the History of R. Jacob Ettlinger" (Hebrew), *Ha-Ma'ayan* 12:2 (1972): 25–35; and A. Abraham, "The True Guardian of Zion" (Hebrew), *Yated Ne'eman*, Nov. 29, 1991: 10–12.

the modern world.[76] As we shall see, his genuine regard for aspects of secular study was reflected also in the language that he preached, in the curriculum he instituted in his day school in Altona, and in the curriculum he prepared for his proposed rabbinical seminary.

In 1825, Ettlinger was appointed *rosh yeshiva* of the *klaus* in Mannheim, while also serving as district rabbi of Ladenburg and environs. Some seventy students would study under Ettlinger in Mannheim, including, approximately for a year, R. Samson Raphael Hirsch. In 1836, Ettlinger assumed the post of Chief Rabbi of Altona where he would serve with distinction for some three and a half decades until his death. There too Ettlinger served as head of a yeshiva, and among its more illustrious graduates was R. Azriel Hildesheimer. Thus, the two central figures who shaped Orthodoxy in the Western world—R. Samson Raphael Hirsch and R. Azriel Hildesheimer—were disciples of Ettlinger, even as they had been disciples of Ḥakham Bernays.

It was no accident that Ettlinger preached in German. In fact, it was a condition of employment incorporated into his rabbinic contract![77] With the Enlightenment, the nature of the rabbinate changed drastically and rapidly. Whereas the pre-Enlightenment rabbi did not attend a university, did not ordinarily preach every Sabbath, and certainly did not preach in German, by the middle of the nineteenth century, virtually all Orthodox rabbis in Germany were college educated and preached every Sabbath in German.[78] In part this was due to governmental interference, which required rabbis to be college educated or, at the very least, to pass

---

76. A colleague at the yeshiva of Wuerzburg would describe Ettlinger's university years as follows:

> He attended lectures in secular study only for several hours a day, several days a week. This he did because the times required it, in order to be knowledgeable in worldly matters, in order to be able to say to Wisdom "You are my sister" [cf. Proverbs 7:4], and in order to know how to respond to reformers and heretics. Even then, however, his mind concentrated on Torah, never ceasing to study Torah and observe the commandments diligently.

See Horovitz, *She'elot u-Teshuvot,* I, introduction, 13.

77. The contract is reprinted in Horovitz, *She'elot u-Teshuvot,* I, introduction, p. 18. Contrast the view of the Ḥatam Sofer:

> Heaven forbid that you appoint a rabbi who publishes false teaching, reads outside books, or delivers a sermon in a foreign tongue, for learning Torah from such a rabbi is prohibited.

See *She'elot u-Teshuvot Ḥatam Sofer, Ḥoshen Mishpat* (Jerusalem, 1972), 74b, §197.

78. See Ismar Schorsch, "Emancipation" (above, n. 72), 205–47 (and the appended qualifying remarks by H. A. Strauss). Interestingly, of the 67 rabbis with doctorates in Germany in the 1840s (listed by Schorsch), 13 percent studied under R. Abraham Bing at Wuerzburg. The list, of course, does not include Ettlinger, Bernays, and others who enrolled at the University of Wuerzburg but did not earn the Ph.D. degree while studying under

equivalency examinations in secular study; in part it was due to the new social setting in which rabbis found themselves. After all, logic dictates that a rabbi preach in the language his congregants understand. In many parts of Germany, government agencies did all they could to curtail the powers of the rabbinate. Their ultimate goal was to control and speed the process of Jewish acculturation to German culture. Thus, for example, rabbis were no longer to decide civil disputes in accordance with Jewish law. Jews, as budding citizens of the realm, were to petition the same courts of justice as everyone else. Ettlinger, who served in Altona, then under the aegis of the kingdom of Denmark, retained the right to adjudicate civil disputes among the Jews under his authority. This state of affairs continued until 1863, when Denmark adopted the policy of virtually all the principalities in Germany and revoked the dispensation it had provided for Ettlinger.

Ettlinger's use of the German language and of new literary formats for Jewish expression was part of a carefully crafted plan to use the very tools of the Enlightenment against its more corrosive aspects. He founded two major periodicals of Jewish thought—long before it had become fashionable to do so in Orthodox circles. They were *Der Treue Zions-Waechter*, a German periodical which appeared as a weekly from 1845–1850 and as a bi-monthly from 1851–1854; and *Shomer Ẓiyyon ha-Ne'eman*, a bi-monthly Hebrew periodical which appeared from 1846–1856. These pioneer periodicals paved the way for the later, more influential Orthodox journals, such as Hirsch's *Jeschurun*, Lehmann's *Israelit*, and Hildesheimer's *Die juedische Presse*.

In 1839, Ettlinger founded a Jewish day school in Altona. It featured an integrated curriculum of Jewish and secular study that included the study of the Danish language. Nine to thirteen hours per week—approximately 30 percent of weekly instructional time—were devoted to Jewish studies. Boys and girls were taught in separate classes from the start—in contrast, for example, to Hirsch's *Realschule*. Jewish and non-Jewish teachers taught in the school; the non-Jewish teachers taught secular studies. The appointment of non-Jewish teachers was made necessary by the dearth of Orthodox teachers adept in secular study and by Ettlinger's refusal to appoint non-Orthodox Jews to his faculty.[79] Once again, Ettlinger served as a trailblazer, restructuring the form and substance of traditional Jewish education in order to render Orthodoxy viable in a modern world.[80]

Bing. Was it the proximity of the yeshiva to the university that best accounts for this statistic, or is it possible that Bing played a more active, perhaps even pivotal, role in the transition of the rabbinate from the premodern to the modern period? The matter deserves investigation. See, tentatively, Isaac Bamberger's biography of Bing in R. Abraham Bing, *Zikhron Avraham* (Pressburg, 1892), 5–12.

79. The appointment of Christian rather than non-Orthodox Jewish teachers of secular studies was first instituted by Ḥakham Bernays in the day school at Hamburg. See Goldschmidt, *Geschichte*, 57–58.

80. In a carefully worded manifesto on behalf of Torah study in the *yishuv* in Palestine,

Perhaps the boldest of Ettlinger's educational programs was one that never got off the ground. It was a proposal for the establishment of a rabbinical seminary with him as its head. Given the radical transformation of the rabbinate and the lay community during the Enlightenment period, Ettlinger felt that it was essential that Orthodoxy train a new generation of rabbis and teachers who could cope with modernity and earn the respect of the lay community. While yet in Mannheim in 1829, Ettlinger received a tentative invitation to serve as head of a projected rabbinical seminary in Amsterdam. Although the appointment never materialized, he indicated in his response to the authorities in Amsterdam that he had already given much thought to a similar proposal which would have transformed the *klaus* in Mannheim into a rabbinical seminary.[81] Ettlinger then describes in some detail the curriculum he envisioned for the rabbinical seminary in Mannheim. Beyond what would be studied at any *yeshivah gedolah*, it included instruction in Hebrew grammar, biblical exegesis, Jewish philosophy and theology, and in the art of preaching. An even more ambitious proposal, once again involving Ettlinger, appeared in his *Der Treue Zions-Waechter* in 1846. The anonymous proposal appeared as the lead article and could only have been printed with Ettlinger's approval. After justifying the need for an Orthodox rabbinical seminary, the detailed proposal delineates the administrative structure, student requirements, and curriculum of the projected

written by R. Eliyahu Guttmacher (d. 1874) and cosigned by Ettlinger, the two rabbis called for the establishment of "universal" yeshivot in Jerusalem, Hebron, Tiberias, and Safed. Diaspora Jewry was urged not only to support the yeshivot, but to send its youth to study in these new world centers for Torah study. Regarding the students at these new yeshivot, the manifesto predicts:

> They will surely excel in secular wisdom in a holy way, as did our holy forefathers, in comparison to whom present day sages, even those knowledgeable in secular study, are as naught. . . . Consider Saadia Gaon, Maimonides, Ravad, and the tens of thousands of others who mastered all of secular wisdom, yet merited ultimate perfection from the light of Torah that shone over them. . . . The day will come, perhaps, when every parent who wishes to instill Torah, fear of God, and secular wisdom in his child . . . will send him to the Holy Land . . . and after [studying Torah at the yeshiva] he will learn how to engage in business, then marry, thus combining Torah with worldly success.

The manifesto should hardly be viewed as an endorsement of the introduction of secular studies into the yeshivot in the Holy Land. One suspects that the two rabbis had a far more subtle—and innocuous—notion in mind, i.e., the notion that if Torah is studied properly and intensively all wisdom can be derived from it. Nonetheless, the formulation—intended to attract European students to the yeshivot in the Yishuv—is striking and worth noting. Also noteworthy is the rather clear indication that graduates would not be bankrolled indefinitely by Kollel funds or by the *ḥalukkah*; they were expected to join the work force. The full text of the manifesto, dated 1862, is available in Guttmacher's *Mikhtav me-Eliyahu* (Jerusalem, 1990), 124–37; and in Horovitz, *She'elot u-Teshuvot,* II, 140–45.

81. Ettlinger's response is printed in Jaap Meijer, *Moeder in Israël* (Haarlem, 1964), 80–91.

rabbinical seminary. Applicants aged fifteen to eighteen would be accepted into the program upon presenting documents attesting to their background in Jewish and secular study, and upon passing a required entrance examination. The purpose of the entrance examination was to enable the student to demonstrate his proficiency not only in Talmud, but also in German, mathematics, history, and geography. Those accepted into the program would follow an eight-year course of study that included courses in German, philosophy, mathematics, logic, history, and geography. As Judith Bleich has shown, the seminary was to have been established in Altona, and Ettlinger was to have served as president of its Board of Directors. It failed only because of the sudden death of the benefactor upon whom the entire proposal was dependent "and without flour there can be no Torah" (*M. Avot* 3:17).[82] What Ettlinger could only dream about would be implemented by his disciple, R. Azriel Hildesheimer.

Ettlinger was first and foremost a traditional rabbinic scholar whose talmudic commentaries and responsa follow in the footsteps of his predecessors, the *gedolei ha-Torah* of Germany. Remarkably, without any apparent diminution in either the quality or quantity of his Torah teaching and publication, he laid the foundations for the Orthodox response to modernity. His guarded blending of the old and the new is perhaps best exemplified by this brief citation from his responsum endorsing the use of machine-made *mazzot* during Passover:

> I, together with all those who fear God and have a clear understanding of how the machine—in these lands—works, take delight at the improvement it has wrought. In my native city, Karlsruhe, it is already several years that the rabbis instituted the practice that *mazzot* are made by machine. So too the Chief Rabbi of Wuerzburg [R. Seligmann Baer Bamberger (d. 1878)], author of *Melekhet Shamayim*, instituted the same practice in Wuerzburg and in the district under his authority. We are all in agreement in praising the improvement it has wrought in the production of kosher *mazzot*. I am therefore surprised that you write that several rabbis in your country have banned its use. It would appear that those rabbis, despite the finest of intentions, have no idea how the machine works. Hearing reports about the machines is no substitute for seeing them first hand. If they reject the machines precisely because they are new, know that we—the authentic rabbis of Germany—also keep our distance from all that is new pertaining to Torah and the commandments. But why shouldn't we accept the advances in modern technology that aid us in understanding and observing God's commandments even better than before?[83]

---

82. See the full account in Bleich, *Jacob Ettlinger*, 276–90. It should be noted that Ettlinger's approval of rabbinical seminaries was not indiscriminate. See Horovitz, *She'elot u-Teshuvot*, 160 and 270.

83. The responsum was reprinted in Horovitz, *She'elot u-Teshuvot*, II, 26–27.

R. Samson Raphael Hirsch

The passages listed below, drawn from the writings of R. Samson Raphael Hirsch's (1808–1888) contemporaries—admirers and opponents—bear eloquent testimony to his powerful impact on German Jewry.

> Hirsch has great influence over me; he has made life very sweet for me here at Bonn. . . . I already knew him at Heidelberg. . . . One evening both of us bemoaned the loneliness of the Jewish students of theology and we decided to found an orator's club. This club has exercised a distinct influence over me and has led to the formation of the strongest ties of friendship between Hirsch and myself. After his first lecture, we talked at very great length, and I learned to admire his exceptional eloquence, the keenness of his intellect, and his quick and lucid grasp. This debate, however, did not draw us close to each other, since we touched at times upon the religious aspect as well. . . . That winter and the following summer we studied the tractate *Zebaḥim* together. Gradually, there resulted mutual love and esteem. I respected his lofty qualities of spirit, his rigorously moral deportment, and I loved the goodness of his heart. His comradeship brought me great benefit and pleasure.
>
> *Abraham Geiger*[84]

> To Samson Raphael Hirsch, the spirited champion of historic Judaism, the unforgettable teacher, the fatherly friend, in love and gratitude.
>
> *Heinrich Graetz*[85]

> The man who exerted the greatest influence upon my young life and imbued me with the divine ardor of true idealism was none other than the representative of what was called Neo-orthodoxy, Samson Raphael Hirsch, the pupil of Isaac Bernays, the Ḥakam of Hamburg, author of the anonymous book, *Der Bibel'sche Orient*,[86] and of Jacob Ettlinger when Klaus rabbi in Mannheim. Though he kept himself at a distance from his pupils, as he never invited us to his home nor manifested any personal interest in our welfare or progress, his strong personality was such as to work like a spell upon his hearers. Whether he spoke in the pulpit or expounded the Scripture to large audiences, or led us through the discussions of the Talmud, there was a striking originality and the fascinating power of genius in his grasp of the subject. His method of reading and explaining the Scripture or the Talmud was quite different from the usual way; he made us find the meaning of the passage independently, though his own system of thought was peculiar. His was a strange combination of Hebrew lore and German culture, which culminated in his concept of the 'Jisroel-Mensch,' that is of a humanity which finds its highest expression in loyal, traditional Judaism. Every Saturday night in my letter to the

---

84. Abraham Geiger, *Nachgelassene Schriften* (Berlin, 1878), V, 18–19. The translation cited here is from Mordecai Breuer, "Samson Raphael Hirsch," in Leo Jung, ed., *Guardians of Our Heritage* (New York, 1958), 268.

85. Heinrich Graetz, *Gnosticismus und Judenthum* (Krotoshin, 1846), dedication page.

86. See n. 41.

dear ones at home I gave a faithful synopsis of the sermon I heard in the morning and the impressive teachings laid down in the 'Horeb' and other works by Hirsch became part and parcel of my innermost life.

Kaufmann Kohler[87]

Hirsch made it a point to appear always in faultless apparel, almost stylish, according to the fashion of the period. Nothing in his manner or figure was to be strange to the crowd. This remained so during his whole life and I can still see him as an octogenarian, immaculately dressed in the finest black suit and top hat, like a born aristocrat. A striking feature was his head, so well-shaped and adorned with the most beautiful and brilliant eyes, which kept their fiery lustre up to the last moments of his life. I think nobody could ever forget his countenance, animated by the magnetic glance. And whilst his outward manner was prepossessing and attractive, his character showed a strength and earnestness uncommon for any man, almost too earnest. He did not freely make friends and even his friends he kept at a distance; nor was he easily approached, his serenity and dignity warded off intimacy. Bold and fearless he upheld his convictions. Only once did he yield to outside pressure, when—in Oldenburg—he allowed *Kol Nidre* to be abolished.[88] In later years he made no concessions, no adjustment of views was possible and, in questions of principle, he never accepted any compromise, nor did he permit any of his communities to interfere with his opinions and beliefs.

As a scholar he lived his own life. His intercourse with other scholars was scanty. He did not need them. Feared as an antagonist, he was born a fighter and he hit hard. Mendelssohnian tolerance was unthinkable for him. He lived in his study amidst his books and papers, where the air was thick with smoke clouds, issuing from his long much-loved pipe.

Needless to say, the Religionsgesellschaft was very proud of their rabbi. His reputation as one of the greatest living scholars was a source of the deepest satisfaction, but it was in the first place his eloquence that thrilled their minds. He spoke always spontaneously, without any notes; all his addresses were presented extemporaneously. He was a marvelous orator; his noble language, the rapid flow of his speech, the originality of his thoughts, the force of his arguments, together with his whole personal appearance, made his sermons irresistible and secured him a magic influence.

Saemy Japhet[89]

One word about his success as a preacher. With a preacher like Hirsch it is as with a great singer. The effect of the performance must be felt but cannot be described and is lost to posterity. Whenever in his sermons some struggle, some hesitation was noticed, it was because he was applying to himself the reins, not the spur. He had to restrain the great

87. Kaufmann Kohler, "Personal Reminiscences of My Early Life," in his *Studies, Addresses, and Personal Papers* (New York, 1931), 475.

88. For details regarding this episode, see Mordecai Breuer, "Chapters in the History of Samson Raphael Hirsch: The Annulment of the Recital of *Kol Nidre* at Oldenburg" (Hebrew), *Ha-Ma'ayan* 4:2 (1964): 7–12

89. Saemy Japhet, "The Succession From the Frankfurt Jewish Community under Samson Raphael Hirsch," *Historia Judaica* 10 (1948): 104–6.

copiousness in the outpour of ideas, in the exuberant flow of words which suggested themselves to him; and with the greatest skill he selected on the spur of the moment those that were most fitting. The effect his addresses had on his audience was always electric. Suffice it to say that the instances were by no means few, that men of culture and education entered the synagogue with opinions antagonistic to his, and left it again with serious doubts as to the correctness of their views, to end in becoming his most ardent followers.

But it was by his pedagogical achievements in the founding of and presiding over schools, and by his statesmanlike qualities in the organization of communities, that he exhibited himself most as a man of action. That he knew his own mind and never acted at random, but always in accordance with settled principles, is evidenced by his many articles on communal affairs. Again I am unable to discuss them, and must therefore request my readers to inquire for themselves if they wish to know Hirsch in quite another character. That his theories were sound, that his activity proceeded in the right direction, cannot be shown better than by pointing to the congregation which he created in Frankfort-on-the-Main.

Samuel A. Hirsch[90]

Hirsch was an awesome figure. Much has been, and will continue to be, written about him—with little fear that what remains to be said is anywhere near exhaustion. Following a brief biographical sketch, we shall focus primarily on Hirsch's central teaching: *Torah and derekh ereẓ*.[91]

90. Samuel A. Hirsch [no relation to Samson Raphael Hirsch], "Jewish Philosophy of Religion and Samson Raphael Hirsch," *Jewish Quarterly Review*, old series, 2 (1890): 136.

91. Biographical studies of Hirsch abound. No one has written more intelligently about him than the historian Mordecai Breuer in a series of essays published in *Ha-Ma'ayan* and elsewhere, several of which are cited in these notes. In general, see Eduard Duckesz, "Zur Genealogie Samson Raphael Hirsch's," *Jahrbuch der Jüdisch-Literarischen Gesellschaft* 17 (1926): 103–32; Isaac Heinemann, "Studies on R. Samson Raphael Hirsch" (Hebrew), *Sinai* 24 (1949): 249–71; idem, "Samson Raphael Hirsch: The Formative Years of the Leader of Modern Orthodoxy," *Historia Judaica* 13 (1951): 29–54; Isidor Grunfeld, "Samson Raphael Hirsch: The Man and his Mission," in his edition of Samson Raphael Hirsch, *Judaism Eternal* (London, 1956), I, xiii–lxi; idem, "Introduction to Samson Raphael Hirsch's *Horeb*," in his edition of Samson Raphael Hirsch, *Horeb* (London, 1962), I, xix–cliii; Pinchas E. Rosenblüth, "Samson Raphael Hirsch, sein Denken und Wirken," in Hans Liebeschütz and Arnold Paucker, eds., *Das Judentum in der Deutschen Umwelt 1800–1850* (Tübingen, 1977), 293–324; Robert Liberles, *The Resurgence of Orthodox Judaism in Frankfurt am Main* 1838–1877 (Westport, 1985); Yonah Immanuel, ed., *Rabbi Samson Raphael Hirsch: His Teaching and System* (Hebrew), (Jerusalem, 1989); and the numerous studies strewn throughout *Nachalat Ẓewi* (1930–1938) and *Ha-Ma'ayan* (new series: 1964 on)—two periodicals devoted largely to the thought of Samson Raphael Hirsch. Regarding Noah Rosenbloom's iconoclastic *Tradition in an Age of Reform: The Religious Philosophy of Samson Raphael Hirsch* (Philadelphia, 1976), see Mordecai Breuer's review in *Tradition* 16:4 (1977): 140–48. An informative biography of Hirsch is R. Eliyahu M. Klugman's "Treatise on 'There Was a King in Jeshurun'" (Hebrew), in Samson Raphael Hirsch, *Shemesh Marpe* (Brooklyn, 1992), 273–

Born in Hamburg in 1808, Hirsch studied mostly with private tutors until 1821, when Bernays was appointed to the Hamburg rabbinate. Hirsch was profoundly influenced by Bernays; in effect, he would devote his life to transforming Bernays' teachings into a living reality for Orthodox Jewry in Germany.[92] Even before Hirsch had graduated from the local *Gymnasium*, and at his parents' request, he began serving as an apprentice for a business concern—the typical profession engaged in by Hamburg Jews. But Hirsch's heart was set on the rabbinate. At Bernays' suggestion, Hirsch, at age twenty, left for Mannheim to study at the yeshiva of R. Jacob Ettlinger.[93] His studies at the yeshiva lasted for little more than a year, after which Hirsch enrolled for a year of study at the University of Bonn, where he studied, among other topics, classical languages and literature and experimental physics.[94] This was clearly part of a carefully laid-out plan that would provide him with the education and credentials necessary to succeed in the German rabbinate. Like Bernays and Ettlinger, Hirsch did not earn a college degree. In 1830, Rabbi Dr. Nathan Adler—who would later serve with distinction as Chief Rabbi of the British Empire—resigned his post as Chief Rabbi of Oldenburg, just northwest of Bremen in Lower Saxony. Upon the receipt of a strong letter of recommendation from Bernays, Adler recommended Samson Raphael Hirsch, then only twenty-two years old, as his successor.[95] Hirsch served eleven years in Oldenburg.[96] There he would marry, father the first of his ten children, and write *The Nineteen Letters* (1836) and *Horeb* (1837), two works that would catapult the young Hirsch to the front line of leadership of Orthodox Jewry in Germany. In 1841, he accepted an appointment to serve as Chief Rabbi of the districts of Aurich and Osnabrueck in the province of Hanover and took up residence in Emden. It was in Emden that Hirsch issued for the first time the rallying call for *Torah and derekh ereẓ*.[97] In 1846, Hirsch was appointed Chief Rabbi of Nikolsburg, and *Landesrabbiner* of Moravia and Silesia. His predecessors at Nikolsburg included the Maharal of Prague, R. Yom Tov Lipmann Heller, R. David Oppenheim, and R. Mordecai Benet.

This should have been his most distinguished and perhaps final appointment as

367. Far more comprehensive, even magisterial, is his recent *Rabbi Samson Raphael Hirsch: Architect of Torah Judaism for the Modern World* (New York, 1996).

92. For Bernays' impact on Hirsch, see Isaac Heinemann, "The Relationship Between S. R. Hirsch and his teacher Isaac Bernays" (Hebrew), *Ẓion* 16 (1951): 44–90.

93. See Mordecai Breuer, "Chapters in the History of Samson Raphael Hirsch: At the Yeshiva of R. Jacob Ettlinger in Mannheim" (Hebrew), *Ha-Ma'ayan* 12:2 (1972): 55–62.

94. See Raphael Breuer, *Unter seinem Banner: Ein Beitrag zur Würdigung Rabbiner Samson Raphael Hirschs* (Frankfurt, 1908), 214–15.

95. For the text of Adler's recommendation, see Trepp, *Die Oldenburger Judenschaft*, 119, and the accompanying photograph between pp. 120–21.

96. The definitive study of Hirsch's Oldenburg years is Trepp, *Die Oldenburger Judenschaft*, 119–207.

97. See n. 112.

Chief Rabbi. But events proved otherwise. Despite some successes at Nikolsburg, e.g., Hirsch successfully led the struggle for the emancipation of Austrian and Moravian Jewry, factionalism took its toll on Hirsch. The traditional Orthodox viewed his modern dress as well as some of his innovations, such as the broadening of the yeshiva curriculum and the performance of weddings in the synagogue, with suspicion. Liberal Jews were scandalized by Hirsch's refusal to introduce reforms in the liturgy and in Jewish practice. Not able to satisfy either constituency, Hirsch sought a new venue for his rabbinical talent and aspirations.[98] Upon the death of Bernays in 1849, Hirsch informed the Jewish communal authorities in Hamburg that he was prepared to leave Nikolsburg and assume Bernays' post. The Jewish communal authorities, however, were not prepared to meet Hirsch's terms.[99] Instead, in 1851, Hirsch accepted an invitation to serve as a rabbi of a small breakaway group of Orthodox Jews in Frankfurt who wished to preserve an island of Orthodoxy within the predominantly Reform Jewish community of that city. Here, Hirsch would realize his life's mission by becoming the champion of Orthodoxy. For the first time in his rabbinic career, Hirsch was not responsible for addressing the religious needs of an entire Jewish community, consisting of the full spectrum of Jews from the most liberal to the most Orthodox. Instead, he could focus all his energies on establishing an ideal Jewish community. This he did with great gusto and considerable skill. He shaped the synagogue service, designed the school curricula, created the institutions, and authored the literature that would revive Orthodoxy not only in Frankfurt but throughout Germany and Western Europe.

In 1850, the predominantly Reform-minded Jewish community in Frankfurt consisted of some 5,000 Jews. Eleven Jews, representing a larger group of approximately fifty to 100 Orthodox Jews, petitioned the Frankfurt Senate for the right to create a religious society committed to Orthodox teaching and practice, and for the right to appoint a rabbi. The petition was approved and the separatist *Israelitische Religionsgesellschaft* (henceforth: IRG) came into being. The Senate made it clear, however, that the IRG was recognized as a society, not as an independent Jewish community. Thus, all members of the society remained members of and paid dues to the official Jewish community of Frankfurt.[100] When Hirsch arrived in

98. For details concerning Hirsch's tenure at Nikolsburg, see Yiẓḥak Ze'ev Kahana, "Nikolsburg," in Yehudah Leib Maimon, ed., *'Arim ve-Immahot be-Yisrael* (Jerusalem, 1950), IV, 285–301; and Gertrude Hirschler, "Rabbi and Statesman: Samson Raphael Hirsch, *Landesrabbiner* of Moravia," *Review of the Society for the History of Czechoslovak Jews* 1 (1986–1987): 121–49.

99. Poppel, "The Politics of Religious Leadership: The Rabbinate in Nineteenth Century Hamburg," 464.

100. In 1876, through the efforts of Hirsch, the Prussian parliament approved a law of secession that enabled Orthodox Jews to withdraw from the official Jewish community without abandoning their Jewish status and without jeopardizing their status as citizens of the realm. Hirsch urged all members of the IRG to withdraw from the official Jewish

1851, the IRG had neither synagogue nor school. By the time he died, the IRG consisted of a community of over 400 families with a total population of 1,000 to 2,000 Jews; a day school and high school with over 500 students; and a synagogue that seated 1,000 congregants.[101] Hirsch was first and foremost an educator. His spirited oratory and facile pen essentially accomplished his mission for him. His first work, *The Nineteen Letters*, was a foundation document that encapsulated virtually all that Hirsch would teach throughout his life. Its electrifying effect alone assured Hirsch a permanent place in the history of the revival of Orthodoxy in modern times. This was followed by *Horeb*, a comprehensive digest of Jewish law which made available to the Jewish youth of Germany the essence of Torah teaching in an updated, palatable, even attractive format. Aside from a rich polemical literature against Reform and incipient Conservative Judaism, Hirsch published his monumental *Commentary on the Torah, Commentary on Psalms, Commentary on the Siddur,* and *Commentary on the Passover Haggadah.* In 1854, he founded the periodical *Jeschurun*, a forum in which he published many of the well-over 100 essays, articles, and pamphlets he would author aside from his books. Many of these essays were gathered together and published posthumously in his *Gesammelte Schriften.*[102] Although his published work was written almost exclusively in German, Hirsch also wrote in fluent, even eloquent Hebrew. Many of his *ḥiddushim* and legal responsa were written in classical Hebrew—and they have been gathered together and published in recent years.[103] These recent publications explode the myth that

---

community of Frankfurt, with little success. Some 75 percent of Hirsch's *kehillah* preferred to retain membership in (and pay dues to) both the official Jewish community and the IRG. In general, see Japhet, "The Secession" and Judith Bleich, "The Frankfurt Secession Controversy," *Jewish Action* 52:1 (1991–1992): 22–27, 51–62. For its repercussions in a later period, see Matthias Morgenstern, *Von Frankfurt nach Jerusalem: Isaac Breuer und die Geschichte des 'Austrittsstreits' in der deutschjüdischen Orthodoxie* (Tübingen, 1995).

On the relationship between Hirsch's commitment to secession and his espousal of *Torah and Derekh Ereẓ*, see Jacob Katz, "R. Samson Raphael Hirsch: Rightist and Leftist" (Hebrew), in Mordecai Breuer, ed., *Torah 'im Derekh Ereẓ* (Ramat Gan, 1987), 13–31.

101. See Liberles, *The Resurgence*, passim.

102. Samson Raphael Hirsch, *Gesammelte Schriften* (Frankfurt, 1902–12), 6 vols. An English edition, entitled *The Collected Writings* (New York, 1985–95), 8 vols., has been published by Philipp Feldheim, Inc.

103. See, e.g., the list of printed responsa in Isidor Grunfeld's edition of S. R. Hirsch, *Judaism Eternal*, 1, lxi; R. Barukh Goitein, *Zikhron Avot* (Tel Aviv, 1971), 167–68, responsum 77; Mordecai Breuer, ed., "R. Samson Raphael Hirsch's Essay on Aggadah in Rabbinic Literature" (Hebrew), *Ha-Ma'ayan* 16:2 (1976): 1–16 [for an English translation of this essay, see Joseph Munk, "Two Letters of Samson Raphael Hirsch: A Translation," *L'Eylah* 27 (1989): 30–35]; idem, ed., "Letters by R. Samson Raphael Hirsch" (Hebrew), *ha-Ma'ayan* 29:1 (1988): 17–34; idem, ed., "Responsa, Letters and Handwritten Documents by R. Samson Raphael Hirsch" (Hebrew), *Ha-Ma'ayan* 29:2 (1989): 1–18; Yonah Immanuel, "An Exchange of Letters between Rabbi S. B. Bamberger and Rabbi S. R. Hirsch on Hirsch's Commentary

Hirsch was a second-rate Talmudist who really couldn't hold his own against his contemporaries in Frankfurt. When he wanted to, Hirsch could joust with the outstanding Talmudists of his day—and on their own terms.[104] His mission, however, was not to the intellectual elite but, rather, to the lay community. Hirsch would produce a community of committed lay Orthodox Jews that would become the envy of the decaying, splintered, and beleaguered Jewish communities of Eastern Europe. He would not produce *gedolei yisrael.*

In 1835, the young Hirsch would write as follows:

> Our century wants to think, and that is the greatest merit. Whatever can be rationally explained and is capable of being presented as idea and concept and can stand the test of rational thinking, has nothing to fear. But one can only analyze, test and meditate upon things with which one is acquainted. Among Jews, however, nothing is less well known than Judaism itself. I dare to submit Judaism as it appears to me to intellectual analysis; I shall perhaps be blamed for it from all sides. But just because of that I must not and will not be silent. If I knew of even one person more capable than myself of pleading the true cause of Israel, my incapable and inexperienced pen would have rested for a long time yet. As it is, however, I see an older generation in which Judaism has become an inherited mummy; a generation which shows veneration for Judaism, it is true, but a veneration without spirit; some of that generation, therefore, see only tombstone inscriptions in Judaism and thus despair of the eternal validity of the only thing that makes life worth living. On the other hand, I see a younger generation aglow with noble enthusiasm for Judaism—or rather for Jews. These young men do not know about authentic Judaism, and what they believe they know of it they consider as empty forms without meaning. One must admit, however, that this ignorance is not entirely their fault; and thus the young generation is in danger of undermining Judaism while striving for Jews. I see no one in our day capable of disclosing to the young generation the meaning behind what they wrongly consider as empty forms, of reviving the mummy and taking our young generation to a vantage point from which they can behold the shining light of Judaism. And in such conditions should we condone a dreamy, inactive silence? No; it is a duty to speak out if one is only to hint at a route which others might valiantly follow. I must speak simply because no one else does so; this is the only justification for my coming forward. God will help me.
>
> The weakest feature in Israel's present parlous condition is in respect of Jewish scholarship, the way in which Bible, Talmud, and Midrash have been studied for the last

---

to Leviticus 11:36" (Hebrew), *Ha-Ma'ayan* 29:2 (1989): 35–58; and Els Bendheim, ed., *Liepman Philip Prins: His Scholarly Correspondence* (Hebrew; Hoboken, 1992), which includes letters by Hirsch. A treasure trove of unpublished Hirschian correspondence in Hebrew, including halakhic responsa, rests in an archive at Bar Ilan University. See tentatively David Farkas, ed., *Guide to Manuscripts and Printed Matter from the Legacy of R. Samson Raphael Hirsch: The Sänger Collection* (Hebrew; Ramat Gan, 1982). Many, but hardly all, of Hirsch's responsa and talmudic novellae have been gathered together in S. R. Hirsch, *Shemesh Marpe* 1–269.

104. See R. Yaakov Perlow, "Rav S. R. Hirsch: The Gaon in Talmud and Mikra," in R. Eliyahu Glucksman, et al., eds., *The Living Hirschian Legacy* (New York, 1988), 75–89.

hundred years. We are now paying dearly for this mistaken method of Torah study. Because life has long since been banished from the study of the Torah, the Torah has been banished from life.[105]

Hirsch's writings reflect a dual commitment to rationalism and German idealism. Clearly influenced by a host of Enlightenment and post-Enlightenment philosophers, Hirsch rarely mentions their names.[106] At once a rationalist and romantic, Hirsch's writings, though carefully reasoned and sober, are addressed more often to the heart than to the mind. A hortatory tone pervades his writings. A typical passage reads as follows:

> Although the Jewish community must be administered by its official representatives, the success of Jewish communal life is not dependent on these leaders. Neither boards nor committees, neither rabbis nor preachers make a Jewish community. *For if you will guard faithfully* (Deuteronomy 11:22) "It is you, you who must rally around the Torah as its guardians," the Rabbis (*Sifre, ad loc.*) say to the people—or to the "laity," the elegant term used in modern theology. Do not say, "We have elders, or notables, or prophets for that purpose;" it is you and you alone that must stand on guard for the Torah. The Torah that Moses brought to us is the heritage of the community of Israel. . . . All of you must stand together before the Lord, your God, the totality of Jewish men, including the woodcutter and the water carrier. If the Jewish community as a whole does not bear responsibility for the preservation of the Torah, the Torah will perish.
>
> Therefore the Jewish individual should not think he has acquitted himself of his duty to the community just because he has made his contribution to the communal treasury and cast his vote in the communal elections. If the men you have elected do not perform their duties in such a manner as to promote the religious welfare of your community, if the penny you have turned over to the communal treasury is not spent for the religious welfare of your community, if, despite a rabbi, a board and committees, religion does not fare well in your community, then you have not discharged your obligation towards the community. You must find out why the sacred values of Judaism are doing badly in your community and you must summon all your energies to improve the situation. Remember, in heaven there are no "laymen" or "clergymen." There are only Jewish men and women; there is only a "priestly community," all of whom will be held accountable for the welfare of the sacred values that have been entrusted to their care and who cannot shift this awesome responsibility to the shoulders of others.

---

105. "Letter to Z. H. May," in I. Grunfeld's edition of Hirsch, *Horeb*, I, cxlii–cxliii.

106. See Noah H. Rosenbloom, "The Nineteen Letters of Ben Uziel: A Hegelian Exposition," *Historia Judaica* 22 (1960): 23–60; Howard L. Levine, "Enduring and Transitory Elements in the Philosophy of Samson Raphael Hirsch," *Tradition* 5 (1963): 278–97; and Mordecai Breuer, *Jüdische Orthodoxie im Deutschen Reich 1871–1918* (Frankfurt, 1986), also available in Hebrew under the title *'Edah u-Deyoknah* (Jerusalem, 1990), and in English under the title *Modernity Within Judaism: The Social History of Orthodox Jewry in Imperial Germany* (New York, 1992). Cf. R. Shelomoh E. Danziger, "Clarification of R. Hirsch's Concepts—A Rejoinder," *Tradition 6* (1964): 141–58.

> As a matter of fact, even if you feel you can tell yourself happily that the sacred values of Judaism are flourishing within your own circle, that the men to whom you have entrusted the care of your sanctuary are performing their functions properly, that the school, the synagogue and all the institutions needed for the religious life of any Jewish community are thriving, you have not done your part entirely unless you have been able to convince yourself beyond doubt that this flowering is not an accident but the gratifying fruit of the way in which the community is run, a flowering that will withstand decay. You must be able to assure yourself that some day you may go quietly to your eternal rest, knowing that the flowering you hailed will continue under the care of your children, and that when the men who are now guiding the affairs of the community are gone, they will be replaced only by men with the same attitude and spirit. As long as you cannot be certain of all this, you also have not yet performed your duty as a Jew.[107]

Hirsch was not a philosopher. He nowhere presented a systematic account of his thought. But his voluminous writings are incredibly consistent and often repetitive. The avid reader will have little difficulty grasping the essence of his teaching. In his earliest works, Hirsch criticized severely what he considered to be the skewed form of Judaism of the ghetto:

> The spirit predominant in the most recent form of Jewish education was chiefly devoted to abstract and abstruse speculation. A vivid awareness of the real world was lacking, and therefore study was not conducted with a view to application in life, or to the acquisition of understanding for the world and our duty. Study became the end instead of the means, while the actual subject of the investigation became a matter of indifference. People studied Judaism but forgot to search for its principles in the pages of Scripture. That method, however, is not truly Jewish. Our great masters have always protested against it. Many pages of the classic works of Jewish literature are filled with the objections of their authors to this false and perverted procedure. The Bible and the Talmud are to be studied with one sole object in view, namely, to ascertain the duties of life which they teach, "to learn and to teach, to observe and to do." There is no science which trains the mind to a broader and more practical view of things than does the Torah, pursued in this manner.
>
> A life of seclusion devoted only to meditation and prayer is not Judaism. Study and worship are but paths which lead to action. "Great is study, for it leads to the practical fulfillment of the precepts," say our sages, and the flower and fruit of our devotions should be the resolve to lead a life of action, pervaded with the spirit of God. Such a life is the only universal goal.
>
> Certain misunderstood utterances were taken as weapons with which to repel all higher intellectual interpretation of the Talmud. No distinction was made between the question "What is stated here?" and the query "Why is it so stated?", and not even the category of *Edoth*[108] which, according to its whole nature, was designed to stimulate the mind to activity, was excluded from the excommunication of the intellect. Another

107. S. R. Hirsch, *The Collected Writings* (New York, 1990), VI, 14–15.

108. *Edoth* is the Hirschian term for the symbolic commandments, i.e., commandments obviously intended to reflect an idea or to stimulate thought. See *Nineteen Letters*, chapter 13,

misunderstood passage (*Sanhedrin* 24a, *Tosafot*, s. v. "*belulah*") even led to the suppression of Bible study, an error against which almost prophetic warning had been given long ago (*Soferim* 15: 9). The inevitable consequence was, therefore, that since oppression and persecution had robbed Israel of every broad and natural view of the world and of life, and the Talmud had yielded about all the practical results of life of which it was capable, every mind that felt the desire for independent activity was obliged to forsake the paths of study and research open in general to the human intellect, and to take recourse in dialectic subtleties and hair-splittings.[109]

Nor did the Enlightenment improve matters:

For a spirit had come from the West which mocked at everything holy, and knew no greater pleasure than to make the commandments sound ridiculous. Together with it there entered a longing for sensual enjoyment, which eagerly embraced the opportunity to rid itself so easily of burdensome restrictions. These motives combined to induce people to tear down the barriers erected by the Law, until human conduct became one dead, dull level.[110]

Hirsch's solution was a call for the restructuring of Jewish education, one that would allow for the revival of Judaism in modern times.

There is one way to salvation—atonement must begin where the sin was committed. That one way is to forget the inherited views and prejudices concerning Judaism; to go back to the true sources of Judaism, to the Bible, Talmud and Midrash; to read, study and comprehend them in order to live by them; to draw from them the teachings of Judaism concerning God, the world, mankind and Israel, according to history and precept; to know Judaism out of itself; to learn from its own utterances its wisdom of life. The beginning should be made with the Bible. Its language should first be understood, and then, out of the spirit of the language, the spirit of the speakers therein should be inferred. The Bible should not be studied as an interesting object of philological or antiquarian research, or as a basis for theories of taste, or for amusement. It should be studied as the foundation of a new science. Nature should be contemplated with the spirit of David; history should be perceived with the ear of an Isaiah, and then, with the eye thus aroused, with the ear thus opened, the doctrine of God, world, man, Israel and Torah should be drawn from the Bible, and should become an idea, or system of ideas, fully comprehended. It is in this spirit that the Talmud should be studied. We should

---

and cf. Isidor Grunfeld's discussion of Hirsch's classification of the commandments in Hirsch, *Horeb*, I, lii-lxx.

109. S. R. Hirsch, *The Nineteen Letters on Judaism*, ed. J. Breuer (New York, 1960), 99–100, 121. Breuer's translation, followed here, is based upon S. R. Hirsch, *The Nineteen Letters of Ben Uziel*, trans. B. Drachman (New York, 1899; reissued: New York, 1942). See also the new translation by Karin Paritzky, with commentary by R. Joseph Elias, in *The Nineteen Letters* (Jerusalem, 1995).

110. Hirsch, *The Ninteen Letters on Judaism*, 126.

search in the Halachah only for further elucidation and amplification of those ideas we already know from the Bible, and in the Aggadah only for the figuratively disguised manifestation of the same spirit.

The results of such study must be carried over into life, transplanted by the schools. Schools for Jews! The young saplings of your people should be reared as Jews, trained to become sons and daughters of Judaism, as you have recognized and understood and learned to respect and love it as the law of your life. They should be as familiar with the language of the Bible as they are with the language of the country in which they live. They should be taught to think in both. Their hearts should be taught to feel, their minds to think. The Scriptures should be their book of law for life, and they should be able to understand life through the word of that Law.

Their eye should be open to recognize the world around them as God's world and themselves in God's world as His servants. Their ear should be open to perceive in history the narrative of the education of all men for this service. The wise precepts of the Torah and Talmud should be made clear to them as designed to spiritualize their lives for such sublime service to God. They should be taught to understand, to respect and to love them, in order that they may rejoice in the name of "Jew" despite all which that name implies of scorn and hardship. Together with this type of instruction they should be trained for breadwinning, but they should be taught that breadwinning is only a means of living, but not the purpose of life, and that the value of life is not to be judged according to rank, wealth or brilliance, but solely in terms of the amount of good and of service to God with which that life is filled.[111]

For Hirsch, the Torah was a living Torah to be applied to all spheres of life, including—as he would make abundantly clear in his later writings—general culture. In effect, Hirsch affirmed general culture by declaring it, like all other aspects of life, subservient to Torah. The theological notion that all aspects of life, including general culture, are shaped by and subservient to Torah was summed up by Hirsch in the phrase *Torah and derekh ereẓ*. Although the phrase does not occur in Hirsch's earliest writings, its theological underpinnings were already adumbrated in them. The phrase itself would first appear in an 1844 broadside against Reform.[112] In it, Hirsch called repeatedly for the establishment of Jewish schools whose teachers are expert in Torah and *madda*,[113] and whose curriculum would combine Torah and *ḥokhmah* or Torah and *derekh ereẓ*.

111. Hirsch, *The Nineteen Letters on Judaism*, 127–29.

112. S. R. Hirsch, "Open Letter in Response to the Braunschweig Rabbinical Conference" (Hebrew), in Ẓevi H. Lehren and Eliyahu A. Prins, eds., *Torat ha-Kenaot* (Amsterdam, 1844), 3b–5b; reissued in *Nachalat Ẓewi* 1 (1930–1931): 102–12, in Yonah Immanuel, ed., *Rabbi Samson Raphael Hirsch*, 323–35, and in Hirsch, *Shemesh Marpe*, 188–96.

113. Thus, Hirsch provided an early precedent for what would become the motto of Yeshiva University, "Torah and Madda." For the history of the term and its use at Yeshiva University, see Jacob J. Schacter, "Torah u-Madda Revisited: The Editor's Introduction," *Torah u-Madda Journal* 1 (1989): 1–22.

Before assuming his new post in Frankfurt, Hirsch issued his last circular to the Jewish communities in Moravia. It read in part:

> Neither should you lend your ears to those who alienate themselves from life and science, believing that Judaism must fear them as its worst enemies. They are mistaken in believing that Judaism and all that is holy to it can only be saved by shutting off the sanctuary of Israel within its four walls and by locking the door against any gust of the fresh wind of life, or any beam of the light of science. Listen only to the voice of our Sages (who said): If there is no Torah there is no *derekh ereẓ*, and if there is no *derekh ereẓ*, there is no Torah.[114]

So central was the theme of *Torah and derekh ereẓ* in Hirsch's *Weltanschauung* that it was embedded in the foundation stone of his synagogue. The text of the scroll buried in the foundation stone read:

> May we merit to raise up together our sons and daughters to *Torah and derekh ereẓ*, as we were instructed by the founding fathers of our nation, the true sages.[115]

Similarly, emblazoned in gold letters on the banner of the Jewish day school founded by Hirsch was the phrase: *yafeh talmud torah 'im derekh ereẓ.*[116]

In his writings from the Frankfurt period, Hirsch would address the issue of the relationship between Torah and general culture again and again. Well aware that the phrase *Torah and derekh ereẓ* lent itself to misinterpretation—some Jews would equate the terms *Torah and derekh ereẓ*; others would make Torah subservient to *Derekh Ereẓ*—Hirsch attempted to nip these misinterpretations in the bud. We allow Hirsch to speak for himself:

> We hereby declare before heaven and earth that if our religion indeed required us to renounce that which men call civilization and culture, we would be ready to do so without hesitation, precisely because we truly regard our religion as religion, because it is to us the Word of God in which all other considerations must defer. . . .
>
> But is this really necessary? Judaism was never alien to genuine civilization and culture. In almost every era, its followers stood at the very heights of the culture of their day; indeed, they often outstripped their contemporaries in this respect. If, in recent centuries, the German Jews remained more or less alien to European culture, the fault lay not in their religion but in the coercion, the tyranny from the outside that forcibly

114. See Mordecai Breuer, "'Torah and Derekh Ereẓ' According to the Teaching of R. Samson Raphael Hirsch" (Hebrew), *Ha-Ma'ayan* 9:1 (1969): 1–16, 9:2 (1969): 10–29. Cf. the English version, Mordecai Breuer, *The "Torah-im-Derekh-Eretz" of Samson Raphael Hirsch* (Jerusalem, 1970), 47.

115. Breuer, "Torah and Derekh Ereẓ," 9.

116. Breuer, "Torah and Derekh Ereẓ," 9. Cf. Hermann Schwab, *The History of Orthodox Jewry in Germany* (London, 1950), 43.

confined them to the alleys of their ghettos and shut them off from communication with the outside world. . . .

If, then, our own objectives, too, include the earnest promotion of civilization and culture, if we have expressed this objective in unambiguous terms in the motto of our *Religionsgesellschaft*, "Torah study combined with derekh ereẓ is a good thing," thus merely building upon the same foundations as those set as standards by our Sages of old, what is that separates us from the followers of "Religion Allied with Progress?"

Just this, What *they* want is *religion allied with progress*. We have already seen how this principle, from the outset, negates the truth of what they call religion. What *we* want is *progress allied with religion*.

To them, progress is the absolute on which religion is dependent. To us, religion is the absolute on which progress depends.

They accept religion only to the extent that it does not interfere with progress. We accept progress only to the extent that it does not interfere with religion. . . .

The more we understand that Judaism reckons with all of man's endeavors, and the more its declared mission includes the salvation of all mankind, the less can its views be confined to the four cubits of one room or one dwelling. The more the Jew is a Jew, the more universalist will be his views and aspirations, the less alien will he be to anything that is noble and good, true and upright in the arts and sciences, in civilization and culture. The more the Jew is a Jew, the more joyously will he hail everything that will shape human life so as to promote truth, right, peace and refinement among mankind, the more happily will he himself embrace every opportunity to prove his mission as a Jew on new, still untrodden grounds. The more the Jew is a Jew, the more gladly will he give himself to all that is true progress in civilization and culture—provided that in this new circumstance he will not only maintain his Judaism but will be able to bring it to ever more glorious fulfillment. [117]

The merciful father of mankind has, in our days, stirred up the spirit of righteousness and humanity in the world, a spirit that has opened the gates of the ghettos and introduced the sons of authentic Judaism into the sphere of European civilization as equal citizens. Could the Jew, under these conditions, find a loftier task than to preserve his ancestral heritage beneath the light of justice and religious freedom, even as he did during the centuries of darkness and under the oppression he suffered in a world of error and delusion? Can the Jew not absorb everything in European culture that is noble and good, godly and true, everything that accords with the teachings of his own ancestral faith? For is not European culture itself, in all its finer and nobler aspects, a daughter of that Divine heritage which the Jew himself has introduced among mankind? Now that his energies have been liberated and he has been given freedom of movement, can he not utilize these opportunities to activate all the lofty, sacred, godly, true, noble and good qualities of his own historical, eternal Judaism with even more zeal and devotion? Can he not bring these qualities out into the light of the larger world, so that the Jews, as Jews, may compete with all their neighbors of European humanity in working to promote the happiness and salvation of all mankind?[118]

---

117. Hirsch, *The Collected Writings* (New York, 1990), VI, 120–23.
118. Hirsch, *The Collected Writings,* VI, 21–22.

Let us assume that Moses were to visit our communities today to see whether, thousands of years after his death, we still were *his* communities. Of course, welcoming committees of communal trustees would be waiting to show him our resplendent synagogue edifices and our beautiful Torah arks; they would let him listen to our choirs singing jubilant hymns; they would take him to visit the offices of our trustees, the treasuries and properties of our communities, the humanitarian institutions of our charities. But Moses would turn away from the bewildered trustees and go looking, first of all, for our children. He would stop the first Jewish boy he encountered in the street and ask him, "What biblical verse did you study today?" Let us assume that the lad would answer him with a patronizing smile, "Strange old man! I do not understand your question. A biblical verse? What is that? I had classes today in German, French, English geography, history, physics and natural science. And now I am on my way to my class in religion. I will be Bar Miẓvah this summer, and that is why I am having two hours of religion each week with my teacher." Moses would leave the trustees alone with their synagogues and choirs, their offices and treasuries, their properties and institutions, and sadly walk away, because they would not be his communities. Not without good reason did Moses repeat, over and over again, in the Name of God, the words "You shall keep my commandments; you shall keep my laws; you shall keep my statutes; you shall keep and observe." Not without good reason did he consistently emphasize the keeping of the Law. "To keep means to study." This is the constant refrain with which the Divine oral tradition exhorts us to study the Law. To keep means to study; "that which is not studied will not be practiced," that which is neglected in theory will be lost in practice. In vain do you build synagogues, write Scrolls of the Law and clothe them in purple and gold, gather books and establish libraries. With all this, you have done nothing to help preserve the Torah, that treasure which God has entrusted to you for safekeeping, unless you study the Law yourselves and have your children study it. If you do not know the Law and the youth does not study it, if the Law does not live within the spirit of the nation, then the arks in your synagogues and your libraries are nothing but magnificent mausoleums of the Law.[119]

Ever since we have attempted to make some small contribution with voice and deed and pen within the Jewish community and for the cause of Judaism, it has been our endeavor to demonstrate precisely and how intimately Judaism—we mean Judaism in its unabridged totality—is wedded with the spirit of all true science and knowledge. It has been our aim to show that this Judaism, this *complete* Judaism, "The Lord's Torah is perfect," does not belong to an antiquated past but to the vigorous, pulsating life of the present. In fact, all the future, with the answers that men expect from it to all their social and spiritual problems, belongs to that very Judaism, that whole, complete Judaism. The gap that still separates our actual achievements from what we seek to accomplish is not the point under discussion here. But the fact that precisely this is our aim and our ambition can be seen clearly from our each and every word, and this is the subject of our discussion. And precisely because this is our objective, precisely because we want to see Jewish life and Jewish scholarship understood in the light of true science and knowledge, because (to the extent of our limited insight) we can see the survival and future flowering of Judaism only in terms of an intimate union with the spirit of true science and knowledge in every

119. Hirsch, *The Collected Writings,* VI, 77–78.

age, we are the most avowed foes of all spurious science and knowledge and of any attempt, under the misappropriated mask of scientific research, to lay the ax to the very roots of our sacred Jewish heritage. Any spurious scholarship of this sort undermines not Judaism—because Judaism will outlive us all—but the flowering of true scholarship in Judaism, for such "research" must of necessity give any sincere Jew who is not familiar with scholarship the impression, based on his own limited experience, that any endeavor at scientific, scholarly research is a threat to Judaism.

And that is why we regard Dr. Beer[120] and his associates as the most dangerous enemies of scholarly research in Judaism. For if it were indeed true that there was no alternative, if any attempt at scholarly research *per se* were indeed capable of shaking the very foundations of Judaism as it was given to the House of Israel for its eternal mission, never to be abridged, if we had only a choice between Judaism and science, then we would simply have no other alternative. In that case, every Jew would decide, without a moment's hesitation. "Better to be dubbed a fool all my days than to be wicked before God for even a moment." (*M. Eduyoth* 5:6) *Better a Jew without science than a science without Judaism.*[121]

In sum, the primacy of Torah and the subservience of *derekh ereẓ* were central to Hirsch's affirmation of *Torah and derekh ereẓ*.

Yet another fundamental misunderstanding of *Torah and derekh ereẓ* is the claim that Hirsch himself believed that his attitude toward general culture was a *hora'at sha'ah*, e.g., a timebound stance. The argument runs that Hirsch did what he had to do in order to stem the tide of Reform. His theme of Torah and *Derekh Ereẓ* was intended for nineteenth century German Jewry alone. Hirsch, it is claimed, would not have called for an openness to general culture in Eastern Europe or anywhere else where circumstances differed substantively from those of nineteenth century Germany.[122] It is, of course, impossible to know with certainty how Hirsch would

---

120. Dr. Bernhard Beer (1801–1861), scholar and bibliophile, was a close associate of Zechariah Frankel, founder of the "positive historical" school of Judaism, i.e., what is known today as Conservative Judaism. Hirsch was a bitter opponent of Frankel, and Beer had come to Frankel's defense. For the Hirsch-Frankel controversy, see Hirsch, *The Collected Writings,* V, 209–330.

121. Hirsch, *The Collected Writings,* V, 287.

122. For vigorous rebuttal of this fundamental misunderstanding of Hirsch, see Jacob Rosenheim, *Samson Raphael Hirsch's Cultural Ideal and Our Times* (London, 1951), 44; R. Yeḥiel Y. Weinberg, *She'elot u-Teshuvot Seridei Esh* (Jerusalem, 1977), IV, 366–69; R. Joseph Breuer, "Torah and Derekh Ereẓ—A Timebound Measure?" (Hebrew), *Ha-Ma'ayan* 6:4 (1966): 1–3; and R. Shimon Schwab, *These and Those* (New York, 1966), 16.

Such misrepresentation of Hirsch's views needs to be distinguished carefully from those who understood Hirsch's views correctly but disagreed with them. Thus, many East European *gedolim,* while expressing genuine admiration for Hirsch, denied that the principle of *Torah and derekh ereẓ* was applicable outside of Germany. Some even expressed reservations about the results of its implementation in Germany. See, e.g., R. Israel Salanter's comments cited in R. Isaac J. Reines, *Shnei ha-Me'orot* (Piotrkow, 1913), II, 44–48; in R. Yeḥiel Y. Weinberg,

have responded to differing sets of circumstances. It is quite clear, however, that Hirsch viewed *Torah and derekh ereẓ* as an operating principle that applied to Jews at all times and at all places. In any given epoch and in any given locality, Torah was to be applied to all spheres of life, including general culture. In his tragic confrontation with R. Seligmann Baer Bamberger,[123] Hirsch wrote:

> The *Religionsgesellschaft* has set a shining example, evoking widespread enthusiasm and emulation, showing that our timeless Judaism is capable of rebirth and of proving itself in the midst of all modern trends. It has become visible testimony to the fact that this ancient, timeless Judaism, with its Law and its scholarship, does not belong to a past that has already been buried or that is ripe for burial but is a most vital part of the present and the future. It attests most cogently to the truth of the saving and healing principle of *Torah and derekh ereẓ*, which the *Religionsgesellschaft* wrote upon its banner at the time of its establishment and with which it has entered the arena of the present day. It is true that you, dear Rabbi, are not altogether in favor of this principle, but *Torah and derekh ereẓ* is nevertheless the one true principle conducive to "truth and peace," to healing and recovery from all ills and all religious confusion. The principle of Torah and *Derekh Ereẓ* can fulfill this function because it is not part of troubled, time-bound notions; it represents the ancient, traditional wisdom of our sages that has stood the test everywhere and at all times. These sages and they alone, have always been, and still are, our true sages.[124]

We have already seen that Hirsch applied the principle of *Torah and derekh ereẓ* to the Jewish communities of Moravia.[125] The same is true regarding the Jewish communities in Lithuania. In 1881, Hirsch wrote a letter of recommendation on behalf of the Kolel Perushim of Kovno, an institute for the advanced study of Talmud founded by R. Israel Salanter and R. Isaac Elḥanan Spektor. Apparently, Hirsch had been informed that the members of the institute would study, aside from Torah, the vernacular and science. Hirsch wrote:

> This institution trains brilliant young men to become great scholars, while at the same time imparting to them a knowledge of the language of the country as well as of other subjects important for their general education. This institution seems to be a true

Serdei Esh, II, 14, §8; and in Immanuel Etkes, *Rabbi Israel Salanter and the Beginning of the Musar Movement* (Hebrew; Jerusalem, 1984), 307. Cf. R. Ḥayyim 'Ozer Grodzenski's view of the Orthodox rabbinate in Germany, in R. Abraham I. Karelitz, *Iggerot Ḥazon Ish* (second edition, Bnei Brak, 1956), II, 171–73 (reissued in: R. Ḥayyim 'Ozer Grodzenski, *Aḥiezer: Koveẓ Iggerot* [Bnei Brak, 1970], II, 443–44, and in R. Ben Ẓion Shapiro, ed., *Iggerot le-Ra'ayah* [second edition, Jerusalem, 1990], 457–58, letter 318). See too the carefully worded formulation in R. Shlomo Wolbe, *'Alei Shur* (Jerusalem, 1988), I, 296, §§5 and 8.

123. See Hirsch, *The Collected Writings*, VI, 189–317. Cf. the references cited above, n. 100.

124. Hirsch, *The Collected Writings*, VI, 221.

125. See above, p. 191 and n. 114.

> salvation for the religion which has been on the retreat in that great realm for many years. As a matter of fact, this is the first case, and the only one for the time being, of leading rabbis and Torah scholars of distinction proclaiming the study of the local language and the study of the general sciences a permitted and even desirable undertaking. This way the principle on which our community, too, is based, is safeguarded against attack from different quarters and especially on the part of our brothers in Eastern Europe. And, indeed, this is the principle in which we see the only remedy against the regrettable religious aberrations of our time, and here we see it declared above all doubt as a model example worthy of imitation.[126]

A year later, Hirsch addressed the following letter to R. Isaac Elḥanan Spektor:

> I have come to inform you that on behalf of the publishers of the periodical "Jeschurun" in Hanover, some pages will be sent to you in which there is an article on the problem of the Jews in your country. Special reference is made to the desire of the government to bring about a closer proximity between the Jews and the other citizens regarding the knowledge of their language and the wisdom of their writers. It is the purpose of the article to find a true solution to this matter, as follows: Although it is necessary and very useful to comply, in this respect, with the wishes of the government, whose intentions are undoubtedly good, at the same time an even greater duty will devolve upon every man in Israel not to leave the path of the Torah and the fear of God which have been our heritage forever; for the Torah and the true *Derekh Ereẓ* and their sciences fit together and do not contradict each other at all, and only by disregarding the truth have the rulers of your country failed to achieve their aim so far, nor will they ever achieve it, as long as they regard the Jewish religion and true general culture as contrary to one another, imagining that the rabbis and learned men are full of hatred for the sciences, and as long as they try to turn the hearts of the Jews toward love of knowledge with the help of rabbis and teachers who are neither faithful nor God-fearing and are lacking in the knowledge of Torah.[127]

Similarly, Hirsch advocated the spread of *Torah and derekh ereẓ* to Hungary. In 1869, when a struggle relating to secular study ensued between various factions of the Hungarian Orthodox rabbinate, Hirsch wrote:

> Let no one cast aspersions on the memory of the rabbis of yore, may they rest in peace, or on their living counterparts among our brethren in Eastern Europe. Their suspicions regarding general culture are to be respected. They emanate from genuine concerns about all that is holy in Israel. These concerns are easily comprehended in the light of the corrupt practices of their opponents. Nonetheless, they are in error. Indeed, there is no hope for the future of the Jewish community until this error is rectified, and until those very rabbis become the leaders of the faction that welcomes general culture into its midst. They must inscribe on their banner with total dedication the adage taught us by

126. Breuer, *The "Torah-Im-Derekh Eretz" of Samson Raphael Hirsch,* 48.
127. Breuer, *The "Torah-Im-Derekh Eretz" of Samson Raphael Hirsch,* 49.

> the true sages—the slightest deviation from which has cost us dearly in the past—*the study of Torah with derekh erez̤ is an excellent thing*, this is to say, the cultivation of general culture in conjunction with Torah study, while living in accordance with the Torah, is an excellent thing.[128]

Clearly, according to Samson Raphael Hirsch, *Torah and derekh erez̤* was intended for all Jewish communities, for all times, and for all places.

Torah and Derekh Erez̤: Practice

It was one thing to preach *Torah and derekh erez̤*; it was quite another to implement it. In reality, Hirsch had to contend with a right and left wing within Orthodoxy—even in Frankfurt—that often viewed Hirsch with suspicion, either as being too liberal or too fundamentalist. More importantly, he had to contend with Reform, Orthodoxy's most successful rival in the Post-Enlightenment period in Germany. He also had to contend with governmental interference relating to the implementation of his educational program. Thus, for example, Hirsch's schools devoted more time to secular than to religious study—despite his commitment to the subservience of *derekh erez̤* to Torah—precisely because educational institutions were rigorously regulated by governmental agencies.[129]

In light of the above, Hirsch's openness to general culture took a variety of forms. In the early years of his rabbinate he was either clean shaven or wore a closely trimmed beard. He grew a fuller beard upon assuming the rabbinate in Nikolsburg, and retained it thereafter. Throughout his rabbinate (with the exception of the years in Nikolsburg) he wore canonicals.[130] He introduced a choir and communal singing into the synagogue service. These and similar innovations were bold moves designed to make the synagogue service decorous and aesthetically pleasing, while defeating his Reform competitors at their own game.

Hirsch, of course, would preach, teach, and write in German. Aside from his college study, Hirsch read widely and could cite copiously from Greek and Latin literature, Shakespeare, and German philosophical literature. In 1859, Hirsch's day

---

128. S. R. Hirsch, "Die jüdischen Hoffnungen in Ungarn," *Jeschurun* 15 (1869): 20–22, cited in Mordecai Breuer, "Outside the Partition" (Hebrew), *Ha-Ma'ayan* 21:3 (1981): 43.

129. See Eliav, *Ha-Ḥinukh*, 227–32. Cf. Breuer, *Jüdische Orthodoxie im Deutschen Reich: 1871–1918*, 91–139 (Hebrew edition: 91–136; English edition: 91–147).

130. See the various portraits of Hirsch in Rosenbloom, *Tradition in an Age of Reform*, opposite the title page; in Rubens, *A History of Jewish Costume*, 171; in Trepp, *Die Oldenburger Judenschaft*, opposite p. 120; in Liberles, *The Resurgence of Orthodox Judaism*, between pages 135 and 138; and in Grunfeld's *Judaism Eternal*, I, opposite the title page. Regarding canonicals, see the references cited in n. 56.

school joined in the commemoration of the one hundredth birthday of Friedrich von Schiller, the distinguished German dramatist, poet, and historian. Aside from the school's participation at a public ceremony in Frankfurt, where the school's banner with its *Torah and derekh ereẓ* insignia was unfurled and displayed for all to see, Hirsch convened an assembly in his school. As headmaster, he delivered a stirring address filled with quotes from Schiller's poetry, which paid homage to this German cultural hero, while pointing to parallels to Schiller's teaching in biblical and rabbinic literature.[131]

While serving as Chief Rabbi of Oldenburg, Hirsch provided quarters in his home for a budding young scholar—later the famed historian—Heinrich Graetz. The nineteen-year-old Graetz was in the throes of a spiritual crisis when Hirsch's *Nineteen Letters* appeared in print. Upon reading the book, Graetz petitioned Hirsch to serve as his mentor and tutor, and Hirsch agreed. In his diary, Graetz recorded the curriculum that Hirsch had prepared for him.[132]

4–6 A.M.	Talmud; *Shulḥan 'Arukh*
6–8 A.M.	Prayer and breakfast
8–10 A.M.	Talmud
10–12 A.M.	Greek
1–3 P.M.	History, Latin, Physics
3–5 P.M.	Mathematics, Geography
6–8 P.M.	Bible, *Halakhah*

Here was an early adumbration of the curriculum that Hirsch would implement in his schools.

Clearly, Hirsch's greatest success came in the day school and later the two high schools—one for boys and one for girls—that he founded in Frankfurt.[133] Here he moved beyond Bernays and Ettlinger by founding the first Orthodox Jewish high schools. These would serve as models for all the Orthodox Jewish high schools that would follow elsewhere in Germany and Western Europe, and ultimately in the United States and Israel.

No rabbinic leader articulated the need to incorporate secular study into the Jewish curriculum more forcefully and boldly than Samson Raphael Hirsch:

> Who among us did not know Mr. Y., that wonderful man who was so thoroughly imbued with the true Jewish spirit, with Jewish learning, Jewish punctiliousness and Jewish religious fervor? His home was a well-known shining example of a pious Jewish abode in which the Torah was studied and the commandments were practiced so that it stood out like an oasis in the wilderness of present-day moral and spiritual corruption. Anything

131. See Herman Schwab, *Memories of Frankfort* (London, 1955), 9.
132. Heinrich Graetz, *Tagebuch und Briefe* (Tübingen, 1977), 47–48.
133. See the references cited in n. 129.

that bore even the faintest tinge of un-Jewish thought or un-Jewish belief was kept far away from the threshold of that home. Is there anyone who does not remember this father as one of the outstanding and devoted champions of tradition in Jewish communal life, how he fought against all forbidden innovations at the synagogue and at our school, and saw to it that the religious institutions of our community should remain painstakingly faithful to the requirements of Jewish law? He regarded ignorance of things Jewish as the greatest of all evils. He viewed so-called modern education as the worst threat to Jewish survival because he felt it would supplant Jewish learning. Mr. Y. therefore regarded it as a sacred matter of conscience not only to get his sons to perform the duties of Judaism most scrupulously but also to make them competent Torah Jews by seeing to it that the sacred writings of Judaism should remain virtually their only intellectual and spiritual nourishment. Moreover, in order to protect them from the poison of modern education, he not only anxiously isolated them from every contact with the "moderns" but filled them with arrogant contempt for all other knowledge and scholarship that he deemed as nothing compared to the study of the knowledge given us by God.

It is said that this man died of a broken heart, grief-stricken because not even one of his sons remained Jewish in feeling and practice. All of them, as youths and later in manhood, had been spiritually ruined by the very tendencies from which he had so zealously sought to protect them in their education. Anyone who knew this man and knows his sons today will see no reason to doubt the truth of this tragedy.

But anyone who would have evaluated his father's educational approach by the standard of *Train a lad in accordance with the path he will have to follow* (Proverbs 22:6), our maxim of education, could have predicted these sad results from the outset. The best way to have our children catch cold the very first time they go out of doors is to shelter them most anxiously from every breeze, from every contact with fresh air. If we want our children to develop a resistance to every kind of weather, so that wind and rain will only serve to make them stronger and healthier, we must expose them to wind and rain at an early age in order to harden their bodies. This rule holds good not only for a child's physical health but equally for his spiritual and moral well-being.

It is not enough to teach our children to love and perform their duties as Jews within the home and the family, among carefully chosen, like-minded companions. It is wrong to keep them ignorant of the present-day differences between the world outside and the Jewish way of life, or to teach them to regard the un-Jewish elements in the Jewish world as polluting, infectious agents to be avoided at all costs.

Remember that our children will not remain forever under the sheltering wings of our parental care. Sooner or later they will inevitably have contacts and associations with their un-Jewish brethren in the Jewish world. If, in this alien environment, they are to remain true to the traditions and the way of life in which they were raised at the home of their parents; if we want them to continue to perform their duties as Jews with calm, unchanging determination, regardless of the dangerous influences and, even more dangerous, the ridicule and derision they may encounter; indeed, if the contrast they note between their own way of life and that of the others will only make them love and practice their sacred Jewish heritage with even greater enthusiasm than before, then we must prepare them at an early age to meet this conflict and to pass this test. We must train them to preserve their Jewish views and to persevere in their Jewish way of life precisely when they associate with individuals whose attitude and way of life are un-Jewish. We must train our children, by diligent practice, to be able to stand up against ridicule and wisecracks. We must train them so that they may be able to draw upon the deep wellsprings of Jewish awareness and upon their own sound judgment based on true Jewish knowledge in order to obtain the armor of determination and, if need be, the naked weapons of truth and clarity, from which frivolity and shallowness will beat a hasty retreat.

Finally, it would be most perverse and criminal of us to seek to instill into our children a contempt, based on ignorance and untruth, for everything that is not specifically Jewish, for all other human arts and sciences, in the belief that by inculcating our children with such a negative attitude we could safeguard them from contacts with the scholarly and scientific endeavors of the rest of mankind. It is true, of course, that the results of secular research and study will not always coincide with the truths of Judaism, for the simple reason that they do not proceed from the axiomatic premises of Jewish truth. But the reality is that our children will move in circles influenced and shaped by these results. Your children will come within the radius of this secular human wisdom, whether it be in the lecture halls of academia or in the pages of literature. And if they discover that our own Sages, whose teachings embody the truth, have taught us that it is God Who has given of His own wisdom to mortals, they will come to overrate secular studies in the same measure in which they have been taught to despise them. You will then see that your simpleminded calculations were just as criminal as they were perverse. Criminal, because they enlisted the help of untruth supposedly in order to protect the truth, and because you have thus departed from the path upon which your own Sages have preceded you and beckoned you to follow them. Perverse, because by so doing you have achieved precisely the opposite of what you wanted to accomplish. For now your child, suspecting you of either deceit or lamentable ignorance, will transfer the blame and the disgrace that should rightly be placed only upon you and your conduct to all the Jewish wisdom and knowledge, all the Jewish education and training which he received under your guidance. Your child will consequently begin to doubt all of Judaism which (so, at least, it must seem to him from your behavior) can exist only in the night and darkness of ignorance and which must close its eyes and the minds of its adherents to the light of all knowledge if it is not to perish.

Things would have turned out differently if you had educated and raised your child *in accordance with the path he will have to follow*; if you had educated him to be a Jew, and to love and observe his Judaism together with the clear light of general human culture and knowledge; if, from the very beginning, you would have taught him to study, to love, to value and to revere Judaism, undiluted and unabridged, and Jewish wisdom and scholarship, likewise unadulterated, in its relation to the totality of secular human wisdom and scholarship. Your child would have become a different person if you had taught him to discern the true value of secular wisdom and scholarship by measuring it against the standard of the Divinely-given truths of Judaism; if, in making this comparison, you would have noted the fact that is obvious even to the dullest eye, namely, that the knowledge offered by Judaism is the original source of all that is genuinely true, good and pure in secular wisdom, and that secular learning is merely a preliminary, a road leading to the ultimate, more widespread dissemination of the truths of Judaism. If you had opened your child's eyes to genuine, thorough knowledge in *both* fields of study, then you would have taught him to love and cherish Judaism and Jewish knowledge all the more.[134]

Hirsch's legacy to modern Judaism was his vision of *Torah and derekh erez*. His openness to general culture even as he understood the primacy of Torah teaching was largely responsible for the revival of Orthodoxy in Western Europe, and set the tone for contemporary non-isolationist Orthodoxy in the United States and Israel.

R. Azriel Hildesheimer

Rabbinic leaders in [nineteenth century] Germany were experts in the field of Jewish education. That is why they succeeded in raising whole generations of Jews who were at once pious and secularly educated. No such success can be ascribed to the rabbinic leaders of Lithuania and Poland. They did not know how to attune Jewish education to their time and circumstance. R. Israel Salanter, after returning to Eastern Europe from Germany, told how he had witnessed R. Azriel Hildesheimer teaching Bible and Codes to young women. He commented: If a Lithuanian rabbi would ever institute such a practice in his community, he would be fired, and justly so. Nevertheless, may my share in the World to Come be the same as that of R. Azriel Hildesheimer!

R. Yeḥiel Yaakov Weinberg[135]

I am not of sufficient stature to provide a letter of approbation for the great Gaon, disseminator of Torah and fearer of the Lord in Germany, our master, Rabbi Azriel Hildesheimer, of blessed memory. He lived in the generation that preceded the previous generation; great was his fame due to his good deeds. The Gaon R. Yiẓḥak Elḥanan of Kovno referred to him as the "the great Gaon;" many others praised him for his greatness in Torah and for his fear of God. Who am I to follow in the footsteps of kings? (Who are "the kings"? The rabbis.) Moreover, it is stated in Scripture: *Do not stand in the place of nobles* (Proverbs 25:6). Now that his grandson has undertaken to publish his (i.e., Hildesheimer's) novellae on various tractates of the Talmud, we wish him every success. . . . May the merit of his grandfather, the Gaon, assure him success in every matter.

R. Eleazar Menaḥem Shach[136]

A younger contemporary of R. Samson Raphael Hirsch, R. Azriel Hildesheimer was born in Halberstadt in 1820.[137] He attended Halberstadt's Orthodox day

---

134. See S. R. Hirsch, "Pädagogische Plaudereien: Erziehe den Knaben nach Massgabe seines einstigen Lebenweges," in his *Gesammelte Schriften* IV, 408–16. The translation presented here is from Hirsch, *The Collected Writings,* VII, 413–17.

135. Weinberg, *She'elot u-Teshuvot Seridei Esh,* II, 14, §8.

136. Letter of approbation to A. Hildesheimer, *Ḥiddushei Rabbi Azriel: Yebamot, Ketubot* (Jerusalem, 1984), 7.

137. In general, see David Ellenson, *Rabbi Esriel Hildesheimer and the Creation of a Modern*

school—the first elementary school combining Jewish and secular study whose express purpose was the perpetuation of traditional Judaism[138]—then left for Altona-Hamburg, where he studied under Bernays and Ettlinger. In 1843 Hildesheimer enrolled at the University of Berlin where he studied physics, mathematics, history, philosophy, and classical and Semitic languages. He continued his studies in the University of Halle, where he earned his doctorate in Jewish studies in 1846. The very fact that he earned a doctorate (in contrast to Bernays, Ettlinger, and Hirsch who did not do so), and that his field of concentration was Jewish studies, would serve as harbinger of a life-long commitment to *Wissenschaft des Judenthums.* That same year Hildesheimer assumed his first role in public affairs by accepting an appointment to the post of "secretary" of the Jewish community of Halberstadt. Here, Hildesheimer's administrative talents came to the fore, though hardly at the expense of time devoted to Torah study. While administering the affairs of the Jewish community, and, in effect, serving as Assistant Rabbi to the aging Chief Rabbi of Halberstadt, R. Mattathias Levian, Hildesheimer found time to lecture to a small cadre of devoted disciples. One of them, Marcus Lehmann—who would later serve as rabbi of the separatist Orthodox community of Mainz and editor of *Israelit*—recorded for posterity Hildesheimer's schedule of lectures in Halberstadt:

> Each morning, R. Azriel lectured on *posekim* from 4 to 6 A.M. From 8 to 10 A.M. he lectured on tractate *Gittin*, and from 10 A.M. to noon he read German literature with his students.[139] From 2 to 4 P.M. he lectured on tractate *Ḥullin*, and from 8 to 10 P.M. he

Jewish Orthodoxy (Tuscaloosa, Alabama, 1990). Earlier biographies (not mentioned by Ellenson) include G. Karpeles, *Dr. Israel Hildesheimer: Eine biographische Skizze* (Frankfurt am Main, 1870); and Yaakov Mark, *Gedolim fun unzer zeit* (New York, 1927), 174–90 [Hebrew edition: (Jerusalem, 1958), 154–67]. See also the excerpt from Henriette Hildesheimer Hirsch's "Memoirs of My Youth" (unpublished manuscript) published in Monika Richarz, ed., *Jewish Life in Germany: Memoirs from Three Centuries* (Bloomington, 1991), 173–80; Esriel Hildsheimer, "A Pioneer in the Renaissance of Orthodox Jewry: Rabbi Esriel Hildesheimer," *Jewish Action*, Fall 1993: 86–88; and Hans-Joachim Bechtoldt, "Dr. Israel Hildesheimer, Rabbiner und Seminar-Direktor," in his *Die jüdische Bibelkritik im 19. Jahrhundert* (Stuttgart, 1995), 53–63; and Jacob H. Sinason, *The Rebbe: The Story of Rabbi Esriel Glei-Hildesheimer* (Jerusalem, 1996).

My colleague, Dr. Marc Shapiro, recently discovered a copy of Hildesheimer's doctoral dissertation (long considered lost), together with a short biography prepared by Hildesheimer himself. For an annotated text of the autobiography, see M. Shapiro, "An Autobiography of Rabbi Azriel Hildesheimer" (Hebrew), *'Alei Sefer* 17 (1992–1993): 149–50. For a photograph of the autobiography, see the essay by Esriel Hildesheimer listed above.

138. See above, p. 165.

139. The study of German literature (in this context) surely reflects the extent to which Orthodox Jews in nineteenth-century Germany were immersed in German culture and *Bildung.* Hildesheimer's daughter, Esther Calvary, records the following interesting episode in her memoirs:

lectured again on *posekim*. On Sabbath we prayed at an early service, and then studied tractate *Shabbat* from 8 A.M. to 12:30 P.M. Friday evenings during the winter season he lectured on tractate *Shavu'ot*.[140]

In 1851—the same year that Hirsch assumed his historical rabbinic post in Frankfurt—Hildesheimer was appointed Chief Rabbi of the Austro-Hungarian community of Eisenstadt. Almost upon his arrival in Eisenstadt, Hildesheimer founded the first yeshiva (i.e., secondary and post-secondary Jewish talmudical academy) to include secular study in its curriculum.[141] Moreover, the language of instruction was the vernacular (German), not Yiddish. In its early years, the faculty consisted almost exclusively of Hildesheimer. He taught all the Jewish studies courses, totalling some 25 hours per week. He also taught most of the secular studies courses, including German language and literature, Latin, mathematics, history, and geography, totalling some 12 hours per week. Starting with 6 students in 1851, Hildesheimer's yeshiva eventually became the second largest in Hungary, with over 150 students in 1869. Leading rabbis in Hungary, including R. Judah Aszod (d. 1866) and R. Moses Schick (d. 1879), sent their sons to study at Hildesheimer's yeshiva.[142]

Nonetheless, Hildesheimer's success did not come without a struggle. He was severely criticized from the right and the left. For the most part, Hungarian Orthodoxy was not prepared to grant legitimacy to a yeshiva that included secular study in its curriculum. Fundamentalists such as R. Akiva Joseph Schlesinger (d. 1922) labelled Hildesheimer a heretic and had him placed under the ban.[143]

> On *Yom Tov*, between *minḥah* and *ma'ariv*, when no *zemirot* were sung, Father would seat himself in the large armchair in the bedroom, we children around him. I remember sitting at his feet on the footstool, with my brothers Levi and Aaron standing beside him, and Mother and the little ones on the sofa. Then Father would sing to us German *Lieder*. And each time for us, his children, the high point was when he sang his favorite, Heine's *Die Zwei Grenadiere*.

See Esther Calvary, "Kinderheitserinnerungen," *Bulletin des Leo Baeck Institute* 8 (1959): 187–93. Cf. Gertrude Hirschler and Shnayer Z. Leiman, "Esther Hildesheimer Calvary: The Hildesheimers in Eisenstadt," *Tradition* 26:3 (1992): 87–92.

140. Cited in Meir Hildesheimer, "Toward a Portrait of Rabbi Azriel Hildesheimer" (Hebrew), *Sinai* 54 (1964): 73.

141. See Mordecai Eliav, "Torah and Derekh Ereẓ in Hungary" (Hebrew), *Sinai* 51 (1962): 127–42.

142. Hildesheimer, "Toward a Portrait," 75. Cf. idem, "R. Judah Aszod and R. Azriel Hildesheimer" (Hebrew), in Azriel Hildesheimer and Kalman Kahana, eds., *Sefer ha-Zikkaron le-Rav Yeḥiel Yaakov Weinberg* (Jerusalem, 1969), 285–302; and Hildesheimer's moving tribute to Aszod in *Ẓefunot* 13 (1992): 78–80.

143. See, e.g., Schlesinger's *Kol Nehi mi-Ẓiyyon* (Jerusalem, 1872). Cf. R. Hillel Lichtenstein's *Tokhaḥat Megullah* (Jerusalem, 1873) and his *Teshuvot Bet Hillel* (Szatmar, 1908), 10b–11b, §13.

Hildesheimer was undeterred. He engaged in polemical exchanges with the right, treating the critics with respect even as he defended his approach to modernity.[144] There was never a trace of apology, regret, or compromise in the positions he staked out for himself. He genuinely believed that his approach to modernity was the only one that made sense for Orthodoxy. His critics from the left—the leadership of the Reform movement in Hungary—were relentless in their pursuit of him. They understood clearly that a successful rapprochement between Orthodoxy and modernity would pull the rug out from under their feet. Upon reading the first annual report of Hildesheimer's yeshiva and seeing the list of courses taught by him, Leopold Loew (d. 1875), the leading Reform rabbi in Hungary at the time, published a scathing review in which he referred sarcastically to Hildesheimer as "Rabbiner, Direktor und Professor aller Wissenschaften."[145] Hildesheimer responded to the substance, but not to the style, of Loew's critique.[146] Indeed, like Hirsch, much of Hildesheimer's career was devoted to countering Reform.

Despite his differences with the right wing, Hildesheimer felt sufficiently comfortable in Hungary—even as late as 1862—that he seriously considered an offer to become Assistant Rabbi of Pressburg, sharing the rabbinate of Pressburg with R. Abraham Benjamin Sofer (d. 1871), son and successor of the Ḥatam Sofer.[147] Indeed, in order to attract Hildeshimer, Rabbi Sofer was prepared to incorporate secular study in the Pressburg yeshiva curriculum, following the model of Hildesheimer's yeshiva in Eisenstadt.[148] Apparently, word of the pending concession reached the right wing, which intervened and prevailed upon the Pressburg authorities to rescind the offer to Hildesheimer. Hildesheimer began to realize that the differences that separated him from his colleagues on the right were in fact irreconcilable. When the possibility of a government sponsored rabbinical seminary was being considered by Hungarian Jewry in 1864, Hildesheimer urged that Orthodoxy support such a seminary so long as it remained under Orthodox auspices. Hildesheimer was bitterly opposed by the right, which was not prepared to recognize the legitimacy of a rabbinical seminary that incorporated secular study in its curriculum. Since the major supporters—other than Hildesheimer—of the government sponsored rabbinical seminary were the Reformers, Hildesheimer was placed in the untenable position of seemingly being aligned with the Reformers

144. Hildesheimer responded to Schlesinger in a major essay on the importance of secular study which, although extant, has never been published. See Mordecai Eliav, "Rabbi Azriel Hildesheimer's Role in the Struggle to Shape the Image of Hungarian Jewry" (Hebrew), *Ẓion* 27 (1962): 67.

145. Leopold Loew, "Neuester Fortschritt der juedisch-theologischen Studien in Ungarn," *Ben-Chananja* 1 (1858): 248.

146. Azriel Hildesheimer, *Offener Brief an den Redacteur der Monatsschrift Ben-Chananja Leopold Loew in Szegedin* (Vienna, 1858).

147. Eliav, "Rabbi Azriel Hildesheimer's Role," 64.

148. Eliav, "Rabbi Azriel Hildesheimer's Role," 65, n. 21.

against the Orthodox. The antagonism unleashed by the Orthodox against Hildesheimer made him painfully aware of just how isolated his position was in Hungary.[149] He certainly was not about to relinquish his vision of Orthodoxy. On the other hand, he realized that a change of venue was essential if he wanted to find a receptive audience for his program. In 1869, he abandoned his yeshiva in Eisenstadt and accepted a call from the separatist Adass Jisroel congregation in Berlin.[150] By 1873, the Orthodox rabbinical seminary that had eluded him in Hungary became a reality in Germany.

Azriel Hildesheimer was keenly aware that Jewish day schools and high schools would, at best, produce committed lay Jews. The teachers' seminaries at Wuerzburg and Duesseldorf could, at best, be counted upon to produce the faculty that would staff the day schools and high schools.[151] Who would producc rabbis? Who would produce the Torah elite that would teach the teachers? The answer, of course, was an Orthodox rabbinical seminary, but none existed in Germany.[152] Hildesheimer often discussed the need for an Orthodox rabbinical seminary during his 18 years in Eisenstadt:

> The only hope for Orthodoxy is the establishment of a rabbinical seminary. Those who agitate against the establishment of a rabbinical seminary, claiming we see the results of the existing rabbinical seminaries, are sorely mistaken. For we see only the results of seminaries headed by the non-Orthodox. If, on the other hand, there would be a rabbinical seminary headed by God-fearing faculty, it would be a sanctification of God's Name. It is the only remedy that remains.[153]
>
> Let us not deceive each other. Although our common goal is to magnify Torah and glorify it, the different means toward realizing the goal that we espouse are as far removed from each other as East is from West. I say frankly that in the years ahead the only solution will be the establishment of a rabbinical seminary. Similarly, there is no hope except through the establishment of schools where students study primarily Torah but also all the secular disciplines taught in Christian and leftist schools. Not only are we obligated to tolerate the existence of such institutions, i.e., we may not oppose them, we are also obligated to support them. I am convinced that there is great danger in always

---

149. Aside from Ellenson (n. 137) and Eliav (n. 144), see Aron Moskovits, *Jewish Education in Hungary: 1848–1948* (New York, 1964) and Moshe Carmilly-Weinberger, ed., *The Rabbinical Seminary in Budapest: 1877–1977* (New York, 1986).

150. See Mario Offenberg, ed., *Adass Jisroel, Die juedische Gemeinde in Berlin (1869–1942): Vernichtet un Vergessen* (Berlin, 1986).

151. Regarding the teachers' seminaries in Wuerzburg and Duesseldorf, see Breuer, *Juedische Orthodoxie im Deutschen Reich 1871–1918*, 133–37 (Hebrew edition: 131–34; English edition: 140–45) and notes.

152. In general, see Meir Hildesheimer, "Documents Pertaining to the Establishment of the Rabbinical Seminary in Berlin" (Hebrew), *Ha-Ma'ayan* 14:2 (1974), 12–37.

153. Mordecai Eliav, ed., *Rabbiner Esriel Hildesheimer Briefe* (Jerusalem, 1965), Hebrew section, 34, letter 13, dated May 29, 1864.

saying "No! No!," i.e., in always fighting against what others propose, rather than proposing what we really want.[154]

In 1872, Hildesheimer appealed to ten prominent and wealthy Orthodox lay Jews in Germany, asking them to provide the seed money for the establishment of an Orthodox rabbinical seminary in Germany. Hildesheimer explained that nothing less than the future of Orthodoxy was at stake. The Reform and Conservative movements had founded institutions of higher Jewish learning in Berlin and Breslau. If Orthodoxy was to remain competitive, it too would have to establish an institution of higher Jewish learning that would train Orthodox rabbis. Berlin, with its university and its large Jewish population, presented the ideal setting for the creation of an Orthodox rabbinical seminary. Hildesheimer concluded his appeal as follows:

> Only a seminary will strengthen and increase the power of Orthodox Judaism internally and raise its esteem externally. . . . From the day Israel was exiled from its land, no matter has been more important than this.[155]

Hildesheimer's appeal did not fall on deaf ears. In short order, the indefatigable Hildesheimer managed to raise the necessary funds, acquire the building, gather together a distinguished faculty (initially he was joined by Professors David Hoffmann and Abraham Berliner; a year later Professor Jacob Barth joined the faculty), and recruit the students.[156]

---

154. Eliav, *Rabbiner Esriel Hildesheimer Briefe,* Hebrew section, 42–43, letter 18, dated May, 1867.

155. Hildesheimer, "Documents", 17–18.

156. Interestingly, Hildesheimer (throughout his Berlin years) did not hesitate to raise funds in Hungary for the rabbinical seminary in Berlin! When a distinguished Hungarian rabbi took him to task for doing so, Hildesheimer responded:

> It has been appropriate now for more than thirty years that I should take all the Hungarian rabbis to task for not having provided the remedy before the disease took hold, i.e., for not having established a proper rabbinical seminary in Budapest. You accuse me of raising funds in Hungary for my rabbinical seminary, despite the fact that "hundreds of rabbinical scholars, including *geonim,* have banned such a seminary." You ask: "Does not the bibilical rule: 'always follow a majority' [cf. Exodus 23:2] apply in this case?" Let me assure you that it does not apply at all to this case. This case requires no legal decision, which in any event would not require "hundreds of rabbinical scholars" or "*geonim*" in order to render it. The laws that apply to all Jews are promulgated in the *Shulḥan 'Arukh.* Everyone must abide by its decisions. Matters, however, that do not call for a legal decision, e.g., enactments, cannot be decided upon and implemented for an entire country even by a thousand rabbis. Only the Great Sanhedrin had the authority to make enactments and impose its views on the entire Jewish community, as stated in the first chapter of Maimonides' *Code: Hilkot Mamrim.* Rabbis and communal leaders can only make enactments that apply to their city. Indeed, I have never raised funds in a city whose rabbi opposed my cause. Regarding all other cities, permission has been granted to me.

Hildesheimer served as *rosh yeshiva* and administrator of the fledgling institution. Not surprisingly, it came to be known as "Hildesheimer's Rabbinical Seminary." Thus the seeds that had been sown in Eisenstadt came to fruition in Berlin.[157] Two features in particular distinguished the Hildesheimer Rabbinical Seminary from the traditional yeshiva. First and foremost was its commitment to secular study. Students were allowed to matriculate only after earning a high school diploma or its equivalent. More importantly, all rabbinical students also enrolled at the University of Berlin, where they earned doctorates while they pursued their rabbinical studies at the seminary. Second, the Hildesheimer Rabbinical Seminary was committed to the study of *Wissenschaft des Judenthums*. In his inaugural address delivered at the opening of the rabbinical seminary, Hildesheimer said:

> It is impossible that the quest for knowledge in one area of learning will not build bridges to other areas of learning. . . . We have neither the leisure nor the desire to pursue all areas of secular study. Due to our focus on Talmud and ritual practice, we must confine our pursuit of secular study to those of its aspects essential for our learning. This minimal commitment to secular study, however, cannot be compromised. We will engage in these various areas of secular study with the same devotion we apply to religious study, for all our study is for the sake of Heaven. The second half of this century has brought several changes: the new *Wissenschaft des Judenthums* has come into its own, and areas that have been known for a long time, i.e., biblical exegesis, demand investigation from a new perspective and require the use of rich linguistic and philological materials, to the extent possible. In our desire to engage in these areas as our own, we will attempt to work in them with absolute academic seriousness and for the sake of, and only for the sake of, the truth.[158]

See Eliav, *Rabbiner Esriel Hildsheimer Briefe,* Hebrew section, 57, letter 27, dated November 5, 1878.

157. In general, see Moshe A. Shulvass, "The Rabbinical Seminary in Berlin" (Hebrew), in Samuel K. Mirsky, ed., *Mosedot Torah be-Eropa* (New York, 1956), 689–713; Breuer, *Judische Orthodoxie im Deutschen Reich,* 120–33 (Hebrew edition: 118–30; English edition: 125–40) and notes; and the references cited in Hildesheimer, "Toward a Portrait," 80, n. 72. Cf. Isi J. Eisner, "Reminiscences of the Berlin Rabbinical Seminary," *Year Book of the Leo Baeck Institute* 12 (1967): 32–52; and Mordecai Eliav, "Das Orthodoxe Rabbinerseminar in Berlin," in Julius Carlebach, ed., *Wissenschaft des Judentums: Anfänge der Judaistik in Europe* (Darmstadt, n.d. [circa 1992]), 59–73.

158. Azriel Hildesheimer, "Rede zur Eroeffnung des Rabbiner-Seminars," *Jahresbericht des Rabbiner-Seminars fuer das Orthodoxe Judenthum pro 5634* (1873–1874) (Berlin, 1874), 84–89, cited in Hildesheimer, "Toward a Portrait," 80–81. Cf. David Hoffmann, "Thora und Wissenschaft," *Jeschurun* 7 (1920): 498–99. Hoffmann's remarks were delivered at the opening session of the winter semester at the Hildesheimer Rabbinical Seminary, 1919. For an English translation of his address, see Marc B. Shapiro, "Rabbi David Ẓevi Hoffmann on Torah and *Wissenschaft,*" *Torah u-Madda Journal* 6 (1995–1996): 129–37.

Hildesheimer's commitment to *Wissenschaft des Judenthums* was reflected in the faculty he appointed to, and in the curriculum he designed for, the rabbinical seminary and in his scholarly publications. In the recently published volumes of Hildesheimer's novellae on the Talmud (see below), for example, he cites extensively and approvingly from the writings of Jacob Reifmann, an outstanding practitioner and advocate of *Wissenschaft des Judenthums.*[159] In typical Hildesheimer fashion, these citations stand side by side with citations from traditional rabbinic classics such as R. Aryeh Leib b. Asher's *Sha'agat Aryeh,* R. Aryeh Leib Heller's *Keẓot ha-Ḥoshen,* and R. Jacob of Lissa's *Netivot ha-Mishpat.*

Starting with twenty students in 1873, the Hildesheimer Rabbinical Seminary continued to thrive until the notorious *Kristallnacht* in 1938, when its doors were closed forever.[160] The impact of its hundreds of rabbinic graduates on Western Jewry is a matter of record.[161] Some of the more prominent family names (often including father and son; sometimes including brothers) among its graduates were: Altmann, Auerbach, Biberfeld, Cahn, Carlebach, Horovitz, Marx, Munk, Nobel, and Unna. Aside from practicing rabbis, many of its graduates were distinguished Jewish educators, academicians, lawyers, and doctors. Two graduates merit special mention here. R. Moses Auerbach (d. 1976) was the founder and first headmaster of *Ḥavaẓelet,* the Warsaw *gymnasium* for Jewish girls.[162] Dr. Leo Deutschlaender (d. 1935) helped Sarah Schenierer establish the Beth Jacob network of schools for Jewish girls, which still flourishes today in the United States and Israel. He also headed the Beth Jacob Teachers Training College for Women in Cracow.[163] Hildesheimer was an early advocate of Jewish education for women, and it comes as no surprise that graduates of the seminary he founded would devote their lives to this cause.

Hildesheimer succeeded in creating the institution that would provide intellec-

---

159. Hildesheimer's admiration for Reifmann was not confined to citations and words alone. He regularly provided financial support for the poverty-stricken Reifmann, and even went public (in *Juedische Presse*) with a plea for community wide financial support on behalf of Reifmann. See Meir Hildesheimer, "The Correspondence Between R. Azriel Hildesheimer and R. Jacob Reifmann" (Hebrew), *Hadarom* 21 (1965): 148–64.

160. For the failed attempt in the 1930s to transfer the Hildesheimer Rabbinical Seminary to Palestine, see Christhard Hoffmann and Daniel R. Schwartz, "Early but Opposed—Supported but Late: Two Berlin Seminaries which Attempted to Move Abroad," *Year Book of the Leo Baeck Institute* 36 (1991): 267–304. For R. Yeḥiel Yaakov Weinberg's angry critique of the tactics used by those who thwarted the attempt, see Daniel Schwartz, "Between Berlin, Lithuania, and the Distant East" (Hebrew), *Kiryat Sefer* 64 (1992–1993): 1086–87.

161. See Eisner, "Reminiscences."

162. See Auerbach's "Memoirs" (in Hebrew), *Ha-Ma'ayan* 21:3 (1981): 6–36; 21:4 (1981): 10–37; and 22:1 (1981): 3–23.

163. See Judith Grunfeld, "Leo Deutschlaender," in Leo Jung, ed., *Sages and Saints* (New York, 1987), 297–320.

tual leadership for Orthodoxy in the Western world. As such, his efforts complemented those of Samson Raphael Hirsch, whose primary focus was on creating the institutions that served the needs of the laity. Interestingly, Hildesheimer and Hirsch came under the influence of the same set of teachers—Bernays and Ettlinger—and both students became champions of Orthodoxy in its confrontation with modernity. Clearly, there was more Ettlinger than Bernays in Hildesheimer, even as there was more Bernays than Ettlinger in Hirsch. Hildesheimer was first and foremost a Talmudist and *posek*, whereas Hirsch was primarily a Jewish thinker, preacher, and writer. While they had much in common, and knew and respected each other well,[164] they differed considerably.[165] Aside from the differences alluded to above, they differed particularly in their attitude toward general culture.[166] Both subscribed to *Torah and derekh ereẓ*, using the term freely and programmatically.[167] In a certain sense, Hirsch seems to have had a broader view of *derekh ereẓ*. For him, it encompassed any and all aspects of culture that advanced or enhanced civilization. As such, they were worthy of pursuit, valuable in and of themselves, while subservient to Torah. For Hildesheimer, *derekh ereẓ* had instrumental value only. *derekh ereẓ* was important only to the extent that it advanced the cause of Torah. Ironically, Hirsch, despite his broad view, found no place in his curriculum for *Wissenschaft des Judenthums*. Hildesheimer, despite his narrower view, was a staunch advocate of *Wissenschaft des Judenthums*. This parting of the ways between Hirsch and Hildesheimer would be reflected in the institutions they founded and in the communities they influenced. Indeed, some of the very tensions that marked the differences in character between Frankfurt and Berlin are still felt in their successor communities in the United States and Israel.

Despite his serving as rabbi of a congregation, principal of a congregational

---

164. See, for example, Hirsch's reliance on Hildesheimer in halakhic matters in Hirsch, *Shemesh Marpe*, 72, §55. Hildesheimer, on the other hand, openly acknowledged Orthodoxy's "eternal gratitude" to Hirsch for singlehandedly "restoring Orthodoxy in our day." See, e.g., Eliav, *Rabbiner Esriel Hildeshimer Briefe*, German section, p. 119, letter 34, and p. 120, letter 36.

Not insignificant is the fact that Hildesheimer delivered a eulogy at Hirsch's funeral. See Eliyahu M. Klugman's biography of Hirsch, appended to Hirsch's *Shemesh Marpe'*, 364.

165. For a discussion of the basic issues that separated them, see Azriel Hildesheimer, "From an Exchange of Letters Between R. Azriel Hildesheimer and R. Samson Raphael Hirsch and His Supporters" (Hebrew) in Yeḥiel Y. Weinberg and Pinḥas Biberfeld, eds., *Yad Shaul* (Tel Aviv, 1953), 233–51, and idem, "An Exchange of Letters Between R. Azriel Hildesheimer and R. Samson Raphael Hirsch on Matters Relating to the Land of Israel" (Hebrew) *Ha-Ma'ayan 2* (1954): 41–52. Cf. Berthold Strauss, *The Rosenbaums of Zell* (London, 1962), 40–41.

166. See, e.g., Eliezer Stern, *The Educational Ideal of Torah 'im Derekh-Erez* (Hebrew) (Ramat Gan, 1987), 89–112.

167. For Hildesheimer's use of the term *Torah 'im derekh 'ereẓ*, see, e.g., Eliav, *Rabbiner Esriel Hildesheimer Briefe*, German section, p. 118, letter 34, and Hebrew section, p. 58, letter 27.

school, and rector of the Rabbinical Seminary, Hildesheimer managed to publish over 150 books and articles during his lifetime.[168] These include his magnum opus, an almost 700-page critical edition of and commentary on *Halakhot Gedolot* based on a Vatican manuscript (Berlin, 1880–90).[169] Two studies in particular demonstrate his mastery of Greek, mathematics, and astronomy: "Die Beschreibung des herodianischen Tempels im Traktate Middoth und bei Flavius Josephus," *Jahresbericht des Rabbiner-Seminars* (Berlin, 1877); and "Die astronomischen Kapitel in Maimuni's Abhandlung uber die Neumondsheiligung," *Jahresbericht des Rabbiner-Seminars* (Berlin, 1881). Several important works published posthumously include: *She'elot u-Teshuvot Rabbi Azriel* (Tel Aviv, 1969 and 1976), 2 vols.; and *Ḥiddushei Rabbi 'Azriel* (Jerusalem, 1984 and 1992), 2 vols.

Like Hirsch, Hildesheimer lived to a venerable age and saw the fruits of his labor. If the ultimate mark of greatness is the ability to reproduce it in a worthy successor, Hildesheimer was great indeed. Shortly before his death, Hildesheimer designated his disciple in Eisenstadt and colleague in Berlin, R. David Ẓevi Hoffmann, as his successor. Hoffmann would lead the Hildesheimer Rabbinical Seminary into the twentieth century, while serving as the supreme halakhic authority for Orthodox Jewry in Germany until his death in 1921.[170]

Upon Hildesheimer's death in 1899, the Jewish communal leaders of Berlin turned to Hoffmann for a ruling as to whether it was permissible to bring Hildesheimer's bier into the synagogue so that eulogies could be delivered in the synagogue where he had served as rabbi. Hoffmann ruled as follows:

> Although R. Abraham Danzig railed against the practice of bringing a bier into the synagogue, explaining that it was permitted only for the Gaon of Vilna, who was unique in his generation, there is no question that it is permissible in our case. R. Azriel Hildesheimer was unique in his generation. He was endowed with every good quality; sanctity, holiness, sharpness of mind, and erudition. He studied Torah day and night; sought diligently to observe the commandments and to do good deeds; strove mightily

168. See Esriel Hildesheimer, *Rabbi Esriel Hildesheimer: Bibliographie seiner Schriften* (Jerusalem, 1987). The German version is drawn from Azriel Hildesheimer, "Rabbi Azriel Hildesheimer: A Bibliography" (Hebrew), *'Alei Sefer* 14 (1987): 143–62.

169. Many of Hildesheimer's comments have been incorporated in the Makhon Yerushalayim edition of *Halakhot Gedolot* (Jerusalem, 1992). Neither the Hildesheimer nor the Makhon Yerushalayim edition should be confused with the critical edition prepared by Hildesheimer's grandson Azriel, *Halakhot Gedolot* (Jerusalem, 1971–1987), 3 vols.

170. On Hoffmann, see, e.g., the vignettes by Louis Ginzberg, *Students, Scholars and Saints* (Philadelphia, 1928), 252–62; Chaim Tchernowitz, *Massekhet Zikhronot* (New York, 1945), 244–64; Alexander Marx, *Essays in Jewish Biography* (Philadelphia, 1947), 185–222; Yeshayah Aviad-Wolfsberg in Leo Jung, ed., *Guardians of our Heritage* (New York, 1958), 363–419; and David Ellenson and Richard Jacobs, "Scholarship and Faith: David Hoffman and His Relationship to *Wissenschaft des Judenthums*," *Modern Judaism* 8:1 (1988): 27–40. A definitive intellectual portrait of Hoffmann remains a scholarly desideratum.

to work on behalf of the poor in the land of Israel and elsewhere; and fought bravely on behalf of our faith against its detractors. All this he did freely without recompense.[171] He never sought honor. Quite the contrary, he was genuinely humble. He honored all scholars who came into contact with him as if they had been his teachers. The list of virtues could continue *ad infinitum*. It is appropriate indeed that we honor Torah, Worship, and Good Deeds by having his bier brought into the synagogue.[172]

Afterword

The approaches to general culture initiated by the *gedolei yisrael* in nineteenth-century Germany, as well as the educational institutions they founded, would resonate far beyond the confines of time and place in which they first appeared.

The twentieth century, for example, not only witnessed a resurgence of interest in the writings of Hirsch and Hildesheimer in Jewish communities throughout the world, but, more importantly, it yielded a small but disproportionately influential group of *gedolei yisrael* whose attitude toward general culture was remarkably open. Indeed, with respect to the interface between traditional Jewish teaching and modern scholarship in a variety of specific disciplines, these *gedolim* moved well beyond the efforts of their nineteenth-century predecessors. Moreover, their influence were hardly confined to a single geographic or cultural area. Such *gedolim* as Rabbis Isaac Jacob Reines (d. 1915), David Hoffmann (d. 1921), Eliyahu Klatzkin (d. 1932), Abraham Isaac ha-Kohen Kook (d. 1935), Isaac Herzog (d. 1959), Ḥayyim Heller (d. 1960), Yeḥiel Yaakov Weinberg (d. 1966), and Joseph B. Soloveitchik (d. 1993) were among the outstanding Talmudists, *posekim*, rabbis, and *roshei yeshivah* of their generation, even as they confronted general culture and its impact on Torah scholarship and—with regard to the land of Israel in particular—on Jewish life.[173]

---

171. Hildesheimer was married to Henriette Hirsch, daughter of a wealthy Halberstadt industrialist. Due to his wife's family, Hildesheimer would remain a man of independent means throughout his life. Thus, in Eisenstadt, he distributed his salary among the poor. In Berlin, he served gratis as rabbi, principal of the congregational school, and rector of the rabbinical seminary. See Hildesheimer, "Toward a Portrait," 89.

172. *She'elot u-Teshuvot Melammed le-Ho'il* (Frankfurt, 1927; reissued: New York, 1954), II, 110, §106.

173. For their massive contribution to rabbinic literature, see the standard Jewish encyclopaedias and the ever-burgeoning bibliographical entries (under their names) in the card (or on-line computer) files at any of the major libraries of Judaica.

Regarding their attitudes toward general culture, suffice it to note that five of the eight *gedolim* listed—Rabbis Hoffmann, Herzog, Heller, Weinberg, and Soloveitchik—earned doctorates, respectively, at the universities of Tuebingen, London, Wuerzburg, Giessen, and Berlin. Rabbis Reines, Klatzkin, and Kook, while lacking in formal secular education, read

As a native of Lithuania, a graduate of Mir and Slabodka, and last Rector of the Hildesheimer Rabbinical Seminary in Berlin, R. Yeḥiel Yaakov Weinberg[174] certainly spoke with authority when he contrasted the *Torah and derekh ereẓ* approach in Germany with the Torah Only approach in Lithuania:

> Rabbinic leaders in [nineteenth-century] Germany were experts in the field of Jewish education. That is why they succeeded in raising whole generations of Jews who were at once pious and secularly educated. No such success can be ascribed to the rabbinic leaders of Lithuania and Poland. They did not know how to attune Jewish education to their time and circumstances.[175]

In a letter written in 1955, Weinberg thanked Dayyan Isidor Grunfeld for translating Hirsch into English. Weinberg added:

> I am persuaded, as you are, that in our day the only antidote to assimilation and to alienation from Judaism is the spread of the *Torah and derekh ereẓ* approach of the *gedolim* of Germany. Much to my dismay, in certain circles within Agudat Yisrael opposition to this approach has increased. In my opinion, such opposition reflects tunnel vision and narrow-mindedness. It is essential, therefore, that we increase our efforts on behalf of *Torah and derekh ereẓ*. There is no better means of doing so than the dissemination of the writings of the Gaon Rabbi Samson Raphael Hirsch.[176]

Rabbi Weinberg was not the first East European *gadol* who found Jewish education in Eastern Europe wanting, when compared to the new approaches of the

---

widely in, and were deeply influenced by, the philosophical, scientific, and literary classics of general culture. Regarding Rabbi Reines, Ge'ulah Bat Yehudah, *Ish ha-Me'orot: Rabbi Yiẓḥak Ya'akov Reines* (Jerusalem, 1985). Regarding Rabbi Klatzkin, see below, n. 178. Regarding Kook, see, e.g., Benjamin Ish-Shalom, *Rabbi Kook: Between Rationalism and Mysticism* (Hebrew: Tel Aviv, 1990), and idem and Shalom Rosenberg, eds., *The World of Rav Kook's Thought* (New York, 1991).

174. For biographical studies of Rabbi Weinberg, see the references cited by Hoffmann and Schwartz, "Early but Opposed," 271, n. 13. Interestingly, Weinberg was, for a while, an academician by profession. He was a member of the faculty at the University of Giessen. A close associate of the Christian Orientalist and Masoretic scholar, Paul Kahle (d. 1965), Weinberg agreed to collaborate with him on a series of scholarly studies relating to *genizah* fragments of the Mishnah. See Paul Kahle and Jehiel J. Weinberg, "The Mishna Text in Babylonia," *Hebrew Union College Annaul* 10 (1935): 185–222. Although Weinberg's name appears as coauthor, the article was written entirely by Kahle. Weinberg's planned contribution was announced in the article, but (not surprisingly) did not appear in subsequent issues of the *Hebrew Union College Annual*, a scholarly periodical sponsored by the Hebrew Union College in Cincinnati.

175. See above, p. 201 and n. 135.

176. See Melekh Shapiro, "Letters From Rabbi Y.Y. Weinberg" (Hebrew), *Ha-Ma'ayan* 32:4 (1992): 19.

gedolim in Germany. In a scathing indictment of a group of rabbis in Jerusalem who, at the end of the nineteenth century, tried to impose East European style educational standards on West European Jews who immigrated to the land of Israel, R. David Friedman (d. 1917) of Karlin, a leading East European *posek*, wrote as follows:

> Those East European rabbis in the diaspora who banned the study of languages and secular study, never issued a blanket ban, to be applied under any and all circumstances. They kept secular study at a distance so long as circumstances warranted it. Even in this guarded approach, they were not successful, for many students could not cope with the ban and were led astray when exposed clandestinely to secular study. Far more successful were the West European rabbis, leaders of the Orthodox Jewish community, who were zealots for the Lord and His Torah. They established educational institutions that provided Torah study on the one hand, and secular study on the other.[177]

Still other East European *gedolim*, exposed to Western culture and enamored by the response of the *gedolim*, saw—perhaps more profoundly than others—that in the modern world both approaches, *Torah and derekh ereẓ* and Torah only, were indispensable. The issue was no longer one of cultural spheres of influence. Wherever Jews resided in significant numbers both approaches would be necessary if Judaism was to thrive. Thus, R. Eliyahu Klatzkin,[178] a former Chief Rabbi of

177. See his *'Emek Berakhah* (Jerusalem, 1882), 14b. Cf. my discussion "R. David Friedman of Karlin: The Ban on Secular Study in Jerusalem," in *Tradition* 26:4 (1992): 102–5.

178. Rabbi Klatzkin, whose formative years were spent in the talmudic academies of Shklov and Eishishok, developed a profound interest in medicine, pharmacology, chemistry, mathematics, history, and geography. He was a regular subscriber to the *Medizinische Wochenschrift* and an avid reader of the *London Times*. He was conversant in Greek, Latin, German, French, English, Russian, and Polish. Among his favorite masters of belles lettres were Victor Hugo, Guy de Maupassant, and Leo Tolstoy. One observer offered the following vivid description of Klatzkin's insatiable passion for knowledge:

> [His] wide knowledge of geography was incredible. I doubt if there was anyone better acquainted with the subject even among the specialists in the field. No point on the globe was unfamiliar to him. Even small, remote settlements, wildernesses, streams, brooks, swamps, hills, and valleys were an open book to him with their details of boundaries, climate, lines of communication and population. The maps in general use were inadequate for him and he used to carp at their slightest inaccuracy. He tried as far as he was able to obtain the scientific and especially military maps which were issued by cartographic societies. His maps covered every region and province, every city and town, and he would spread them on the floor, examining them until he was familiar with every road in every land, including all auto highways and the streets of every large city. He was conversant with most of the railroads in the world, their stations and schedules, and could recite all the timetables in effect in Russia, Germany, France and England.

See "My Father, Rabbi Eliyahu Klatzkin" (Hebrew), in Jacob Klatzkin, *Ketavim* (Tel Aviv, 1953), 304–20. An abridged English translation of this essay is available in Leo Jung, ed., *Jewish Leaders* (Jerusalem, 1964), 319–41.

Lublin who settled in Jerusalem, where he occasionally joined together on broadsides with members of the rabbinic court of the *'edah ha-ḥaredit*, wrote as follows:

> Those who are exposed to danger in their youth, drinking spring water tinged with arsenic, find themselves invigorated and strengthened in adulthood. Similarly, those inoculated with infectious microbes carrying diphtheria, rabies, and the like, develop a resistance to the disease and suffer no deleterious effects. It is essential, however, that the inoculations be administered in proper dosage and be carefully monitored. Now Maimonides has already explained that disease of the soul is comparable to disease of the body. When secular education is carefully monitored and properly applied, it is possible not only to ward off dangers, but to invigorate one's self and gain strength. Students properly educated are able to neutralize and overcome those who would deprecate the Torah and the commandments, and who would entice them away from Jewish teaching and practice. Due to their solid education, they stand firm in their religious views, despite any peregrinations or other unforeseen circumstances that may overtake them. The experience of our brethren—observers of the Torah and the commandments—in Frankfurt is decisive. Due to the Torah oriented educational institutions they established, they were able to win over many new adherents to the cause of God and His Torah. Yet, aside from those educational institutions, we must also support another type of Jewish educational institution, in which students will devote almost all their time to Torah study alone. These institutions will help train a cadre of experts in Talmud and Jewish law who will fathom the depths of Jewish teaching and wage war on behalf of the Torah, while following in the footsteps of the *geonim* and rabbis of the past.[179]

Interestingly, a prominent contemporary Torah sage, who was raised in Western Europe but studied in the great Eastern European *yeshivot* prior to World War II, arrived at a conclusion strikingly similar to that of R. Eliyahu Klatzkin. Since his remarks were published anonymously, we will—in deference to his preference when he published them—quote him without revealing his identity.

The immediate context of the Torah sage's remarks was the appearance in print, in 1963, of a scathing critique of *Torah and derekh ereẓ* by Rabbi Eliyahu Dessler (d. 1953), leading member of the Musar movement, *mashgiaḥ* of the Ponoviez yeshiva in Bnei Brak, and profound thinker.[180] Labelling *Torah and derekh ereẓ* "the Frankfurt approach," Rabbi Dessler conceded that very few graduates of the *Torah and derekh ereẓ* educational institutions defected from traditional Judaism, and that

179. *Devar Halakhah* (Lublin, 1921), 57. Cf. his *Even Pinnah* (Jerusalem, 1930), introduction.

180. The critique, which first appeared in the periodical *Ha-Ma'ayan* 4:1 (Tishre, 1963): 61–64, is included in Rabbi Eliyahu Eliezer Dessler, *Mikhtav me-Eliyahu* (Jerusalem, 1963), III, 355–60.

Regarding Rabbi Dessler, see Lion Carmell, "Eliyahu Eliezer Dessler," in Leo Jung, ed., *Guardians of Our Heritage* (New York, 1958), 675–99. See also Rabbi Eliyahu Eliezer Dessler, *Ḥiddushei ha-Gaon Rabbi Eliyahu Eliezer Dessler 'al Shas* (Jerusalem, 1992).

was certainly a strength. But, argued Rabbi Dessler, precisely because secular study was incorporated into the curriculum, the Frankfurt approach was doomed to failure. In effect, it produced no *gedolei yisrael* and precious few rabbinic scholars (*lomedim*) of note. In contrast, the East European *yeshivot* had only one educational goal: the production of *gedolei yisrael.* Secular study was banned from the yeshiva curriculum because nothing short of total immersion in Torah study would produce *gedolei yisrael.* The *gedolim* in Eastern Europe were well aware that heavy casualties would result from this single-minded approach to Jewish education. But that was a price they were prepared to pay in order to produce *gedolei yisrael.*

The anonymous Torah sage responded, in part, as follows:

> The rabbis of the previous generation, indeed the ancestors of Rabbi Dessler who were the founders of the Musar movement, R. Israel Salanter and his disciple R. Simḥah Zissel,[181] addressed this issue. I have heard that their view on these matters came very close to that of R. Samson Raphael Hirsch, but that they were outnumbered and opposed by the majority of East European rabbis at the time. It seems to me that this was always the case historically. The majority of rabbis refused to engage in secular study, lest they be ensnared by it. On the other hand, in every generation a minority of Torah sages engaged in secular study, using it as a handmaiden to serve the cause of Torah. That minority pursued its own path and sanctified God's name throughout the universe. . . .
>
> Regarding Germany, the truth is that some 200 years prior to Mendelssohn, great *gedolim,* by and large, were no longer being produced there. Already then, the vast majority of rabbis in Germany and Western Europe were imported from Poland, Lithuania, and Russia. Certainly when Mendelssohn's disciples began to spread their heritical teaching throughout Germany, there were few *geonim* born and raised in Germany. At that time, virtually all the rabbis in Germany and Holland were natives of Lithuania, Poland, and other Eastern countries. Surely in those days none of our ancestors engaged in secular study; nevertheless, they did not produce *geonim* in Torah. Who knows why one country produces Torah sages over several generations, then ceases to do so, and another country produces them instead? In the period following Mendelssohn, the only great *geonim* born in Germany were the Ḥatam Sofer, R. Nathan Adler,[182] and R. Wolf

181. R. Simḥah Zissel Broida (d. 1897), as indicated by the anonymous author, was a disciple of R. Israel Salanter and a pillar of the Musar movement in Lithuania and Russia. He founded Torah institutions in Kelm (in Lithuania) and Grobin (in Latvia) that advanced the educational program of the movement. At those institutions, three hours per day were devoted to secular study, including instruction in Russian language, history, arithmetic, and geography. In general, see Dov Katz, *Tenu'at ha-Musar* (Tel Aviv, 1954), II, 26–219; Eliezer Ebner, "Simḥa Zissel Broida (Ziff)," in Leo Jung, ed., *Guardians of Our Heritage,* 319–35; and Israel Isidor Elyashev, "A Chapter in the History of the Musar Movement" (Hebrew), in Immanuel Etkes, ed., *Mosad ha-Yeshivah be-Shelhi Yemei ha-Beynayim u-ve-'Et ha-Ḥadashah* (Jerusalem, 1989), 204–32.

182. R. Nathan Adler (d. 1800), distinguished talmudist and kabbalist, was a teacher of the Ḥatam Sofer. In general, see Josef Unna, "Nathan Hacohen Adler," in Leo Jung, ed., *Guardians of Our Heritage,* 167–85.

Hamburger.[183] Shortly afterwards there was R. Jacob Ettlinger, author of *'Arukh la-Ner*—but he was learned in secular study, and attended the University of Wuerzburg for one year together with his colleague, the *gaon* R. Mendel Kargau,[184] author of *Giddulei Taharah.* So too Ḥakham Bernays, the teacher of R. Samson Raphael Hirsch, who would follow in Bernays' footsteps. The upshot of all this is that the "Frankfurt approach" alone cannot be blamed for the lack of production of Torah sages in Germany. . . .

Who knows! It may well be that both approaches, *Torah and derekh ereẓ* and "Torah Only," are true, both reflecting the essence of Torah. What is crucial is that one's intent be for the sake of Heaven, always according the Torah primary status, and making secular study secondary. No rabbinic court ever banned secular study. Indeed, the Torah scholars of the various generations never ruled officially in favor of the one approach over the other. Everyone is free to select whichever approach finds favor in his eyes. Let him consult his teachers and follow in the footsteps of his forefathers. The followers of the one approach must respect the followers of the other approach. They may not cast aspersions on the approach they reject. To the contrary, they must provide support for each other. . . .

Those who wish to dedicate their lives to the study of Torah alone, come under the category of "the tribe of Levi" as described by Maimonides. But I worry about all the tribes of Israel . . . the vast majority of Jews cannot live with a ban on secular study. We need to provide institutions that service the needs of the majority of Jews, wherever they may be, even as we view it a great *mizvah* to support the minority who study Torah only. And so I say, both approaches are well-grounded in the sources. Both are necessary ingredients for the continued existence of the Jewish people in our time.[185]

When a Torah sage speaks, the wise listen attentively. How much more so when two Torah sages, nurtured at opposite ends of the European cultural spectrum, arrive at the same conclusion!

---

183. R. Wolf Hamburger (d. 1850), prolific author of rabbinic responsa and novellae, was among the last great *roshei yeshiva* in Germany. He headed the yeshiva in Fuerth, where R. Seligmann Baer Bamberger (see n. 56) was among his many disciples.

184. R. Mendel Kargau (d. 1842; see above pp. 164–165) was a disciple of Rabbis Ezekiel Landau, Nathan Adler, and Pinḥas Horowitz. He too taught at the yeshiva in Fuerth, and was a close associate of R. Wolf Hamburger.

185. Anonymous, "A Letter Regarding the Frankfurt Approach" (Hebrew), *Ha Ma'ayan* 6:4 (1966): 4–7. For another response to Rabbi Dessler's critique of the "Frankfurt approach," see William Z. Low, "Some Remarks on a Letter of Rabbi E. E. Dessler," in H. Chaim Schimmel and Aryeh Carmell, eds., *Encounter: Essays on Torah and Modern Life* (Jerusalem, 1989), 204–18.

4

Torah and General Culture: Confluence and Conflict

Aharon Lichtenstein

Contents

Introduction

The question of Torah and general culture[1] bears a dual aspect. Its core is clearly ideological. The relation, respectively, of reason and revelation, the optional and the normative, the temporal and the transcendental, secularity and sacrality, diversity and uniformity, and, above all, of man and his Creator—these are obviously the

1. The issue to which this essay, and indeed this volume, addresses itself is more commonly denominated as *Torah u-Madda*. I am not fully comfortable with either formulation. Culture—certainly in the anthropological and sociological sense, as opposed to Arnold's "the best that has been thought and said in the world"—includes areas and levels of human experience quite beyond the pale of our topic. On the other hand, in modern usage, as opposed to the Rambam's, the term *madda* has a scholarly and even academic connotation which does not capture either the quality or scope of general culture—as expressed through both secular disciplines and creative arts—whose relation to Torah is here under discussion. In this respect, it has undergone a constriction similar to that of the Latin *scientia* and its offspring (see O. E. D., s.v. science), an interesting phenomenon in its own right. I would much have preferred the term *ḥokhmah* which, from Scripture on, has retained its capacious and flexible character and also has the advantage of having been explicitly juxtaposed with Torah in the celebrated *midrash*, "If a person tells you there is *ḥokhmah* among the Gentiles, believe him; . . . [If he tells you] there is Torah among the Gentiles, don't believe him" (*Midrash Eikhah Rabbati* 2:17).

Nevertheless, mindful of the current status of the phrase *Torah u-Madda* as both an ideological/institutional logo and the forensic focus of much contemporary debate, I have used *madda* extensively although frequently alternating it with *ḥokhmah* with which it is, in several places, twinned in Scripture. See especially II Chronicles 1:10–12. In any event, for our purposes both terms are preferable to *derekh ereẓ*, which in Ḥazal and *rishonim* relates more to the vocational and social arena, with a greater emphasis upon cultivating the world and inculcating the "tradition of civility" than upon developing culture in its "high," spiritual sense. See, e.g., *Abot* 2:2 and commentators; R. Loewe (the Maharal of Prague), *Netivot ʿOlam, Netiv Derekh Ereẓ; Enẓyklopedia Talmudit* 7:672–706; Nahman S. Greenspan, *Mishpat*

primary components. Philosophy and theology aside, however, we are confronted by a second, no less important, element—practical, and particularly educational, in nature. How well, if at all, can Torah and secular wisdom meld within a single personality or institution; the promise and risks—the cost-benefit ratio, if you will—of any projected synthesis; determination of priorities and the appointment of energies; the psychological and sociological impact of differing relations to ambient general culture—these are all issues which need to be candidly confronted by the philosophic devotees of symbiotic integration no less than by its detractors.

These two aspects are clearly related and yet, they are both conceptually distinct and operationally divisible. One may regard the integration of Torah and wisdom as not only legitimate but optimal, and yet hold that, within the context of an overwhelmingly secular modern culture, it is generally best foregone. Contrarily, one may subscribe to the purist ideal of comprehensive singleminded devotion to *talmud Torah* and yet favor an integrated curriculum as an accommodating concession to the Zeitgeist. What is certain is that Torah educationists ignore either aspect at their—and, more importantly, their students'—peril. We must approach the topic rooted in ideology and yet not be entrapped by it; informed and energized by our *weltanschauung* without being fossilized by it. Whatever our orientation, we can hardly afford Procrustean disdain for pragmatic realities. We are charged to confront the issues responsibly, courageously, and sensitively and, if necessary, differentially.

The End of Learning: The Problem in Perspective

From a Torah perspective, the phenomenon of general culture can be regarded as a specific—if you will, formal—halakhic issue, to be adjudicated within the context of *hilkhot talmud Torah*. Given the all-embracing character of the *mizvah* to study Torah and thereby know the *Ribbono Shel 'Olam* and cleave to Him, what can

---

'Am-ha-Arez (Jerusalem, 1946), ch. 1. See also, Rabbi Norman Lamm, *Torah Umadda* (Northvale, N.J., 1990), especially pp. 10–12.

It should be noted that, given the wide range of *hokhmah* in biblical usage, especially in *Mishlei* and *Kohelet*, and in Ḥazal—from prophetic insight to manual craftsmanship—it is not surprising that at times it is also taken to refer to Torah. See, e.g., *Kiddushin* 49b, where Rashi successively interprets *milta de-talya bi-sevara*, denoting the nature of *hokhmah*, as deriving from reason as opposed to tradition (see *Sanhedrin* 36b) rather than its contents; and, several lines later, *Torah ve-derekh erez*.

In certain contexts, of course, the term *Torah u-Madda* is discussed as virtually synonymous with the problem of religion and science; see, e.g., *Torah u-Madda*, ed. Shalom Rosenberg (Jerusalem, 1988).

be the relative value or viability of the pursuit of human culture? Yet, while this aspect surely needs to be explored, we should err grievously in confining discussion of the problem to this issue. Are women exempt from coping with the problem of secular culture simply because, halakhically and historically, they are less committed to *talmud Torah*? Is the question of no import to a gentile? Regardless of the scope of one's normative obligation to study Torah, to the extent that every person needs strive to maximize his spiritual self-fulfillment, he or she is inevitably faced by the question of the relative merit of general culture as opposed to direct contemplation of God and his word.

Hence, the question of Torah and general culture confronts us with some of the most basic and comprehensive issues of religious thought. An analysis of culture per se would be sweeping in its own right; but the attempt to assess its place within the totality of spiritual existence clearly extends our range. What, we need to ask, are man's primary aims and duties, and what, therefore, the possible contribution of *madda* to their realization?

The familiar Gemara near the end of *Makkot* (24a) limns the gradual reduction (logical, not operational) of 613 *miẓvot* to one overarching principle, Ḥabakuk's "But the righteous shall live by his faith." For our purposes, however, with an eye to mapping areas of existence and activity rather than denominating an ultimate and definitive normative mode, we may best speak of three primary categories: environmental, personal, and historical. First in time, although not necessarily foremost in importance, is man's responsibility for the well-being, in all senses, of the world into which he has been born. While the mundane order may be nothing more than a way station, residents who have been entrusted with its care need to keep it clean, bright, and airy—and occasionally spruced up and renovated, both literally and figuratively. As the Rambam put it: "For a person ought not to engage all his days but in matters of wisdom and in the ordering of the world."[2] Transient though he be, the wayfarer launched upon *la pélèrinage de la vie humaine* is no mere nomad. Genuine "pilgrims of eternity," to use Byron's phrase, are few and frequently parasitic. Man, in general, is charged, inter alia, with *yishuvo shel 'olam*—the physical, socioeconomic, and spiritual order of the world.

This trust is at least symbolically reflected in the Torah's account of the position of primal man with respect to his primordial world: "And the Lord God took the man, and put him into the garden of Eden to cultivate it and to guard it."[3] Care for his environment, in the broad sense of the term, is a realization of man's responsi-

2. *Hil. Gezelah va-Avedah* 6:11. The Rambam here codifies a ruling formulated in *Sanhedrin* 24b that one who engages in gambling extensively to the point that he has no gainful pursuit is disqualified from offering testimony. However, while the Gemara only cites the lack of any contribution to *yishuvo shel 'olam,* the Rambam characteristically also speaks of the role of the pursuit of wisdom in human life as well.

3. Genesis 2:15. It is conceivable that the primary emphasis upon caring for the world inherent in this charge is rooted in man's prelapsarian innocence and that, after the fall, it

bility to himself, to his fellow, and to the *Ribbono Shel 'Olam,* whose creation is theologically related to *yishuvo shel 'olam.* "He is God, that formed the earth and made it; He established it, not as a waste He created it, He formed it to be settled."[4]

It should be noted, however, that the *pasuk* speaks of a dual task for man in Eden: *le-'avdah u-le-shamrah,* to cultivate and to guard. These roles are no doubt complementary and yet they can be clearly differentiated. The latter is an essentially conservative function, geared simply to maintaining the status quo. The former, too, bears a preservative aspect—fields need to be tilled and houses painted just to prevent decay—but it patently includes a creative, dynamic element as well. To cultivate is to develop; and development has a vertical as well as a horizontal dimension.

Custodial responsibility is complemented, second, by the molding of self as a spiritual being; this, both as an end in itself and as an avenue to the attainment of ultimate beatitude. "Rabbi Yaakov says: This world resembles a vestibule to the world to come; prepare yourself in the vestibule so that you may enter the banquet hall" (*Avot* 4:16). The ongoing process of preparation encompasses numerous areas and includes a range of components; and its mode and substance—particularly as regards priorities—may vary considerably. The psychomachy envisioned in the opening chapter of *Mesillat Yesharim* differs significantly from the speculative quest described in the conclusion of *Moreh Nevukhim.*[5] Both are, however, bound by a common overriding emphasis upon personal development—*hatken 'aẓmekha*; "prepare thyself."[6]

Development, at both the collective and the personal plane, not only enhances the present but informs an incipient future. Hence, it relates to a third dimension of human existence: responsibility to history as both reality and process. Somewhere between the vestibule and the banquet hall there is an antechamber of a redeemed messianic world; and, quite apart from man's duties to strive for his own spiritual perfection and the maintenance of his world, he is enjoined to help move that world to a higher and ultimately redeemed level. In this connection, some may think, in the concluding words of *In Memoriam,* of "one far-off divine event, to

---

shifted to concern for his own spiritual self. Obviously, however, this is a matter for conjecture and debate.

4. Isaiah 45:18. Cf. *Gittin* 41b.

5. R. Mosheh Ḥayyim Luẓẓatto and the Rambam share a common concern (one might add, a common faith) with regard to direct analysis of one's duty and persistent introspective examination of the degree and mode of its fulfillment as a necessary vehicle of self-preparation. Others—much of Hasidic thought notably comes to mind—lack and perhaps even shun this emphasis while sharing the overall goal.

6. Strikingly, the identical phrase appears in another Mishnah in *Avot* (2:12), in which R. Yose exhorts, "Prepare yourself (*hatken aẓmekha*) to study Torah, as it is not a patrimony unto you."

which the whole creation moves,"[7] as evolution and epiphany conjoin to cap history with a glorious but essentially continuous culmination. Others may conceive, in aeonic terms, of a radical leap into a qualitatively new phase of human existence. In either case, however, the advancement of eschatological realization—or, more modestly stated, contributing towards leaving the world a better place than one had found it—is clearly a basic facet of the human mandate. It is, moreover, directly related to the earlier charges. The prophetic annunciation of the millennium—"They shall not hurt nor destroy in all My holy mountain; for the earth shall be full of the knowledge of the Lord, as the waters cover the sea" (Isaiah 11:9)—clearly envisions the coalescence of the ultimate *tikkun 'olam* with illumination of a multitude of redeemed souls.

Definition of ultimate spiritual goals commends itself, at least, in theory, as a necessary prelude to deciding upon any significant course of action. All the more so, however, with respect to as complex and comprehensive a matter as the relation of Torah and general culture—to what, in current parlance, is generally referred to as the question of *Torah u-Madda*; or, as I would prefer to denominate it, as that of *Torah ve-ḥokhmah*. In dealing with it, we need to address ourselves at the primary level to four basic questions: (1) What is the contribution of *madda* and *ḥokhmah* to the realization of basic human aims? (2) Is that contribution sufficient to warrant diversion of time and effort from pure *talmud Torah*? (3) Whatever the benefits, what of concomitant risks? (4) What is the risk-benefit ratio, and might the dangers not preclude the pursuit of *madda*, however inherently worthwhile? At a secondary level, we need to confront the historical aspect. What, traditionally, has been the place of general culture within Torah Judaism and is that place legitimately subject to significant change?[8]

The Beauty of Japhet: Culture as Supplement

The contribution of *madda* relates, I believe, to all three primary aims: in part, to maintenance of the vestibule; in part, to self-preparation; and, hence, to the extent that all the millennium is a function of human initiative, to the molding of "a new

7. The lines no doubt include a strain of nineteenth-century faith in progress to which Tennyson gave vent in various contexts. The religious moment is clearly predominant, however.

8. I regard this as a significant question and have a fairly clear sense of the general outlines of its answer. Its thorough treatment lies, however, beyond both my expertise and the scope of this essay and is the subject of much of the rest of this volume.

For other formulations of some of the central issues, see the analysis of *mori ve-rabbi*, Rabbi Ahron Soloveichik, *Logic of the Heart, Logic of the Mind* (Jerusalem, 1991), 35–60; Rabbi Jonathan Sacks, "Torah Umadda: The Unwritten Chapter," *L'Eylah* 30 (September, 1990): 10–16; and, of course, the discourse in *The Torah u-Madda Journal*, 1–3.

heaven and a new earth" as well. To begin with the first, I trust that, in an age so deeply pervaded by the impact of science and technology, little needs to be said concerning their contribution to the fabric of human society. Their influence is so profound, even among the most seemingly obscurantist, that they are widely regarded as not only maintaining the present quality of life but as ensuring and enhancing its future progress. Presumably, more needs to be said, however, of two related points. First, *madda*, in this context, is not confined to the natural sciences. Man, after all, is the center of the vestibule, and whatever disciplines relate to his social, economic, and political institutions sustain human society in the most basic sense. It would be a strange Torah perspective, indeed, which regards a sewage system as more related to *yishuvo shel 'olam* than a family agency. Second, the knowledge in question is not merely an instrument of collective import. Even at the purely functional level, it relates to individual fulfillment as well. Quite apart from the spiritual well-being which is the ultimate object of *hatken 'aẓmekha,* orientation towards one's physical and social environment is, presently, itself an integral part of human self-realization.

Beyond its possible independent significance, the assurance of a proper material base for civilization has obvious religious implications. "Without flour there is no Torah";[9] in the absence of the necessary infrastructure, spiritual existence too is stifled. Nevertheless, this effort is, in a real sense, devoid of any direct link to Torah or even spirituality in general. The case is quite different with respect to other Torah benefits of general culture. One might single out three, in particular, each of various spiritual import but all directly related to Torah rather than a mere precondition. *Madda* helps elucidate the content of Torah; it enhances its optimal implementation; and it provides a spiritual complement. In many respects, these functions are interrelated, both conceptually and practically. Nevertheless, they are also clearly distinct and may be independently treated seriatim.

To begin with elucidation, at the most obvious plane, *madda* enhances our understanding of basic sources. We can harness linguistics to the explication of both *Torah she-bikhtav* and *Torah she-be'al peh* (Scripture and Oral Law), not only to decipher obscure texts but in order to illuminate many which are, at a superficial level, readily intelligible. We presumably all recognize the importance of discovering the literal meaning of "difficult" words and willingly recognize the aid of etymology and semantics in dealing with them. We are probably less mindful of the significance of the nuances of sensitive terms and therefore are less aware of the potential role of *madda* in analyzing them. Ultimately, however, the latter is more significant. One need not be a disciple of Wittgenstein or I. A. Richards to recognize the centrality of precise definition. The example of the first part of the *Guide to the Perplexed* is evidence enough. Can anyone really question the impor-

9. *Avot* 3:17. The reciprocal interdependence cited in the Mishnah does not, of course, confer axiological parity.

tance, both conceptual and practical, of accurately defining the phrase *haẓnea' lekhet* in that critical *pasuk* in Micah?[10] And does not the precept and practice of *rishonim* attest to the uses of philology in arriving at such truths?

Analogously, various disciplines can shed much light on many areas of *halakhah*. Mathematics, so much esteemed by the Rambam and the Gaon of Vilna for other reasons, illumines relatively few *sugyot* directly. But history, for instance, is quite another matter. Knowledge of Ḥazal's world—its agriculture, medicine, economics, or politics—enhances understanding of numerous *gemarot* and is often valuable if not essential in order to arrive at definitive halakhic conclusions. Looking to later ages, the reciprocal relation between historical research and responsa literature is self-evident. If professional historians, on the one hand, scour the Rivash or the Ḥatam Sofer for data, *benei Torah,* for whom *teshuvot* (responsa) are incomparably more than academic lodes, often conversely find recourse to scholarship critical for their proper understanding.

Madda's elucidation of Torah is not confined, however, to minutiae. At its best, it affords not only information but insight. Our understanding of Tanakh may be enhanced by criticism as well as by philology; and that relates not just to phrases but to entire texts, events, epochs, and personalities. "Biblical criticism" is, of course, for us anathema; and, by and large, rightly so. If the term denotes, as to many it predominantly does, a school which denies the transcendental truth of Torah; if it signifies a fusion of heresy and blasphemy whose advocates alternately gut and grade *kitvei ha-kodesh* as they pass judgment upon Torah and the *Ribbono Shel 'Olam*—then, clearly, we shall have no truck with it. But there can be biblical criticism of a very different order—one which wholeheartedly accepts the integrity of Torah and, precisely for that reason, strives maximally to divine its message. As Harry Levin has pointed out, the Greek root *krino* relates primarily to distinction and differentiation and only secondarily to evaluation.[11] From criticism geared to apprehending texts and contexts in their multiplanar complexity, the Torah world's reading of Scripture can profit considerably. Whether one accepts Meir Weiss' suggestion that "New Criticism," in particular, can be harnessed to traditional biblical study,[12] or whether one opts for a variety of approaches, the value of

10. See Micah 6:8; and cf. *Makkot* 24a. English translations, including the Jewish Publication Society's version, generally render the phrase as "to walk humbly." However, humility is only one aspect of this multifaceted term. While the *pasuk* clearly denigrates arrogance and exhibitionism, the alternative need not be weakness, but may rather entail firm resolve and quiet determination. The self-effacing simplicity and retiring shyness which, among other qualities the phrase connotes, are not inconsistent wtih self-esteem. For an interesting discussion of this phrase, see D. Winton Thomas, "The Root צנע in Hebrew and the Meaning of קדרנית in Malachi III, 14," *The Journal of Jewish Studies* 1 (1948): 182–86. (I am indebted to Rabbi Dr. Dov Frimer for this reference.)

11. See *Perspectives of Criticism*, ed. Harry Levin (Cambridge, Mass., 1950), introduction.

12. See Meir Weiss, *Ha-Mikra Kidemuto* (Jerusalem, 1967), especially 9–27.

perceiving Torah via penetrating observation through both sides of the telescope is clear.

The need is felt in some areas more than in others. Under the impact of the midrashim and a lengthy homiletic tradition, the Torah world is highly sensitive to imagery and symbolism; but as to structure, sequence, sound patterns, and thematic development, less so. These are, however, genuinely relevant to a total experience of the text. "The voice of the Lord is powerful, the voice of the Lord is majestic,"[13] and whatever sharpens our apprehension of the power and beauty of resonant revelation enhances our spiritual existence.

Above all, criticism accentuates awareness of the human element. Toward its appreciation, a literary sensibility, trained to observe perceptively and to respond empathetically, its imagination honed to grasp a scene or a moment as the focus of complex interaction, is inestimable. Criticism sensitizes to both what is said and—what the Ramban so acutely perceived—unsaid. The omission of even single factual points, after all, may have significant implications. Did Yaakov Avinu ever learn of the sale of his beloved Yosef? What is the import of whether Avraham ever saw Sarah after the *'akedah* or, in a wholly different era, of whether Yithro came before or after *matan Torah?*[14] Surely, a *talmid ḥakham* wholly bereft of any literary exposure could conceivably answer these questions intelligently and sensitively. Which academy did the Neẓiv attend? In most cases, however, he would not even fully appreciate their cutting edge. From a certain point of view, this is, of course, regarded as all to the good. Advocates of hagiographic *parshanut,* which portrays the central heroic figures of scriptural history as virtually devoid of emotion, can only regard the sharpening of psychological awareness with reference to Tanakh with
a jaundiced eye. But for those of us who have been steeped in midrashim, the Ramban, and the *Ha'amek Davar*—in a tradition, that is, which regards our patriarchal *avot* and their successors as very great people indeed but as people nonetheless, and which moreover sees their greatness as related to their humanity—enhanced literary sensibility can be viewed as a significant boon.

The potential contribution of *madda* to our understanding of Torah is thus not merely technical or exegetical—important as that would be in its own right—but, in a broader and deeper sense, thoroughly substantive. Specifically, as should be clear from the foregoing, we should take note of the methodological factor. In this connection, two elements may be singled out. The first is order. In practice, *madda*

13. Psalms 29:4. In context, the *pasuk* of course does not describe attributes of the revealed Word but rather conversely proclaims that where power and majesty obtain—the reference is presumably to nature—they are effectively the voice of the Lord. Nevertheless, the conjunction between *kol Hashem* and these qualities is clearly established and one ought therefore search for them within revelation.

14. See the Ramban's commentary on Genesis 45:27, 23:2, and Exodus 18:1, respectively.

or *ḥokhmah* for us is primarily Western culture.[15] That culture was largely molded by Greek thought; and the Greek world—as the very term, cosmos, indicates—was deeply pervaded by the quest for order. Our own spiritual and intellectual world developed along very different lines. Judaism neither attained nor cherished the level of systematization characteristic of Hellenism, as reflected particularly in Aristotle. It presumably regarded man, the universe, and, above all, the transcendental order, as far too mysterious and far too dynamic for that. But whatever the theological and philosophical reasons, there was a price.

The best case in point is our greatest collective achievement: the Gemara. I love Gemara passionately; and part of what I love, over and above its status as *devar Hashem* (the Divine word), is precisely its disheveled character. Its student is not confronted by the judicious formulations of Justinian or Coke. Rather, he enters a vibrant *bet midrash,* hears and, with reverential vicariousness, participates in discourse animated by dynamic interaction, frequently marred by associative digression, and rarely formulated with integrative thoroughness. For the initiate, it is all very exhilarating, and the sense of the pulsating vibrancy of living Torah is pervasive. But this heady environment creates certain problems. The difficulties confronting the tyro are all too familiar. These are by no means confined to modern day-school students, ignorant of Aramaic vocabulary or syntax. They had been succinctly described in the early fourteenth century by Rabbenu Aharon Halevi, one of the foremost disciples of the Ramban. Explaining why he has chosen to write a commentary upon the Rif, who had in effect, edited the Gemara, he writes:

> And upon it (i.e., the mishnah) many claims were made, numerous thoughts and nice inferences out of which was built the Babylonian Talmud which is deep water, consisting of obscure and lengthy matters, to the point that the Sages denominated it as "[a place of] darkness". Most of those who have sought to enter have found its gates shut, except with regard to individuals in favored eras. . . . And the students venture forth fatigued and pressured, their thoughts then sapped by the extensive dialectic discourse. So that when I noted that the labor was great and the *gemara* [nevertheless] closed and shut, access and exit being generally barred, I composed a [commentary] work called *Nezer ha-Kodesh,* following the order of the *gemara.* . . . And yet, the ways of the Talmud are obscure, closed with a tight seal, and its matters are wearying and not all are fortunate to have fixed daily and nightly periods [i.e., of Torah study], and, because of their temporal

15. I stress "in practice." No value judgment is intended here. When Ḥazal affirmed the presence of *ḥokhmah ba-goyim,* they did not restrict the assertion to Occidental gentiles. In fact, however, the Jewish world's contact with general culture has been almost overwhelmingly with the West. Even the medieval relation to Islam focused primarily upon its Hellenistic component.

The reader will note that literary allusions in the course of this essay have been disproportionately weighted, with a great many drawn from English literature. That is, of course, simply a reflection of the author's ignorance. Clearly, the same points could have been equally exemplified by drawing upon other cultures.

travails, learn Torah by hours and moments, and many need short summaries and orderly codes, such as shall find favor in their eyes, like radiant sapphires.[16]

It should be emphasized, however, that it is not just the neophyte or the dilettante who senses the difficulty. As the multifarious history of the *Mishneh Torah* indicates, *talmidei ḥakhamim* likewise feel the need and the urge for comprehensive and systematic ordering of *halakhah.* To this end, *madda,* systematic both intrinsically and by dint of its classical roots, has much to contribute. Above and beyond the Rambam's personal genius, surely there is some link between his philosophic studies and his remarkable bent for structure and order. On a broader scale, it is no accident that Sephardic *rishonim* demonstrated a systematic capacity far greater than that of their Ashkenazic counterparts; nor, looking to later ages, that the author of the best-known classical halakhic encyclopedia, *Paḥad Yiẓḥak,* was university-trained, or that the current *Enzyklopedia Talmudit* is being written within the context of a *madda*-oriented culture.[17]

To be sure, compendia are secondary works in two senses of the term, being both later and lesser. One would not exchange *Ḥiddushei Rabbenu Ḥayyim Halevi* for the entire spate of summary monographs currently inundating the Torah world. But that is not the issue. We are not confronted by an either/or choice. Whatever the respective merits of various talents, the Torah world in its entirety is best served by the fusion of various qualities, of which the systematic impulse is surely not the least important. And that impulse is greatly energized by general culture.

Rewarding as the quest for order may be with respect to *halakhah,* it is of even greater significance as concerns *maḥshavah.*[18] The intrinsic nature of legal discourse as well as the structure of the Mishnah assures at least a modicum of structure with respect to *Sanhedrin* or *'Eruvin.* No such assurance exists with regard to faith or morality. Ḥazal's *weltanschauung* was expressed primarily through numerous aggadic statements, usually scattered through Shas and midrashic literature. These are mostly aphoristic, homiletic, or exegetical, more hortatory or expository than analytical. Of course, these statements—they are, after all, Ḥazal's—individually and collectively, enlighten, stimulate, and inspire. Historical comments limn the portrait of a personage or a period while moral and philosophic dicta both inculcate values and communicate truths. The fact remains, however, that the means are primarily illuminative flashes and penetrating insights rather than systematic exposition or discursive analysis. This is, of course, said descriptively, not as a value

16. *Pekudat ha-Leviyyim,* ed. S. and N. Bamberger (reprinted, Jerusalem, 1962), preface, 11.

17. R. Yiẓḥak Lampronti (1679–1756) studied medicine at the University of Padua and practiced it for a number of years. Most of the contributors to the *Enzyklopedia* lack academic education but the impact of *madda* upon the enterprise is transparent.

18. Literally "thought," with particular reference to Jewish thought, especially as articulated in Ḥazal and in classical exegetical and philosophic texts. The overall connotation is, however, less technical than "philosophy," and the existential component more prominent.

judgment. Ḥazal undoubtedly had their reasons. Order, after all, is not the foremost spiritual value. Would anyone wish Pascal's *Penseés* more orderly? Nevertheless, for most of us, be we, in terms of Isaiah Berlin's familiar dichotomy, hedgehogs or foxes,[19] some passion for order persists. Its satisfaction, particularly with respect to our religious world, is greatly enhanced by general culture and strains of Jewish thought that have felt its impact.

Quite apart from direct elucidation, *madda* enriches our understanding of Torah via a second indirect channel: by providing a basis for comparison. The natural sciences generally deal with subject matter which is not part and parcel of Torah. Their relation to it is therefore peripheral or incremental. The social sciences and the humanities, by contrast, are directly concerned with many issues which are of the woof and warp of Torah proper. The structure and substance of law, the fabric of state and society, the nature of man and his cosmic context all fall within the purview of general as well as Torah thought. Knowledge of how such questions, legal and/or philosophic, have been treated in different traditions can frequently enhance our understanding of Torah positions, as regards either broad outlines or specific detail.

Comparison, the closer the better—"between blue and green" more than "between blue and white" (*Berakhot* 9b)—highlights not only the difference between phenomena but the respective character and content of each. At the conceptual plane, comparison may focus our attention upon facets of Torah we might otherwise have missed, as the import and importance of distinctive Torah positions may be insufficiently appreciated so long as they are unwittingly taken for granted. While confined to one's native linguistic and cultural tradition and devoid of universal categories and perspective through and from which to perceive it, one is often totally oblivious to much of its substantive content; and the study of a foreign language may teach a person much about his mother tongue, as well as about man as a verbal being, in general. Analogously, the knowledge that an issue of Jewish import—say, the subject of this essay, the status of general culture within a religious tradition—has been prominently treated within Islam and Christianity, can surely enrich its treatment by adding to the halakhic analysis—which, for us, is, of course, fundamental and decisive—universal human and spiritual dimensions.

To be sure, comparison may be a two-edged sword, to be wielded with proper caution. Despite its clear benefits, it may perilously undermine the sense of the uniqueness and objective truth of Torah; and more on this anon. This is, however, a primarily educational consideration—not the less weighty on that account—and in no way vitiates, in principle, the role of comparison in elucidating Torah.

19. See Isaiah Berlin, *The Hedgehog and the Fox* (New York, 1957). Berlin speaks primarily of substantive world-views rather than form; and, hence, counts Pascal among the hedgehogs animated by a dominant and comprehensive unitary vision (p. 8). The two are, however, often closely related. The general issue raised by Berlin has much relevance with regard to Jewish thought, especially as regards the interaction of *halakhah* and *maḥshavah*.

Properly developed, its contribution is once again real and significant. Within a context of true commitment, it not only sheds light upon the totality of Torah as an objective entity but stimulates our understanding and appreciation of it. Such, I presume, was the position of R. Yehudah Halevi. It seems most unlikely that the format of the *Sefer ha-Kuzari*—a summary overview of the respective merits of Judaism, Islam, and Christianity—was dictated by literary and forensic considerations alone; and if, as I believe, there are substantive rewards to be reaped from its relatively low-keyed comparisons, all the more so from more intensive recourse to *ḥokhmah* and *madda,* in their full range and depth.

Madda's contribution to the elucidation of Torah is just that. It enhances, enriches, illuminates, adds information and insights; extends dimensions of clarity, range, and depth. Nevertheless, in this context, that role is generally—although the Rambam, for one, may, in certain respects, be an exception—not pivotal. Moving on to a second area, however, the implementation of Torah, we enter a realm within which *madda* is indeed often crucial. A full Torah life, personal or collective, revolves around two foci: *talmud* and *ma'aseh,* study and action. *Madda* advances both, but in different ways and varied proportions. *Talmud* is relatively self-contained. While much of the subject-matter of *halakhah* concerns the real physical and/or social order, significant knowledge of that world or immediate contact with it is generally no prerequisite to halakhic study. That consists primarily of the analysis of sacred texts and normative concepts, the method being largely deductive, the focus ideational rather than factual. Within this context, knowledge of the realia is helpful but, with respect to much if not most of the endeavor, not indispensable. I recall hearing that Professor Saul Lieberman was once shocked, in the midst of an animated discussion with an eminent *talmid ḥakham* about *rediyat ha-pat,* upon discovering that his interlocutor did not know just what phase of the baking process the phrase denoted. I understand the shock fully; but is the knowledge truly necessary in order to deal with the major crux of the nature of the proscription of *ḥohkmah she'en 'immah melakhah*?[20] Or, to take a more basic area, could not one discuss most aspects of *ḥameẓ* with true *lomdut* without being able to identify that substance or define its chemical properties? To be sure, many problems can only be treated seriously and intelligently in the light of external knowledge; and I am not suggesting that it can be ignored with impunity. Yet, the fact remains that the world of basic halakhic discourse as a whole—and not only as it has developed within *yeshivot*—is largely insular.

The situation is radically different with respect to the implementation of Torah. That takes place within the physical or social world, and intimate knowledge of

20. See *Rosh Hashanah* 29b and *Shabbat* 4a as well as Rif, *Ba'al ha-Ma'or* and *Milḥamot Hashem,* ad loc. The term *rediyat ha-pat* refers to removal of bread from the oven upon conclusion of its baking. It is denominated as "a craft unaccompanied by labor" which is, therefore, only rabbinically proscribed—and, to a lessser degree, at that—unlike *melakhah* (labor) which is biblically prohibited.

that world is its sine qua non. Ignorance of realia is a major impediment even at the level of theoretical *pesak;* as regards application, it simply disqualifies. At the juncture of the *Shulḥan 'Arukh* and the barnyard, the apocryphal story about the *lamdan* who opined that, if what he had been shown was indeed its craw, then the chicken was *terefah,* is no joking matter.

Hence, *madda* figures far more prominently in the world of active *ma'aseh* than in that of contemplative *talmud.* To the extent that it is a recognized source of knowledge about the object and locus of halakhic realization, it is an integral and essential element of Torah existence, broadly conceived. The point is presumably self-evident, but many in the Torah world are not sufficiently mindful of its ramifications. We take it for granted with respect to certain areas but ignore it, blandly and perhaps even blithely, with regard to others. Recourse to biology or physics is de rigueur with respect to patently scientific questions. The approach is best exemplified by Rav, who is quoted in the Gemara (*Sanhedrin* 5b) as stating that he had spent eighteen months with a shepherd, "in order to know which is a permanent defect and which is a transitory defect." Few subsequent *posekim* have found the time, or possibly, the inclination, to acquire such first-hand knowledge so intensively. They have, however, routinely consulted experts (although not fully agreeing over how much weight to assign their reportage) in line with the practice of seeking out doctors cited in the Gemara (*Yoma* 83a; *Niddah* 22b). Would any responsible *posek* determine the Shabbat status of hot-water systems or elevators bereft of the relevant engineering data?

Logically, the same principle should presumably apply to other areas, of *halakhah* and of human life, as well. To an extent, this is true even with respect to the inner psychic realm (of which more anon) but surely so, in relation to the behavioral and particularly the interpersonal sphere. *Halakhot* regarding the social, economic, or political order, generally formulated with reference to several variables, simply cannot be properly implemented unless one has or had access to knowledge concerning the situation to which they are to be applied. One cannot translate ordinances concerning neighborly relations into contemporary terms without some knowledge of both the classical and modern socio-economic scene. One cannot properly apply *halakhot* governing labor relations without the capacity for extrapolating from one milieu to another. Determination of the current equivalent of Ḥazal's regulations concerning the collection and distribution of *ẓedakah* is only possible through an informed comparison of their world and ours. *Madda* is a significant repository of requisite factual knowledge; and, what is often no less important, a vehicle of developing sensitivity to intangibles which mark respective eras.

General culture is thus of value in implementing Torah even at the relatively narrow, formal—and, if you will, mechanical—level of the application of specific rule to particular situation. Its value is measurably increased, however, if it is brought to bear not upon the normal halakhic process of normative application but within the context of innovation and initiative. This can take the form, within legitimate halakhic limits, of either deviant retrenchment or expansive extension.

The former is, of course, quite limited in scope; but it does exist. License for such deviation, when mitigated by historical circumstances, is derived by the Gemara (*Yevamot* 90b) from the archetypal example of Eliyahu ha-Navi who offered a sacrifice in the course of his confrontation with the votaries of Baal, this in apparent violation of the injunction against proffering sacrifices outside of the *mikdash*. This source might lead us to assume that only single deviant acts could be countenanced as one-time exceptions. The Rambam, however, clearly posits otherwise. After stating that, in certain instances, a later *bet din* cannot annul ordinances legislated by its predecessors, he qualifies, in *Hil. Mamrim* (2:4).

> However, the court, even if it be inferior, is authorized to dispense for a time even with these matters. For these decrees are not to be [regarded as] more stringent than matters of the Torah itself, as even Torah matters proper can be suspended by any court by a temporary decree. . . . If, in order to bring back the multitudes to religion or in order to save many Jews from stumbling with respect to other matters, the court may act in accordance with the needs of the hour. Even as a physician will amputate a person's hand or foot in order to save his life, so a court, at a given time, may direct to transgress some commandments temporarily in order that their corpus may be preserved. This, in accordance with what the early Sages said: "Desecrate on his account one Sabbath that he be able to observe many Sabbaths."

This formulation seems to imply that the Gemara's term, *le-sha'ah* (for a period), does not necessarily refer to a single emergency, but is rather to be contrasted with *le-dorot* (for posterity) and to be regarded as denoting a temporary initiative, as opposed to permanent revisionist legislation. Needless to say, determination of the needs of a given period requires intimate and incisive knowledge of the contemporary scene and, to that end, general culture is often invaluable. In the absence of such convincing knowledge, one might either take misguided initiatives or remain understandably passive. In either case, the consequences of mistaken judgment could be grievous. Who would decide about surgery bereft of relevant data?

Even on the Rambam's view, however, such authoritative deviation is quite limited in scope—in all likelihood, confined to a formally constituted Sanhedrin. Far more prevalent is retrenchment of a different sort, pithily summed up by another citation from the Rambam, with reference to the failure to implement proper juridic procedure: "For we lack the power to establish religious laws on their [proper] basis."[21] The comment—it refers to abandonment of the requirement that witnesses and the parties stand during certain stages of a trial—was made with regard to the *halakhah*'s home court, a defined arena of its own creation and subject to its ground rules. Obviously, the problem is greatly exacerbated in dealing with the broader social scene, frequently the locus of confrontation between the normative halakhic order and an often intractable human reality. The Rosh,

21. *Hil. Sanhedrin* 21:5.

grappling with the total disregard of *shemittat kesafim* (remission of debts at the conclusion of the Sabbatical year) he encountered in Spain, moving from outrage to resignation and even apologetics[22]; the *Noda' bi-Yehudah* winking at the disregard of his instructions concerning the preparation of a hot *mikveh* for Shabbat[23]; the Rama vigorously rejecting and yet conjecturally explaining widespread indulgence in gentile wines[24]—these exemplify situations which have persistently arisen throughout the ages.

Response to them is guided by a famous Gemara in *Yevamot* (65b):

> R. Il'a further stated in the name of R. Eleazar son of R. Shimon: "As one is commanded to say that which will be accepted, so one is commanded not to say that which will be rejected." R. Abba stated: "It is a duty; for it is written, 'reprove not a scorner, lest he hate thee; reprove a wise man and he will love thee.'"

Clearly, the implementation of this Gemara is dependent upon accurate prognosis of how a given message is likely to be received. To this end, *madda* can be doubly helpful. First, it can possibly provide psychological and sociological tools which can enhance the capacity for evaluation in general. Second, to the extent that the prospective audience is itself suffused with secular values and sensibility, knowledge of general culture is invaluable toward the understanding of its particular character and projected response. Even if one contends that the theoretical knowledge is superfluous, as perspicacity is more readily attained through Torah proper, the application of insight to a given social reality obviously is largely dependent upon familiarity with its characteristic features.

Hence, the relative resurgence of *Torah u-Madda* in the modern period—the concept had been largely quiescent if not dormant for several centuries[25]—was not due solely to the stimulation provided by the intrinsic cultural and intellectual challenges of modernity or to secular seepage into the religious world (although that, too, has probably been a factor). It was no less the result of a perceived need to respond for pristine Torah reasons to a changed communal situation. Within a relatively homogeneous ghettoized community, Torah leadership sans *madda* can communicate effectively with its constituents and accurately assess their needs and inclinations. The situation is quite different when a cultural gap—at times, a chasm—divides the shepherd from his flock. In an age, unlike Lycidas', in which the sheep may not even realize they are hungry, ministering to their needs becomes incomparably more difficult and the impetus to understand their sensibility and language far greater.

---

22. See *She'elot u-Teshuvot ha-Rosh*, 77:4. Cf. *Bet Yosef, Ḥoshen Mishpat* 67:4, who expresses astonishment at the Rosh's acquiescence and conjectures a possible explanation.

23. See R. Yeḥezkel Landau, *Noda' bi-Yehudah*, Mahadura Tinyana, Oraḥ Ḥayyim, 24.

24. See R. Mosheh Isserles, *She'elot u-Teshuvot ha-Rama*, §124.

25. At least, as regards the center court of the Torah world. Peripherally, it of course persisted throughout.

The issue extends well beyond the specific halakhic question of the proper fulfillment of the *mizvah* of reproaching one's fellow. That is, of course, crucially important in its own right and never easy. Rabbi Tarfon and Rabbi Eleazar ben 'Azaryah wondered whether anyone in *their* generation knew how to receive or express rebuke, respectively.[26] However, beyond judgment as to whether—and what kind of—exhortation or excoriation will be effectively heeded, we must cope with the formulation of public policy in general, especially on its spiritual side. In which direction should contemporary society be moved and at what pace? In which direction *can* it be moved? What are the present priorities? What is the optimal current balance between Torah and *hesed,* as regards the apportionment of time, energy, or resources, the determination of educational emphases, or the development of communal institutions? Should social justice be pressed, even at the possible expense of pietistic fervor, or vice versa? How is effective leadership best developed? Ought the religious community be largely self-contained, its base narrow but deep, or should it reach out to the moderately committed and even to an unregenerate *klal Yisrael*?

Answers to such questions—most of which have halakhic ramifications, but are not purely halakhic themselves—are clearly grounded in basic sources and traditional practice. But, again, their substantive guidance requires intelligent application to an era, properly understood and evaluated. At the level of public policy, what is needed is not just knowledge of clumps of facts but a broader and profounder understanding of social forces and historical currents. *Madda* can be enormously helpful in enhancing such understanding. On the one hand, it inculcates a sense of historical perspective in general; on the other, it enables one to grasp the zeitgeist better by familiarizing him with its background and major components. By limning the contours of a period, it helps define its needs and directions at the broadest and highest planes.

To be sure, Judaism, by and large, can be regarded as inclining to the sound classical emphasis upon the fundamental constancy of human nature. Nevertheless, it is wholly fallacious to assume, as do many in the Torah world, that all ages can be regarded as largely identical and, normatively speaking, can be approached as such. Ḥazal, at any rate, had no such misconception. A celebrated statement by Hillel, touching upon both educational and public policy, clearly endorses a differential approach—somewhat surprisingly, even toward the dissemination of Torah:

> During a time of ingathering [i.e., of Torah] disseminate; during a time of dissemination, gather in. When you see that Torah is cherished by all of Israel and everyone is happy with it, disseminate it, as is stated: "There is that scattereth and yet increaseth." When you see that Israel is oblivious to Torah and everyone does not pay attention to it, gather it in, as is stated, "When it is time to work for the Lord, they make void Thy law."[27]

26. See *'Arakhin* 16b.
27. *Tosefta, Berakhot* 6:24; cited in the *Bavli, Berakhot* 63a. The Meiri, ad loc., takes the

If the realization of so central a value is a function of the spirit of the age, sensitivity to the zeitgeist is a fortiori essential to other aspects of communal life.

To many, the point will, quite rightly, appear elementary. And yet, it needs to be stressed. Modern secular culture is, on the whole, excessively historicistic; the Torah world, insufficiently so. Failure to grasp the essence of contemporary society and to perceive it in proper historical perspective cost Orthodoxy dearly in Eastern Europe. Some of the disintegration and demoralization which affected Polish, Russian, or Lithuanian Jewry earlier in this century—much of it obscured today by nostalgic romanticization but painfully real at the time—was no doubt inevitable. But not all. Better collective grasp of the forces which were buffeting those great bastions could have arrested the decline measurably. To that end, *madda*—which could have sharpened insight into social dynamics, generally, and, say, Socialism, particularly—could have contributed significantly.

But need one resort to the past for supportive examples? Contemporary Israel is, unfortunately, an excellent case in point. Within the religious community, concern for the country's spiritual character is genuine and widespread; but attempts to cope with the problem are often grievously misguided and inept. Culture shock has left some elements of its Torah world in bewilderment and disarray. Others, particularly within the political realm, are confident to the point of being overweening, but often fight the wrong battles with the wrong tools; and while some of these are nevertheless won, many of the triumphs are Pyrrhic victories which already exact an immediate toll but whose full cost—in the form of *ḥillul Hashem*, anti-religious resentment, and national divisiveness—is deferred to the future. Those who lack the capacity to understand the secular mind properly may find it easier to misconstrue or disregard it. The result is a blatant obliviousness to Ḥazal's admonition (*Mo'ed Katan* 17a): "'And put not a stumbling-block before the blind,' that text applies to one who beats his grown-up son," because, as Rashi explains, he is thereby possibly inciting him to rebel in recoil. A true *gadol,* such as Rav Shlomo Zalman Auerbach, *zẓ"l* intuits the situation fully and is, indeed, consequently dismayed. For most, however, a measure of *madda* can be vital toward illuminating both the present scene and the ramifications of prospective courses of action.

Perfumers and Cooks: Culture as Complement

Madda thus contributes effectively to both *talmud* and *ma'aseh,* the understanding as well as the realization of Torah. Nonetheless, its most significant potential contri-

---

text to be one continuum, with the opening statement being subsequently expounded. However, Rashi interprets the opening as a separate directive to the effect that, when outstanding Torah scholars are derelict in disseminating Torah, lesser lights should take up the slack. If, however, the former do teach assiduously, others should inhibit themselves.

bution to Judaism, as well as its most controversial, inheres in yet a third capacity; as a spiritual complement or, if you will, supplement. *Ḥokhmah* can inform and irradiate our spiritual being by rounding out its cardinal Torah component. It effects this, either by casting light, if not upon the stuff of Torah proper—its basic texts and concepts, with all their derivatives—then upon the issues to which they relate; or, alternatively, by expanding our spiritual and intellectual horizons through exposure to other areas of potential religious import. Of course, to many the notion that Torah can be rounded out at all is pure anathema. Moreover, prima facie, this position is securely anchored in Ben Bag Bag's aphorism (*Avot* 5:26): *Hafakh bah ve-hafakh bah dekhola bah,* "Engage in it and engage in it for all is withen it." It is important, however, to discern what precisely is intended by "it" and in what sense Torah narrowly defined—that whose study constitutes a fulfillment of the *miẓvah* of *talmud Torah*—is "all ye know on earth and all ye need to know."

The Ramban, in any event, had no such qualms. Referring to the forty-nine portals of wisdom to which Mosheh Rabbenu had been granted access, he describes them as encompassing virtually all planes of cosmic reality—terrestrial and celestial, physical and metaphysical, animal and human—and he goes on to expound that Mosheh, having been initiated into these worlds of wisdom and mastered them, was consequently invested with penetrating psychological insight. Suffused with the understanding related to the gate concerning man, he was able

> to contemplate the secret of the soul, to know its essence and its power in its palace [i.e., the body], and to attain to the level alluded to in the saying of the Sages: "If a person stole, he [who has the aforesaid understanding] knows and recognizes that in him; if he has fornicated, he knows and recognizes that in him; if he is suspect of having had relations with a *niddah,* he knows and recognizes that in him. Greater yet, he recognizes masters of witchcraft." And hence, one can ascend to the understanding of the spheres, the heavens and their hosts, for pertaining to each of these there is one gate of wisdom which is unlike any other.

And he goes on to expound how all this universal knowledge is mystically imbedded in the Torah:

> Everything that was transmitted to Moses our teacher through the forty-nine gates of understanding was written in the Torah explicitly or by implication in words, in the numerical value of the letters or in the form of the letters, that is, whether written normally or with some change in form such as bent or crooked letters and other deviations, or in the tips of the letters and their crownlets. . . .
>
> In the *Midrash Shir ha-Shirim Rabbah,* they [the Sages] have also said: "It is written, 'And He declared unto you His covenant,' which means: He declared unto you the Book of Genesis, which relates the beginning of His creation; 'which He commanded you to perform even the ten words,' meaning the ten commandments, ten for Scripture and ten for Talmud. For from what source did Elihu the son of Barachel the Buzite come and

reveal to Israel the secrets of the behemoth and the leviathan? And from what source did Ezekiel come and reveal to them the mysteries of the Divine Chariot? It is this which Scripture says, 'The King hath brought me into his chambers,' meaning that everything can be learned from the Torah. King Solomon, peace be upon him, whom God had given wisdom and knowledge, derived it from the Torah, and from it he studied until he knew the secret of all things created even of the forces and characteristics of plants, so that he wrote about them even a Book of Medicine, as it is written, 'And he spoke of trees, from the cedar that is in Lebanon even unto the hyssop that springeth out of the wall.' "[28]

In one sense, this is a ringing affirmation of *hafakh bah ve-hafakh bah,* and a clear rejection of *Torah u-Madda.* In another, however, it is a far-reaching assertion of the value of general knowledge and hence a *locus classicus* for its advocates. At the primary level, the problem of *Torah u-Madda* has two components. First, what, if anything, apart from Torah narrowly defined is worth knowing? Second, how is its knowledge to be attained? The Ramban unequivocally designates the text of Torah as the repository of all wisdom; but only after he has posited the importance of so much we ordinarily regard as *madda.* What, for us, are the practical ramifications of this two-edged message?

I believe they are clear. Of the two questions I have singled out, the first is axiological, the second—at least at the educational level—largely empirical. As regards the former, we extract from this text the principled assumption of the importance of knowing man and nature. With respect to the latter, the passage challenges our sensitivity and candor as we judge how to relate to it. The Ramban's assertion of the comprehensive self-sufficiency of Torah is patently couched in mystical terms. Even, however, as we can share his conviction at that plane, we need to ask ourselves honestly what are the implications for the mundane rational plane at which we ordinarily and normatively function. Does any devout Jew ignore modern medical progress out of reliance upon the "secret of all things created" inherent in the Torah? Confronted with a medical crisis, we rightly assume that the requisite knowledge may indeed be imbedded in Torah but that, in the absence of Shlomo, Elihu, or Yeḥezkel to mine its secrets, we are constrained to turn to alternative sources. What is so readily taken for granted in so critical an area applies to many others as well. If, indeed, we wish to enhance that knowledge of man and his world so highly esteemed by the Ramban, we can benefit greatly from general culture.[29]

---

28. See R. Mosheh ben Naḥman, *Commentary on the Torah, Genesis,* tr. Rabbi C.B. Chavel (New York, 1971), 9–11.

29. The Ramban's view of general culture—which, for him, largely meant Greek philosophy and science or their tributaries—was, however, ambivalent. On the one hand, he studied and applied them, even at times bending his prima facie interpretation of Scripture in order to accommodate them; see, e.g., his commentary on Genesis 9:12. On the other hand, he took pains to insist upon their problematic aspects as avenues to truth and to

The benefits extend over a range of disciplines, relating to various facets and levels of revelation. The natural sciences manifestly decipher and describe a divinely ordained order whose knowledge both inspires praise and thanksgiving to the *Ribbono Shel 'Olam* and stimulates our reverential response to him. "The heavens declare the glory of God, and the firmament showeth His handiwork," David declares in *Tehillim* (19:2); and, as R. Yehudah Halevi stressed in the *Kuzari* (3:17), the glory of the heavens is paralleled and perhaps, on Pascal's view, even surpassed by that which is manifested through the infinitesimal microcosm of minute organisms. The whole, as the Rambam postulated in a passage (*Hil. Yesodei ha-Torah* 2:2) worn thin by quotation, stimulates not only wonder but love and awe:

> And what is the way to attain love and fear of HIm? When a person contemplates His great and wondrous works and creatures and will see from them His incomparable and infinite wisdom, He will immediately love, praise, and glorify and be filled with great passion to know His great name; even as David said, "My soul thirsteth for God, for the living God."

To a religious sensibility, that response—albeit, in the modern era, shorn of the quality of proof often associated with it by *rishonim* in other contexts—has lost nothing of its force. In and of itself, contemplation of nature does relatively little, at present, to resolve religious doubt. Tennyson's testimony—"I found Him not in world or sun,/Or eagle's wing, or insect's eye,/Nor thro' the questions man may try,/The petty cobwebs we have spun"[30]—is probably typical of modern sensibility as a whole. Newman's comment, that he did not believe in God because he saw design in nature but, rather, saw design in nature because he believed in God, is characteristic. Given the substratum of faith, however, the study and experience of nature can unquestionably deepen our religious commitment.

If science probes one facet of immanent revelation, history describes another. Its sphere, however, is not God's exclusively but the interaction of the human and the divine. From the perspective of faith, historical study consists of the exploration and analysis of the events and records of the drama of conjunction and confrontation between providential direction and creaturely freedom. The nature and proportions of that interaction constitutes a major crux of religious philosophy. Its analysis lies beyond the scope of this essay; but the significance of understanding the historical scene, however perceived, is beyond question. And this with respect

---

note that recourse to them, while perhaps necessary in certain circumstances, reflected spiritual weakness rather than strength, perhaps even with respect to the scientific or medical realms. See, e.g., his letter to the northern French rabbis in *Kitvei Rabbenu Moshe ben Naḥman*, ed. Rabbi C. B.Chavel (Jerusalem, 1964), I, 339. (I am indebted to Dr. David Berger for calling my attention to this reference.) This attitude parallels to some extent his position with respect to the dichotomy between the natural and supernatural standing of Jewry, depending on the degree of collective religious commitment.

30. Alfred Lord Tennyson, "In Memoriam," 124:5–8.

to both (*salve reverentia*) participants. On the one hand, history at once challenges us to seek an insight into the modus operandi of Providence and provides tools and materials requisite for the quest. To be sure, modern man is far less predisposed than his predecessors to read the past theologically. While alternative philosophical readings had been fully developed from antiquity—the polar contentions that either necessity or chance ruled all had been clearly articulated in the Greco-Roman world and widely discussed in the Middle Ages—the prevalent vision of ages of faith, at both the professional and popular level, included the perception of immanent divine presence and involvement; and it was left to secularized modern culture, even as it was increasingly sharpening its sense of history, to interpret it in more natural categories.

Admittedly, no serious contemporary historian can, would, or for that matter, should emulate Bossuet, whose *Discours sur L'Histoire Universelle,* replete with theological interpretations, sketched the course of God's dealings with humanity down to Louis XIV's France. Nevertheless, to the committed Jew, the spiritual significance of viewing God's historical handiwork remains paramount. The Torah's injunction, "Remember the days of old, consider the years of many generations" (Deuteronomy 32:7), confronts him with all its pristine force. That call—in part, hortatory and in part normative—refers in some measure to universal history, as the next *pasuk* clearly implies: "When the Most High gave to the nations their inheritance, when He separated the children of man, He set the borders of the peoples according to the number of the children of Israel." Primarily, however, it challenges us to master the history of *knesset Yisrael,* not out of mere chauvinistic insularity but rather out of a profound sense that it is in the context of God's unique relation to His chosen people that the workings of Divine Providence are most fully manifested and can be most readily perceived. Not that a Jew regards his history simply as a sourcebook providing instructive insight into the ways of the *Ribbono Shel 'Olam.* Are love letters read primarily with an eye for their style? Rather, he perceives it as an engagement with an epiphanous Shekhinah which has forged special ties with His people and singled it out for particular attention: "For the portion of the Lord is His people, Yaakov the lot of his inheritance." Obviously, however, this conception—anathema to universalists but the linchpin of the traditional Jewish view of history—only reinforces the need for historical knowledge and sensitivity.

These cannot be attained by hagiography or moralizing alone. As the glory of God which the heavens declare is apprehended by scientific observation as well as esthetic appreciation—to the point that Ḥazal could assert that "whoever knows how to calculate the cycles and planetary courses, but does not, of him Scripture says, 'But they regard not the work of the Lord, neither have they considered the product of His hands,'"[31]—any meaningful attempt at perceiving the role of

31. *Shabbat* 72a. See the Ramban's comment upon *Sefer ha-Mizvot le-ha-Rambam, Shoresh* 1 (p. 12a in the standard editions), in which he explains that when the *Ba'al Halakhot Gedolot*

Providence in history must rest upon some knowledge of its course. Nor can Jewish history be wholly severed from universal culture. Quite apart from possible impact or influence—of which, in one form, we hear much in Tanakh—the mere fact that alien settings have often served as the context of our existence frequently renders knowledge of their annals invaluable for an understanding of our own experience. Moreover, to the extent that patterns can be discerned in general history, its study can by analogy shed light on our own. To be sure, faith in chosenness clearly implies the conviction that our path must be substantively different, not only axiologically but factually. "Israel," said R. Joḥanan (*Shabbat* 156a), "is immune from planetary influence. For it is said, 'Thus saith the Lord, Learn not the ways of the nations, and be not dismayed at the signs of heaven, for the nations are dismayed at them; they are dismayed but not Israel.'" What is here stated with reference to astrological impact, is true, *mutatis mutandis,* with respect to other causal modes; and the Ramban repeatedly stressed that God's covenantal relation to Israel—as formulated in His declaration to Avraham, "I am God Almighty; walk before me, and be thou whole hearted. And I will make my covenant between me and thee, and will multiply thee exceedingly"[32]—effectively supersedes the ordinary forces of nature and history. Nevertheless, as the Ramban well knew, distinct parallels obviously exist; and the proper study of Jewish history against its universal background requires attaining a balance between the senses of uniqueness and similarity respectively. To that end, the *madda* of historical science can contribute significantly.

The study of history offers, then, limited apprehension of the working of Providence, perceived through a glass darkly. How much more powerfully, though, does it illumine for us its second aspect—the actions and peregrinations of man, collective and individual. This, too, is of spiritual, rather than merely pragmatic, moment. The truism that history helps us plan and implement the future apart, the understanding it affords us of human character and destiny as manifested throughout the ages, provides insight into *ẓelem E-lokim* (the image of God) qua agent and sentient. At one level, it portrays social and cultural dynamics as concrete realities rather than sociological abstractions. At another, it enables us to see how and why individuals have made a difference and, what is no less important, to see those

---

enumerated attaining astronomical knowledge as a *mizvah,* he was referring to its subsequent application to designating and possibly intercalating months and years and thus determining the dates of the *yamim tovim.* But see R. Mosheh of Coucy, *Sefer Mizvot Gadol, Mizvot 'Assei,* §47, who speaks of both the knowledge per se and its halakhic application; and see the comment of *Berit Mosheh,* ad loc.

32. Genesis 17:1–2, and see the Ramban, ad loc. Presumably, the Ramban did not wholly deny the force of ordinary causation even with reference to collective Jewry; see David Berger, "Miracles and the Natural Order in Naḥmanides," in *Rabbi Moses Naḥmanides (Ramban): Explorations in His Religious and Literary Virtuosity,* ed. I. Twersky (Cambridge, Mass., 1983), 107–28, especially p. 122. He did, however, circumscribe it severely.

individuals. The extent to which Carlyle's view of history as biography should be adopted is open to constant question. Given Judaism's tremendous emphasis upon free will, I, for one, find it highly consonant with a Torah perspective. Hero-worship aside, however, exposure to those who, through initiative, wisdom, and courage, have had a decisive impact upon events; who have significantly affected the substance, quality, and direction of experience; who, beyond that, have, in Bacon's phrase, enlarged the bounds of human empire—such exposure can be of profound spiritual import. Can anyone read R. W. Chambers' *Man's Unconquerable Mind*[33] without feeling both humbled and inspired?

This brings us, in turn, to a third area in which *madda* complements Torah. If science deals with God's handiwork and history with the conjunction of the human and the divine, the humanities—broadly defined to include the humanistic social sciences—deal with homo sapiens proper: with his existence and experience, his responses and reflections, with the insights of his rational faculties and the progeny of his creative powers. The impact of different areas of the humanities obviously varies. As Aristotle emphasized, abstract philosophic discussion of moral verities cannot compare with their imaginative dramatic manifestation[34]; and, one might add, vice versa. Broadly speaking, however, the humanities' basic shared concert confers common spiritual import—and hence, to a degree, common status—as a complement to Torah.

This import has not always been fully appreciated. Advocates of *madda* have often contended that its study ought be confined to the natural sciences through which one can engage in direct contemplation of divine creation and thus, in the spirit of the Rambam, attain both illumination and inspiration. Confronted by apparent contradiction between disparate sources pro and con secular studies, many propose to resolve it by suggesting that they be taken to refer, respectively, to the scientific pursuits they espouse and to the humanistic disciplines they denigrate.[35] On this view, the famous midrashic aphorism, "If a person tells you there is *ḥokhmah* among the Gentiles, believe him; that there is Torah among the Gentiles, don't believe him,"[36] distinguishes, in effect, between the humanities (spurious Torah) and the natural sciences, here denominated as *ḥokhmah*. Where the philosophical evidence for these convenient definitions is to be found or how the presumed meaning of the latter term squares with its pervasive use in *Mishlei* or *Kohelet*, we are left to figure for ourselves. Of greater importance, however, is the argument per se.

In certain respects, the attitude is thoroughly understandable. On the one hand, to the extent that physics or microbiology involve direct perception of God's creative power, they presumably have more to offer religiously than literature or

33. (London, 1939). The title, drawn from a Wordsworthian sonnet, should not mislead. The book is suffused with the spirit of religious humanism.

34. See Aristotle, *Poetics,* sec. 9.

35. See, e.g., Leo Levi, *Sha'arei Talmud Torah,* 3rd ed. (Jerusalem, 1987), 282.

36. *Midrash Eikhah Rabbati* 2:15.

philology. Moreover, their subject matter has greater universal scope—and, hence, it is argued, deeper spiritual significance—than the study of national cultures. On the other hand, to the extent that the natural sciences are axiologically neutral they do not challenge tradition unless their conclusions accidentally appear to contravene sacred texts or dogmas, as many value-oriented endeavors do. Puritans who regarded Elizabethan drama as an abomination were among the enthusiastic founders of the Royal Society; and their analogues within our own community often entertain a similar distinction.

And yet, at bottom, the notion that Shakespeare is less meaningful than Boyle, Racine irrelevant but Lavoisier invaluable, remains very strange doctrine indeed. In effect, it constitutes a variation of Plato's critique of the arts[37] and, as such, is open to the same objections that has engendered. In banishing poets from his ideal republic, Plato based himself, in part, upon the moral contention that they exercised a nefarious influence by arousing questionable passions. Primarily, however, he advanced the metaphysical and epistemological argument that, far from enhancing knowledge of truth, they distanced us from reality. Regarding the phenomenal natural order as merely a copy of the ultimate noumenal world of ideas, he viewed art, perceived as a copy of a copy, as presenting truth at two removes and, hence, to be rejected as an inferior rendering of true being.

Advocates of poetry (i.e., the creative arts) responded with two primary rejoinders. Aristotle contended that, even by the standard of proximity to metaphysical truth, art is to be valued because its mimetic portrayal is not so much a copy of nature as its distillation. Unlike the naturalist or historian, the poet is free to focus upon archetypal physical and psychological patterns; and, in transcending accidental detail and portraying essential qualities and forms, he offers a more universal—and hence, philosophical—account of reality. "The poet's function is to describe, not the thing that has happened, but a kind of thing that might happen, i.e., what is possible as being probable or necessary. . . . Hence, poetry is something more philosophic and of graver import than history, since its statements are of the nature rather of universals, whereas those of history are singular."[38]

Plotinus, on the other hand, saw the value of art as deriving from its being not the quintessential epitome of nature but its analogue and competitor.[39] Creative rather than descriptive, it is no mere imitation but an alternative—and, on this view, not necessarily inferior—rendering of metaphysical and moral reality. This position was set forth cogently in the best-known critical essay of the English Renaissance, Sir Philip Sidney's "An Apology for Poetry." Whereas scientists and philosophers "build upon the death of Nature," the creative artist harnesses his imagination to

37. See Plato, *Republic,* in *The Dialogues of Plato,* tr. B. Jowett (New York, 1937), 1:864 (606).

38. Aristotle, *Poetics,* 1:9, in *The Basic Works of Aristotle* (New York, 1941), 1463–64.

39. See, particularly, the exposition set forth in Plotinus, *Enneads,* 5:8.

limn his own universe. "Only the poet," Sidney contends, "disdaining to be tied to any such subjections, lifted up with the vigours of his own invention, doth grow in effect another nature, in making things either better than nature bringeth forth, or quite anew, forms such as never were in Nature." And he does not flinch at the thought that the poetic order may indeed be superior. "Nature never set forth the earth in so rich tapestry as diverse poets have done—neither with pleasant rivers, fruitful trees, sweet-smelling flowers, nor whatever else may make the too much love earth more lovely. Her world is brazen, the poets only deliver a golden."[40]

This debate over the status of poetic creation has obvious implications for discussion of the value of its study. A religious version of the Huxley-Arnold controversy over the merits of modern scientific and literary education, respectively, would have harped less upon pragmatic ramifications—how best to understand modern culture or the place of a sense of beauty as a primary psychological component—and focused instead upon the position of human creation in relation to the divinely ordained natural order. To those who extol chemistry because it bespeaks the glory of the *Ribbono Shel 'Olam* but dismiss Shakespeare because he only ushers us into the Globe Theater, one must answer, first, that great literature often offers us a truer and richer view of the essence—the "inscape," to use Hopkins' word—of even physical reality. The judgment of Whitehead, himself a first-rate mathematician, that it was the Romantic poets' intuited perception of the vital, organic character of nature which righted distorted eighteenth-century views of a denuded mechanical universe,[41] is not readily paralleled with respect to other periods. But the basic sense that literature sharpens our experience and, hence, our understanding of various aspects of reality has broad application. Can anyone doubt that appreciation of God's flora is enhanced by Wordsworth's description of "a crowd/ a host, of golden daffodils;/ Beside the lake, beneath the trees,/ Fluttering and dancing in the breeze?"

Secondly, for all the importance of elucidating the world of God to man, the value of imaginative works does not rest upon their descriptive or interpretive aspect exclusively. In Plotinus' vein, we may recognize the worth of human artifacts in their own right—be they, beyond mimesis, ideologized analogies of familiar mundane reality or wholly independent creations. Whether impelled by demonic force or profound equanimity, conjoined to inchoate terror or incandescent aspiration, great literature, from the fairy tale to the epic, plumbs uncharted existential and experiential depths which are both its wellsprings and its subjects.

---

40. In *Criticism: The Major Texts*, ed. W. J. Bate (New York, 1952), 85. For an incisive discussion of this issue in relation to Sidney, see C. S. Lewis, *English Literature in the Sixteenth Century* (Oxford, 1954), 318–22. Plotinus' view finds its analogue in Romantic theory and practice, but primarily with reference to the artist's inner world. See M. H. Abrams, *The Mirror and the Lamp* (Oxford, 1953), passim.

41. See Alfred North Whitehead, *Science and the Modern World* (New York, 1948), chs. 4–5.

In doing so, it realizes a major aspect of human spiritual existence. If, on the one hand, primal Adam is defined functionally as invested with a clear moral and pragmatic charge, to conserve and develop his locus in Eden, he is, on the other, initially defined essentially as "a living soul," which Onkelos renders as *ruaḥ memalela*, "a speaking spirit"; i.e., more generally, as the creator of symbols—verbal, cognitive, imaginative.

Hence, far from diverting attention from the contemplation of God's majestic cosmos, the study of great literature focuses upon a manifestation, albeit indirect, of his wondrous creation at its apex. In one sense, to be sure, human artifacts may be regarded as competing with divine handiwork. Yet, in another, they themselves reveal the spiritual potential which God's creative will had implanted in man. If the heavens bespeak the glory of their Maker, the imaginative powers of man all the more so. To return to Sidney:

> Neither let it be deemed too saucy a comparison to balance the highest point of man's wit with the efficacy of Nature; but rather give right honor to the heavenly Maker of that maker, who, having made to His own likeness, set him beyond and over all the works of that second nature: which in nothing he showeth so much as in Poetry, when with the force of a divine breath he bringeth things forth far surpassing her doings."[42]

To those who might find Sidney's position not only just saucy but nearly blasphemous, one should respond first, that veneration of "the heavenly Maker of that maker" can be attained through appreciation of great works quite independently of any contrasts with nature. Second, his view closely parallels that of Rabbi Akiba, as cited in a famous midrash. Anticipating Taurnus Rufus' attack upon circumcision as constituting a violation of divinely ordained nature, he avers, in response to a query, that "human artifacts are finer than God's," and he goes on to prove the point: "Rabbi Akiba brought him stalks [of grain] and rolls, pointing out that these were God's handiwork and those man's; and he said to him: 'Aren't these [rolls] superior to the stalks?' "[43]

This brings us, in turn, to the most obvious and telling rejoinder. The contention that a Torah *hashkafah* should sanction scientific studies to the exclusion of the humanities, as only they deal with God's world, blithely ignores man's position as part of that world. To the extent that the humanities focus upon man, they deal not only with a segment of divine creation but with its pinnacle. The dignity of man is not the exclusive legacy of Cicero and Pico della Mirandola. It is a central theme in Jewish thought, past and present. Deeply rooted in Scripture, copiously asserted by Ḥazal, unequivocally assumed by *rishonim*, religious humanism is a primary and persistent mark of a Torah *weltanschauung*. Man's inherent dignity and sanctity, so radically asserted through the concept of *ẓelem E-lokim*; his hegemony and steward-

42. Bate, *Criticism*, 86.
43. *Tanḥuma*, "*Parshat Tazria'*."

ship with respect to nature; concern for his spiritual and physical well-being; faith in his metaphysical freedom and potential—all are cardinal components of traditional Jewish thought. On a number of issues, differences obviously abound. The Kabbalists placed man above the angels while the Rambam reversed the order.[44] Likewise, he rejected as presumptuous the notion, familiar in the midrash, that the world had been created for man.[45] These are, however, matters of degree and nuance. The overall humanistic thrust is abundantly and unassailably clear.

How, then, can anyone question the value of precisely those fields which are directly concerned with probing humanity? Granted that no religious Jew can countenance the priority expressed by the definite article in Pope's dictum, "The proper study of mankind is man."[46] *The* proper study of mankind is, of course, God. But surely, among disciplines which deal with the phenomenal world, those which focus upon its pinnacle deserve recognition if not preeminence. Our rejection of Protagoras' estimate of man as the measure of all things in no way denigrates the need to understand human nature. Within the context of the Ramban's appreciation of the importance of knowing the natural order, we can share his scale which places knowledge of man above that of nature: "And thence he ascends to [knowledge of] the creation of those invested with a verbal soul, so that he understands the secret of the soul and knows its essence and its power within its chamber."[47]

That knowledge is gained from any of several fields; often, from their interdisciplinary relation. The study of language elucidates both the modalities of *ru'aḥ memalela,* and, in conjunction with history, the record of its past development. One need hardly be a devotee of analytic philosophy to understand the importance of the former nor an acolyte of philology to appreciate the import of the latter. As even a brief glimpse at a historical dictionary reveals, the course traced by a particular word over centuries provides fascinating insight into the matrix out of which it sprang. In many cases, the insight may be trivial, but in others it is central to an understanding of a culture or, for that matter, of mankind. C. S. Lewis' *Studies in Words*—an incisive analysis of the course of such basic terms as *world, life, nature, sense, wit, conscience, simple*—focuses upon English but its implications are

44 See R. Mosheh ben Maimon, *Guide,* 3:12. See, also R. Ḥayyim of Volozhin's attempt to reconcile these conflicting views in *Nefesh ha-Ḥayyim,* 1:10.

45. See *Guide,* 3:13. Earlier, in the preface to *Perush ha-Mishnayot,* the Rambam had embraced the midrash's view wholeheartedly.

46. Alexander Pope, *An Essay on Man,* 2:2. The assertion, of course, occurs within a context which deals with man's place in the cosmos in religious terms. Nevertheless, it is Jewishly, clearly problematic.

47. R. Mosheh ben Naḥman, *Commentary to the Torah,* Preface. The Ramban goes on to speak of knowledge of the celestial order—spheres, intelligences, angels, etc.—as an even greater level of understanding. However, man clearly is at the apex of the hierarchy of the perceptible phenomenal world.

universal.[48] Likewise, omissions may be significant. The Rambam's contention (*Guide* 3:8) that the sanctity of Hebrew was either derived from or reflected in the paucity of its sexual vocabulary illustrates the point; and while the Ramban rejected both the interpretation and its factual base, he did not question the underlying approach.[49]

From related and yet different perspectives, knowledge of man is afforded, as previously noted, by history, particularly from its biographical aspect; and, more directly, albeit also often more technically, by psychology and its kindred discipline, sociology. Popularly, psychology is often regarded as a modern innovation, its emergence loosely related to psychoanalytic theory and practice. In part, this perception is quite soundly based; but only in part. The sense that man can be understood and consequently treated with precision comparable to that of the natural sciences is of relatively recent vintage. The emergence of science as the dominant force of modern culture and the concomitant growth of mechanistic and deterministic views of human nature provided the conceptual base of current professional psychology and its persistent claim to scientific status. Obviously, however, the concern with understanding human nature and ministering to it is of long standing; and general culture, throughout history, has shed much light upon this critical area. Moreover, classical writings on this topic are relatively less dated. We properly treat Aristotelian biology as an anachronistic element of the history of science, of interest solely to students of that somewhat arcane field; but the comments upon human nature strewn throughout his writings remain pertinent if not invaluable. Few would now regard seriously the detailed portrait of the soul limned in *De Anima* or its potpourri of physiology and psychology which issued in the medieval doctrine of the humors. But which student of Western man and society would dare ignore the *Politics* or *Nicomachean Ethics*?

For profounder insight into human nature, however, we look beyond professional treatises and practitioners. "The heart is involuted above all things, and it is exceeding weak—who can know it?"[50] The question is rhetorical and, with

---

48. C. S. Lewis, *Studies in Words* (Cambridge, England, 1967). See, especially, Introduction.

49. See his remarks on Exodus 30:13. The controversy clearly reflects different approaches to the matrix and possibly the nature of *kedushah*: to what extent is it moral and spiritual, or mystical and/or metaphysical. However, it need not necessarily reflect differing appreciations of sexuality. See Ramban, commentary on Leviticus 18:6. The *Iggeret ha-Kodesh*, long ascribed to the Ramban, takes a very positive view. The ascription is probably erroneous, however. See the remarks of Rabbi Chavel in his edition of *Kitvei Rabbenu Mosheh ben Naḥman* (Jerusalem, 1964), II, 315–19.

50. Jeremiah 17:9. The original J. P. S. translation rendered *'akov* as "deceitful." This interpretation had been previously advanced by the Radak. I do not find it warranted, however, by either the context—the next verse states, "I the Lord probe the heart, search the mind, to repay every man according to his ways, with the proper fruit of his deeds,"

respect to the human plane, the presumed response "no one" clearly implicit. Yet, of those who have at least attained and revealed some measure of knowledge, great writers are preeminent. In reading them, we can confront the human spirit doubly, as creation and as creator; Clytemnestra or Hamlet on the one hand, Aeschylus and Shakespeare on the other. As regards enriching our understanding of *ruaḥ memalela,* imaginative artists have been more illuminating than theoreticians—not only because they have described more powerfully but because they have also probed more deeply. For sheer insight, can Locke or James compare with Dickens or Dostoyevsky? The comparison is perhaps unfair. The psychologist, practicing or theoretical, must perforce resort to technical jargon, sophisticated abstractions, and schematic bifurcations. The artist, for his part—particularly, the dramatic artist—melds precision and sensitivity, intuition and acuity, to perceive and portray concrete personal and social reality. But the fact remains; and it underscores the spiritual value of great literature.

The measure of that value can be most fully grasped in light of De Quincey's familiar distinction between two types of literature and their respective characters and functions. "There is, first, the Literature of *Knowledge;* and, secondly, the literature of *Power*. The function of the first is—to *teach*; the function of the second is—to *move*; the first is a rudder; the second, an oar or a sail. The first speaks to the mere discursive understanding; the second speaks ultimately; it may happen, to the higher understanding or reason, but always through affections of pleasure and sympathy."[51] One need not share De Quincey's Romantic predilection for oars and sails to recognize the trenchancy and significance of the distinction. By virtue of immediacy and concreteness, literature which addresses itself to the imagination—and through it, to the intellect and emotions both—becomes highly charged. Its force can be perceived even at the purely descriptive plane. Aristotle's contention that poetry presents a truer and fuller account of events than history was grounded upon its deeper impact no less than upon its more philosophical character. With respect to the exposition of moral truth, analogously, Arnold was palpably correct in arguing that literature often communicates it more trenchantly and more effectively than the pithy syllogisms or discursive analyses of bald philosophy.[52] Art speaks through the whole man and to the whole man in tones that generally elude the logician. Recognition of this fact need not, of course, issue in anti-intellectual romanticization. Philosophy, rigorous philosophy, certainly has a place

---

without in any way intimating that these ways and deeds are wicked—or other biblical uses of the term. Deceit is clearly intended in II Kings 10:19, Jeremiah 9:3, and Genesis 27:36. However, in Isaiah 40:4 and Job 37:4, only physical crookedness is denoted. The revised J. P. S. version (1978) translates "devious," but this, too, strikes me as excessively pejorative.

51. Thomas De Quincey, "The Literature of Knowledge and the Literature of Power," in *Selected Writings of Thomas De Quincey* (New York, 1945), 1099–1100.

52. See Matthew Arnold, "Literature and Science," in *The Portable Matthew Arnold* (New York, 1949), 405–29.

in the world of moral discourse. But not the sole—perhaps not even the primary—place.

How much more telling, however, is the element of power at the prescriptive or persuasive level. For sheer impact, can anyone compare two seventeenth-century works, each avowedly written to "assert eternal Providence and justify the ways of God to man"—Leibniz' *Essais de Théodicée* and Milton's *Paradise Lost?* That prescriptive moment obtains, of course, in much which is not directly aimed at persuading. One thinks of the concerted thrust of even single sonnets—vehicles for Shakespeare's reflections upon the eternal themes of time and change, Milton's grappling with gradual blindness, Keats' confronting impending early death as "then on the shore/ Of the wide world I stand alone, and think/ Till Love and Fame to nothingness do sink."[53] Nor are implicit "messages" absent from the literature of self-expression. Yeats' comment that men write rhetoric about their conflicts with others but poetry about their struggle with themselves does not imply that those struggles issue in no resolution or that their protagonist has no purpose beyond baring his soul. Tennyson's *In Memoriam* is a case in point; and even when one has acknowledged the critical shibboleth that its skepticism rings truer than the expressions of faith, the spiritual import remains impressive. Or, with reference to Yeats himself, are we to suppose that *Sailing to Byzantium* or *The Second Coming* are devoid of broadly didactic intent?

Of course, we can hardly be so naïve as to regard humanistic studies as guarantors of humaneness. Not, surely, in this post-Holocaust generation. The point was made with telling force by one of the most learned of contemporary literary critics. In his soul-searching preface to *Language and Silence,* George Steiner writes:

> We come after. We know now that a man can read Goëthe or Rilke in the evening, that he can play Bach and Schubert, and go to his day's work at Auschwitz in the morning. To say that he has read them without understanding or that his ear is gross, is cant. In what way does this knowledge bear on literature and society, on the hope, grown almost axiomatic from the time of Plato to that of Matthew Arnold, that culture is a humanizing force, that the energies of the spirit are transferrable to those of conduct?[54]

This is, no doubt, a terrifying question for believers in the self-sufficiency of secular humanism—and a formidable one even for advocates of religious humanism. Nevertheless, I believe the abiding valuation of culture as a civilizing and ennobling force which, when harnessed to moral and religious commitment, can help energize and uplift the human spirit, remains basically sound. On its own, it did not—evidently, cannot—prevent brutalization. However, within a spiritual context, it can make a genuine contribution.

This brief survey of the benefits of *madda* might best conclude with some

53. John Keats, "When I Have Fears."

54. George Steiner, *The Language of Silence: Essays, 1958–1966* (London, 1967), 15–16.

discussion of what has traditionally been regarded as both the most promising and the most problematic of *ḥokhmot:* philosophy. Its contribution straddles the various areas we have mapped. It serves to elucidate Torah, indirectly, by honing methodological tools and conceptual categories; and directly, by guiding exegesis. Allusion has already been made to the first part of the *Guide* in which the Rambam, animated by philosophical and theological assumptions, interprets basic scriptural terms in light of the parameters established by his premises. His recourse to allegory in order to mediate between sacred texts and a priori concepts raises obvious questions and became one of the flash points of subsequent polemics. But there is no questioning its significance as an exemplar of the interface of philosophy and exegesis.

Implementation is no less well-served by a gamut of practically oriented subdisciplines, of which moral and political theory are the most prominent. Philosophy's most significant role, however—again, as well as its most controversial—clearly concerns its serving as a complement to Torah. Within a context of deeply rooted commitment, the process of inquiry not only sharpens and amplifies faith but purifies it. This is not a trifling matter. The Rambam's lifelong struggle against predominantly popular anthropomorphism was animated by the sense that its crudities were tinged with idolatrous elements which philosophic sophistication could eradicate. Asking the right questions and groping for proper solutions is no guarantee of enhanced faith. The return to theological basics may just as well undermine commitment, and even as tenets and perceptions are presumably being illuminated, they may also be recast. The promise of concurrent enlightenment and inspiration certainly exists, however, and it has brought many to a truer and richer perception of the *Ribbono Shel 'Olam* and of their relation to Him.

For All Is in It: Self-Sufficient Torah

In its various manifestations, general culture can, then, be of considerable spiritual significance. It can help us understand and confront the human situation; to know what we are, who we can be, and who we should be; to define our needs, develop our abilities, and mobilize our energies; to enhance both our desire and our capacity for spiritual development. And it can render us more sensitive and perceptive not only with regard to ourselves but also with respect to the physical and social world within which and in relation to which that development is to be realized. "The end, then, of learning," wrote Milton, "is, to repair the ruins of our first parents by regaining to know God aright, and out of that knowledge to love him, to imitate him, to be like him, as we may the nearest, by possessing our souls of true virtue, which, being united to the heavenly grace of faith, makes up the highest perfection."[55] That knowledge and virtue being then properly applied, universal wisdom

55. John Milton, "On Education," in *Areopagitica and Other Essays* (London, 1950), 44.

can abet the fulfillment of our multiple mandate: soul-making, world-shaping, advancing the millennium.

Yet, inexorably and inevitably, the obvious question arises. Granted that general culture promotes the attainment of these primary and lofty ends, but why should a Jew turn to *it* for sustenance? "Is there no balm in Gilead? Is there no physician there?" (Jeremiah 8:22). Having been chosen as a covenantal community and uniquely endowed with the truest and richest of spiritual treasures in the form of Torah in all its manifestations, need we—nay, may we—mine alternative nodes? True, it will be contended, the Ramban's preface clearly values knowledge of the areas to which much of general culture addresses itself. But is its pursuit consonant with his subsequent affirmation that all of this knowledge is adumbrated within Torah, having been revealed to Mosheh Rabbenu and mystically enshrined within its text?

I do not take the question lightly. On the contrary, I am fully cognizant of both its cogency and its urgency. I do not regard its proponents as parochial, obscurantist, or xenophobic, nor do I harbor delusions of superior enlightenment or perspicacity by dint of not raising it. For, in fact, I do raise it. Could a *ben Torah* do otherwise? However, it is, to repeat an earlier point, a factual question, to be confronted with reference to experience. Admittedly, a satisfactory response is highly elusive. At the personal plane, subjective bias, rendering even pure observation suspect, is of course notorious. Moreover, one cannot be content with a retrospective review of the path he has pursued, which he presumably knows, but must also ponder the gamut of hypothetical alternatives, whose permutations he can only conjecture. And beyond observation, proper evaluation of personal or communal data is complicated by the fact that, like Einstein's imaginary timekeeper, we find that our movements affect our clocks. Decisions taken at one juncture often determine the standards subsequently applied both to mold and to assess thought and action—and this not only out of a natural proclivity to self-justification but because one has honestly adopted those standards. The road taken, in Frost's familiar image, can indeed make all the difference.

So, difficulties abound. But, with respect to an issue such as *Torah u-Madda,* what is the alternative to maximally honest confrontation? Apodictic fiat? Knee-jerking rejection? Mechanical head count? With respect to a major hashkafic issue, concerning which no clear historical consensus exists—although a prevalent majority view (in this case, probably not my own) may be perceived—recourse to intelligence and conscience, provided that both have been properly irradiated by Torah, is not only licit but mandatory.

In this spirit, I submit that indeed some of the knowledge and experience which the Ramban admired is not, currently, readily available from our own sources, so that there are portals and levels of wisdom to which access is attained and/or facilitated by the proper supplementary use of non-Jewish material. To be sure, the Ramban asserts that all knowledge is literally imbedded within the Torah's words and script—and of course we accept the assertion in humble faith. But what of the capacity to discover and extract it? Wisdom, understanding, and insight—which, inter alia, enhance fear and knowledge of God—are to be sought as silver and searched for "as for hid treasures."[56] But if we find a given layer impregnable, should we be content with spiritual strip mining or pretend that we have plumbed the nether depths? Or should we, rather, have recourse to the best available tools? The Ramban speaks of the mystical import of Torah, every minute *koẓo shel yod*, each curlecue incorporated as part of an all-embracing concatenation of ineffable divine names. But, for ordinary mortals, bereft of antennae attuned to the music of the spheres, what of the need, desire, and obligation to understand Torah and to build a spiritual world at a rational plane? As previously noted, no one ignores modern medicine or technology because the Ramban declares of Shlomo, "that God had given him wisdom and knowledge, all of it coming to him from Torah, from which he studied until he knew the secret of all gestations . . . to the point that he even wrote a medical text."[57] Should one, correspondingly, be blithely oblivious to other elements of general culture? When Elisha sought prophetic inspiration, he declared (II Kings 3:15): "'But now bring me a minstrel.' And it came to pass, when the ministrel played, that the hand of the Lord came upon him." And the Rambam generalized: "For the spirit of prophecy does not descend upon one who is melancholy or indolent, but comes as a result of joyousness. And therefore, the Sons of Prophets had before them psaltery, tablet, pipe and harp, and thus sought a manifestation of the prophetic gift."[58] If inspiration can be drawn from pipes and harps, why not, conceivably, from poetry?

But should we indeed seek first-rate poetry, we shall have to look elsewhere.[59] Our moral and religious lights did not address themselves with equal vigor to every

---

56. Proverbs 2:4. In context, it is not fully clear what is to be sought, as the referent of *im tevakshenah*, "if you seek *it*." The entire passage reads: "My son, if you accept my words and treasure up my commandments; if you make your ear attentive to wisdom and your mind open to discernment; if you call to understanding and cry aloud to discernment; if you seek it as you do silver and search it as for hidden treasures—then you will understand the fear of the Lord and attain knowledge of God" (2:5). "It" may refer to the antecedent wisdom, its various manifestations lumped together as a single referent, which is then discussed again in the next *pasuk;* or it may relate to the fear of the Lord mentioned subsequently (albeit in tandem with knowledge). The Meiri and Rabbenu Yonah, ad loc., assumed the former; R. Mosheh Ḥayyim Luẓẓatto, in the preface to *Mesillat Yesharim*, the latter. The Gaon of Vilna, ad loc., strikes a median course, holding that the silver refers to Torah and the treasures to *mizvot.*

57. Mosheh ben Naḥman, *Commentary to the Torah*, Preface.

58. R. Mosheh ben Maimon, *Hil. Yesodei ha-Torah* 7:3. Rashi, ad loc., interpreted that the minstrel had been called to mute anger; the Radak, to dispel grief. The Rambam, however, saw it as part of the normal quest for prophetic inspiration—this, evidently on the basis of *Shabbat* 30b which, on the one hand, speaks of sadness, indolence, frivolity, levity, idle chatter, etc. as barriers to prophecy and, on the other, posits, on the basis of Elisha's call, the joy of *mizvah* as a precondition. See also *Guide* 2:36.

59. A number of biblical books—perhaps most notably, *Tehillim*—are, of course,

area of spiritual endeavor. Ḥazal engaged little in systematic theology or philosophy and their legacy includes no poetic corpus. Their *hashkafah* was undoubtedly anchored in a comprehensive, if partly intuited, *weltanschauung*, and their inner experience surely reflected profound and passionate sensibility. However, the record with respect to these areas is almost bare. That patent fact may constitute a cogent argument against pursuing such directions, although Rav Saadya Gaon—as both his *Treatise of Beliefs and Opinions* and his great *bakkashot* attest—the Rambam, and the Maharal clearly thought otherwise. But be that as it may, for those who do acknowledge the merits of such pursuits, it is preposterous to pretend to find in our own tradition that which, at a given level and with a certain range, simply is not there.

Assuredly, many aspiring *talmidei ḥakhamim* have experienced religious moments profounder than Petrarch's ascent to Mont Ventoux. But how many have then sent their *rebbi* a descriptive account concluding with the poignant supplication: "And thus, most loving father, gather from this letter how eager I am to leave nothing whatever in my heart hidden from your eyes. Not only do I lay my whole life open to you with the utmost care but every single thought of mine. Pray for these thoughts, I beseech you, that they may at last find stability. So long have they been idling about and, finding no firm stand, been uselessly driven through so many matters. May they now turn at last to the One, the Good, the True, the stably Abiding. Farewell."[60] An account of Rabbi Akiva's spiritual odyssey could no doubt eclipse Augustine's. But *his* confessions have been discreetly muted. The rigors of John Stuart Mill's education—and possibly, their repercussions—are not without parallel in our history. But what corresponds to his fascinating *Autobiography?* Or to the passionate *Apologia Pro Vita Sua* of his contemporary, John Henry Cardinal Newman? Our Johnsons have no Boswells.

The point is not confined to the biographical realm. The substance of Hawthorne's "message" in *The Scarlet Letter* or "Young Goodman Brown"—that serpentine passion may lurk, not hypocritically but substantively, within a nobly respectable soul—is familiar in our tradition. Ḥazal went so far as to assert, with reference to illicit sexual passion, that "the greater the man, the greater is his Evil Inclination" (*Sukkah* 52a). But its imaginative portrayal is not. Raw material for a study such as Henri Brémond's *Prière et Poésie,* a study of the relations between two major modes of spiritual experience, the prayerful and the poetic, abounds. But with the possible exception of some of Rav Kook's writings, where in the Torah world shall such an analysis be found? Or, to cite an area in which the personal and the objective coalesce, while Stoic and existential strains are common in the world

---

among the greatest of literary treasures (and much more). They are, however, very much a special case.

60. Francesco Petrarea, "The Ascent of Mont Ventoux," in *The Renaissance Philosophy of Man* (Chicago, 1948), 46.

of Jewish thought, their concentrated expression in works such as Marcus Aurelius' *Meditations* or Pascal's *Pensées* is not.

If I may cite a personal example, I recall vividly that when my father *zẓ"l* was suddenly blinded at the age of eighty-one, I felt, on the one hand, that I could better appreciate and commiserate with his suffering because the cadences of the great relevant Miltonic passages still reverberated in my mind. I recalled the searing power of Samson's opening speech:

> O dark, dark, dark, amid the blaze of noon,
> Irrecoverably dark, total Eclipse
> Without all hope of day!
> O first created Beam, and thou great Word,
> Let there be light, and light was over all:
> Why am I thus bereav'd thy prime decree?
> The Sun to me is dark
> And silent as the Moon,
> When she deserts the night,
> Hid in her vacant interlunar cave.[61]

Or the majestic plaintiveness of the autobiographical proem to the third book of *Paradise Lost* (3:40–50):

> Thus with the Year
> Seasons return, but not to me returns
> Day, or the sweet approach of Ev'n or Morn,
> Or sight of vernal bloom, or Summer's Rose,
> Or flocks, or herds, or human face divine;
> But cloud instead, and ever-during dark
> Surrounds me, from the cheerful ways of men
> Cut off, and for the Book of knowledge fair
> Presented with a Universal blanc
> Of Nature's works to mee expung'd and ras'd,
> And wisdom at one entrance quite shut out.

On the other hand, I felt that, for the same reason, I could better understand his dual response: the determination to overcome and the struggle to accept. I shall never forget the fervor with which, on the first Rosh Ḥodesh after he was stricken, he so resolutely intoned in Hallel: *Lo amut ki eḥyeh va-asaper ma'asei Y-ah,* "I shall not die but live, and declare the works of the Lord." How similar, in essence, to the continuation of the proem, "So much the rather thou Celestial light/ Shine inward, and the mind through all her powers/ Irradiate, there plant eyes, all mist from thence/ Purge and disperse, that I may see and tell/ Of things invisible to mortal

61. John Milton, *Samson Agonistes,* 80–89.

sight;"[62] or, in a different vein, to the sublime reconciliation expressed in the remarkable conclusion to one of the greatest of English sonnets: "They also serve who only stand and wait."[63]

I suppose some will regard these ruminations as a symptom of spiritual weakness. Why hadn't I thought of our own spiritual giants who had suffered a similar fate—of patriarchal *avot ha-'olam*, blind Yiẓḥak and dim-sighted Yaakov? Or, among *amoraim*, why hadn't Rav Yosef and Rav Sheshet come to mind? The answer is that of course they had. A prefatory note to a halakhic discourse I published at the time on the subject of a blind person's status with respect to lighting Hanukkah candles dedicated the article to "the descendants of Yiẓḥak and Yaakov, the disciples of Rav Sheshet and Rav Yosef, who accept their lot with love and serve their Creator in silent anticipation"[64]—the last phrase an oblique reference to the Miltonic sonnet. The point is, however, that the respective recollections were not mutually exclusive but, rather, reciprocally resonant. The stature which the *avot* or *amoraim* enjoy in the eyes of a *ben Torah* is of course, qualitatively, wholly different from that of even so great a poet as Milton—and that not only as regards intellectual prowess but with respect to the entire range of spiritual and emotional experience. But, whereas Milton's response was recorded for posterity with great power and depth, *their* response can only be conjectured.

Whence, however, the capacity for conjecture? In part, of course, from Milton. Literary exposure to a broad range of social, historical, and personal experience helps us transcend the insular bounds of our own niche in time and space—to disengage the local and accidental from the permanent and universal, to understand, both intellectually and empathetically, situations we had not otherwise confronted or even possibly envisioned. All the more so, when that experience has been communicated through culture at its finest, by great souls capable of feeling deeply and expressing feeling powerfully. The tragedy of personal affliction, in particular, is thus more acutely perceived because the tragedy of a great soul—Milton in the throes of blindness, Beethoven on the threshold of deafness—as well as its passionate response bears the imprint of that greatness and imparts to us a keener sense of the nature of the experience.

Milton can sensitize us, then, to understand Yiẓḥak Avinu better. Some, no doubt, need no such enrichment, either being endowed with native intuitive sensitivity or having developed it by alternate means. Many, however, lacking empathetic capacity, prefer the easier path of pretending that it is unnecessary. The proclivity, evident in much recent *parshanut,* to dehumanize our greatest, springs in part from ideological considerations—from the conviction that nothing short of almost total etherealization will do justice to those whom, if we regard ourselves as

62. John Milton, *Paradise Lost,* 3:51–55.
63. John Milton, "On His Blindness," 14.
64. "Be-'Inyan Ḥiyyuv Suma be-Ner Ḥanukkah," *Hadarom* 50 (1980): 184–205.

human, we are to perceive as angelic. In part, however, it derives from sheer ineptitude, from the inability to engage in what midrashim, the Ramban, or the Neẓiv did so impressively and so boldly: to understand and portray nuances of spiritual profundity; to seize upon the moral and psychological complexity of a personage or situation; to recognize that giants too may, at their level and in their own way, be involuted. The result may be distortion through superficiality—pious distortion, to be sure, but still no mean matter when at issue is the proper understanding of *kitvei ha-kodesh.*[65]

I am neither so overweening as to contend that such understanding cannot be attained without general literary education nor naïve to the point of assuming that it is invariably conferred by it. Knowledge of *Paradise Lost* is neither a necessary nor a sufficient condition for the best grasp of *Sefer Bereshit.* But, to the extent, and I believe it can be significant, that the particular fusion of knowledge and power, insight, and inspiration provided by great literature enables us to relate to *ru'aḥ memalela* and to enrich our spiritual lives, we shall often profit from grazing in foreign pastures. Where, in our treasure, shall we encounter a despondent and tragically deserted father to compare with King Lear? Of thousands who have been imprisoned, who has left a record of his experience on a par with Boethius' *De Consolatione Philosophiae* or Bonhoeffer's *Letters from Prison?* Do we have a paean of inspired passion to wedded love to match Spenser's *Epithalamion?* Far from constituting mere straying in alien fields, study of general culture can become a vehicle for enhancing our Torah existence.

TIME'S WINGED CHARIOT: THE DILEMMA OF APPORTIONMENT

Conviction of the value of general culture does not necessarily issue in programmatic advocacy of *Torah u-Madda.* As in all decision making, having established the inherent desirability of a given phenomenon, one must still determine its concomitant costs. Even with respect to *miẓvot,* Ḥazal have counselled us to "calculate its loss against its rewards" (*Avot* 2:1); and this can be interpreted to refer not only to the

65. The question of sensitivity or the lack of it, of course, has ramifications which extend well beyond the realm of *parshanut.* I vividly recall a comment I heard from *mori ve-rabbi,* Rav Hutner *zẓ"l,* when I went to be *menaḥem avel* after his wife's death. Our discussion turned upon the capacity to feel and its current dearth in relation to assumptions prevalent in certain circles that learning alone was wholly sufficient; and he, alluding to the midrashic statement, "Any *talmid ḥakham* who has no insight (*da'at*)—a carcass is superior to him" (*Vayikra Rabbah,* 1:15), intoned vigorously: "*Is er dokh a talmid ḥakham . . . un fort* (So he is indeed a *talmid ḥakham . . .* and yet)." Much of his own personal greatness, of course, lay precisely in the interplay of intellectual force and profoundly passionate sensitivity.

juxtaposition of material rewards and spiritual losses *sub specie aeternitatis* but to the balancing of loss and gain within the religious realm proper. It is not akin to a patient's calculating the merits of continued indulgence against possible medical repercussions but to a doctor's figuring risk-benefit ratios from a purely professional perspective. To continue the analogy further, we must evaluate, qua costs, both price and possible side effects. Translated into the terms of our specific issue, we need to consider first the extent, if any, to which personal and/or communal resources (time, energy, funding) may or should be allocated for the pursuit of culture; second, the danger that religious commitment may be diluted by exposure to secular culture, especially as that may occur within a context of constricted Torah study.[66]

Each question is itself reducible to two components, or rather, may be posed at two distinct levels: that of rigorous halakhic norm and that of general spiritual desirability. To the committed Jew, the latter is of course critical, but it must, generally, be raised within the parameters of the former. Except in rare situations—with respect to which the extraordinary principle, "When it is time to work for the Lord, they make void Thy law,"[67] is invoked—one must determine whether a course of action is permissible before he presumes to judge whether it is beneficial. I shall therefore open discussion of each of the aforementioned issues with a summary halakhic discourse.

With respect to the first point, the *mizvah* of *talmud Torah* and the concomitant *issur* of *bittul Torah*, the *locus classicus* is a Gemara in *Menahot* (99b). Commenting upon Rabbi Yose's statement that at the weekly changing of the *Lehem ha-panim* in the *hekhal* there could be an interval between the removal of the old bread and the placing of the new, even though the Torah stipulates, "And thou shalt set upon the table show-bread before me *always*,"[68] the Gemara expounds:

66. N. Lamm, *Torah Umadda*, 86–100, also focuses upon a third issue as a critical objection to *Torah u-Madda*: the concept of *yeridat ha-dorot* ("the generational decline") and the concomitant contention that pursuits which may have been legitimate in earlier times are no longer licit because of our greater spiritual fragility. This issue, important in its own right, is not so much an independent objection as a detail related to the treatment of the basic dangers. Its exponents advance this thesis by way of neutralizing the evidence of precedent which might legitimize the pursuit of *madda*. Moreover, I think the thrust of this contention does not focus so much upon the historical decline as upon the singular status of rare individuals, seen by advocates of this objection as special cases even within the context of their own generations.

67. See *Berakhot* 63a. The clear limits of this principle are an important topic but one which lies beyond my present scope.

Of course, in certain areas, spiritual benefit is itself the criterion of halakhic license, but not always.

68. Exodus 25:30. The *lehem ha-panim* consisted of twelve loaves of bread which lay on a table in the *hekhal* (inner sanctum) of the *bet ha-mikdash* for a week, were then replaced by others on the Sabbath, and eaten by the *kohanim* on duty. The controversy in the Mishnah deals with the mode of the exchange, with the majority opinion being that

R. Ammi said, "From these words of R. Yose we learn that even though a man learns but one chapter in the morning and one chapter in the evening he has thereby fulfilled the precept of 'This book of the law shall not depart out of thy mouth.'"

R. Yoḥanan said in the name of R. Simeon b. Yoḥai: "Even though a man but reads the Shema morning and evening he has thereby fulfilled the precept of '[This book of the law] shall not depart.' It is forbidden, however, to say this in the presence of *'ammei ha-areẓ* (the unlearned)." But Raba said, "It is a meritorious act to say it in the presence of *'ammei ha-areẓ.*"

Ben Damah, the son of R. Ishmael's sister, once asked R. Ishmael, "May one such as I who has studied the whole of the Torah learn Greek wisdom?" He thereupon read to him the following verse, "This book of the law shall not depart out of thy mouth, but thou shalt meditate therein day and night." "Go then and find a time that is neither day nor night and learn then Greek wisdom."

This, however, is at variance with the view of R. Samuel b. Naḥmani. For R. Samuel b. Naḥmani said in the name of R. Yonatan, "This verse is neither duty nor command but a blessing. For when the Holy One, blessed be He, saw that the words of the Torah were most precious to Joshua, as it is written, 'His minister Joshua, the son of Nun, a young man, departed not out of the tent,' He said to him, 'Joshua, since the words of the Torah are so precious to thee, [I assure thee,] this book of the law shall not depart out of they mouth!'"

In light of the two controversies cited, as to whether the *pasuk* is normative and how "day and night" is to be understood, we are left with three textual interpretations and, presumably, with three positions concerning the *miẓvah* of *talmud Torah.* Rabbi Yonatan could conceivably hold that, as regards the *pasuk* drawn from Shema, "And thou shalt talk of them . . . when thou liest down, and when thou riseth up,"[69] minimal study morn and eve suffices per se, in the same manner as hearing the requisite shofar sounds once suffices on Rosh Hashanah. Rav Ammi, however, as evidenced by the analogy from Rabbi Yose's position, clearly holds that fundamentally and conceptually *talmud Torah* is indeed to be perpetual; it is only that, in practice, if it frames a basic unit of time, it is regarded as being indeed pervasive and perpetual so that the whole span can be defined as devoted to Torah study. Both seemingly agree, however, that one need not actually learn continually. Hence, they can interpret the Mishnah's familiar inclusion of *talmud Torah* among *miẓvot* "for which no definite quantity is prescribed"[70] as referring to both upper

---

there must be literal continuity, the old bread being removed only as the new takes its place.

For another recent discussion of this text in relation to *Torah u-Madda,* see R. Soloveichik, *Logic of the Heart,* 57–60.

69. Deuteronomy 6:7. Of course, a more demanding standard could conceivably be posited on the basis of other *pesukim.* But the Gemara does not raise this possibility here.

70. *Pe'ah* 1:1. See the commentary of the Gaon of Vilna, *Shenot Eliyahu,* ad loc., who explains that, on this view, even recitation of the Shema is not requisite. Even a single word

and nether limits.[71] Rabbi Ishmael, however, holds that, insofar as possible, Torah study should literally be throughout and not just by day and night; and, on this view, the requisite quantity of the *miẓvah*—in a sense, both minimum and maximum, albeit not uniformly defined—constitutes a halakhic requirement.

No definitive decision emerges from the *sugya,* and the Rambam's position is likewise unclear. Rejecting Rabbi Yose's opinion, he states (*Hil. Temidin u-Musafin* 5:4) that the *leḥem ha-panim* must literally be on the table constantly, so that the basis of Rav Ammi's proof is, of course, obviated. But in dealing with Torah study, he contents himself with the formulation (*Hil. Talmud Torah* 1:8) that every Jewish man "is obligated to set for himself time for Torah study by day and by night as it is stated, 'And thou shalt meditate therein day and night'," leaving open the question of the duration of these periods or of what, if anything, might be required beyond them. The impression conveyed *de silentio,* however, is clearly that he has adopted Rabbi Yonatan's minimalist position. This is buttressed by the fact that, elsewhere, in defining a monarch's obligation, he writes (*Hil. Melakhim* 3:5–6) that "he should be engaged in Torah [study] and in [dealing with] the needs of Israel, by day and by night, as it is stated, 'And it shall be with him, and he shall read therein all the days of his life. . . . 'For his heart is the heart of the whole community of Israel; therefore Scripture has cleaved him to Torah more than the rest of the people, as it is stated, 'All the days of his life'." Rav Mayer Dan Plotzky infers that the Rambam held that "even *mi-derabbanan* (rabbinically) there is no obligation to learn constantly . . . for he apparently thinks that the verses which state that one should always study Torah refer solely to a monarch but the rest of Israel is not included."[72] Likewise, Rav Isser Zalman Meltzer asserted that, on the Rambam's view, only a king is enjoined from indulging in pleasures which may divert him from Torah study, "but for the common man, only *bittul Torah* for no cause whatsoever is proscribed."[73]

If this indeed be the Rambam's position, it is nonetheless a decidedly minority

---

suffices at the barest level of minimal fulfillment, although, of course, if one can, he is obligated to learn more.

71. The more general question of whether this Mishnah deals with maxima or also with minima is discussed in the *Yerushalmi,* ad loc.

72. *Keli Ḥemdah, Devarim,* 330.

73. *Even ha-Azel,* ad loc. R. Isser Zalman's view is very far-reaching. Even if the Rambam held that the specific *miẓvah* of *talmud Torah* is limited, it seems almost incredible that he might have regarded the pursuit of unnecessary pleasures as neutral, even for the ordinary person. The whole thrust of the *Guide,* as well as of the animated concluding chapter of *Hilkhot Teshuvah,* the heart of *Hilkhot De'ot,* and the codas of many of the books in *Mishneh Torah,* clearly militate otherwise. Beside Torah study and indulgence, there is a third alternative: pursuit of the *Ribbono Shel 'Olam* in other modes, including the speculative. At the very least, one should qualify that for the spiritual elite (and not necessarily monarchs) the effective religious use of time is paramount.

view. This is amply illustrated within the context of discussions of a related Gemara in *Nedarim* (8a) which states that even if obligating oaths be confined to optional matters, if a person were to swear that he shall rise early and learn a given chapter, the oath would be valid, "inasmuch as, if he wished, he could absolve himself [i.e., from the obligation to study Torah] by reciting Shema morning and evening." In a sixteenth-century responsum, the Radbaz takes the statement at face value, contending "that a person is not biblically obligated to study Torah constantly."[74] This is consonant with the view of R. Yehudah he-Ḥasid who—commenting upon the controversy between R. Shimon b. Yoḥai and R. Ishmael as to whether a Jew should ordinarily undertake full scale economic activity, or, in order to engage in Torah study, should reduce his vocational involvement to a minimum—notes: "Not because R. Shimon holds that it [i.e., extensive Torah study] is obligatory, for it is he who states in *menaḥot* that even though a man but read the Shema morning and evening he has thereby fulfilled the precept of '[This book of the law] shall not depart etc.'; but he only speaks of a *miẓvah* in general, because of *bittul Torah*."[75] This view was echoed by the Rosh who also saw R. Shimon as regarding such total commitment as a matter of superogatory piety.[76] Additional Torah study is, on this view, meritorious, but in no way normatively demanded.

Of *rishonim* who addressed themselves to the issue, however, most apparently recoiled from this position, and they qualified R. Shimon's statement accordingly. The Ritba comments that it only applies *bidela efshar lei tefei*, "when one cannot do more, as he must devote part of the day to his living; otherwise, he is not thus absolved, as is stated in *Menaḥot*."[77] The Ran more fully asserts: "It seems to me that one does not truly discharge his obligation thus, for, after all, every person is required to learn constantly day and night, in accordance with his capacity (*kefi kokho*). Moreover, we state in the first chapter of *Kiddushin* (30a), 'Our Rabbis taught: "And thou shalt teach them diligently"—that the words of the Torah shall be clear-cut in your mouth, so that if anyone asks you something, you should not show doubt and answer him etc.; and reciting Shema, morning and evening, surely does not suffice to that end.' But . . ."[78] and he goes on to use this Gemara as support for his position that oaths can take effect even with regard to *miẓvah*

74. *She'elot u-Teshuvot ha-Radbaz*, 3:416.

75. *Tosafot Rabbenu Yehudah he-Ḥasid*, ad loc., *s.v. R. Shimon.*

76. See *Tosafot ha-Rosh*, ad loc., *s.v. R. Shimon.*

77. *Ḥiddushei ha-Ritva*, ad loc., *s.v. amrinan.* The allusion to *Menaḥot* is problematic, as the issue is certainly not clear-cut there.

78. *Nedarim* 8a, *s.v. ha.* The Radbaz surprisingly includes the Ran among *rishonim* who subscribe to his position. The Ran's language clearly dictates otherwise, however. Nevertheless, support can be adduced from an anonymous citation in the *Shittah Mekubeẓet*, ad loc., to the effect that additional study has not been commanded at all: "*ve-afilu 'assei leka.*"

In the passage cited, there is a play upon two senses of the root SNN, denoting recitative study and sharpness, respectively.

matters, if only they have not been explicitly mentioned in Scripture. Among *posekim,* likewise, the *Sefer Mizvot Gadol,* the central halakhic compendium of medieval Ashkenazic Jewry, declares that "in times of pressure, when a person is in disarray and has no time to learn, he can rely upon Rav Yoḥanan's statement,"[79] that is to the effect that recitation of Shema suffices; and thence, transmitted, inter alia, by the *Hagahot Maimuniyot,*[80] this formulation was incorporated by the Rama into the *Shulḥan 'Arukh*[81] as a codicil to Rav Yosef Karo's citation of the Rambam.

Important as this question may be and however far-reaching its ideological and practical ramifications, it is, for our purposes, not the sole, or perhaps even the primary, problem. At least two major additional points need to be considered. We have heretofore dealt with *talmud Torah* as process and experience, as part of the woof and warp of a Jew's lifelong religious existence. This is a crucial aspect, in many respects unique to Judaism. However, Torah study may also be result-oriented. This is amply illustrated by the Gemara's statement, "If his father has not taught him, he is obligated to teach himself," or by its discussion of "to what point is a person obiigated to teach his son Torah?"[82]—a discussion which focuses upon children's education but clearly has implications for personal learning as well. Presumably, the *mizvah* of *talmud Torah* imposes a dual demand: (*a*) continual if not continuous Torah study; and (*b*) attainment and maintenance of a certain quantitative and qualitative level of Torah knowledge.

That being the case, the prospect of engaging in other pursuits at the expense of Torah must be weighed with an eye to both factors. Even if, in accordance with R. Shimon's view, one's program of study meets the minimal standards, if it nevertheless fails to achieve the requisite result it cannot be countenanced. This is clearly indicated by the previously quoted passage of the Ran in which he contends, first, that maximal Torah study is obligatory per se; and, second, that the necessary level simply cannot be attained by minimal learning. It is also a central motif of a trenchant analysis of the problem—albeit with an eye to vocational education rather than to general culture—in a small treatise, *Hilkhot Talmud Torah,* the first published work of R. Shneur Zalman of Lyadi, author of the *Tanya.* Addressing himself to the controversy previously noted between R. Ishmael and R. Shimon, and the apparent contradiction between the latter's positions as set forth in *Berakhot*

79. *Mizvot 'Assei,* 12. Cf. *Or Zarua,* "Alpha Beta," 19, who cites the Gemara in *Menaḥot* in conjection with a passage from *Midrash Tehillim* (1:17; in S. Buber's ed., p. 16) in which R. Yehoshua and Bar Kappara express views essentially similar to R. Shimon b. Yoḥai's, a position the *Or Zarua* eventually accepted.

80. On *Hil. Talmud Torah* 1:7.

81. *Yoreh De'ah,* 246:1.

82. *Kiddushin* 29b and 30a, respectively. The description of personal learning as an autodidactic process reflecting an overall emphasis upon teaching, which is very clear in the Rambam, is highly instructive. Presumably, it is related to awareness of tradition as opposed to the modern focus upon venturesome exploration.

and *Menaḥot,* respectively, he suggests a basic distinction between the two texts. The first *sugya* deals with an aspiring *talmid ḥakham* in his formative stages, still in the process of acquiring his store of requisite knowledge. That being the case, R. Shimon prescribes that he devote himself wholly to Torah study, even to the point of adopting a subsistence-level standard of living, while R. Ishmael counsels normal economic activity even in this situation. In *Menaḥot,* on the other hand, the Gemara deals with a person who simply wishes to fulfill the *miẓvah* of *talmud Torah* as a normative activity without regard for the accumulation of knowledge—either because like Ben Dama, he has already attained that goal; or because, contrarily, lacking the necessary intellectual tools, he has no meaningful chance of achieving it. With respect to the study as opposed to the mastery of Torah, R. Shimon holds that a minimal portion suffices.[83]

This position raises an obvious problem: What is the level of proficiency, as regards both depth and scope, which constitutes basic adequate knowledge? To the best of my knowledge, no clear-cut definition emerges from Ḥazal. Statements about the importance of Torah study and the value of its knowledge, of course, abound, but the line between the hortatory and the normative, between laudable aspiration and halakhic duty, is not drawn. Some light may perhaps be shed, however, by reference to an analogous obligation: the *miẓvah* to teach one's son Torah. This point is raised by the Gemara in *Kiddushin* (30a). After initially suggesting that the father must teach "*mikra* (Scripture), Mishnah, Talmud, *halakhot,* and *aggadot,*" it then scales back drastically and concludes that *mikra* alone suffices, to the exclusion even of Mishnah.

Presumably, what is intended is not just knowledge of the literal text but its understanding in accordance with traditional interpretation. Perhaps, beyond that, the *miẓvah* requires imbuing knowledge which can assure commitment. Thus, the Meiri comments: "A father is but required to teach his son the written Torah, to the point that he shall understand the substance of *miẓvot* and fulfill them properly."[84] Even this, however, is a relatively modest requirement. R. Meir Halevi Abulafia (the Ramah) seriously qualified the Gemara's conclusion, however, by postulating that it only applied to cases of hardship which prevent a father's doing more. However, "If one only can, he is obligated to teach Mishnah, Talmud, *halakhot,* and

83. See R. Sheur Zalman of Lyadi, *Hilkhot Talmud Torah* (Brooklyn, 1968), 38–41. The treatise was first published independently in 1794, but was then frequently included as an appendix to *Shulḥan 'Arukh ha-Rav.* For a summary analysis of the Ba'al ha-Tanya's views, see Rav S.Y. Zevin, *Le-Or ha-Halakhah* (Jerusalem, 1957), 204–12. A distinction between different personages as a way of reconciling the apparent contradiction between the *sugyot* was also advanced by the *Keren Orah, Menaḥot* 99b. See also *Midrash Tehillim* 1:17 which, analogously, limits Bar Kappara's view—similar to R. Shimon's—to a given group.

84. *Bet ha-Beḥirah,* ad loc. See also Rav Yehuda Gershuni, *Kol Yehudah* (Jerusalem, 1990), 437–38.

aggadot."[85] The Rambam, for his part, took the Gemara at face value, but formulated the *halahkah* with reference to the financial obligation to pay for a child's education, possibly conveying the impression that the duty to teach per se ranges further.[86] Even if these qualifications be accepted, however—and the Ramah's was incorporated into the *Shulḥan 'Arukh (Yoreh De'ah* 246:1)—the message that *mikra* enjoys special status, so that the absolute obligation, if any, to know the rest of Torah, is of a lesser order, is clear.

Obviously, this point has possible ramifications beyond the specific realm of parental duty. Certainly, mastery of the totality of Torah, of every nook and cranny within its many mansions, is an ideal towards which every *ben Torah* strives. Even those who know that they shall probably never realize such mastery are animated by Browning's sense that "a man's reach must exceed his grasp, else what's a Heaven for," and proceed accordingly, as best they can. Yet, whether it is regarded as absolute duty or laudable aspiration will clearly make a great deal of difference; surely so, with regard to the prospect of devoting time, even for spiritually worthwhile reasons, to other pursuits. The discussion centering upon the Gemara in *Kiddushin* may therefore be highly relevant to resolving the question of *Torah u-Madda.*

Nevertheless, it should be borne in mind that one cannot necessarily infer the range of obligatory personal Torah knowledge from this Gemara, as it may very well exceed the scope of what one is bound to teach his children. Thus, Rashi, commenting upon the father's exemption from teaching Mishnah, notes explicitly: "The obligation with respect to the son only applies to *mikra;* beyond that, he [i.e., the son] will teach himself."[87] He did not, however, stipulate what degree of mastery might be required "beyond that": which areas and how much of each. As regards *mikra,* the Rambam speaks of the child's reading "the whole of *Torah she-bikhtav;*"[88] but, given the range of Torah, it seems unlikely that such comprehensiveness would also be required with respect to the other areas—as regards either teaching one's son according to the Ramah,[89] or one's personal obligation to know Torah on other views.

Some *aḥaronim* have clearly held otherwise, however. The Ba'al ha-Tanya himself speaks of *kol ha-torah kulah,* "Torah in its entirety," and he explicitly states that there exists "a *de-oraita* obligation to study and to know all the details of the

85. Cited in *Tur Yoreh De'ah,* 245.

86. See *Hil. Talmud Torah* 1:7 and *Leḥem Mishneh,* ad loc.

87. *S.v. eno.*

88. *Hil. Talmud Torah* 1:7. Rashi, *Kiddushin* 30a, *s.v. Torah,* holds that only *Ḥumash* is required, not the whole of Scripture. See also *Siftei Kohen, Yoreh De'ah,* 245:5.

89. The Gaon of Vilna, *Be'urei ha-Gera, Yoreh De'ah,* 245:15, sees the Ramah's position as based on the standard of personal knowledge, the inference being that, at a secondary level, one is obligated to teach his child that which he himself as any Jew must know. It is conceivable, however, that for the Ramah, the obligation to inculcate Torah in one's child is greater than with respect to himself. See, however, *Kiddushin* 29b.

halakhot"[90] at the plane of requisite basic knowledge, although only for those capable of becoming genuine *talmidei ḥakhamim*. More recently, R. Barukh Baer Leibowitz expanded upon this theme extensively in a responsum written shortly before World War II, which analyzes various aspects of the *miẓvah* of *talmud Torah*. Basing himself, in part, upon the Ramah and, in part, upon the Gemara the Ran had cited, "'And thou shalt teach them diligently'—Let Torah matters be honed on your tongue, so that if a person should ask you something, do not stammer in answering him."—he postulates, first, that, as regards his sons, one is duty-bound "to make and train them to be *geonim* and Torah scholars;" and second, that it is likewise incumbent upon one to attain this level personally.[91]

R. Barukh Baer further assumes that, quite apart from the need to attain a given level of proficiency, the *miẓvah* of Torah study per se requires continuous learning, unless absolute physical, economic, or religious necessity (i.e., the need to perform some immediately pressing *miẓvah*) precludes it. This, as we have seen, is a matter of dispute. Even if this contention be rejected, however, his earlier definition is of considerable moment with respect to *Torah u-Madda*. If that be the standard of minimal compulsory knowledge, then the question of the scope of the injunction against *bittul Torah* per se becomes, for all but a handful, largely irrelevant as they must learn constantly in any event simply to pass muster. On this view, little room is left even for the acquisition of a trade or a profession, much less, for general culture. Presumably, R. Barukh Baer, too, his legendary naïveté notwithstanding, recognized that the parental and/or personal educational enterprise he envisioned was doomed to failure, as most would become immersed in earning a livelihood long before they could even dream of becoming "*geonim* and Torah scholars." That, however, could be sanctioned as a matter of sheer personal necessity (the societal aspect he largely ignored). Not so, with respect to *madda*. R. Barukh Baer himself, of course, despised it on other grounds. The responsum in question, reflecting the polemical atmosphere of the time, includes a blistering attack upon university education as a subversive force and categorically rejects it as a legitimate option. Even for those who do not share his revulsion, however, acceptance of his definition effectively precludes the pursuit of *Torah u-Madda*.

It is, however, with respect to absolutely normative knowledge, a radical definition; and inasmuch as *rishonim* did not speak in this vein, one can probably assume that they did not entertain it. Nonetheless, even if more modest standards be posited, a second major issue independent of the scope of the *miẓvah* of lifelong learning must be considered: the axiological and existential place of Torah in our lives and our total relation to it. The enormous (in many respects, incomprehensible) attachment which, practically and ideologically, *knesset Yisrael* has had historically to Torah study has not been solely grounded in its being, *primus inter pares*, an

---

90. *Hilkhot Talmud Torah*, 38.
91. See *Birkat Shemuel, Kiddushin*, sec. 27.

important *mizvah.* Upon that too to be sure. "None of all the *mizvot,*" writes the Rambam (*Hil. Talmud Torah* 3:3), "is equal to *talmud Torah* but *talmud Torah,* rather, is equal to all the *mizvot,* as study leads to practice." But not upon that alone. It springs from deep rooted faith in the sanctity and significance of Torah at the cosmic, sociohistorical, and personal planes; as that which sustains the creation, binds His covenantal community to the *Ribbono Shel 'Olam,* and purgatively sanctifies the individual Jew. Above and beyond its normative thrust, Torah study is a central aspect of the Jew's destiny. "If you have learned much Torah," said Rabban Yoḥanan b. Zakkai, "do not claim credit for yourself, as it is to this end that you were created" (*Avot* 2:8). It affords him access, as far as humanly possible, to God's revealed will and, hence, informs and inspires him on the one hand and brings him closer to his Maker on the other. It ennobles and enriches, investing its votary with a transfiguring "crown of Torah."

Even if alternate courses of study be halakhically permissible, then, can they be commended? Certainly not. For a Jew, there is no substitute for Torah. It is the unchallenged central driving force, molding, directing, and informing his spiritual and intellectual life. But that is hardly the question. At issue is not whether Torah ought be central but whether it should be exclusive. Emphasis and comprehensiveness are obviously not identical. The metaphysical dialectic which so intrigued Rav Ḥayyim of Volozhin—on the one hand, *ein 'od milevado,* "There is nothing but He," and yet much else obviously exists[92]—is paralleled cosmically by the relation between the sacred and the profane, generally, and between Torah and *ḥokhmah,* specifically. The problem arises at one level with respect to the overall range of spiritual existence. "Whoever asserts that he has nothing but Torah," Ḥazal states (*Yevamot* 109b), "does not even have Torah," as he is lacking its realization. In a more limited vein, it is clearly relevant to the status of *madda* as well. Spuriously rigorous logic dictates that more of the best is always best. But sound common sense knows that additional bread does not take the place of butter.

To be sure, some scorn butter as a mark of self-indulgence. But must the whole Torah world be comprised solely of spiritual ascetics? Can it not harbor with honor, not effete sybarites but vibrant and vigorous souls who wish to explore, create, and enjoy within a more ambient range of the *Ribbono Shel 'Olam*'s spiritual world, so as to relish a variegated fare? Others spurn it out of anxiety over the deleterious impact of the spiritual equivalent of cholesterol content. This is, of course, legitimate concern. But it is a matter of detail; and, and as long as the principle is clear, the point can be made with reference to relatively innocuous margarine or jam.

At times, moreover, the spread may be transmuted by the absorbent roll. A halakhic analogy may illustrate the point. The Gemara (*Pesaḥim* 35a) cites a

92. See *Nefesh ha-Ḥayyim,* pt. 3, especially ch. 3–8. The *pasuk,* cited from Deuteronomy 4:35, can of course be understood as denying the existence of other deities but not of other beings. See also Rambam, *Hil. Yesodei ha-Torah* 1:4.

controversy between Rabbi Yoḥanan b. Nuri and his peers as to whether rice is included in the list of species out of which bread can be made. The majority view, denying this status, prevailed. Nevertheless, the Mishnah (*Ḥallah* 3:7) states: "If one makes dough out of wheat and rice, if the taste is that of grain, it requires [tithing of] *ḥallah,* and a person may use it to discharge his obligation [i.e., to eat *mazah*] on Pesaḥ. If, however, it does not have the taste of grain, it is exempt from *ḥallah* and a person cannot use it to discharge his obligation on Pesaḥ." The *Yerushalmi (Ḥallah* 1:1) explains that the rice is "pulled" by the wheat, that is, it does not merely absorb the flavor of the latter while retaining its own identity, but is, in effect, transubstantiated. As the Ramban elaborated: "Hence, we understand that the mishnah's reason is that although the rice is exempt, as it is not bread, nevertheless, when it is mixed with grain and tastes like grain, the grain pulls it so that the whole becomes bread which is obligated with respect to *ḥallah*."[93] Similarly, there may be aspects of culture which per se are in no way part of Torah nor on a par with it; and yet, within a Torah context, may be harnessed by it and, in its broader sense, adumbrated to it. Only some to be sure. The *Yerushalmi* concludes that only rice is subject to such transmutation and then only by wheat. Still, even within limits, the phenomenon can be of moment.

Of course, the line of reasoning I have metaphorically suggested is wholly irrelevant if one argues that Torah is both bread and butter; if one contends that, while the desire for a spread is indeed both legitimate and laudable, of this celestial fare, too, one might say what Ḥazal homiletically adduced (*Yoma* 75a) with respect to manna: "Just as the infant finds many a flavor in the breast, so also did Israel, as long as they were eating manna, find many a flavor in it." Adherents of this view would no doubt echo the words of R. Avraham Yiẓḥak Bloch who, although he evidently recognized the merits of general culture, when asked by a yeshiva student about its pursuit, answered categorically: "As to the study of literature and its reading, as well as all other popular studies which have no practical utility, surely it is not worthwhile to expend time upon them when one can attain development of personality through our sacred Torah; all the more so, as Gentile literature includes erotic and proscribed matters. And in any event, it is not worthwhile to search for gold amidst slime and mud when one can gather pearls from a pure place, from a source of living water, the written and oral Torah, of which it is said, 'Engage in it and engage in it, for all is in it.'"[94]

As I have previously indicated, I have no quarrel whatsoever with those who for themselves wish to adopt this position. But surely it is no less legitimate to desire to "taste and see," not just mystically but perceptibly, and to acknowledge the limitations of our own taste buds. Those who seek positive spiritual dimensions and

93. *Hilkhot Ḥallah,* 31b (in the Vilna shas). Cf. *Zevaḥim* 78a and *Ḥiddushei Rabbenu Ḥayyim Halevi, Hil. Ḥamez u-Maẓah* 6:5.

94. Printed in L. Levi, *Sha'arei Talmud Torah,* 339.

experiences which aspects of general culture palpably convey in a way that their direct Torah study does not will then perforce devote time to its pursuit.

We are brought back, inexorably, to the factual question, but with an even keener sense of the difficulty of confronting it forthrightly. Where shall the proper bar be found? An essay in a volume devoted, in part, to the subject of *Torah 'im derekh ereẓ* extolled the contribution of relativity, quantum mechanics, microbiology, set theory, particle physics, and others to a religious perception of the universe.[95] But how are those who are leading intensive Torah lives in abysmal ignorance of these developments to evaluate them? Are they truly attaining this perception by alternate means—it can presumably be achieved without state-of-the-art physics—or are they in effect partially forfeiting it? In a parallel essay, after noting that "scope, system, power, concentration and focus—these are often found in the world of *ḥokhmah* more than in our own; it was not for naught that the Rambam was so impressed by Aristotle,"[96] I went on to pose a series of rhetorical questions intimating that general literary sources might impart certain spiritual insight more effectively. I concluded with the statement: "Whoever does not know this material will find it difficult to answer these questions—and hence, is inclined to dismiss them glibly." This is true of many but surely not of all. Let us bear in mind that, among the opponents of secular studies, *gedolei Yisrael* have figured prominently. And it is, in some respects, an unfair statement. *Vita brevis.* We cannot examine and/or experience in depth every cultural phenomenon upon which we need to pass judgment. Nevertheless, mindful of Rabbi Eliezer's dictum (*Niddah* 7b), "We do not say to him who has not seen the new moon that he should come and testify but, rather, to him who has seen it," we should, at the very least, lend as careful an ear to those who, out of their direct experience, have countenanced secular studies as to those who have damned them.

These remarks have tentatively been put forth within the context of the view of the Radbaz and probably the Rambam, that is, on the assumption that maximal continuous *talmud Torah* is not absolutely obligatory. According to the Ran, who does regard such study as mandatory, there is presumably no latitude for allocation to other pursuits. In truth, however, a similar argument can be advanced with reference to the Ran's view as well. A number of *aḥaronim* have juxtaposed two of R. Ishmael's dicta and noted an apparent contradiction. In *Menaḥot* 99b, as we have seen, he, in effect, counselled against the study of "Greek wisdom," not because of its content but because such study countermanded God's mandate to Yehoshua, "But thou shalt meditate therein day and night." Yet, in *Berakhot* 35b it is he who asserts that, this mandate notwithstanding, one may engage in normal economic activity: "Inasmuch as it is stated, 'This book of the law shall not depart out of thy

95. See R. Eliyahu Zeeny, "Kera be-Aḥdut," in *Mamlekhet Kohanim ve-Goy Kadosh*, ed. Y. Shaviv (Jerusalem, 1989), 68–85.

96. "Tovah Ḥokhmah 'Im Naḥalah," in *Mamlekhet*, 31–32.

mouth,' is this possibly to be understood literally? Therefore it says, 'And thou shalt gather in thy corn?' To wit: Combine them [i.e., matters of Torah study] with a worldly occupation."[97] In fact, however, there is no contradiction at all. R. Ishmael holds that one ought not devote spare time to inane endeavors. How "spare time" is to be defined is another matter, however. He recognizes that there are legitimate needs to be met, whose pursuit does not constitute *bittul Torah*. Drawing upon the Ran's formulation, we note that the obligation for each person to learn constantly is qualified by the phrase, *kefi koḥo*, "in accordance with his capacity;" and to the extent that one's capacity is limited by the need to earn a livelihood, the *mizṿah*, too, is constricted.

It should be emphasized, moreover, that this is not a case of obligation being overridden by necessity. As R. Yaakov Kaniewsky ("the Steipler") pointed out in explaining why, according to some *rishonim*, the principle of *ha-'osek be-mizṿah patur min ha-mizṿah* ("whoever engages in one *mizṿah* is exempt from another") did not apply to one who was engaged in Torah study: "With respect to other positive Torah commandments, even when one is forcibly prevented from fulfilling the *mizṿah*, and no claim or demand can be brought against him over its annulment, nevertheless the obligation is incumbent upon him. . . . However, as concerns the *mizṿah* of *talmud Torah*, inasmuch as the Torah has not delineated it quantitatively, the obligation is, inescapably, in accordance with one's capacity; and with regard to time during which one is forcibly prevented from learning, this is not in the nature of canceling a *mizṿah* out of constraint. Rather, that is the limit of one's obligation."[98]

Just what can be subsumed under the rubric of "legitimate needs" is, however, obviously of critical importance. R. Ishmael presumably speaks directly of economic need. But as this license is not based upon a dispensation of *piku'aḥ nefesh* (the

97. The concluding phrase *hanheg bahem minhag derekh ereẓ* might also be rendered "Relate to them in accordance with normal practice."

See L. Levi, *Sha'arei Talmud Torah*, 233–36 and 269–79 for a summary of various approaches with regard to resolving the apparent contradiction between the *sugyot*. The question of *pesak*, particularly as regards the Rambam, is unclear. R. Barukh Baer (ibid., 27:6) quotes R. Ḥayyim Soloveitchik as assuming that the Rambam accepted the view of R. Shimon, and this on the basis of the conclusion of *Hil. Shemittah ve-Yovel*. His position, of course, is contravened by the *Even ha-Azel* and *Keli Ḥemdah* previously cited. However, even if one rejects their much more radical view, it seems difficult to establish a *pesak* with regard to so crucial an issue in light of a clearly hortatory peroration in a wholly different context while the purported decision was pointedly omitted in *Hilkhot Talmud Torah*; doubly so, in light of the Rambam's vigorous opposition to the economic dependency of *talmidei ḥakhamim*.

98. *Kehillat Ya'akov, Shabbat* 10a; cited in L. Levi, *Sha'arei Talmud Torah*, 203. For a discussion of the principle of *ha-'osek be-mizṿah* with respect to Torah study, see the letter of Rav Y. Hutner, printed in *Sefer ha-Zikkaron le-Maran Ba'al ha-Paḥad Yiẓḥak zẓ"l* (Jerusalem, 1984), 340–44; L. Levi, *Sha'arei Talmud Torah*, 201–05; and my "be-'Inyan ha-'Osek be-Torah Patur Min ha-Mizṿah," in *Kevod ha-Rav* (New York, 1984), 187–201.

saving of life), we hardly assume that only maintenance of the barest subsistence level is intended. I suppose we would take it for granted that physical or psychological need would likewise be recognized. Why not, then, psychic spiritual needs such as general wisdom and culture help satisfy? But, it will be rejoined, those are not needs at all, just intellectual indulgence. That, however, is precisely the point at issue. One cannot reject *madda* categorically on the ground of *bittul Torah* unless one has already dismissed it in part on other grounds; unless one has already decided, independently of the question of diverting time from Torah study, that it serves no truly meaningful purpose in human life.

Deeply engraved upon every *ben Torah*'s heart is R. Nehorai's exposition of the phrase, *ki devar Hashem bazah,* "For he hath despised the word of the Lord," as referring to "whosoever can engage in the study of the Torah but fails to do so."[99] But how is this ability to be defined? An evening the Rambam spent on Aristotle was not devoted to refining his *Mishneh Torah;* an hour during which R. Yaakov Ettlinger read Schiller, composition of the *'Arukh la-Ner* ground to a halt. Would anyone dare describe them in R. Nehorari's terms? One can appreciate only too well the full force of R. Shimon b. Yoḥai's plaintive statement, "Had I been present at Mount Sinai at the time that Torah was given to Israel, I would have asked that two mouths be created for each person, one to study Torah and one to deal with all [other] matters."[100] Man having been created single-mouthed, however, when he is engaged in a legitimate pursuit, he is ipso facto not defined as one who can then study Torah. Of course, inasmuch as there are more legitimate pursuits, Torah being primary and unique among them, than time in which they can be realized, choices must be made, priorities determined, and some overall balance struck. At that plane, if one acknowledges its spiritual value, the possibility that some time will be allotted to culture cannot be precluded purely on the grounds of *bittul Torah.*

This was, manifestly, the view of the Rama who, on the one hand, cites the Rivash to the effect that one should devote his intellectual endeavors to Torah, "as it is thus that he shall acquire [his place in] this world and the next, but not through the study of other wisdoms;" and yet then continues: "Nevertheless, it is permissible to study other wisdoms, incidentally."[101] This formulation probably does not wholly satisfy either the advocates of *Torah u-Madda* or its adversaries. The former may find the license grudging, while the latter may find it incomprehensible.[102] There is no question, however, but that, as regards the specific issue of *bittul Torah,* the Rama in principle espoused the position I have outlined.

As to his qualifications, the statement that salvation is attained through Torah and not through other disciplines may very well refer to the prospect of their being

99. *Sanhedrin* 99b; the *pasuk* is from Numbers 15:31.

100. Yerushalmi, *Berakhot,* 1:2.

101. *Yoreh De'ah,* 246:4.

102. See *Birkat Shemuel,* 27:7–8 who cites and discusses the Rama but sees him as agreeing with his own position—a palpably difficult interpretation.

posited as an alternative to Torah—a course no champion of *Torah u-Madda* would countenance. The limitation of *be'akrai,* that other studies be incidental, rests upon the centrality although not the exclusiveness of Torah; and it is analogous to the Gemara's statement (*Yoma* 19b), "Make them [i.e., Torah matters] permanent and do not make them transitory." It is an important qualification, but a flexible one, to be implemented in practice with an eye to specific conditions, while always retaining the basic conception of the primacy of Torah.

Decision to embrace or reject the pursuit of *ḥokmah* turns, then, not only upon its factual evaluation but upon definition of the standard to be applied. We cannot determine whether it may be regarded as a legitimate need unless we perceive what degree of need is the yardstick. Is it that of bread, butter, or some intermediate food or condiment? If the first, the answer shall of course be resoundingly negative. The asseveration we recite daily in our evening prayers, *ki hem ḥayyenu ve-orekh yamenu,* "For they are our life and longevity," can only be expressed with reference to *Torah u-mizṿot ḥukkim u-mishpatim, otanu limadta,* "Torah and commandments, statutes and ordinances, which Thou hast taught us." No exponent of *Torah u-Madda,* no matter how ardent, can question that one may lead a wholesome—albeit, in some cases, superficial—Jewish life sans culture. Does anyone envision basic personal salvation as a function of philosophy or philology? While its adherents may contend that *madda* can enrich and purify piety, they dare not regard culture as either the sine qua non or the litmus test of its very existence.

If, however, the standard be something less than that of the staff of life, there is certainly room for thought. On the premise that aspects of *madda* enhance a person's spiritual existence, *kefi koḥo* may very well be defined with some allocation for general culture in mind. I fully admire and appreciate those who single-mindedly take their literal cue from the text in *Kinyan Torah* (*Avot* 6:4): "Thus is the way of Torah: You shall eat bread with salt, drink water by ration, sleep on the ground, and live a life of hardship, while toiling in the Torah." I am awed by the rigor of R. Ḥayyim Volozhiner who contends that, even according to R. Ishmael, only the most minimal diversion from Torah study is permissible and that, moreover, "Also, during the same time and brief period that you engage in earning a livelihood because of the need and compulsion to subsist, in your mind's thoughts, in any event, you should be thinking only of Torah matters."[103] But I fail to understand opponents of *Torah u-Madda* who think it is perfectly legitimate to labor long and engrossing hours in order to eat lamb chops, drive a Volvo, or vacation in St. Moritz, but illicit to devote those hours instead to exploring, with Plato or Goethe, vistas of thought and experience. I do not, of course, equate Plato with lamb chops. I just hope we are not so Philistine as to value him less.

With regard to those aspects of *ḥokhmah* which perceptibly enhance optimal implementation of *halakhah,* the problem of *bittul torah* is mitigated in another respect. Even on the most rigorous view, the relevant criterion is not whether one

103. *Nefesh ha-Ḥayyim,* 1:8.

is actively fulfilling the *miẓvah* of studying Torah. Enabling its realization suffices. Rav, as we have noted, spent eighteen months on a farm so that he should be better equipped to decide halakhic questions regarding the blemishes of firstlings. In all likelihood, he did not thereby engage in *talmud Torah*.[104] Would he have uttered the blessings over Torah before examining animals or felt constrained to abstain from his studies on *Tish'ah Be'Av*?[105] Yet, given their character qua *hekhsher* (preparatory enablement of) *miẓvah*, he had no qualms about them. The point is readily understood with regard to narrow questions of halakhically relevant realia, especially within the scientific realm. It is, however, equally applicable to less technical areas. If we are to heed the injunction against *ona'at devarim*, "verbal aggression,"[106] we must be sensitive empathetically to others' responses and aware introspectively of our own motives. Great literature may then be the farm of *ona'at devarim*. On a broader scale, knowledge of man, society, and history is often essential to realizing Torah values at the public level and its acquisition, too, constitutes *hekhsher miẓvah*. The Ḥazon Ish's caveat, "The pitfalls of false correlation [i.e., of rule to situation] are greater than those of basic halakhic formulation,"[107] has relevance beyond carbuncles and capacitors.

---

104. Just where the line is to be drawn with regard to definition of the *miẓvah* is, of course, an important question. I take it for granted that calculations made in the midst of *sugyot* in *Kil'ayim* would qualify. At the same time, I think it is clear that the antecedent study of mathematics as a propaedeutic measure so that, when encountered, the *sugya* could be studied properly, could only count as *hekhsher miẓvah*. Just how immediate must be the relation to the context of *talmud Torah* proper is, however, a moot point; and, a priori, an entire intermediate spectrum can be envisioned. R. Yosef Kapaḥ, "Limudei 'Ḥol' be-Mishnat ha-Rambam," *Teḥumin*, 2 (1981): 248–51, contends that, on the Rambam's view, study of fields regarded as prerequisites to the knowledge of divine science constitute a fulfillment of the *miẓvah* of the love of God. That is, however, separate from *talmud Torah*, although the latter is itself a means of attaining the former. Rabbi Lamm does advance the qualified possibility that *madda*, when studied for the sake of *talmud Torah*, can be regarded as a literal fulfillment of the *miẓvah*—evidently even if at the time of study, it is contextually divorced from Torah study. He advances this view with reference to both the Rambam and his own elaborated view of *madda* as a "textless subject of Talmud Torah" (*Torah Umadda*, p. 163), lower in the hierarchy of Torah than its texts but still included within the range of the *miẓvah*; see, especially, chs. 4, 9, and 10. I find this far-reaching, however, and am not inclined to agree.

The relevant halakhic sources, with reference to various areas, are treated in a lengthy article by R. Aharon Kahn, "Li-Kevi'at ha-Ḥefẓah Shel Torah be-Miẓvat Talmud Torah," *Beth Yosef Shaul* 3 (1989): 305–403.

105. It is, however, conceivable that these *halakhot* were formulated with respect to Torah qua object rather than with regard to the *miẓvah* of its study—in which case, they would not be relevant to our discussion.

106. The term is not easily translated. It includes taunts, building up false hopes, insults, even a moralizing reproach to a sufferer; see *Baba Meẓia* 58b.

107. *Iggerot Ḥazon Ish*, 1:31; cited in Y. Levi, *Sha'arei Talmud Torah*, 203.

The position I have suggested is open to an obvious objection. If some measure of cultural activity can be recognized as a legitimate need, why, then, did R. Ishmael enjoin Ben Dama from studying "Greek wisdom"—and this on grounds of *bittul Torah* rather than because of its inherently objectionable character? The question was, in effect, raised by the Maharal of Prague, and he offers the most likely solution. The *ḥokhmat yevanit* in question is not genuine wisdom at all but an amalgam of various disciplines which are bereft of spiritual import, "lacking any relation whatsoever to Torah. But the *ḥokhmot* whose purpose is the perception of reality and the structure of the world, it is certainly permissible to study."[108] In different variations, this confined—some would contend, self-serving—definition of *ḥokhmat yevanit* had been advanced by *rishonim,* starting with the Rambam;[109] and if one adopts this course in principle, then those aspects of culture that one regards as spiritually significant are not subject to R. Ishmael's proscription.[110]

Let me reiterate as vigorously and as emphatically as I can, that *madda* can only be championed when it is placed in proper perspective—as subsidiary if not subservient to Torah. We subscribe, without trace of sophisticated embarrassment, to the prevalent medieval conception of secular studies as handmaidens to the divine. The overarching principle is that of the *Sifra:* "'To walk therein'—Make them primary and do not make them subordinate. 'To walk therein'—that your business be but with them, that you not commingle other things with them, that you not say, 'I have learned Jewish wisdom, [now] I shall learn Gentile wisdom.' To wit, it is stated, 'To walk therein': You are not empowered to rid yourself of them."[111] The primacy of Torah is axiomatic. That primacy should of course ordinarily be reflected in the division of time and energy between *talmud Torah* and secular studies, particularly during critical formative years. Even if the proportion should be shifted, however, in the course of subsequent professional development, the axiological relation remains immutable. It is solely on that basis that *Torah u-Madda* can be advocated. There can be no parity—"that you not commingle other things with them"—much less, a reversal of roles—" that you not say, 'I have learned Jewish wisdom, [now] I shall learn Gentile wisdom.'" The caption, "make them primary and do not make them subordinate," clearly implies that in an ancillary capacity, qua *tafel,* there can be room for other things properly proportioned. But on that condition alone.

It is in this context that Ben Bag Bag's dictum is to be understood. Encouragement to study Torah persistently need hardly be based on the assumption that,

108. *Netivot 'Olam,* "Netiv ha-Torah," ch. 14.

109. See *Perush ha-Mishnayot, Sotah* 9:15. For a succinct summary of the variations, see *Enzyklopedia Talmudit,* s.v. *ḥokhmot ḥiẓoniyot,* 15:59–64.

110. The Maharal seems to have had the natural sciences particularly in mind, but the principle is more broadly applicable.

111. *Sifra, Aḥarei Mot,* 13:11. Cf. *Sifre, Va'etḥanan,* sec. 9. See also Mordecai Breuer, "Torah 'im Derekh Ereẓ be-Yamenu," in *Mamlekhet,* 44–67.

directly and immediately, its corpus narrowly defined includes everything worth knowing. Such exhortation can surely be based upon the conviction that it is the key to ultimate knowledge—all being "in it" in this sense—and, hence, is to be the focus of a Jew's intellectual experience. One is enjoined to "engage in it and engage in it," i.e., to posit Torah as a permanent facet of his spiritual life rather than as a phase of his formative development; and this out of recognition of its centrality within the inner world and the world at large. Explaining the repetition of the phrase, *va-hafakh bah* in the Mishnah R. Mosheh Almosnino comments: "The first refers to engaging in Torah proper; the second, that one should engage, through it, in everything else. To wit: when one studies other disciplines, he will relate them to it, so that he will strive to harmonize what he studies with what is written in the Torah. . . . For it is impossible that you should say that Torah and other sciences are, respectively, separate, for everything is in it. . . . And this is what is intended by 'for all is within it.'"[112] This interpretation probably bears the stamp of R. Mosheh's advocacy of the study of philosophy and astronomy, which he avidly pursued. Nevertheless, the thrust of his understanding of *dekhola bah* seems eminently reasonable.

After Your Own Eyes: The Corruption of Morals

The second major concern, the deleterious potential of exposure to general culture and its study, is even more pressing than the first, and this in two respects. First, at issue here is not just the failure to fulfill a *mizvah* optimally or to attain maximal spiritual structure, but the threat of corrosive influence; not only the realization of good but the avoidance of evil. Second, it is, in essence, a universal concern. The problem of *bittul Torah* is, by and large, narrowly ours. While the optimal use of time is, of course, a broad human goal and the "work ethic" not our parochial patrimony (although its Puritan, and subsequently Victorian, version may very well have Jewish roots), its cutting edge for us is the normative and axiological force of Torah study. Infection is a universal scourge, however, and from Plato on, it has been dealt with accordingly.

Nevertheless, it should be noted that eminent recent *gedolim* have apparently found this problem manageable. The clearest test of whether reservations about secular education are grounded in concern about *bittul Torah* or in anxiety about spiritual subversion is the resolution of the issue with respect to women, whose

112. Cited in *Midrash Shemuel,* ad loc. The Meiri neutralizes somewhat the relevance of this Mishnah to our problem by interpreting that it refers to a mode of Torah study, repeated and intensive, rather than the place of that study within the total intellectual universe; see *Bet ha-Beḥirah,* ad loc.

relation to Torah study is of a lesser order but whose moral and ideological integrity is not. By this standard, the prevalent attitude of the first-rank leaders of the American Torah world during the last generation seems clear. Daughters of Rav Mosheh Feinstein, Rav Yaakov Kamenetzky, and Rav Yaakov Ruderman, *zẓ"l,* graduated from college; daughters of Rav Aharon Kotler, of *mori ve-rabbi,* Rav Yitẓḥak Hutner, *zẓ"l* and of *rabbi muvhak,* Rav Yosef Dov Soloveitchik *zẓ"l* received doctorates—all presumably with paternal blessing. Today, the situation is, of course, quite different, in part, because the academic scene has changed, but primarily because attitudes have shifted. Be that as it may, these *gedolim*'s positions regarding this point—again, without reference to the element of *bittul Torah,* so critical in other respects—is unquestionably clear.

The content of their message is threefold. First, I do not for a moment imagine that they were heedless of the moral and religious damages attendant upon exposure to secular culture. Recognizing those, however, they evidently felt, secondly, that these could be overcome; and, thirdly, that the benefits of general education rendered the effort of coping worthwhile. That in sum is a position to which adherents of *Torah u-Madda* can readily subscribe. From my own perspective, I should like to flesh it out somewhat.

The dangers are many and varied, but, broadly speaking, fall under two categories which Ḥazal singled out as foci of the Torah's familiar admonition against spiritual vagrancy. With references to the *pasuk,* "And that you go not about after your own heart and your own eyes, after which you used to go astray," the Gemara comments: "'After your own heart'—this refers to infidelity, as is stated, 'The fool hath said in his heart: There is no God.' 'After your own eyes'—this refers to lustful thoughts, as is stated, 'And Samson said unto his father: Get her for me for she finds favor in my eyes.'"[113] Morals and faith—these are at once the core of religious existence and the potential storm center of spiritual danger.

Both concerns are well-known and longstanding. It is important, however, that we recognize their full scope. In modern times, immorality in the arts has been largely identified with eroticism. Public outrage and concomitant controversy over censorship have tended to be generated by causes célèbres—from Restoration drama to Madame Bovary, D. H. Lawrence, and beyond—which have offended standards of sexual morality. Important as this area may be—*ẓeniut* is a cardinal Jewish virtue and Ḥazal even placed great stress upon niceties of "clean language" (*Pesaḥim* 3a)—we must beware lest its emphasis mute other moral concerns. When Plato banished poets from his ideal republic because "poetry feeds and waters the

113. *Berakhot* 12b. The term *minut,* used in the Gemara, is both sharper and more comprehensive than the word "infidelity" by which Soncino renders it. There are clear overtones of heresy and even apostasy and many formal halakhic applications. I know, however, of no single term that would render it fully.

passions instead of drying them up,"[114] he was not referring solely to amorous passion. And of course it is not just a matter of lust versus reason. Even those who reject Socratic rationalistic ethics and regard desire more charitably can recognize the potential impact of the arts upon the whole range of moral being: action, attitude, impulse. The respective roles of reason and emotion, as well as the kind and degree of emotion; the level of spirituality, of purpose if not of mission, in human life; aggrandizement, arrogance, egotism, and dissoluteness, as opposed to accommodation, humility, altruism, and discipline; the various catalogues of cardinal virtues and deadly sins—can these be less the stuff of ethical being and moral philosophy than prurience and chastity? Inasmuch as, for better or for worse, culture patently affects us with respect to the gamut of moral existence, our concern with its content and over how we relate to it should be wide-ranging.

However one regards Plato's solution, his grasp of the problem—of both its urgency and scope—cannot be faulted. The pros and cons of formal censorship need no recounting; but personal wariness as to what and how one reads and experiences is a sine qua non of a Torah existence. It is precisely votaries who believe in the power of culture who should be most concerned about its impact. Given their modern liberal cast, many find it convenient and convincing to subscribe to the substance of one of the most celebrated passages in English Renaissance prose. Milton wrote in *Areopagitica:*

> Good and evil we know in the field of this world grow up together almost inseparably; and the knowledge of good is so involved and interwoven with the knowledge of evil, and in so many cunning resemblances hardly to be discerned, that those confused seeds which were imposed upon Psyche as an incessant labor to call out, and sort asunder, were not more intermixed. It was from out the rind of one apple tasted, that the knowledge of good and evil, as two twins cleaving together, leaped forth into the world. . . . I cannot praise a fugitive and cloistered virtue, unexercised and unbreathed, that never sallies out and seeks her adversary, but slinks out of the race, where that immortal garland is to be run for, not without dust and heat. Assuredly, we bring not innocence into the world, we bring impurity much rather; that which purifies us is trial, and trial is by what is contrary. That virtue therefore which is but a youngling in the contemplation of evil, and knows not the utmost that vice promises to her followers, and rejects it, is but a blank virtue, not a pure; her whiteness is but an excremental whiteness. Which was the reason why our sage and serious poet Spenser, whom I dare be known to think a better teacher than Scotus or Aquinas, describing true temperance under the person of Guion, brings him in with his palmer through the cave of Mammon, and the bower of earthly bliss, that he might see and know, and yet abstain.[115]

114. Plato, *Dialogues,* 1:864 (*Republic,* 10:606).

115. John Milton, *Areopagitica,* 13. Guion is the Knight of Temperance who is the central figure in Bk. II of Edmund Spenser's *The Faerie Queene.*

As to the relevance of the passage to our own problem, however, several points should be noted. First, the implicit preference of exposure and resistance to temptation to blissful ignorance of it—or, in Renaissance parlance, between continence and temperance—is itself a matter of longstanding debate, epitomized in Ḥazal by an incident described in the Gemara:

> R. Ḥanina and R. Jonathan were walking on the road and came to a parting of ways, one of which led by the door of [a place of] idol worship and the other led by the door of harlots. Said the one to the other: "Let us go by the place of idolatry, the inclination for which has been destroyed." The other responded: "Let us rather go by the harlots' place and suppress our inclination and we receive our reward."[116]

While the incident revolves around the ancillary question of compensation, at the heart of the debate clearly lies the substantive spiritual question of the merit and stability of pristine and tested virtues, respectively. Even if the prospect of succumbing is discounted, many moralists, general and Jewish, have rejected Milton's premise, holding that naïve innocence is superior to restraint, so that a process which may issue in nothing better than what Shaftesbury scornfully described as the virtue of "a caged tiger" is better left untried.[117]

Second, even if the premise be acknowledged, a third alternative can hardly be ignored: neither continence nor temperance but concupiscence and possibly indulgence. We are not all Guions, and seeing and knowing—essentially the two "brokers of sin" which the Yerushalmi (*Berakhot* 1:5) identified with heart and eyes—need not culminate in abstinence. Better a "blank virtue" surely than colorful vice. As has often been noted, Milton himself evidently came to doubt that this ebullient optimism was warranted. Two decades later, the thrust of much of his own earlier argument became a symptom of Eve's incipient moral weakness in *Paradise Lost.*[118] The ability to withstand dust and heat is no doubt commendable, but prudence dictates that before setting out on a marathon we check our stamina.

Third, unlike Spenser's Guion triumphantly winding his way through the alluring paths of the Bower of Bliss, many who venture into the gardens of culture lack an accompanying palmer. In "sage and serious" works, elements of motifs that

116. *'Avodah Zarah* 17a. With regard to the destruction of the idolatrous impulse, see *Yoma* 69b.

117. This question has a long history, dating from Aristotle. Its best-known Jewish discussion is in the Rambam's *Shemoneh Perakim*, ch. 6.

118. See John Milton, *Paradise Lost*, 9:270–384. It has been correctly noted that Milton would probably have distinguished between the prelapsarian state of Eve within which pristine untested virtue was ideal and the desire to confront temptation a snare, and the historical human condition within which the encounter with dust and heat are the spiritual order of the day. Nevertheless, it seems likely that the change in his situation and his views also had some impact upon the contrast between the two passages.

might be problematic in their own right are depicted within a context, grounded in the artist's ethical vision, which passes implicit judgment upon them and provides moral perspective. Not all resemble *The Faerie Queene,* however. Many works are neutral and some beyond. Modern literature, in particular, often seeks not only to arouse passion but to provide moral and philosophic sanctions for acceding to it. Blake's dictum, "Sooner murder an infant in its cradle than nurse unacted desires,"[119] is singularly stark, but his basic message pervades much nineteenth and twentieth-century imaginative writing, especially at the popular level.

Finally, the danger is not confined to works in which libido or macho are purveyed straight. Intravenous poison is no less deadly than hemlock potions. In many respects, a novel in which authority is invariably vested in the hands of rigid pedants while its opponents are imaginative and gentle is more insidious than nihilist manifestos. Precisely because it is less perceptible, subliminally insinuated influence may be doubly nefarious.

Thorns and Thistles: The Corrosion of Faith

The second major concern is religious, especially as regards the sensitive area of faith and dogma: "'After your own heart'—this refers to infidelity." This, too, is multifaceted, relating in part to faith in its universal aspect, and in part to specific dogmatic elements. The study of philosophy may issue in agnosticism or atheism or, less radically, in denial of revelation. History often purports to present findings which contravene Scripture or tradition; or, alternatively, it may distort the tensile balance between the eternal and temporal aspects of Torah by overemphasizing the contextual cultural matrix within which it flourished. Schools of psychology and sociology tend to embrace determinism while life sciences may portray man as devoid of the divine spark of *ẓelem E-lokim.*

Beyond confrontation, moreover, lurk subtler dangers—some, the flip side of palpably positive elements. Comparison with other civilizations is a case in point. On the one hand, it heightens and sharpens our awareness of the genuine character of Torah. "Just look at the difference between my progeny and that of my father-in-law," Ḥazal (*Berakhot* 7b) would have Leah, and *knesset Yisrael* after her, exhorting; and they, in the same spirit, permitted the violation of a rabbinic injunction if necessary to provide a basis for comparison. A *kohen* was thus permitted to leap over coffins en route to seeing gentile kings, "so that if he should be privileged, he should be able to distinguish between Jewish and Gentile kings."[120]

On the other hand, the very act of comparison often jades a sense of uniqueness. The question posed in the familiar *pasuk* in *Yeshayahu* (40:25), "'To whom then will

119. William Blake, "Proverbs of Hell," 35.

120. *Berakhot* 19b; see my note in *Mamlekhet,* 29, n.

ye liken Me, that I should be equal?' said the Holy One,"[121] presumably precludes the very process of comparison rather than just a particular outcome. And while even the assertion of uniqueness often implies a measure of comparison, as in the familiar, "Who is like unto Thee, O Lord, among the transcendental"[122] or, in *Shemoneh 'Esrei*, "Who is like unto Thee, master of power, and who resembles Thee," the quintessence of those rhetorical questions is, after all, the assertion—very much in the spirit of Onkelos' paraphrastic translation: "There is none of your kind, Thou art God, O Lord,"—that there can be no comparison.

In contrast with such an asseveration, academic comparative religion bears, virtually by definition, a problematic aspect: with regard to its objective content, insofar as it does not confine itself to descriptive analysis of modes of worship or experiential response but rather focuses upon deity proper; with respect to its subjective impact, almost regardless of the focus. As nineteenth-century Europe, to cite one major example, amply illustrates, within certain contexts exposure to varied religious traditions, particularly if sudden, can have a corrosive impact upon faith. And so it is with the Torah world. If comparison reveals difference, relativistic pluralism rears its head; if similarity, homogenizing universalism. So long as the sense of Torah's uniqueness is not truly ingrained, comparative studies can be both doctrinally and experientially unsettling. In some instances, they lead to shallow conclusions about the source of certain facets of Torah. Even where that does not occur, they may affect one's personal relation to them. There is a mindset whose attitudes towards the triad of a Jewish man's daily blessings concerning his creation (*Menaḥot* 43b) is undermined upon learning that "it is reported variously of Socrates or of Plato that each morning he thanked heaven for having been born male and not female, free and not slave, Greek and not barbarian."[123] A different mentality could of course, as did Newman analogously, revel in the scope of its tradition's prevalence—even if, as with respect to gender here, for radically different reasons—and not feel threatened at all. But that hardly obviates the point. The dangers are clear and present. Moreover, what is true of comparative religion is equally relevant *mutatis mutandis* to other areas. The recoil induced in many *bnei Torah* by the very term *mishpat 'Ivri* derives from the implicit equation (assuredly rejected by many in the field) of *devar Hashem* with various juridic corpora (Roman, common, Napoleonic, et alia) and the concomitant muting of its singular divine origins and character. Or again, tracing the course of a halakhic tradition may issue in treating it in historicist terms.

Even when instructive light is cast upon an aspect of Torah, the shading may be questionable. Caraveggio's portrait of Avraham at the *'akedah* is profoundly sensi-

121. See, in this connection, Rudolf Otto's *The Idea of the Holy*, tr. J.W. Harvey (London, 1950), passim.

122. Exodus 15:11. I have here followed the view of Ibn Ezra and the Ramban that *elim* denotes supernatural beings. Rashi explains that it refers to "the strong."

123. Moses Hadas, *The Living Tradition* (New York, 1969), 31.

tive. But not all would agree that the fusion of fright, awe, and determination captured in those piercing eyes corresponds to the Avraham they envision. The problem is particularly acute with respect to *Wissenschaft des Jüdentums,* many of whose disciplines provide valuable insights and information but whose total impact, as regards nuances of both faith and sensibility, is often distorting.

These concerns, too, are disconcertingly real and they pose, moreover, a genuine halakhic problem. It is not prominently treated by Ḥazal, but the Rambam articulated it sharply; perhaps surprisingly, given his philosophic range, but not so surprisingly, in light of his theological cast. After postulating that we have been commanded not to read books composed by idolaters detailing their principles and practices, "nor to mediate upon idol-worship, nor upon anything appertaining to it," he continues:

> We are likewise admonished, with respect to any thought which might cause one to reject one of the Torah's fundamental principles, that we are not to entertain it in our minds nor to divert our attention to it, so that, by pondering it, we be drawn after the ruminations of our hearts. For a person's mind is limited, and not all can attain truth in its integrity; and if every person will follow the vagaries of his heart, the result, because of the limitations of his mind, would be universal ruin. . . . With respect to this, the Torah has admonished, as is stated therein, "And that ye go not about your own heart and your own eyes, after which ye use to go astray." To wit: You shall not be drawn, each of you, after his own limited intelligence, imagining that his thought is attaining truth.[124]

The formulation is sweeping and seemingly unequivocal and yet, two major qualifications should be noted. The first is that despite the apparent equation—"And it is not after idolatry alone that we are forbidden to be drawn in thought but we are likewise admonished with respect to any thought which might cause one to reject one of the Torah's fundamental principles"—the Rambam clearly distinguishes between idolatry and heresy. Study of the former is proscribed by the *pasuk* in Leviticus (19:4): "Turn ye not unto the idols," and a later analogue in Deuteronomy (12:30): "And that thou inquire not after their gods, saying: 'How used these nations to serve their gods? Even so will I do likewise.'" As regards the latter, the relevant injunction, as we have seen, is drawn from Numbers: "And that ye go not after your own heart and your own eyes." This difference translates into substantive distinctions between the respective prohibitions. With respect to idolatry, the Rambam states categorically that perusal per se is forbidden, evidently irrespective of the result or the concomitant disposition. As regards the study of heresy, by contrast, the prohibition evidently consists in entertaining it as a serious option and is

124. *Hil. 'Avodah Zarah* 2:3. In the *pasuk* cited, the word *zonim,* rendered by J. P. S. as "go astray," actually has much sharper connotations as it relates to fornication.

conditioned upon its subsequent impact.[125] The distinction is more sharply articulated in the *Sefer ha-Mizvot,* where the Rambam initially classifies the respective studies as two separate negative prohibitions between which he clearly distinguishes. He speaks expansively of the injunction against dealing with all forms of idolatrous material (ideology, lore, art) and only cites the prospect of apostasy as a reason.[126] With regard to heresy, however, he states: "That He has admonished us not to turn after our heart to the point that we believe views which are contrary to the views which the Torah has obligated us [to accept], but we should rather inhibit our thought and place upon it a limit—namely, the Torah's commandment and its admonitions."[127]

Secondly, while the formulation in *Mishneh Torah* appears categorical, it seems to be clearly at variance with the Rambam's own example. The gap between precept and practice—he not only read heretical material extensively but, in the *Guide,* cited it copiously—invites two responses. The first is that the Rambam, and any *gadol* analogous to him, is a rather special case. On the one hand, by virtue of his public position he is presumably under greater pressure to confront alien ideologies he must first master. On the other, by dint of both the range of his knowledge of Torah and the depth of his commitment to it, he is relatively inured to their pernicious influence. Some, of course, questioned even the Rambam's immunity. The possible admixture of Greco-Roman elements in his thought was a focal point of the controversy which swirled around him in his lifetime and shortly thereafter; while even much later, long after his position in our spiritual firmament had been secured, the Gaon of Vilna could assert that with respect to his views regarding sorcery and kindred phenomena he had let himself be drawn by "accursed philosophy."[128] Be that as it may, many have contended that only singular individuals thoroughly steeped in Torah, those—to borrow a phrase the Rambam (*Hil. Yesodei ha-Torah* 4:13) coined in a parallel connection—"whose belly had been filled with bread and meat" could indulge in ingesting alien substances.

The second response relates to the motive and hence, in all likelihood, the mode of studying aberrant material. With reference to the *psauk,* "Thou shalt not learn to do in accordance with the abominations of those nations" (Deuteronomy 18:9), which presumably addresses itself to study per se, Ḥazal comments: "You may not learn [in order] to do but you may learn [in order] to understand and instruct."[129]

125. The resultant lapse is culpable in its own right but also constitutes a condition of the prohibition against straying. If it eventuates, one has violated that *issur* as well.

126. See *Mizvot Lo Ta'aseh,* 10.

127. *Ibid.,* 47. See R. Y. F. Perlow, *Sefer ha-Mizvot le-Rabbenu Saadyah Gaon,* 2:47, who notes that *rishonim,* including the Rambam, did not cite the *issur* of *lo tilmad* as an independent prohibition.

128. *Be'urei ha-Gera, Yoreh De'ah,* 179:13. In later editions, the critique was softened by omission of the epithet *ha-arurah.*

129. *Sanhedrin* 68a. The term *le-horot* may denote either "to instruct" or "to rule."

The thrust of this qualification is clear but its latitude is not. The familiar applications cited in the Gemara are narrowly focused: construction of models of celestial bodies, ordinarily forbidden as tinged with idolatry; practice of sorcery and witchcraft; study of magical incantations.[130] These deal with very specific phenomena and can be regarded as justified by the need to pass halakhic judgment upon them. "'To understand,'" Rashi explains, "that you should be able to deal with them, so that if a false prophet should perform these before you, you should understand that he is a sorcerer."[131]

However, the text of the *baraitha* in the *Sifre,* ad locum, is baldly formulated and certainly lends itself to broader scope than the instances to which, by happenstance, it was addressed in the Gemara. That is the impression conveyed in one vein by Rashi's elaborated citation of the *Sifre* in his commentary on the *pasuk:* "'But you may study in order to understand and instruct (*le-havin u-le-horot*);' to wit, to understand how corrupt are their practices, and to instruct your children, 'Do not do such and such as this is a Gentile ordinance.'" Moreover, at least one specific application does intimate that the qualification extends beyond the range of those previously cited. The Gemara (*'Avodah Zarah* 18a) explains that Rabbi Ḥanina b. Teradyon engaged in verbalizing and explicating the ineffable divine name—a practice which, on one view, is so grievous as to constitute a barrier to beatific bliss, as he did so for instructional purposes. While still relating to the arcane (albeit in this case the sacred arcane), this instance clearly enlarges the bounds of the license of *le-havin u-le-horot,* both because additional material is included and because the specific telos of subsequent evaluation is omitted. Hence, the question of what the scope of the concept may be, which of course arises a priori, is clearly reinforced; and indeed, commenting upon this Gemara, one of the Tosafists noted: "There is need to examine which material is requisite to understand and instruct and which is forbidden."[132]

However this need was perceived in medieval France, it is for our purposes, with reference to the ideology and practice of *Torah u-Madda,* much more keenly felt today. It exists presumably at two levels: theoretical definition and factual determination. The latter is obviously conducted with respect to specific contexts, albeit in light of precedents and guidelines. The former, however, cries out for classic conceptual formulation. Unfortunately, however, *rishonim* have shed little explicit

130. See *Rosh Hashanah* 24b, *Sanhedrin* 68a, and *Shabbat* 75a.

131. *Shabbat* 75a, *s.v. le-havin.*

132. *Tosafot Rabbenu Elḥanan, s.v. aval.* It is not clear to me whether he is referring to conceptual definition of a standard or its application in specific evaluation. The term *veẓarikh 'iyyun* used by Rabbenu Elḥanan is generally used in later rabbinic literature to refer to a difficulty, often to one for which one has no solution. It can, however, simply denote an intellectual task on the agenda and is used by *ba'alei ha-Tosafot* in this sense. See *Tosafot, Mo'ed Katan,* 12b, *s.v. makhni*; 13a, *s.v. ein*; 24a, *s.v. ki*; and 26b, *s.v. kakh.* I am indebted to Yoḥanan Breuer for these references.

light upon the matter. In *Mishneh Torah,* the Rambam in effect omitted the qualification of *le-havin u-le-horot* entirely. Others related to it sparingly. Some, as we have seen, contented themselves with commenting upon the specific instances cited in the Gemara, perhaps because they held that indeed the concept encompassed no more; or, then again, perhaps because they were not engaged in comprehensive juridic formulation. R. Meir Halevi Abulafia, the Rambam's younger contemporary and adversary, did expand the license somewhat simply by constricting the prohibition. What is forbidden, he explains, is "engaging in them for personal gratification, in accordance with the abomination of those nations, but you may study *le-havin u-le-horot.*"[133] In a different vein, the thirteenth century exegete, Rabbenu Baḥya ben Asher, included an encyclopedic range of knowledge within the *hetter,* but did not forgo the narrow telos of halakhic judgment:

> And thus we find, with reference to the seventy [members of the] Sanhedrin that they needed to be thoroughly versed in all areas of knowledge, even that of witchcraft, so that they can pass true judgment in accordance with Torah law with respect to all matters.[134]

The parameters of the injunction and the license, respectively, thus remain somewhat murky; and they constitute today, as they have over the centuries, a major crux of the ongoing controversy over *Torah u-Madda.*

Le-havin u-le-horot pertains not only to the motive of study but to its mode. To an extent, the purpose defines the attitude. Clearly, what is envisioned is study of general and, particularly, deviant material from a critical perspective in light of basic ideological and methodological premises. Hence, the two factors that have been suggested with respect to the Rambam's precept and practice may very well conjoin. If the license to pursue general culture is predicated upon its being approached through the prism of Torah, it should presumably be restricted to those who are suitably equipped to effect such an approach or who, at the very least, are properly guided in the course of its study. It would thus be limited to those who subscribe to the modality of *le-havin u-le-horot* in principle and who have the spiritual wherewithal—both the religious commitment and the critical faculties—to implement it in practice. This would not necessarily restrict serious exposure to questionable material to singular individuals who have ingested bread and meat on the Rambam's scope, but it would firmly establish a functional relation between the depth of one's Torah roots and the range of his cultural branches. The linkage between the twin variables of Torah stature and cultural exposure is obvious: the more sensitive and problematic the material, the greater the caution and selectivity with which it is to be approached. However, its practical implementation is not, and it requires genuine wisdom.

---

133. *Yad Ramah, Sanhedrin* 68a, *s.v. piska.*

134. *Rabbenu Baḥya 'al ha-Torah, ad loc.* For the reference to the Sanhedrin, see *Sanhedrin* 17a.

Of course, this proposition touches upon the familiar dichotomies of faith and reason, authority and individuality, credo and freedom. And to many—certainly, to many modern Jews—the position I have assumed is pure anathema. They accept as almost axiomatic the body of liberal doctrine, so succinctly summed up by one of its most brilliant and perceptive opponents in a lengthy appended note to Newman's *Apologia.* This includes the tenets, "No revealed doctrines or precepts may reasonably stand in the way of scientific conclusions;" or, "There are rights of conscience such that every one may lawfully advance a claim to profess and teach what is false and wrong in matters religious, social, and moral, provided that to his private conscience it seems absolutely true and right."[135] Rejection of such self-evident propositions they associate with dogmatists, religious or secular, but surely not with their cherished Judaism.

One can understand, and to the extent that it is animated by regard for *ẓelem E-lokim,* even respect this position. Yet, virtually by definition, an Orthodox Jew cannot agree with it. It is, of course, a truism that dogma figures less prominently in Judaism than in Christianity, or to a lesser degree, Islam. But Mendelssohn's contention that it does not figure at all is patently false. Once dogma is acknowledged, the prospect of a conflict between its content and the conclusions of personal inquiry naturally arises; and there is no question as to how, ultimately, a Torah-committed Jew ought resolve it. In the first instance, every effort will obviously be made to avert a collision. Within limits whose bounds may at times admittedly be open to debate, one will strive to explore various avenues: to reexamine data, reinterpret texts, or rethink propositions. But always out of a profound recognition that at the last frontier, *Mosheh emet ve-Torato emet,* the supremacy of revealed truth is acknowledged.

This view is part of the heritage of the *'akedah.* The divine call, "Take now thy son, thine only son, whom thou lovest, even Isaac, and get thee into the land of Moriah; and offer him there for a burnt-offering upon one of the mountains which I will tell thee of" (Genesis 22:2), demanded of Avraham not only his progeny but his conscience. Paternal mercy aside, had he not been commanded, that paradigm of *ḥesed* surely would not, in his most terrifying nightmares, have countenanced such an act. Every fiber of his moral being, every strand of his conscience would have been revolted by the very prospect. And yet, once the command was issued and he ascertained that it was genuine, his response was alacritous and categorical: "And Abraham rose early in the morning, and saddled his ass, and took two of his young men with him, and Isaac his son; and he cleaved the wood for the burnt-offering, and rose up, and went unto the place of which God had told him." He did not for a moment abandon either morality nor his belief in a moral God. But in the face of the divine imperative, he subordinated his judgment to that of his Taskmaster.

135. "Note A: Liberalism," in *English Prose of the Victorian Era,* ed. C. F. Harrold and W. D. Templeman (New York, 1938), 651.

The call and response of Moriah find their parallels in later ages. The message of the *'akedah* reverberates through Jewish history, and inter alia it dictates our ultimate relation to secular culture. Hence, while there can hopefully be fruitful interaction between the two, Torah is the ultimate measure of culture and not vice versa. As regards our reading, then, we fully adopt in principle T. S. Eliot's assertion that "literary criticism should be completed by criticism from a definite ethical and theological standpoint;" or his admonition that it is necessary for religious readers "to scrutinize their reading, especially of works and imagination with explicit ethical and theological standards."[136] In practice, we are counselled to ascertain what levels of heat we can stand before we enter the kitchen.

Even if problematic studies be deemed permissible, given the right motive and the right person, it does not follow that they are necessarily advisable. As with respect to the moral realm, potential gain and loss must be weighed carefully. Qualifying variables aside, the bottom line of course is that the risks remain. Taking them can only be justified by the faith that they can be counterbalanced by genuine spiritual beliefs, not by the pretense that they are either fictitious or flimsy. A would-be philosopher who had attended Rav Soloveitchik's *shiur* once turned to him for counsel as to whether he should pursue graduate studies in the field—and in a denominational university, at that. The Rav responded that airplanes are known to crash and yet people fly. The questioner subsequently confided that several years later he woke up one morning with an urge to call the Rav to tell him that the plane had just crashed, as indeed it thunderously had.

The Rav's reply is nevertheless understandable, but only if we bear in mind (as he of course did) first, that very few repeatedly run even the minimal risks of flight for the sheer thrill of the adventure; and, second, that the incidence of crashes be reasonably low (however that is defined), so that the risk-benefit ratio is acceptable. Those who contend that questionable material confers no benefits either because it has nothing of value to offer or because its positive content can better be attained otherwise sans possible complications are perfectly justified, given their premise, in avoiding all contact with it. Only where the possibility of true spiritual benefit is perceived, tested faith being regarded as either sturdier or worthier, or if exposure is valued as enhancing the ability to cope with the *apikoros* without or within, or if, in a more positive vein, the material itself or the encounter with it is deemed as stimulating meaningful insight into Judaism, can the prospect of ideologically problematic pursuits be countenanced.

With basic values at stake, real dangers cannot be blithely ignored in the name of liberal openness. Responsible commitment to Torah dictates that we err, if we must, on the side of caution. Prudence need not entail radical rejection, however. If the dangers are real so are the benefits, so that where the risks can be sufficiently neutralized and counterbalanced, a wide range of cultural experience may be

136. T. S. Eliot, "*Selected Essays, 1917–1932* (New York, 1932), 343.

rendered not only palatable but desirable. The keys are selectivity and judgment: discrimination between the proverbial fruit and rind of worldly wisdom, and critical awareness, informed by Torah knowledge and commitment, as a mode of absorbing and evaluating general culture. The capacity for these varies greatly and so should the kind and degree of advisable exposure. But whatever the nature of these variables, the guiding principle, at once ideological and educational, is responsibility.

The issue is familiar but must be recurrently judged anew with regard to the contemporary context. In the preface of his classic work on *Duties of the Heart,* Rabbenu Baḥya argues fervently in favor of philosophic examination of even the most basic of religious tenets on the ground that faith rooted in rational conviction is more profound and more securely anchored than that solely nurtured by tradition and milieu. Writing in a pervasively religious era, he virtually ignored the possibility that the result of the examination—in terms of Newman's familiar dichotomy, investigation rather than inquiry—might be the loss of faith rather than its reinforcement. Could any responsible modern counterpart do likewise? On the darkling plain, the footing is often slippery and exploration requires careful planning and execution.

Such planning obviously takes into account a range of variables, as regards both the prospective benefits of different disciplines and their respective risks. In principle, we are naturally drawn to the position articulated by Averroes:

> And if someone errs or stumbles in the study of these books owing to a deficiency in his natural capacity, or bad organization of his study of them, or being dominated by his passions, or not finding a teacher to guide him to an understanding of their contents, or a combination of all or more than one of these causes, it does not follow that one should forbid them to anyone who is qualified to study them. For this manner of harm that arises owing to them is something that is attached to them by accident, not by essence; and when a thing is beneficial by its nature and essence, it ought not be shunned because of something contained in it by accident.[137]

In practice, however, several factors need to be weighed carefully. Apart from the overall religious knowledge and commitment of an individual as determining his ability to read critically from a Torah perspective, one must gauge the specific material in question. There are pitfalls and there are minefields and different kinds of each. Each generation has its own ideological flash points, each community its soft underbelly. Nor is the degree of danger a function of proximity to traditional thought. Quite often precisely the opposite is true. Today, knowledge of Greek or Norse mythology will entice virtually no one to embrace paganism. It is perhaps

137. From *The Decisive Treatise, Determining What the Connection is Between Religion and Philosophy,* in *Medieval Political Philosophy: A Sourcebook,* ed. R. Lerner and M. Mahdi (Glencoe, 1963), 168.

conceivable, in line with the view of the *Ḥavot Ya'ir* with respect to the *issur* of pronouncing the names of pagan deities that once idolatry has lost its prevalence, its material may be studied even without recourse to the license of *le-havin u-le-horot.*[138] On the other hand, aspects of biblical and talmudic criticism unquestionably pose a truly serious threat greater by far than the New Testament or the Bhagavad-Gita, and they do so not only by assailing the integrity of sacred texts but also by revising their content—whether by distorting their substantive thrust or by subtly recasting perceptions of the *avot* or Ḥazal. If some subvert faith radically by advancing agnostic secularism, others sap it—in a very different vein, of course—by inducing heterodox sensibility.

Admittedly, it is conceivable that even with the best safeguards the encounter with *madda* may lead some astray. Given mass exposure, it is likely that not all will be able to sustain the tensile balance between respective realms. This, in turn, raises the obvious question as to whether the pursuit of general culture can be justified, regardless how worthwhile on balance. The problem is genuine, but it should be noted that we are here confronted educationally with a dilemma analogous to that regarding the use of say, automobiles. If we were presented with the grisly proposition that vehicular traffic could be maintained on the sole condition that a number of designated innocent people be executed, we should certainly respond—as did Alyosha in *The Brothers Karamazov* in an analogous situation—that the proposal was morally revolting.[139] Yet, while we know full well that, despite all exhortation to caution and regardless of the safeguards, many will perish in traffic accidents, we regard this as the inevitable price for the comfort and convenience of automotive travel; and we pay it socially and morally inasmuch as we are dealing with statistical projections rather than willful carnage or specific victims. By the same token, if we were told that *madda's* overall enrichment of our collective spiritual life was conditional upon the apostasy of specific individuals, we would certainly forgo its contribution. We should then assert with C. S. Lews, "that the salvation of a single soul is more important than the production or preservation of all the epics and tragedies in the world."[140] At the statistical plane, however, even if one recognizes sadly that, caveats notwithstanding, some will probably lapse, the advocacy of *Torah u-Madda* can very well still be sustained, depending, of course, on the overall balance of benefit and loss.

---

138. See R. Ḥayyim Ya'ir Bakhrakh, *Ḥavot Ya'ir,* 1.

It is of course quite conceivable that exposure to pagan literature will lead one to evaluate it more charitably, as some of its aspects may be viewed as having religious significance as an attempt to arrive at and to formulate certain truths, rather than simply being regarded, en bloc, as a farrago of abominable nonsense. This is very different from being drawn into its orbit, however.

139. See Bk. 5, ch. 4.

140. C. S. Lewis, "Christianity and Literature," in *Rehabilitations and Other Essays* (London, 1939), 196.

BUT WITH A WHIMPER: THE CHILLING OF FERVOR

I have heretofore spoken of possible risks with respect to two factors, the moral and the religious. There is, however, a third danger which in a sense straddles both areas. Even where sensibility and ideology are not directly affected, the quality of spiritual existence may be impaired by sheer dilution, and this in one of two ways. First, diffusion per se may undermine the centrality of one's primary base. T. S. Eliot once wrote that he became deeply interested in Sanskrit culture but abandoned its pursuit after two years when he sensed that it was starting to affect the attitudes for whose sake he had undertaken that study in the first place. Some trade-off between the singular thrust of monochromatic commitment and the comprehensive breadth of a more balanced perspective is virtually inevitable, but its proportions are obviously critical. A plethora of cultural interests, each valuable in its own right, can divert attention from the supreme challenges of religious existence even to the point of distracting from the quest for the *unum necessarium*, that *yir'at shamayim* (fear of Heaven) of which R. Yoḥanan tells us (*Shabbat* 31b), that the *Ribbono Shel 'Olam* "has nothing else in his world;" may leave one, like the young Augustine, "weeping the death of Dido for love to Aeneas, but weeping not his own death for want of love to Thee, O God."[141]

Second, culture—largely identified by one of its best known apostles with "sweet reasonableness"[142]—often reduces spiritual intensity generally. At times, the dispassionate objectivity upon which its votaries pride themselves issues in the loss of spiritual nerve and verve, in blandness bordering upon frigidity. Seven and one-half minutes (I've clocked it) spent at *minḥah* with a *minyan* of academicians at a university library provide a more effective argument against *Wissenschaft*-centered Judaism than reams of *Yated Ne'eman*. If, as some would have it, the so-called *ḥaredi* world is marred by excessive passion, the modern Orthodox community is often afflicted by endemic lassitude; and it can ill afford the diminution of spiritual enthusiasm.

Dangers abound, then, and we ignore them at our personal and collective peril. But we also ignore *ḥokhmah* at some cost, albeit of a very different order. It may be communal or personal—at times, straddling both; and it is reflected more acutely in the lack of imagination, discrimination, and complexity. In the public arena, as current experience amply illustrates, the lack of culture and, likewise, of any genuine understanding of the society which is animated by it often issues in gross misreading of the sociopolitical scene, and hence, in skewed priorities, missed opportunities, and sheer blunders. Flushed with heady exuberance over recent, admittedly impressive successes, we are, in the absence of historical perspective and cultural sensitivity, at times lured into pursuing muscular approaches which promise tempting short-term rewards but bode no long-range spiritual good.

141. *Confessions*, tr. E.B. Pusey (New York, 1949), 16.
142. See Matthew Arnold, *Culture and Anarchy*, ch. 1.

At the personal level, too, the lack of *madda* poses potential problems. To be sure, as long as one remains securely ensconced within his bastion, insulation offers comforting security, although as recent Eastern European and North African history demonstrated, if the walls are penetrated they may come crashing down. At the same time, it may render one's view shallow and even crude—delineating too precisely He who can at most only be vaguely apprehended, and only perceiving in general outline that which can be carefully analyzed; bereft of imaginative sweep, and thus confined, not just spatiotemporally but spiritually, within the four ells of a very pedestrian existence. Spiritual experience may thus be admirably profound and intense in one sense and yet simplistic and superficial in another.

What may occur at the interface of both sectors can be illustrated by a concrete example. I recall the respective funerals of two of the giants of our generation, Rav Aharon Kotler *zẓ"l*, and Rav Mosheh Feinstein, *zẓ"l*. Of those who delivered eulogies about the former, only one—Mr. Irving Bunim, a layman—provided any real insight into his personality. All the others lamented the loss of a great *gaon* and *ẓaddik* and appropriately exhorted the audience to take stock and to take heart, but nary a word of genuine portrayal. The scene was pretty much repeated at Rav Mosheh's funeral (in Jerusalem). Again, the familiar dirge over the loss of a *gaon* and *ẓaddik*, some account of his profound commitment and prodigious diligence, but barely the faintest trace of a portrait. Incredibly, the most basic aspect of his contribution to the Torah world, the scope and nature of his activity as a *posek*, was virtually ignored for reasons which can only be surmised.

It was all very true, very sincere, and terribly deficient. One reflected in dismay and disbelief that a listener who had had no previous knowledge of either would have come away from both funerals with the impression that there was relatively little difference between the *gedolim*. He could think of both under the rubric of several abstractions and genuinely mourn their loss. But he would have very little idea of who, specifically, they had been. He would surely have no inkling of their being, respectively, a perpetual dynamo, almost a firebrand, and a remarkable blend of boldness and meekness; of their approaching both the study and the implementation of Torah in very different ways. It was astounding that *talmidei ḥakhamim* who were habituated to noting the finest distinctions in a halakhic *sugya* could so utterly fail to delineate and define persons they had known and admired; and it seemed unlikely that this was simply because they were now overcome by grief. I sensed that the requisite powers were simply lacking; and I reflected that a measure of certain aspects of general culture could have remedied the deficiency.

Whoever has attended similar funerals can probably attest to parallel experiences. Nevertheless, it will be rejoined, is this truly significant? Does it really matter if one thinks and speaks of these *geonim* as archetypal *gedolim*, without reference to their individual personalities? Even if one grants that *ḥokhmah* would have helped flesh out these portraits, would that be genuinely material? For myself, I must answer in the affirmative. To be sure, such insight does not deserve the very highest priority. One can lead an upstanding Jewish life without it, and yet it is no pittance.

Frequently emphasizing the need to understand people properly, Rav Soloveitchik—taking note of the biblical account, *zeh sefer toledot adam* ("this is the book of the generations of Adam;" Genesis 5:1)—was wont to remark, "A man must be studied like a book." All the more so, if he is a *gadol;* if grasping his essence accurately in a fulfillment of "But thine eyes shall see thy teachers."[143]

What has been asserted with respect to this particular point is true of *madda* generally. It is not a necessity, but neither is it quite a luxury. It is certainly not a sine qua non of spiritual existence, but it can enhance it measurably. Let us bear in mind Rava's statement that, when a person stands for eternal judgment, he is asked not only whether he had dealt honestly, designated times for Torah study, and engaged in procreation, but also, "Did you pursue wisdom? Did you perceive one matter from another?"[144]

I am of course mindful of the homily's conclusion: "Yet even so, if 'the fear of the Lord is his treasure,' it is well; if not, [it is] not well. This may be compared to a man who instructed his agent, 'Take up for me a *kor* of wheat to the loft,' and he went and did so. 'Did you mix in a *kab* of *humton*?' he asked him. 'No,' he replied. 'Then it were better you had not carried it up,' he retorted."[145] I trust, however, as I presume did Rava, that we need not ordinarily choose between pietistic *yir'at Hashem* and intellectual *ḥokhmah ve-da'at,* but can strive for both. To the extent that choices do need to be made as regards both priorities and risks, they should of course be made carefully, responsibly, and above all honestly; and they should be based on a clear sense that they need not (rather, ought not) be the same for all. In this respect, the counsel of Rav Pinḥas Menaḥem Alter *zẓ"l* who, as the rosh yeshiva of the Gerer *Yeshivat Sefat Emet* of course approached the question of *Torah u-Madda* out of a background quite different from my own, is instructive: "In my opinion, each person should consult with his *rebbi,* or with a *moreh hora'ah* who is a *yerei shamayim,* in order to suit for him the most useful path, and to direct him in the plane

---

143. Isaiah 30:20. Rashi explains that the *pasuk* refers to a promised vision of God. However, Ḥazal, as in *'Eruvin* 13b, take it as referring to spiritual masters, so that a note of exhortation is included.

144. Shabbat 31a. The word *be-ḥokhmah* could be translated either as (1) "in wisdom," with a locative *bet,* so that wisdom is the object of intellectual pursuit; or (2) "wisely," with an instrumental *bet,* so that the word designates a mode of pursuing an area not here defined, quite possibly Torah. I believe the former is inherently more likely, but according to the second, the query is more analogous to the first question (regarding the mode of conducting business) and the last (regarding depth of understanding). In any event, as previously noted, even if *ḥokhmah* is here the object of pursuit, it may refer to Torah.

145. *Shabbat* 31a. The whole statement is an exegetical exposition of a *pasuk* in Isaiah (33:6) which lists various spiritual goods—taken by Rava as associated with different spheres of endeavor about which one may be questioned—and concludes, "The fear of the Lord is his treasure." It might be added that Rava sees the treasure as man's; elsewhere (*Berakhot* 33a), R. Shimon b. Yohai, with respect to this very verse, sees it as God's.

of Torah and *yir'ah*—for in our generation particularly the matter requires special caution."[146] Some may cavil at the stress upon authority in the process of personal decision, but surely no one can question the wisdom of the basic differential approach. The variables are both individual and cultural. The Israeli scene, for instance, is in many respects different from the American. But whatever their nature, they are essential to the process of wise educational decision—to be based on the awareness of self and the world to which it must relate, as an optimal spiritual response to what F. H. Bradley aptly termed "my station and its duties."[147]

Looking Before and After: Epilogue

Conventional wisdom currently holds that appreciative readers for this essay are a vanishing breed. Academicians may be scandalized by the very questions and perturbed by the solutions. To many in the yeshiva world, much of the terrain is foreign, some of the issues irrelevant, and the overall direction possibly dubious; while those who are deeply rooted in neither Torah nor *madda* are unlikely to be profoundly and intimately concerned with the problem altogether. All may be dismayed by a needlepoint approach to themes many pound with sledgehammers. Who, then, is left to lend a sympathetic ear?

That wisdom may turn out to be entirely correct. And then again, it may turn out to be only conventional. Only time will tell. In the interim, for those of us who feel that, personally and communally, the problem is substantive and significant, it needs to be confronted squarely and candidly out of genuine disinterested concern for *klal Yisrael* and Reb Yisrael.

It is in this spirit that the piece was written and in this spirit that it should be read: not as a manifesto, certainly not as an *apologia pro vita sua,* but rather as an attempt to come to grips with an important, difficult, and sensitive issue. Its essence may be symbolically expressed through a comment made in *Abot de-Rabbi Natan* with respect to an analogous problem:

> Rabbi Judah ben I'lai says: He who makes Torah matters primary and worldly affairs secondary will be made primary in the world to come; [but he who makes] worldly affairs primary and Torah matters secondary will be made secondary in the world to come. A parable is told: to what may this be likened? To a thoroughfare which lies between two paths, one of flames and the other of snow. If one walks alongside the flames, he will be scorched by the flames; and if he walks alongside the snow, he will be frostbitten. What then is he to do? Let him walk between them and take care of himself that he not be scorched by the flames and not be frostbitten.[148]

146. From a prefatory letter to L. Levi, *Sha'arei Talmud Torah,* n.p.
147. See F. H. Bradley, *Ethical Studies,* 2nd ed. (London, 1962).
148. *The Fathers According to Rabbi Nathan,* tr. Judah Goldin (New Haven, 1955), ch. 28,

Finding that path has proven to be an elusive undertaking, particularly for those who have not been satisfied with a literally intermediate way but have sought a mode of commingling, as miraculously in Egypt of yore, "fire flashing up amidst the hail." The quest nevertheless continues, of importance at all times but fraught with special significance in the modern world. The nature of modern culture and of the interaction between the secular and the religious which occurs in its pervasive shadow has, on the one hand, added a measure of urgency. On the other hand, it has generally transformed the rejection of *madda,* which in the past has often consisted of benign indifference, into active and often pugnacious opposition with attendant spiritual and material consequences. Hopefully, this essay, which certainly pretends to neither halakhic nor philosophic exhaustiveness, will nevertheless contribute—as this volume in its entirely—to reasoned and responsible discussion of the issue.

Over thirty years have passed since I first addressed myself to this topic in print. During that time, the Torah world has been swept by wide-ranging changes, many for the better, some decidedly for the worse; and the balance of power within it, particularly as it relates to *Torah u-Madda,* has shifted dramatically. Looking back over that period, I find myself almost inexorably drawn to two complementary and yet possibly contradictory conclusions. My sense of the need for *Torah u-Madda* has sharpened, particularly in light of public events throughout the Jewish world. So, however, has my awareness of the difficulties of realizing it; of the very considerable spiritual and educational cost—regrettably far in excess of what is inexorably necessary—which the proponents of *Torah u-Madda* often pay for their choice. Jointly, these conclusions—and I am not alone in subscribing to both—pose a challenge which needs to be conscientiously and creatively confronted.

For the foreseeable future, the magnitude of the challenge is unlikely to be diminished. It is intensified, moreover, by the fact that those who could profit from *madda* most and can afford it best desire it least. What one hopes will change is the climate within which the ongoing debate has been conducted. The rancor, mutual recrimination, verbal aggression, and delegitimization which have marred much of the controversy have no place in the serious discussion of an age-old Torah crux. Advocates of *Torah u-Madda* can certainly stake no exclusive claims. It would be not only impudent but foolish to impugn a course which has produced most *gedolei Yisrael* and has in turn been championed by them. Neither, however, should exclusionary contentions be made by its opponents. While *Torah u-Madda* is not every one's cup of tea, it certainly deserves a place as part of our collective spiritual fare. Hopefully, the current exploration of the issue will help create a climate within

p. 118. Goldin renders the phrase, *divrei Torah,* as "the words of the Torah." This is far too narrow a construction and I have substituted "Torah matters." For a comparable formulation in a different connection, see Tosefta, *Ḥagigah* 2:2.

which this *maḥloket le-shem shamayim* can be conducted in a spirit animated by two powerful *pesukim* drawn from *tamnei appyan*:

> Open Thou mine eyes, that I may behold wondrous things out of Thy Torah.
>
> גל עיני ואביטה נפלאות מתורתך.
>
> Teach me good discernment and knowledge; for I have had faith in Thy Commandments.[149]
>
> טוב טעם ודעת למדני כי במצותיך האמנתי.

149. Psalms 119:18 and 119:66.

GLOSSARY

aggadah / -ot (pl.): passages in classical literature treating nonlegal issues (e.g., Jewish thought and theology)
aḥaronim: later rabbinic masters (post fifteenth century)
'akedah: binding of Isaac
Amidah: the central prayer in the daily liturgy
Amoraim: rabbinic scholars who flourished from the third to the fifth centuries
apikoros: heretic
asmakhta: a biblical citation utilized to support a point without regard for the straightforward meaning of the verse
av bet din: head of a rabbinic court who also serves as chief rabbi
avot: forefathers, the Patriarchs
baraitha: collection of early rabbinic teachings
ben Torah: student and devotee of the Torah (pl. **benei Torah**)
bet din: court of law
bet ha-mikdash: Temple
bet midrash: Torah study hall
birkat ha-hokhmah: the blessing for wisdom, found in the **Amidah**
birkat ha-Torah: the blessing recited over Torah study
bittul Torah: the waste of time from Torah study
dayyan / -im (pl.): rabbinic judge
de-oraita: of biblical, as opposed to rabbinic, authority
derash: homily
derekh ereẓ: general culture, secular study, gainful employment, or proper conduct (depending upon context)
devar Hashem: the divine word
'edah ha-ḥaredit: ultra-Orthodox, anti-Zionist religious community in Jerusalem
gadol: a halakhic authority and spiritual leader (pl. **gedolim, gedolei Yisrael**)
gemara: the Amoraic stratum of the Talmud, or a text thereof (pl. **gemarot**)

Geonim: rabbinic scholars who flourished between the eighth and eleventh centuries; colloq: great rabbinic scholars of all times (sing. **Gaon**)
halakhah: Jewish law
ḥalukkah: institutionalized distribution of funds for the needy in the land of Israel before the establishment of the State
ḥameẓ: unleavened bread
ḥaredi: ultra-Orthodox
hashkatah: outlook
ḥaver: one who has received certification of mastery of portions of the Talmud (the lowest level of ordination in some Jewish communities)
Ḥazal: the talmudic sages
ḥeder: traditional Jewish primary school (pl. **ḥadarim**)
hetter: license
ḥiddush / im (pl.): an original interpretation of, or solution to, a difficult rabbinic passage or problem
ḥilul Hashem: desecration of God's name
ḥokhmah: wisdom, generally of secular nature
issur: prohibition
kedushah: holiness
kehillah: institutionalized Jewish communal structure
kiddushin: betrothal
kilayim: various mixtures of certain types of animals and materials prohibited by Torah law
kitvei ha-kodesh: scripture
klal Yisrael, knesset Yisrael: the Jewish people
klaus: a yeshiva primarily for postgraduate students whose study is subsidized by communal funds
Kohelet: Ecclesiastes
kohen: a Jew of priestly descent (pl. **kohanim**)
kol nidre: a solemn formula concerning the annulment of vows, recited Yom Kippur eve
levi: a Jew descended from the tribe of Levi, but not of Aaronide descent
lamdan: scholar
lomdut: intensive, careful analysis of the Talmud
ma'ariv: evening prayer service
madda: science; general knowledge
mashgiaḥ: faculty member of a yeshiva primarily responsible for the moral development of students
matan Torah: the revelation of the Torah at Sinai
maẓẓah: unleavened bread consumed on Passover (pl. **maẓẓot**)
midrash: classic rabbinic interpretation and exposition of biblical passages
mikdash: Temple in Jerusalem
minḥah: afternoon prayer service

minut: heresy
Mishlei: Proverbs
Mishnah: compendium of rabbinic legal teaching edited by R. Judah the Prince (ca. 200 C.E.)
miẓvah: commandment (pl. **miẓvot**)
mo'eẓet gedolei ha-Torah: governing rabbinic board of Agudat Israel
moreh hora'ah: an authority on Jewish law
morenu: a form of rabbinic ordination
mori rabbi: my revered teacher
Neẓiv: R. Naftali Ẓevi Yehudah Berlin (1817–1893), noted nineteenth-century rabbinic scholar
nissu'in: marriage
parshanut: traditional biblical exegesis
pasuk: a biblical verse (pl. **pesukim**)
pesak: halakhic decision
peshat: literal meaning
posek: halakhic decisor (pl. **posekim**)
rabbi muvhak: my primary teacher
rebbi: teacher
Ribbono Shel 'Olam: the Almighty
rishonim: medieval rabbinic masters, ca. 1050–1500
rosh bet din: head of a rabbinic court who does not serve as chief rabbi
rosh yeshiva: head of a yeshiva (pl. **roshei yeshiva**)
Shas: the Talmud
Shema: central part of the daily liturgy, beginning with "Hear O Israel . . ."
shiur: Talmud class
Shulḥan 'Arukh: code of Jewish law authored by R. Joseph Karo (sixteenth century)
sugya: a talmudic section, dealing with a given topic (pl. **sugyot**)
talmud ḥakham: a rabbinic scholar (pl. **talmidei ḥakhamim**)
talmud Torah: Torah study
tamnei appyan: Psalms 119

Contributors

David Berger, who received his doctorate from Columbia University and his rabbinic ordination from the Rabbi Isaac Elchanan Theological Seminary at Yeshiva University, is Professor of History at Brooklyn College and the Graduate School of the City University of New York, a fellow of the American Academy for Jewish Research, and Chairman of the American Section of the International Association of Societies for the Study of Jewish History. He is the author of *The Jewish-Christian Debate in the High Middle Ages,* which was awarded the John Nicholas Brown Prize by the Medieval Academy of America, and of numerous studies on medieval Jewish history, Jewish-Christian relations, and the intellectual history of the Jews.

Gerald J. Blidstein, who received his B.A., Ph.D., and rabbinic ordination from Yeshiva University, is Hubert Professor of Jewish Law at Ben-Gurion University. He is the author of *Political Concepts in Maimonidean Halakha* for which he was awarded the Jerusalem Prize in Jewish Studies in 1985. He has also written many papers and monographs on Jewish law and social ethics, from both historical and phenomenological points of view, and is a recognized student of Maimonides' work. His latest work is *Maimonides on Prayer.* Prof. Blidstein has also served as Dean, Faculty of Humanities and Social Sciences, Ben-Gurion University.

Shnayer Z. Leiman is Professor of Jewish History and Literature in the Department of Judaic Studies at Brooklyn College of the City University of New York, and Visiting Professor at the Bernard Revel Graduate School of Yeshiva University. He has also served as Visiting Professor of Jewish History at Harvard University, and as Visiting Professor of Bible at the Hebrew University. Prior to his arrival at Brooklyn College, where he served as Chairman of the Department of Judaic Studies from 1981–1987, he served as Dean of the Bernard Revel Graduate School and Director of Graduate Jewish Education at Yeshiva University (1978–

1981). Prior to that, he served as Professor of Jewish History and Literature at Yale University, where he administered graduate and undergraduate programs in Judaic Studies (1968–1978). He has lectured widely and published on Jewish ethics, and served as Visiting Scholar in Jewish Law and Ethics at the Kennedy Institute of Ethics at Georgetown University in Washington, D.C. He is the author of *The Canonization of Hebrew Scripture* (second edition: 1991), editor of *The Canon and Masorah of the Hebrew Bible* (1974), and has contributed articles to the *Encyclopedia Britannica*, the *Encyclopedia Judaica*, and *Encyclopedia Miqra'it.* He earned his doctorate from the Department of Oriental Studies at the University of Pennsylvania, and his rabbinical ordination from the Mirrer Yeshiva in New York.

Aharon Lichtenstein is co-Rosh Yeshiva of Yeshivat Har Etzion and teaches Talmud and rabbinic thought at the Gruss Center of Yeshiva University in Jerusalem. Ordained by the Rabbi Isaac Elchanan Theological Seminary and the recipient of a Ph.D. in English literature from Harvard University, he has written numerous articles on halakhic topics and on aspects of Jewish thought, and is the author of *Henry More: The Rational Theology of a Cambridge Platonist.*

Index

About the Editor

Jacob J. Schacter is the editor of *The Torah u-Madda Journal* and the rabbi of The Jewish Center in New York City. He holds a Ph.D. in Near Eastern Languages from Harvard University, and received his rabbinic ordination from Mesivta Torah Vodaath. Jacob Schacter has edited *Reverence, Righteousness and Rahamanut: Essays in Memory of Rabbi Dr. Leo Jung* (1992) and *Jewish Tradition and the Nontraditional Jew* (1992), coedited *The Complete Service for the Period of Bereavement* (1995), coauthored *A Modern Heretic and a Traditional Community: Mordecai M. Kaplan, Orthodoxy, and American Judaism* (1997), and has written numerous articles and reviews. Jacob Schacter is currently working on a critical edition and English translation of the autobiography of Rabbi Jacob Emden.